Microsoft

Fundamentals of
Audio and Video Programming
for Games

Peter Turcan
Mike Wasson

PUBLISHED BY
Microsoft Press
A Division of Microsoft Corporation
One Microsoft Way
Redmond, Washington 98052-6399

Library of Congress Cataloging-in-Publication Data
Turcan, Peter, 1957-
    Fundamentals of Audio and Video Programming for Games / Peter Turcan, Michael Wasson.
      p. cm.
    Includes index.
    ISBN 0-7356-1945-X
    1. Computer games--Programming. 2. Computer sound processing. I. Wasson, Michael,
1968- II. Title.

QA76.76.C672T84   2003
794.8'1536--dc22   2003060144

Printed and bound in the United States of America.

1 2 3 4 5 6 7 8 9   QWE   8 7 6 5 4 3

Distributed in Canada by H.B. Fenn and Company Ltd.

A CIP catalogue record for this book is available from the British Library.

Microsoft Press books are available through booksellers and distributors worldwide. For further information about international editions, contact your local Microsoft Corporation office or contact Microsoft Press International directly at fax (425) 936-7329. Visit our Web site at www.microsoft.com/mspress. Send comments to *mspinput@microsoft.com*.

Acquisitions Editor: Robin Van Steenburgh
Project Editor: Lynn Finnel

Body Part No. X10-09361

Contents at a Glance

Table of Contents

Introduction

Welcome to *Fundamentals of Audio and Video Programming for Games.*

This book is for software developers who want to add sound, music, or video to their programs. Not just any sound, music or video, but fancy stuff: special effects, 3-D effects, random and ambient effects, and so on. Although you'll learn how to do a straight rendition of a piece of music, sound byte, or video clip, this book focuses on how to create applications that impress. Typically, this application would be a game, although it could be any application requiring an impressive user interface. For example, video effects could be used in the title screens for many applications.

The primary philosophy of the book and its accompanying CD is to *show and tell.* In many ways, this publication is actually more of a CD with an accompanying book. In most chapters, we first direct you to a sample on the CD (written especially for this book), ask you to run it, and then examine the code required to achieve the effects. The samples exercise Microsoft technologies in ways that we hope will inspire you to add similar effects to your own programs. These samples are designed not just to show, but to show off, so, perhaps more accurately, this book's philosophy is to *show off* and tell.

This book is for programmers who are already adept at Visual C++. You should already have written a number of C++ applications or tools, and understand topics such as objects, inheritance, compiling, and debugging. Primarily, the main software tools we will be using are C++, with the development environment provided by Visual Studio.

If you are reading this book, you have probably already experimented with graphics and sound. The more experience that you have with Microsoft DirectX, the easier coding will be, although if you have no experience of the audio, music or video Software Development Kits (SDKs) within DirectX, you will be fine because we start from the beginning. The typical DirectX programmer understands Direct 3D much better than any of the other DirectX components. It has become a matter of pride, especially in the games development community, to be able to write your own 3-D matrix manipulation functions, mesh rendering code, and other hard-core 3-D graphics code. Games developers looking for a competitive edge might consider making awesome audio and imaginative use of video key components in their projects.

DirectX is based on Microsoft's Component Object Model (COM), which performs well, and is expected to be around for a long time. Since its mechanics are usually kept out of the way in most applications, we will do the same in this book.

The team writing this book is from the documentation group of Microsoft's Digital Media Division (DMD). Our division develops the company's audio/visual technology, both for programmers in the form of a whole range of SDKs, as well as the technology for audio and video components that go into Windows itself (such as Windows Media Player and Windows Movie Maker).

In this book, we will mainly be using the Microsoft DirectSound SDK and the Microsoft DirectShow SDK to explain the methods and functions that directly manipulate the output of sound or video, although we will also be referencing other Microsoft SDKs.

The book starts with an introduction to sound effects: first mono, then stereo, then 3-D, then 3-D with special and environmental effects. Following this, we examine the important topics of streaming sound and the use of property sets to get EAX environmental reverb effects to work. We'll also look at what's possible with 5.1/6.1/7.1 surround sound.

In many of today's games, there is a move away from using video clips (often referred to as cut scenes), partly because of the difficulty in obtaining good clips, and the lack of options in rendering them. This difficulty is partly due to the lack of connectivity between DirectShow (the video capture and rendering SDK) and the rest of DirectX. DirectX 9 has gone a long way towards remedying this issue, and the video chapters describe how to take advantage of this improvement. The video-based samples that accompany these chapters are fun and impressive, showing how to make a game out of rendering the video, and how to render video to a Direct3D surface (for example, onto a wall in a room).

The book also explains the techniques involved in capturing raw sound and video, such as cleaning noise out of samples, and going through the process of preparing them for repeated rendering. In this case, we will be using some tools developed outside of Microsoft.

So, close your door, install the book CD, go to the directory of executables, and pump up the volume.

Fun was never meant to be quiet.

Acknowledgements

One of the main differences between SDK documentation and a book is that since the SDK documentation comes out with the product, it usually lacks the benefit of experience using the material. A book should not simply be a rehash of the SDK docs, but a genuine attempt to add experience that only comes with time, consequently, all of the chapters and samples have been written especially for this book. This takes some resources, and thankfully, I have been able to leverage input from a number of people who have a lot of experience in particular areas of audio and video.

First mention goes to Mike Wasson, a programming writer with several years to his credit on the Microsoft DirectShow documentation team. He is responsible for the chapters on video, and the wonderful samples that go along with them. Next there is Bill Birney, a veteran of Hollywood as well as a technical writer for Microsoft, who contributed the two chapters on audio and video quality, along with a number of the music and sound tracks available on the book CD. Jim Travis, also a programming writer at Microsoft, contributed the chapter on audio special-effect parameters. Audio effects are Jim's specialty, coming from a background in theatrical presentations.

Cornel Moiceanu, a tools programmer at Microsoft, contributed some of his own compositions to the music tracks available on the CD.

Originating the content of a book is of course only part of the story. Cathy McDonald took on the awesome task of editing our prose, sagely advised by Terry Dorsey, and ably assisted by Steve Hug and Katherine Enos, while Greg Lovitt mastered the layout and production, assisted by Henry Bale.

At Microsoft Press, Juliana Aldous Atkinson helped the book proposal become reality, before handing over the publishing task to Robin Van Steenburgh. Thanks also to Lynn Finnel, an editor at MS Press, for her hard work and persistence with the project, Tess McMillan for building the CD, and to Joel Panchot, the MS Press artist, for so many inspired pieces of artwork.

There are also those who contributed their time in technically reviewing the content and code samples. Stephen Estrop and Dennis Evseev provided invaluable feedback on the VMR chapters, while Dugan Porter, Stephen Handley and Alan Ludwig provided insightful feedback on the audio chapters.

From the management side, User Education manager Tom Woolums' approval of the budgets and resources for the project was, of course, essential, and I also appreciate the support of managing editor Karen Strudwick and production manager Keith Gabbert.

Finally I must thank the development teams here at Microsoft who created Direct-Sound and DirectShow, far too many people to mention by name.

For my contribution, I wrote seven of the eight chapters on audio, and the samples that go along with them.

Thanks for buying this book, and I hope you enjoy working with it as much as we did putting it together.

Dr. Peter Turcan
SDK Writing Manager
Digital Media Division
Microsoft Corporation

Corrections, Comments, and Help

Every effort has been made to ensure the accuracy of this book and the contents of the sample files. Microsoft Press provides corrections and additional content for its books through the World Wide Web at the following address:

http://www.microsoft.com/mspress/support

To connect directly to the Microsoft Press Knowledge Base and enter a query you have, visit the following address:

http://www.microsoft.com/mspress/support/search.asp

If you have problems, comments, or ideas regarding this book or the sample files, please send them to Microsoft Press. Send an e-mail message to:

mspinput@microsoft.com

Or send postal mail to the following address:

Microsoft Press
Attn: Fundamentals of Audio and Video Programming for Games
One Microsoft Way
Redmond, WA 98052-6399

Please note that product support is not offered through the preceding addresses. For help with Windows Media products, you can connect to Microsoft Product Support Services on the Web at *http://support.microsoft.com.*

Visit the Microsoft Press World Wide Web Site

You are also invited to visit the Microsoft Press World Wide Web site at the following location:

http://www.microsoft.com/mspress

You'll find descriptions for the complete line of Microsoft Press books, information about ordering titles, notice of special features and events, additional content for Microsoft Press books, and much more.

Part I

Audio

1

Getting Started with DirectSound

To examine the samples that accompany this book and develop your own code, you first need to set up your development environment. This chapter covers both setting up your development environment, and getting the first sample to run.

Before going any further, run the install program on the CD that accompanies this book. Then run the High5.exe program, located in the AVBook\bin directory. This sample demonstrates how one sound can be repeatedly mixed to give the impression of complex activity. Try rolling one die, then a number of dice. You will notice that with one die there is no shaking sound and a single rolling sound, and with multiple dice there are multiple shaking and rolling sounds.

Although the High5 sample is simple, it opens up a whole range of issues about the Microsoft DirectX programming environment, which this chapter discusses. After reading this chapter, even if you are new to Microsoft DirectSound, you should have a good idea on how to approach DirectX programming in general, as well as be able to write a small program producing one-dimensional sounds.

Setting Up the Development Environment

First, select a development computer, the fastest and with the most disk space that you can afford. The samples in this book require a computer running Windows 98 or later; we recommend using a Windows 2000 or later operating system.

Since you'll be working with both audio and video, your computer should have a DirectX-compatible video card and a DirectSound-compatible sound card. Although most cards are compatible with these technologies, you should make sure. To get the best performance from the samples, you will also need a good-sized color monitor and stereo speakers. A sub-woofer is also preferable.

If you are going to be working with surround-sound code, you will need to install one of the new sound cards, with the appropriate number of speakers. Figure 1.1 shows the standard layout for 5.1 sound (five speakers and one sub-woofer).

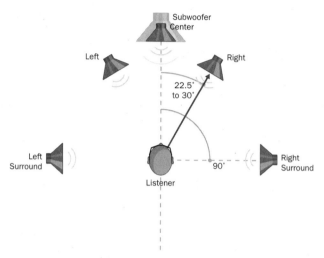

Figure 1.1 Standard speaker layout for 5.1 sound.

However, 6.1 sound is becoming popular, with the addition of one rear speaker, and Figure 1.2 shows the recommended layout.

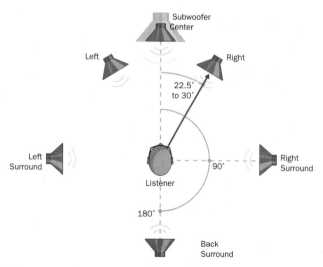

Figure 1.2 Standard speaker layout for 6.1 sound.

For larger rooms and theaters, two rear speakers are recommended, with the 7.1 layout shown in Figure 1.3.

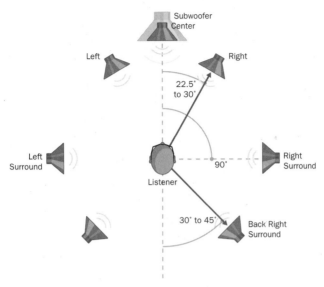

Figure 1.3   Standard speaker layout for 7.1 sound.

By the way, the following enumeration given for speaker configurations defines eighteen speakers – so there is certainly room for even more expansion.

```
#define SPEAKER_FRONT_LEFT              0x1
#define SPEAKER_FRONT_RIGHT             0x2
#define SPEAKER_FRONT_CENTER            0x4
#define SPEAKER_LOW_FREQUENCY           0x8
#define SPEAKER_BACK_LEFT               0x10
#define SPEAKER_BACK_RIGHT              0x20
#define SPEAKER_FRONT_LEFT_OF_CENTER    0x40
#define SPEAKER_FRONT_RIGHT_OF_CENTER   0x80
#define SPEAKER_BACK_CENTER             0x100
#define SPEAKER_SIDE_LEFT               0x200
#define SPEAKER_SIDE_RIGHT              0x400
#define SPEAKER_TOP_CENTER              0x800
#define SPEAKER_TOP_FRONT_LEFT          0x1000
#define SPEAKER_TOP_FRONT_CENTER        0x2000
#define SPEAKER_TOP_FRONT_RIGHT         0x4000
#define SPEAKER_TOP_BACK_LEFT           0x8000
#define SPEAKER_TOP_BACK_CENTER         0x10000
#define SPEAKER_TOP_BACK_RIGHT          0x20000
#define SPEAKER_RESERVED                0x80000000
```

For debugging purposes, especially with video game applications, it is often better to debug remotely over a network. If you want to use this option, obviously you need to have network access. Only the computer running the debugging code needs to have all the multimedia hardware; the development computer is only used to inspect code using the debugging software. However, for the samples in this book that do not exclusively use full-screen video, debugging on the development computer is fine, and there should be little need for remote debugging.

For software, you will need to install Visual Studio .NET, unless you wish to convert the projects back into Visual Studio 6.0, which is still a very common and popular development environment. If you wish to use Visual Studio .NET, but prefer the user interface of Visual Studio 6.0, there is an option that converts the appearance of the UI windows to those of Visual Studio 6.0. This helps keep the view consistent, but a number of the options that you have at your disposal in Visual Studio 6.0 are buried much deeper in Visual Studio .NET, so some developers find the newer UI more awkward.

Although the Windows operating system includes the DirectX run-time bits, you will need to install the latest version of the DirectX SDK (at press time, this was version 9.0), including all the libraries, headers and documentation, by downloading it directly from the Microsoft Web site. The link to the latest download is:
http://www.msdn.microsoft.com/library/default.asp?url=/downloads/list/directx.asp.

If you cannot reach the DirectX SDK from the previous link, go to www.microsoft.com and use the search feature to locate the DirectX download. Make sure that you select the Debug run-time bits option – this enables all sorts of debugging goodies that are not available in the retail version of DirectX. Note also that there is a DirectX entry in the Control Panel, so that you can ensure that hardware acceleration is selected (which it will be by default), and you can change other settings (though we recommend sticking with the defaults for now).

If you already have a DXSDK directory from installing an earlier version of DirectX, you should rename or delete it before installing the latest DirectX SDK, since the DirectX installer will write the new SDK files over the old. However, files that you created or built yourself will be preserved. While this is commendable in that the installer will not delete your work, it can create some confusion in the directory structure. We recommend archiving an older installation so that you know that all the files in the new DXSDK directory are recent.

For the same reason, if you have an earlier version of the DirectX SDK installed, it may be in the directory C:\MSSDK. If so, and if you are converting those older projects to the new version of DirectX, then make sure that the library and include paths in those projects point to the correct location in the DXSDK directory.

DirectX FAQ

A useful Web site that contains frequently asked questions (FAQ) about DirectX is:
http://msdn.microsoft.com/library/default.asp?url=/library/en-us/dndxgen/html/directx9devfaq.asp

---

When you have installed DirectX – which usually means downloading an .exe file to your machine, and then running it to uncompress all the files – it is helpful to examine the SDK directory structure and the sample programs.

The DirectX SDK

If you did not change the installation options from the defaults (we recommend not changing the default settings), you will see that the DXSDK directory has been added to your C drive.

After installation, opening up the DXSDK directory up will give you the Bin, Doc, Include, Lib, Redist, Samples, and SDKDev sub-directories. For the moment, we will concentrate on the Samples directory; open up this directory and look at its contents. Notice that there are a range of samples for C++ and C#. Open up the C++ directory.

The DirectX SDK consists of several components, which are summarized in the following table.

Component	Purpose
DirectSound	Handles the playback of sound, including mono, stereo, 3-D sound, and multichannel sound.
DirectShow	Controls many different video-rendering and capture options.
Direct3D	Renders 3-D objects in a 3-D world.
DirectInput	Controls input from the mouse, keyboard, joysticks, and force-feedback devices.
DirectMusic	Composes and plays all sounds, including music. Based on DirectSound.
DirectPlay	Controls communications in a multiplayer game.

Now that you have installed the DirectX SDK, this is a good time to run some of the DirectSound, DirectShow, and D3D samples in order to test out your audio and video hardware. If you have any problems, it is better to sort them out now before proceeding any further.

It is important to point out that there are few dependencies between the DirectX components; there is no common kernel. Both DirectMusic and the audio components of DirectShow are based on DirectSound, and DirectShow is tightly coupled with D3D, but other than that, the components can be treated as separate SDKs in their own right.

Although DirectMusic is certainly an audio API, experience has shown that it is both too technical for musicians yet too musical for software engineers, not to mention its proprietary file formats and awkward accompanying tool, DirectMusic Producer. We do not cover DirectMusic any further in this book.

The DirectX SDK documentation goes into great detail about the API calls, but goes into much less detail about the utility code that is provided along with the SDK. The utility code is installed along with the SDK, and has names such as dsutil (for DirectSound), dxutil (for basic DX information), and so on.

One of the most important lessons of this chapter is to point out that this utility code should be considered to be part of the SDK; it should not be considered peripheral or unimportant. It contains more than just utility code, and in some cases the functions provided include work-arounds for some of the known problems of the SDK itself.

If you are planning a game based on D3D, we strongly suggest looking through all the source code that is provided when you install DirectX before you begin any coding. By doing so, you could save a lot of time, not to mention a lot of grief.

There are overly confident programmers who feel that all coding should be done to the SDK API calls without considering any layers that are above them. This is just not realistic. Save your problem-solving skills for the unique problems that will develop within your own application. When developing code using DirectX components, such as DirectSound or DirectPlay, it is usual to write a complete layer that wraps up all the DirectX calls, with your application calling only the functions in this upper layer.

This has the advantage of insulating most of your application from handling DirectX pointers and other goop, and also means that this layer can clearly be tailored to exactly the kind of application that you are writing. There are, of course, performance issues to be addressed, although none with a method that is only called once, nor is there any performance improvement to be gained by rewriting code that is already well-written.

The following tables describe all of the utility code that comes with DirectX. Although this book will explain only the audio and video elements, it is good to know all the tools that you have at your disposal – and you should familiarize yourself with them before starting development. The utility code is in the C++/Common directory, with the .cpp files in the Src directory and the .h files in the Include directory.

There is almost a one-to-one correspondence between the .cpp files in the Src directory and the header files in the Include directory. Almost all the utilities have at least one associated header file, and some have two.

DirectX utility	Purpose
Dxutil.cpp	Provides some general functions for handling GUIDs and similar laborious duties. This utility is mostly used by the other utility code and you should not have to change it.

D3D utility	Purpose
D3dapp	Provides the basic initialization and termination for most D3D applications. Reports possible installation errors.
D3denumeration	Provides utilities to enumerate the hardware that is available on the computer that the application is running on.
D3dfile	Supports the .X file format, a complex 3-D file format that can handle a hierarchy of objects, textures and animations. It is compatible, either directly or with conversion tools, with third-party graphics tools such as Discreet's 3ds max.
D3dfont	Provides a range of graphic-text handling functions. Very useful, as there is no explicit text handling in the D3D SDK.
D3dsaver	Provides a framework for screen savers.
D3dsettings	Supports the saving and restoring of window settings – such as whether check boxes have been selected or not, slider positions, and so on. Useful when creating samples.
D3dutil	Initiates essentials for most D3D programs such as lighting, texture, and camera information.
ddutil	Named after the legacy DirectDraw SDK – now subsumed into D3D – this set of utilities is mostly used by the other utility code. You may find some of the low-level functions useful, but many developers will not need to touch the code in this file.

DirectInput utility	Purpose
Didevimg	Provides a framework for the drawing of input device images – and states – on the screen.
diutil	Provides essential, low-level input functions that map devices to input.

DirectMusic utility	Purpose
Dmutil	Supports the playing of DirectMusic segments and scripts. Most DirectMusic functionality is provided within the SDK.

DirectPlay utility	Purpose
Netclient	Provides base classes for enumerating hosts, and for allowing a user to join a session, which is what DirectPlay calls a multiplayer Internet game.
Netconnect	Provides base classes for enumerating hosts and service providers, and enables a user to either join or host a session.
Netvoice	Provides classes to enable the players of an Internet game to talk to each other through sound capture and replay.
SessionInfo	Handles the storage of information required to run a session, such as the players, addresses, messaging, and so on.

DirectSound utility	Purpose
Dsutil	Provides many useful classes for managing the sound system, reading in wave files, handling streaming sound, and hardware and software buffering.

The DirectShow utilities are not in the same folder as all the other DirectX components, but are in their own Common directory within the DShow directory. The sources and headers are all together, and not in separate directories. The following table summarizes the DirectShow utility code.

DirectShow utility	Purpose
Dshowutil	Assists with DShow graph building and debugging.
Mfcdmoutil	Assists in using DirectX Media Objects (DMOs) in Microsoft Foundation Classes (MFC) applications.
Mfcutil	Assists in developing DirectShow applications using MFC.
Namedguid	Converts various DirectShow GUID values to strings, which is useful when debugging.
seekutil	Adds a user interface for file seeking in a DirectShow application.

The DirectShow utilities do not provide as complete a framework as does the utility code for the rest of DirectX. The chapters in this book on special video effects provide a much better framework from which to start.

Another word of warning. There have been some changes to the parameters of methods in the utility code since DirectX 8.1. These changes should not confuse you, and should be obvious when you look at the sources, however, they could cause programs that you wrote for DX 8.1 to not compile.

In addition to the utility code, the samples provided with the DirectX SDK are another great resource. You will find it instructive to check out all the samples and to work through them. However, particularly for audio and video, we found the samples included with the SDK to be somewhat simplistic, and do not show off the capabilities of the product. Partly for this reason, we have included a set of samples for this book that show a fuller range of the capabilities of the DirectX SDK.

The High5 sample is the only DirectSound sample in this book that does not require any changes or additions to the dsutil.cpp utility code provided in the DirectX SDK package. Generally, the utility code is very useful, however, since it does not give you individual buffer-level access to each sound, it is somewhat restrictive. This restriction does not matter when the sounds that you require do not need any manipulation, which is the case for the High5 sample, and for all the samples included with the SDK. However, you will find that you will need individual buffer manipulation for more complex applications.

We will begin our programming tutorial by going through the High5 sample, layer by layer. Now might be a good time to run the High5 sample a few times, to see how it works and to remind yourself just how much life sound can add to graphics.

High5 Sample

Using Visual Studio, open the High5 project file, in the AVBook\Audio projects directory, and then open the High5.cpp file.

Timing

For the High5 sample, timing is simply used to delay an overlapping sound by a small and random fraction of a second in the *playOverlappingSounds* function. As a general rule, especially for games involving animation, timing is extremely important. It is one of the first things that you should address when designing an application. You must reconcile the variables of refresh rate for the screen and the simulated time that the application code is running to, and the variants of these that depend on the speed that the client machine can run your application. Since timing issues affect the structure of such an application so fundamentally, it can be a tough problem if it is not addressed early on.

The first functions in the source file handle timing. The basic timing functions in the Microsoft Win32 SDK do not have the precision we require – each tick takes around 55 milliseconds, which is pretty useless for our purposes. Many developers, and indeed many Microsoft SDKs, instead use the timing functions that are available in the Microsoft Windows Multimedia SDK.

This is an ancient Microsoft SDK long slated for retirement, which is still around due to the usefulness of a few of its functions. The Multimedia SDK includes many early attempts at video reproduction on a computer, in the form of the Video for Windows (VfW) functions, which are also still in use despite their age. However, it does include a number of timing functions that provide fairly good millisecond accuracy. The most frequently used is the *timeGetTime* function.

The *timeGetTime* function returns the number of milliseconds since you started the Windows operating system. The functions in the High5.cpp code that wrap this function are *initMSTimer* and *getMSTime*. The *initMSTimer* function stores the first time that the call is made, and the *getMSTime* function returns the difference between another call and the first call. This means that you can always get an accurate millisecond count since your application started. If you do a search for the use of this function, you will find it used throughout many Microsoft SDKs, since it is a reliable timing function.

There is a remote chance of a problem with *timeGetTime*: as the millisecond count is a DWORD value, it will wrap back to 0 every 49 days or so. For almost all applications, this problem falls in the "won't fix" category, but if you are a purist, you might want to amend the *getMSTime* function to cope with this case (by maintaining a count of 49-day iterations).

The Multimedia SDK run-time bits are included as part of Windows; to use them you need only add the header file, mmsystem.h, to your source files, and include the winmm.lib file for the linker.

Random Numbers

No game program is complete without some random numbers to add chaos to order. Randomness of some sort is essential in ensuring that every puff of smoke, clank of a sword, roll of a dice, or bang of a cannon are not identical each time that they occur.

The *rand* function returns a random number between 0 and the global variable *RAND_MAX* defined in the header file stdlib.h. However, to simulate a dice roll, the numbers required are clearly 1 through 6. To achieve this range, simply use the modulus operator (%) to return the remainder of the returned random number after division by six, and add one to change the result from 0 to 5 to 1 to 6. Purists will notice a tiny flaw in this math, in that if *RAND_MAX* does not evenly divide by six, then there is a small distortion in the results, however one that is too small for us to care about.

The function *srand* should be called to give the random number generation a variable seed, so that the same sequence of numbers is not given out. The most common way of doing this is with the following call.

```
srand( (unsigned)time(NULL));
```

This results in a different stream of random numbers each time that the program is run. For debugging purposes, when you might not want this behavior in order to try to repeat a bug, either set the parameter of *srand* to 1, or comment out the statement, and exactly the same sequence of numbers will be generated every time. Be sure to uncomment the line or change the parameter back when you are ready for prime time.

MFC or Win32

You will note that most DirectX samples are built up from Win32 calls and do not use MFC. Microsoft Foundation Classes (MFC) have turned out, in our opinion, to be somewhat more popular outside of the company than within. You can use MFC to build your applications, and can use the wizards available in Visual Studio to help you get started. However, our samples will follow the convention of coding directly to Win32, so you will not see any projects containing the output from MFC wizards.

There can be tricky issues if you start a programming project using MFC, and then wish to expunge it from the code. For example, the run-time library in the Properties dialog box (in the C/C++ Code generation section) usually needs to be single-threaded for a Win32 application, but multithreaded for an MFC-based application.

Our recommendation for audio/video projects is that if you are not a whiz in MFC, then stick with Win32 and leave learning MFC for a rainy day. A very rainy day.

Having said all that, notice that our *WinMain* function, the entry point to our program, simply calls *InitCommonControls*, then initializes random numbers, stores the instance handle in a handy global, creates a path to the directory containing the wave files, and then fires off the dialog box to do the rest of the work. Delegation at its best.

```
int APIENTRY WinMain( HINSTANCE hInstance,
                      HINSTANCE hPrevInstance,
                      LPSTR lpCmdLine,
                      int nCmdShow)
{
    // Initialize the common control dll.
    InitCommonControls();

    // Use the time to seed the random number generator.
    srand( (unsigned)time( NULL ) );

    // Store the value of the Instance handle.
    g_hInst = hInstance ;

    // Get the sound directory containing the dice sounds.
    GetCurrentDirectory(MAX_PATH, g_soundDir);
    g_soundDir[2] = 0;      // Delete all but the drive.
    strcat(g_soundDir,"\\AVBook\\Audio\\Boardgames\\");

    // Run everything else from the dialog box.
    DialogBox(hInstance, MAKEINTRESOURCE( IDD_HIGH5_DIALOG ), NULL, DlgProc );

    return 0 ;
}
```

Graphics

The High5 sample shows the kind of graphical masterpiece that would have looked fine in the age of games that involved space invaders and ping pong.

For a graphics-based game, which most games are, the rule is to "push the hardware". If you are going to write a 3-D-animated game, and haven't delved into the world of pixel and vertex shaders, then you might want to consider becoming an expert in these skills. However, for our sound samples, we wish to minimize the graphics code in order to isolate the audio programming techniques. You will not learn much about graphics in this book, although it is interesting how passable a user interface can be developed from dialog boxes and character strings. Note that the *sixFaces* structure uses o's and the UI uses multiline edit dialog boxes to mock up the faces of dice.

In other words, dialog-based programs often provide a good base for tool development.

Callbacks

Callback functions are one of the great building blocks of Windows programming. There are many books on this subject, such as *Programming Windows*, by Charles Petzold, and it is a good idea to have such a reference available if you plan to use Windows features in your programming. The callback for the High5 sample is suitably straightforward.

```
int CALLBACK DlgProc( HWND hwndDlg, UINT uMsg, WPARAM wParam, LPARAM lParam )
{
    HRESULT   hr.= S_OK ;

    switch( uMsg )
    {
    case WM_INITDIALOG:
        OnInitDialog(hwndDlg);
        return TRUE ;

    case WM_COMMAND:
        switch (LOWORD(wParam))
        {
        case IDC_RADIO1:
            SetDlgItemText(hwndDlg, IDC_ROLL6, "" );
            g_Dice = 1;
            return TRUE;

        case IDC_RADIO2:
            g_Dice = 2;
            return TRUE;

        case IDC_RADIO3:
            g_Dice = 3;
            return TRUE;
```

```
            case IDC_RADIO4:
                g_Dice = 4;
                return TRUE;

            case IDC_RADIO5:
                g_Dice = 5;
                return TRUE;

            case IDC_ROLL:
                initMSTimer();
                EnablePlayUI( hwndDlg, FALSE );
                return TRUE;

            case IDCANCEL:
                EndDialog( hwndDlg, wParam ) ;
                return TRUE ;

        }

    case WM_TIMER:
        OnTimer( hwndDlg );
        break;

    case WM_DESTROY:
        // Clean up everything.
        KillTimer( hwndDlg, 0 );
        closeDirectSound();
        break;

    }
    return FALSE ;
}
```

Most of the callback function is self-explanatory, so we'll begin by looking at the *OnInitDialog* function, which is called when the *WM_INITDIALOG* message is received by the callback.

```
VOID OnInitDialog( HWND hwndDlg )
{
    HICON    hIcon    = NULL;

    g_hwndDialog = hwndDlg;

    // Load the application icon.
    hIcon = LoadIcon( g_hInst, MAKEINTRESOURCE( IDI_ICON1 ) );
    if( hIcon )
    {
        SendMessage( hwndDlg, WM_SETICON, ICON_SMALL, (LPARAM)hIcon );
        SendMessage( hwndDlg, WM_SETICON, ICON_BIG, (LPARAM)hIcon );
    }
```

(continued)

```
// Load the dialog defaults.
CheckRadioButton(hwndDlg, IDC_RADIO1, IDC_RADIO5, IDC_RADIO1);
g_Dice = 1;

// Create a timer, so we can check for when the sound buffer is stopped.
SetTimer( hwndDlg, 0, 250, NULL );

// Initialize DirectSound.
initDirectSound( hwndDlg );
}
```

There is some pretty standard code for the first few lines of this function, then the dialog box defaults are set, and then there is call to *SetTimer*. This function will set a Windows timer going, and will send the Windows message *WM_TIMER* every time that the timeout value is reached. The first parameter is the ubiquitous handle to the dialog box, the second is an identifier (in case you want to use multiple timers), the third parameter is the timeout value, and the last one can be a procedure name that is called when the timeout value is reached. Windows sends the *WM_TIMER* message if this value is *NULL*, which is the most common use of this function. Note that the timeout value is in milliseconds, so the *WM_TIMER* message is going to be sent every 250 milliseconds (one quarter of a second).

The timer is deleted in the callback function when the dialog box is destroyed with a call to *KillTimer*, using the identifier (0) to indicate which timer is to go.

The next function we'll examine is the *OnTimer* function, remembering that this is called every 250 milliseconds.

```
VOID OnTimer( HWND hwndDlg )
{
    int     result[5];
    int     d;
    int     total;

    // If the shaking sound is required, then load and play it.
    if (rollStatus == status_shaking)
    {
        if (loadSound("DieShake.wav", g_Dice - 1))
            playOverlappingSounds(g_Dice - 1);

        rollStatus = status_starting;

    } else
    // If the die roll sound is required, then load and play it.
    if (rollStatus == status_starting AND
       (g_Dice == 1 OR testSoundStopped() OR getMSTime() >= 1000))
    {
        if (loadSound("DieRoll.wav", g_Dice))
            playOverlappingSounds(g_Dice);

        rollStatus = status_rolling;
```

```
    } else
    // If the dice are rolling, then check to see if it is time
    // to present the results.
    if (rollStatus == status_rolling AND
        (testSoundStopped() OR getMSTime() >= 2000))
    {
        total = 0;
        // For each die, retrieve a random number.
        for (d=0; d<5; d++)
        {
            if (d < g_Dice)
                result[d] = dieRoll(6); else
                result[d] = 0;
            total += result[d];
        }
        // Display the numbers.
        SetDlgItemText(hwndDlg, IDC_ROLL1, sixFaces[ result[0] ] );
        SetDlgItemText(hwndDlg, IDC_ROLL2, sixFaces[ result[1] ] );
        SetDlgItemText(hwndDlg, IDC_ROLL3, sixFaces[ result[2] ] );
        SetDlgItemText(hwndDlg, IDC_ROLL4, sixFaces[ result[3] ] );
        SetDlgItemText(hwndDlg, IDC_ROLL5, sixFaces[ result[4] ] );

        // If more than one die, display a total.
        if (g_Dice > 1)
        {
            SetDlgItemInt(hwndDlg, IDC_ROLL6, total, false);
        }
        // Update the UI controls to show the sound as stopped.
        EnablePlayUI( hwndDlg, TRUE );
    }
}
```

The first test checks a flag to see if the shaking sound should be started. If so, a call is made to *loadSound*, with two parameters: the name of the wave file to load and the maximum number of duplicate sound buffers that might be needed.

Notice that we are loading in the wave file each and every time that it is required. This is hardly efficient, but we do this so we don't have to address the creation of multiple *CSound* objects just yet. We have one *CSound* object, which we will be describing in just a moment, and it needs to be constantly fed with the required wave file and number of buffers that might be needed.

If the file loads correctly, then a call to *playOverlappingSounds* is made. The reason that the number of sounds is one less than the number of dice is simply that the shaking sound represents two dice colliding together, so that two dice only create one shaking sound. For three dice, we play two shaking sounds, and so on.

Following the initiation of any shaking sounds, a flag is set that indicates that the roll has started. The next time *OnTimer* is called, with *rollStatus* set to *status_starting*, we test to see if the shaking sound has stopped, and if it has, starts the rolling sound.

Notice this time that the number of rolling sounds is equal to the number of dice.

Finally, to end the *OnTimer* function, we check to see if the rolling has stopped, and if it has, it is time to update the dialog box and display the dice.

Throughout the previous procedure, we called or implied the existence of five functions that we have not yet explained, but will now discuss: *initDirectSound*, *loadSound*, *playOverlappingSounds*, *testSoundStopped*, and *closeDirectSound*.

DirectSound

The DirectSound utility code, dsutil.cpp, declares two very useful classes: *CSoundManager* and *CSound*. You only need one *CSoundManager* object to manage the audio system, and one *CSound* object for every sound that you wish to play. For this sample, we just have one *CSound* object (hence the need to keep loading the shaking and rolling sounds mentioned previously). This keeps the sample simple for now. The declarations are as follows.

```
CSoundManager* g_pSoundManager = NULL;
CSound*        g_pSound        = NULL;
```

Note that there is a distinct difference between one "sound" (identified by one wave file), and one sound "buffer". Each buffer is a copy of the sound, and can be mixed as a sound effect in its own right. So if one sound is created with four associated buffers, then four copies of the sound can be mixed (overlayed, panned independently, volume changed, processed for special effects, and so on).

initDirectSound

The *initDirectSound* function creates a new sound manager object, and initializes it if all goes smoothly.

```
void initDirectSound( HWND hwndDlg )
{
    g_pSoundManager = new CSoundManager();

    soundWorking = false;

    if (g_pSoundManager != NULL)
    {
        if (SUCCEEDED(g_pSoundManager->Initialize( hwndDlg, DSSCL_PRIORITY)))
            soundWorking = true;
    }
}
```

There is a whole range of errors that can occur when you are trying to initialize the audio system; for example, there can be no sound card, no compatible sound card, no DirectX run-time bits, and so on. However, for the High5 sample we'll simply set a flag on whether the sound system is working correctly or not. It is possible that some users of your application will not have the correct sound card up and running, but that should not mean that the application will grind to a halt. It just won't play any sounds.

The first parameter to the *Initialize* method is the inevitable Windows handle, the second is the cooperative level (how well this application will work with others that are running at the same time). Almost always, this is set to *DSSCL_PRIORITY*, which largely means that, when this application has focus, only its sounds will be audible.

The other cooperative levels that can be set are *DSSCL_NORMAL*, which restricts all sound output to 8-bit, and *DSSCL_WRITEPRIMARY*, which allows the application to write to the primary buffer. The primary buffer contains all the sounds to be played mixed together. Typically, your sounds are loaded into secondary buffers, and then DirectSound handles the mixing into the primary buffer. Use *DSSCL_NORMAL* only if you are nostalgic about poor-quality PC sound, and *DSSCL_WRITEPRIMARY* if you are writing your own mixer. Otherwise, stick with *DSSCL_PRIORITY*.

loadSound

The *loadSound* function checks to see that the sound system is working, and if so, clears the *CSound* object and loads in the requested wave file.

```
bool loadSound(char filename[], int nSounds)
{
    TCHAR      fullFilename[MAX_PATH];

    if (soundWorking)
    {
        // Stop any running sound.
        if( g_pSound )
        {
            g_pSound->Stop();
            g_pSound->Reset();
        }
        // Free any previous sound, and make a new one.
        SAFE_DELETE( g_pSound );

        // Construct the full file name.
        strcpy(fullFilename,g_soundDir);
        strcat(fullFilename,filename);
        // Load the wave file into a DirectSound buffer.
        if (FAILED(g_pSoundManager->Create( &g_pSound,fullFilename, 0,
                                            GUID_NULL, nSounds )))
            return false;

        return true;
    } else
        return false;
}
```

The DirectSound SDK *Stop* method obviously stops a sound that is playing, and the *Reset* method resets the pointer to the sound buffers back to the beginning. This may be somewhat redundant in this sample, but it is usually good practice to go through this procedure when closing down a sound.

SAFE_DELETE is a useful little macro for deleting an object, and is defined in dxutil.h. After first testing that the object exists, *SAFE_DELETE* deletes the object and sets the pointer to it to *NULL*.

The next call does most of the processing required by *loadSound*.

```
g_pSoundManager->Create( &g_pSound,filename, 0, GUID_NULL, nSounds )
```

This call creates a new sound, taking the pointer to the *CSound* object, a file name for the wave file, some creation flags, a GUID identifying a 3-D-sound algorithm (*GUID_NULL* selects the default), and the number of buffers to be created for the sound. The two parameters that require explanation are the creation flags and the GUID for the algorithm.

It is a very common error when programming DirectSound to not set the creation flags to match the sound manipulation that you want. Since we have set the flags to 0 for the High5 sample, nothing can be done to change the sound — not the volume, not the frequency, and certainly not the panning or anything fancy.

For each sound effect, you should set the creation flags to match the processing that you might want to happen later on in the program. The reasoning behind the creation flags is simply one of performance. If DirectSound is notified in advance that very few, or no, processes (such as volume change) will be required, then all the plumbing required to support this processing can be ignored from the beginning, and greater speed efficiency is the result. The downside, of course, is that it is easy to forget to set the creation flags correctly. The following is a list of commonly used creation flags.

Creation flag	Description
DSBCAPS_CTRLVOLUME	The volume of the sound can be changed.
DSBCAPS_CTRLFREQUENCY	The frequency of the sound can be changed.
DSBCAPS_CTRLPAN	The sound can be panned.
DSBCAPS_CTRLFX	The sound can go through effects processing (echo, distortion, and so on). For more information, see Chapter 4.
DSBCAPS_CTRL3D	This creation flag enables 3-D processing. For more information, see Chapter 3.

To set a combination of creation flags, simply OR them together, in a statement such as the following.

```
dwCreationFlags = DSBCAPS_CTRLVOLUME | DSBCAPS_CTRLPAN;
```

For the sake of explanation, we will call sounds that require 3-D processing, 3-D sounds, and those that do not, 2-D sounds.

We will return to this topic for both 2-D and 3-D sound effects, but for our High5 sample, since there is no processing at all, the flags are set to zero.

The second parameter that we need to look at, the GUID for the sound processing algorithm, is easier to explain. For 2-D sound there really aren't any options, so just set it to *GUID_NULL*. However, for 3-D sound, there are a couple of options that trade performance for quality in some situations (see Chapter 3).

playOverlappingSounds

This function randomly waits up to one fifth of a second before playing the same sound over the top of any sounds that are already running.

```
void playOverlappingSounds(int nSounds)
{
    int      n;
    DWORD    current, delay;
    DWORD    dwFlags = 0L;

    if (soundWorking)
    {
        for (n=0; n<nSounds; n++)
        {
            // Wait randomly up to 1/5th of a second (200ms).
            delay   = dieRoll(200);
            current = getMSTime();
            while (getMSTime() < current + delay) {};

            // No need to set volume, frequency or panning parameters
            // as creation flags do not support changing them from the
            // original recording.

            g_pSound->Play( 0, dwFlags, 0 , 0 , 0 );
        }
    }
}
```

The DirectSound *Play* method is an asynchronous call; it starts playing the sound, and then processing immediately returns to continue with the application without waiting for the sound to stop.

Notice that since we have set *dwFlags* to 0, all the parameters to the *Play* call are also set to 0. Yet, we still get the sound that we want, so clearly, the zeros do not mean zero sound.

The first parameter is "reserved for future use" (it will almost certainly never be used), and should be set to 0. The second flag contains the playing flags, not to be confused with the creation flags. However, there is only one playing flag defined, *DSBPLAY_LOOPING*, so set this flag if you want your sound to loop, or set it to 0 if you do not.

The final three parameters contain the required volume, frequency and panning position, assuming that the appropriate creation flags have been set to enable these. As this is not the case here, these parameters will be ignored, and are set to 0.

The Cacophony sample, described in the next chapter, gives a good example of the use of creation flags, and varying volume, frequency and panning positions.

testSoundStopped

This method simply tests to see if a sound has stopped playing.

```
bool testSoundStopped()
{
    if (soundWorking AND g_pSound != NULL)
    {
        if( !g_pSound->IsSoundPlaying())
        {
            g_pSound->Stop();
            g_pSound->Reset();
            return true;
        } else
            return false;
    } else
        return true;
}
```

The *IsSoundPlaying* method returns a Boolean, and if the sound is not playing, it seems wise to call *Stop* and then *Reset* to set the pointer back to the start of the sound buffer.

closeDirectSound

This is a simple function to close things down. Note that you must delete the sound objects before the sound manager object.

```
void closeDirectSound()
{
    if (soundWorking)
    {
        SAFE_DELETE( g_pSound );
        SAFE_DELETE( g_pSoundManager );
    }
}
```

DSUTIL.CPP

The dsutil.cpp utility file is both invaluable and flawed. In the following chapters, we will be changing, removing, and adding methods to our own version of this file. However, it is instructive to summarize here what this file has to offer.

CSoundManager Class

The *CSoundManager* class is well-named, because you will use it to manage the sound in your application. The only data item is a pointer to a *DirectSound8* object. Like all good managers, this object handles initialization, termination, and coordination issues. The definition of the class follows.

```
class CSoundManager
{
protected:
    LPDIRECTSOUND8 m_pDS;

public:
    CSoundManager();
    ~CSoundManager();

    HRESULT Initialize( HWND hWnd, DWORD dwCoopLevel );
    inline  LPDIRECTSOUND8 GetDirectSound() { return m_pDS; }
    HRESULT SetPrimaryBufferFormat( DWORD dwPrimaryChannels,
                                    DWORD dwPrimaryFreq,
                                    DWORD dwPrimaryBitRate );
    HRESULT Get3DListenerInterface( LPDIRECTSOUND3DLISTENER* ppDSListener );
    HRESULT Create( CSound** ppSound, LPTSTR strWaveFileName,
                    DWORD dwCreationFlags = 0,
                    GUID guid3DAlgorithm = GUID_NULL,
                    DWORD dwNumBuffers = 1 );
    HRESULT CreateFromMemory( CSound** ppSound, BYTE* pbData,
                              ULONG ulDataSize, LPWAVEFORMATEX pwfx,
                              DWORD dwCreationFlags = 0,
                              GUID guid3DAlgorithm = GUID_NULL,
                              DWORD dwNumBuffers = 1 );
    HRESULT CreateStreaming( CStreamingSound** ppStreamingSound,
                             LPTSTR strWaveFileName, DWORD dwCreationFlags,
                             GUID guid3DAlgorithm, DWORD dwNotifyCount,
                             DWORD dwNotifySize, HANDLE hNotifyEvent );
};
```

The constructor simply sets the *DirectSound8* pointer to *NULL*, and the destructor cleanly destroys the object and will be called once at the end of your application, through the *closeDirectSound* function in our samples. We have already come across the *Initialize* and *SetPrimaryBufferFormat* methods, but we list them again here for completeness.

Initialize

```
HRESULT Initialize( HWND hWnd, DWORD dwCoopLevel );
```

See the previous description of the *initDirectSound* function for an explanation of this method.

LPDIRECTSOUND8

```
inline LPDIRECTSOUND8 GetDirectSound() { return m_pDS; }
```

This inline method returns the pointer to the DirectSound object. You will probably not need to call this method.

SetPrimaryBufferFormat

```
HRESULT SetPrimaryBufferFormat( DWORD dwPrimaryChannels,
                                DWORD dwPrimaryFreq,
                                DWORD dwPrimaryBitRate );
```

Although it is largely redundant, you will see this method called in many Direct-Sound samples. The method calls through to a DirectSound SDK method, *SetFormat*, which is used to set the format of the primary buffer.

Calling *IDirectSoundBuffer8::SetFormat* on the primary buffer has no effect on Windows Driver Model (WDM) drivers, except in applications that write to the primary buffer. If the application calls *SetCooperativeLevel(DSSCL_WRITEPRIMARY)*, the primary buffer is actually used to play audio data, and *SetFormat* has the effect of immediately changing the format of that data (that is, the format in which DirectSound interprets it to be). However, very few applications use this mode, and on WDM drivers there's no benefit in using it.

WDM drivers were introduced with Windows 98 SE, although it is up to the audio card manufacturers, rather than Microsoft, as to whether they use this model rather than the earlier VxD driver model. If your applications target Windows 98, then you should add a call to *SetPrimaryBufferFormat* when initializing DirectSound. For 16-bit stereo sound, recorded at 22 KHz, that call would be as follows.

```
hr = g_pSoundManager->SetPrimaryBufferFormat( 2, 22050, 16 )
```

Create

```
HRESULT Create( CSound** ppSound, LPTSTR strWaveFileName,
                DWORD dwCreationFlags = 0,
                GUID guid3DAlgorithm = GUID_NULL,
                DWORD dwNumBuffers = 1 );
```

This is one of the most useful and often-used methods of this class, as it loads a sound from a wave file and duplicates the sound into buffers the required number of times. See the previous description of the *loadSound* function for further explanation of this method. Although there are defaults set for the last two parameters for this method, they will not always be what you want, so many times you will want to enter all five parameters. In Chapter 3, you will find an explanation of the *guid3DAlgorithm* parameter.

CreateFromMemory

```
HRESULT CreateFromMemory( CSound** ppSound, BYTE* pbData,
                          ULONG ulDataSize, LPWAVEFORMATEX pwfx,
                          DWORD dwCreationFlags = 0,
                          GUID guid3DAlgorithm = GUID_NULL,
                          DWORD dwNumBuffers = 1 );
```

Calling this method will create a *CSound* object from a waveform held in a buffer. This method is very similar to the previous one, but used far less frequently. The only three parameters that are different from the *Create* method are the pointer to the buffer *pbData*, the length of the buffer *ulDataSize*, and a pointer to a *WAVEFORMATEX* structure describing this data.

This method is not used in any samples in this book.

CreateStreaming

```
HRESULT CreateStreaming( CStreamingSound** ppStreamingSound,
                         LPTSTR strWaveFileName, DWORD dwCreationFlags,
                         GUID guid3DAlgorithm, DWORD dwNotifyCount,
                         DWORD dwNotifySize, HANDLE hNotifyEvent );
```

This method creates a *CStreamingSound* object for a wave file. The advantage of streaming is that it allows a relatively small physical buffer to handle a much larger wave file. This can be very helpful, for example, when playing long music files. The disadvantage of using *CStreamingSound* over *CSound* objects is that there is an added level of complexity in handling the streams. See Chapter 6 for a description and working sample.

CSound Class

Unless your application is as simple as the High5 sample, you will need multiple copies of the object created by this class. A *CSound* object is used to process and play one or more instances of a sound. This is the class that you will need to modify the most for your own application, as we will show in the following chapters. The unmodified declaration of *CSound* follows.

```
class CSound
{
protected:
    LPDIRECTSOUNDBUFFER* m_apDSBuffer;
    DWORD                m_dwDSBufferSize;
    CWaveFile*           m_pWaveFile;
    DWORD                m_dwNumBuffers;
    DWORD                m_dwCreationFlags;
    HRESULT RestoreBuffer( LPDIRECTSOUNDBUFFER pDSB, BOOL* pbWasRestored );
```

(continued)

```
public:
    CSound( LPDIRECTSOUNDBUFFER* apDSBuffer, DWORD dwDSBufferSize,
            DWORD dwNumBuffers, CWaveFile* pWaveFile, DWORD dwCreationFlags );
    virtual ~CSound();

    HRESULT Get3DBufferInterface( DWORD dwIndex,
                                  LPDIRECTSOUND3DBUFFER* ppDS3DBuffer );
    HRESULT FillBufferWithSound( LPDIRECTSOUNDBUFFER pDSB,
                                 BOOL bRepeatWavIfBufferLarger );
    LPDIRECTSOUNDBUFFER GetFreeBuffer();
    LPDIRECTSOUNDBUFFER GetBuffer( DWORD dwIndex );

    HRESULT Play( DWORD dwPriority = 0, DWORD dwFlags = 0,
                  LONG lVolume = 0, LONG lFrequency = -1, LONG lPan = 0 );
    HRESULT Play3D( LPDS3DBUFFER p3DBuffer, DWORD dwPriority = 0,
                    DWORD dwFlags = 0, LONG lFrequency = 0 );
    HRESULT Stop();
    HRESULT Reset();
    BOOL    IsSoundPlaying();
};
```

The creation function for the *CSound* class is called by the *Create* method of the *CSoundManager* class. Although you will probably not need to call the creation function, you will need to modify it later to handle special effects. The destructor will be called through our *closeDirectSound* call.

Get3DBufferInterface

```
HRESULT Get3DBufferInterface( DWORD dwIndex,
                              LPDIRECTSOUND3DBUFFER* ppDS3DBuffer );
```

This method retrieves the 3-D buffer interface associated with one particular buffer for this sound. If you created, for example, a sound with four sound buffers, then *dwIndex* can be 0 through 3 to return one of up to four associated 3-D buffers.

The way that DirectSound handles 3-D sound is that it associates an additional 3-D buffer description with the 2-D sound held in the *CSound* object. This particular method is not used in later samples, because we integrate the 3-D buffer description into the *CSound* class.

FillBufferWithSound

```
HRESULT FillBufferWithSound( LPDIRECTSOUNDBUFFER pDSB,
                             BOOL bRepeatWavIfBufferLarger );
```

This is a very useful method, although it is encapsulated in calls from this and other utility classes. Its purpose is to fill a buffer with the sound that was provided to the class constructor. If the buffer is larger than the provided sound, the remainder will be filled with silence unless you set the *bRepeatWavIfBufferLarger* flag to True, in which case the sound will be repeated until the buffer is full (although none of the calls in the utility code do this). You will probably not need to call this method directly, nor modify it.

GetFreeBuffer

```
LPDIRECTSOUNDBUFFER GetFreeBuffer();
```

This method finds a buffer that is not playing; if it cannot find one randomly, it stops a buffer and selects it. This is not a useful method for building applications, and needs to be replaced (see Chapter 2).

GetBuffer

```
LPDIRECTSOUNDBUFFER GetBuffer( DWORD dwIndex );
```

This is a simple method that retrieves a pointer to a buffer, if the index is valid. You will probably not need to modify this method.

Play

```
HRESULT Play( DWORD dwPriority = 0, DWORD dwFlags = 0,
              LONG lVolume = 0, LONG lFrequency = -1, LONG lPan = 0 );
```

This method plays a buffer, but uses the unreliable *GetFreeBuffer* method rather than allowing the application to select which buffer to play, so this is another method that needs modified. However, this method is useful for discussing the parameters. Volume parameters sent to DirectSound are in the range -100.00 decibels to 0 decibels, which is the attenuation (the reduction in volume) applied to the volume of the wave file. Volume parameters are supplied as 100ths of a decibel in a long variable (so a value of -150 means the original volume is reduced by -1.5 decibels). Frequencies are supplied to DirectSound in hertz, and it is possible to play a sound at a different frequency than it was recorded. Panning values also use the 100th of a decibel unit, and record the attenuation for the left and right speakers. These values are discussed in more detail in Chapters 2 and 3, but the following code shows the defined minimums and maximums (note the increase in maximum frequency supported by DirectSound version 9 or later).

```
#define DSBFREQUENCY_MIN          100
#if DIRECTSOUND_VERSION >= 0x0900
    #define DSBFREQUENCY_MAX          200000
#else
    #define DSBFREQUENCY_MAX          100000
#endif

#define DSBPAN_LEFT          -10000
#define DSBPAN_CENTER        0
#define DSBPAN_RIGHT         10000

#define DSBVOLUME_MIN        -10000
#define DSBVOLUME_MAX        0.
```

Play3D

```
HRESULT Play3D( LPDS3DBUFFER p3DBuffer, DWORD dwPriority = 0,
                DWORD dwFlags = 0, LONG lFrequency = 0 );
```

This is the 3-D version of the previous method. It is helpful in showing how to associate a 3-D buffer with the playing of a sound, but is not a method that should be used without modification (see Chapter 3).

Stop

```
HRESULT Stop();
```

This method stops all the buffers of the sound. You may sometimes want to do this, however, it is usually more useful to stop individual buffers (see Chapter 2). Stopping sounds also involves deactivating special effects (see Chapter 4).

Reset

```
HRESULT Reset();
```

For each sound buffer, there is a pointer that stores where the sound is currently being played from. This method resets all the pointers for all sound buffers back to the beginning. Similar to the previous method, we will need to add a new method that resets the pointer of one specified buffer (see Chapter 2).

IsSoundPlaying

```
BOOL IsSoundPlaying();
```

This method returns True if any sound buffers are playing. Again, a more useful version of this method would be one that determines whether a particular sound buffer is playing or not.

CStreamingSound Class

The *CStreamingSound* class inherits from the *CSound* class, and adds just two methods in addition to the constructor and destructor. A *CStreamingSound* object manages a single streaming buffer, so you cannot create duplicate buffers of the wave file. If you wish to stream multiple copies of the same sound, then you will need to create multiple *CStreamingSound* objects. However, typically it is used to manage large files, such as background music, where having multiple buffers is usually not required (see Chapter 6).

```
class CStreamingSound : public CSound
{
protected:
    DWORD m_dwLastPlayPos;
    DWORD m_dwPlayProgress;
```

```
    DWORD m_dwNotifySize;
    DWORD m_dwNextWriteOffset;
    BOOL  m_bFillNextNotificationWithSilence;

public:
    CStreamingSound( LPDIRECTSOUNDBUFFER pDSBuffer, DWORD dwDSBufferSize,
                     CWaveFile* pWaveFile, DWORD dwNotifySize );
    ~CStreamingSound();

    HRESULT HandleWaveStreamNotification( BOOL bLoopedPlay );
    HRESULT Reset();
};
```

Create a *CStreamingSound* object by calling the *CreateStreaming* method of the *CSoundManager* class. The constructor of the *CStreamingSound* object will call the constructor of the inherited *CSound* object, and will initialize it appropriately.

The parameters of the constructor are, in order, a pointer to a DirectSound buffer, the size of that buffer, the file name of the wave file, and the notification size. Only the last parameter requires much explanation. After that number of bytes has been played, a notification message (*WAIT_OBJECT_0*) will be sent and picked up by a callback function. Respond with a call to *HandleWaveStreamNotification*.

Note that the notification callback is handled in a separate thread, and not in the Windows callback function. This complexity is explained in detail in Chapter 6.

HandleWaveStreamNotification

```
HRESULT HandleWaveStreamNotification( BOOL bLoopedPlay );
```

This method reads data from the wave file, and writes it to the section of the streaming buffer that has just been played. If the end of the data is reached, then the remainder of the buffer will be filled with either silence (*bLoopedPlay* is False) or by reading from the beginning of the file again (*bLoopedPlay* is True).

Reset

```
HRESULT Reset();
```

This method resets the streaming buffer to start reading from the beginning of the file.

CWaveFile Class

The *CWaveFile* class saves a developer the grief of having to write a wave file parser. Although all of the methods are usually called from the previously mentioned classes, occasionally you might need to call the *GetFormat* method to extract some information about the file when you are extending those classes. The *CWaveFile* class provides methods to control both the reading and writing of wave files. We have kept the explanations to a minimum, because we do not recommend amending this class. It works just fine.

```
class CWaveFile
{
public:
    WAVEFORMATEX* m_pwfx;          // Pointer to WAVEFORMATEX structure.
    HMMIO         m_hmmio;         // Multimedia I/O handle for the wave.
    MMCKINFO      m_ck;            // Multimedia RIFF chunk.
    MMCKINFO      m_ckRiff;        // Use in opening a wave file.
    DWORD         m_dwSize;        // The size of the wave file.
    MMIOINFO      m_mmioinfoOut;
    DWORD         m_dwFlags;
    BOOL          m_bIsReadingFromMemory;
    BYTE*         m_pbData;
    BYTE*         m_pbDataCur;
    ULONG         m_ulDataSize;
    CHAR*         m_pResourceBuffer;

protected:
    HRESULT ReadMMIO();
    HRESULT WriteMMIO( WAVEFORMATEX *pwfxDest );

public:
    CWaveFile();
    ~CWaveFile();

    HRESULT Open( LPTSTR strFileName, WAVEFORMATEX* pwfx, DWORD dwFlags );
    HRESULT OpenFromMemory( BYTE* pbData, ULONG ulDataSize,
                            WAVEFORMATEX* pwfx, DWORD dwFlags );
    HRESULT Close();

    HRESULT Read( BYTE* pBuffer, DWORD dwSizeToRead, DWORD* pdwSizeRead );
    HRESULT Write( UINT nSizeToWrite, BYTE* pbData, UINT* pnSizeWrote );

    DWORD   GetSize();
    HRESULT ResetFile();
    WAVEFORMATEX* GetFormat() { return m_pwfx; };
};
```

Open

```
HRESULT Open( LPTSTR strFileName, WAVEFORMATEX* pwfx, DWORD dwFlags );
```

When reading from a file or resource, this method returns the wave format and the data chunk size. The *strFileName* parameter should be set to the file name or resource name. The *pwfx* parameter should point to a *WAVEFORMATEX* structure, and *dwFlags* should be set to *WAVEFILE_READ*.

When writing to a file, fill out the *WAVEFORMATEX* structure with the required format information, and set *dwFlags* to *WAVEFILE_WRITE*.

OpenFromMemory

```
HRESULT OpenFromMemory( BYTE* pbData, ULONG ulDataSize,
                        WAVEFORMATEX* pwfx, DWORD dwFlags );
```

This method reads wave data from memory rather than from a file. We have not used this method in any of the samples in this book.

Close

```
HRESULT Close();
```

This method closes the file, after writing out the RIFF chunk sizes if the file was open for writing.

Read

```
HRESULT Read( BYTE* pBuffer, DWORD dwSizeToRead, DWORD* pdwSizeRead );
```

This method reads data from the wave file, resource or memory location.

Write

```
HRESULT Write( UINT nSizeToWrite, BYTE* pbData, UINT* pnSizeWrote );
```

This method writes data out to the file from the given address.

GetSize

```
DWORD   GetSize();
```

This method will return the size of an opened wave file, in bytes.

ResetFile

```
HRESULT ResetFile();
```

This method resets the pointer used for playing the file back to the beginning.

GetFormat

```
WAVEFORMATEX* GetFormat();
```

This method returns the address of the *WAVEFORMATEX* structure used to describe the wave format.

Summary

The fun side of this chapter involved getting a sample to work that involved mixing sounds.

The serious side of this chapter covered setting up the development environment, installing DirectX, and using and modifying the utility code that comes with it. It also described the importance of timing, the difference between a sound and a sound buffer, and the explanation of the code used by the High5 sample.

Although we used the High5 sample in this chapter to introduce some concepts, for most applications, you will require the modifications to the utility code provided in later chapters. Not until you reach Chapter 8 will the full audio framework that we are describing be fully pieced together.

2

Changing the Volume, Panning, and Frequency of Stereo Sound

The American Heritage Dictionary defines cacophony as "the use of harsh or discordant sounds in literary composition, as for poetic effect." This definition perhaps describes computer game sounds a bit too well, as opposed to words like "harmony" and "melody," although it's fun to use words such as "poetic effect" to describe the racket that you are about to create. This chapter describes the use of a 2-D sound tool aptly named Cacophony, and then dissects its source code.

The Cacophony tool, which is included in the AVBook\bin directory, lets you examine the capabilities of DirectSound in a 2-D world. There are many games and applications that operate in a 2-D world, even if there is an appearance of 3-D on the screen. To use the 3-D capabilities of DirectSound to their best effect, it is preferable to have an underlying 3-D world to base it on. However, a game that uses artwork to create the 3-D appearance, and with what are effectively cartoon characters drawn in front of the artwork, is not based on an underlying 3-D model. This has been used to great effect, particularly with young children's games such as the Microsoft Barney and Magic Schoolbus games. For this type of application, a 2-D sound system may be all that is required.

This chapter also discusses how the utility code in the dsutil.cpp file needs to be extended to support the tool. But first, it's time to create that racket.

The Cacophony 2-D Sound Tool

The Cacophony tool allows you load up to ten sounds, and then alter the following:

- Starting time for the sound

- Starting and ending volume

- Starting and ending panning positions

- Starting and ending frequencies

Clicking on Cacophony.exe will bring up the dialog box shown in Figure 2.1.

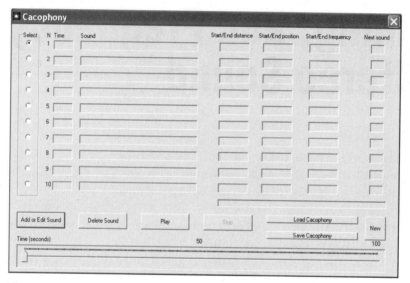

Figure 2.1   Main dialog box of the Cacophony tool.

You can use the Cacophony tool to experiment with small sound compositions to evaluate whether 2-D sound is right for your application. To load in a sound, first click on the radio button under the Select column to pick a slot for the sound to run in, and then click Add or Edit Sound. This will display the dialog box shown in Figure 2.2.

First, you must decide whether the sound is to start at a given time, or if it is dependent upon the completion of another sound. As this is the first and only sound that you are loading for this test, leave the Timed Start (Seconds) check box selected, and keep the start time at 0 seconds. For future reference, any start time up to 100 seconds (which is the maximum playing time of the tool) can be entered in this edit box.

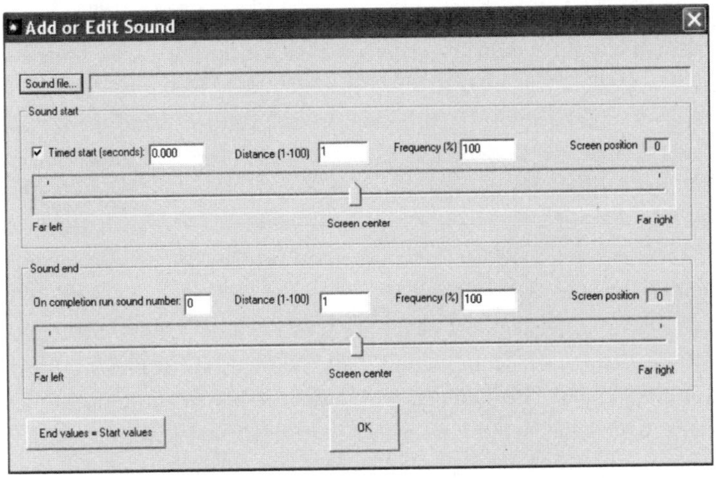

Figure 2.2   Add or Edit Sound dialog box for 2-D sounds.

If you are adding rather than editing a sound, the Add or Edit Sound dialog box will appear blank, as shown in the previous screen. Click the Sound File button, and then load in the LIFTOFF.WAV sound.

The Distance (1-100) edit box determines the volume of the sound. For example, a distance value of 1 means that the sound will be played at its maximum volume (the volume at which the sound was recorded). In other words, a value of 1 means that the object producing the sound is at the same distance from the listener as the original sound source when the sound was recorded. A value of 2 in this box means that the sound volume will match that of an object twice the distance away from the listener as that of the original recording, and so on.

The default start distance is 1 (the maximum), but for this experiment, change this to 4 (which means that the starting volume matches that of an object four times the distance away from the listener as the original recording). Next, move the slider, still within the Sound Start group, over to the Far Left position.

Now, within the Sound End group, leave everything but the slider as is, and move the slider over to the Far Right position. For future reference, positions are based on a linear scale, with -50 being at the far left, and 50 at the far right. The default position of 0 is dead center.

Leave the Frequency settings at 100 to ensure that the sound will be replayed at its original frequency. For future reference, by changing the starting and ending frequencies, for example, to 50 for the start frequency and 150 for the end frequency, the sound will be replayed with the frequency changing from 50% of its original to 150%. However, it is difficult to find the desired sounds by randomly playing with the frequency – you'll get a lot of groans and whines before you find an acceptable effect.

Now click OK to close this dialog box and go back to the main Cacophony dialog box. What you should see on the screen is that for Sound 1, the Time has been set to "0.000," the Sound to "LIFTOFF.WAV," the Start/End Distance to "4 1," the Start/End Position to "-50 50," the Start/End Frequency to "100 100," and the Next Sound to "0".

What this means is that the LIFTOFF sound will start in the far left position at one quarter of its recorded volume, and then move evenly between the left and right speakers, increasing steadily in volume until it is at its maximum when it reaches the far right position. Try it by pressing Play. Although it's a simple application, it encourages you to imagine more complex possibilities.

Going on to other features of the tool, you will notice that the Time cursor at the bottom of the dialog box keeps moving, even though the sound has stopped. To reset this cursor, press Stop. The Time cursor marks the playing time up to the maximum of 100 seconds, which was mentioned earlier in this chapter, and the internal timer for the tool sends a timing message every eighth of a second. This means that sounds can be started accurate to one eighth of a second, and also that changes to the volume, panning position and frequency are updated every eighth of a second. Of course, these latter updates will only occur if the starting and ending values for volume, panning position or frequency are different.

Most of the other buttons in this dialog box are pretty obvious. For example, Delete Sound deletes the sound in the slot identified by the Select radio button, and the New button eliminates all of the sounds.

Perhaps more interesting features of the Cacophony tool are Next Sound, Load Cacophony and Save Cacophony. The Next Sound column contains a sound number if you indicate in the Add or Edit Sound dialog box that, when the sound stops playing, it should start another sound. To do this, enter a number between 1 and 10 (be sure to use a number with a sound actually loaded into that slot) in the On Completion Run Sound Number edit box. Using this fun option, you can hear sound sequences such as a crash being heard just after a screeching, whizzing, or falling sound has ended.

The last option in the Add or Edit Sound dialog box is the End Values = Start Values button. Click this button if you want exactly the same volume, position and frequency for the Sound End group as you do for the Sound Start group, and can't be bothered playing with the edit boxes and slider.

Back in the main dialog box, the Load Cacophony and Save Cacophony options let you save your compositions for the next time that you run the tool. These files are saved as text files (with a .txt file name extension), so they can be examined in Microsoft Notepad, or any other plain text editing tool.

If you click on Load Cacophony, you'll notice that there are a number of cacophony files (all with the .cac file name extension) available to demonstrate different aspects of this tool. If you have not done so already, check out these files, and perhaps create some of your own noises, remembering to save the ones that you would like to hear again. The cacophony file CannonExchange.cac demonstrates the use of panning to create moving effects, and the DistantCannons.cac file shows how the volume is affected by increasing the distance away from the listener (see Plate 1).

The following list contains the contents of the CannonExchange.cac cacophony file. Basically, it consists of the sound number (based 0 to 9 rather than 1 to 10 of the UI), followed by the path and file name of the sound relative to the AVBook directory, and then the settings. Only non-zero settings are saved – the format is the setting slot followed by the value, and ending in the number 999. This method of saving settings makes the tool easier to extend rather than just listing the values. Note that the word empty is used to denote an unused slot. This file format is not a Microsoft format, it is simply a format invented by the creator of this tool.

```
0 Audio\Old military\Cannon.wav* 0 1 2 4 4 100 5 4 7 100 8 3 999
1 Audio\Old military\Cannon.wav* 0 1 1 16 2 5 4 100 5 5 7 100 8 4 999
2 Audio\Old military\WHISTLE.wav* 2 4 4 100 5 1 6 100 7 100 8 5 999
3 Audio\Old military\WHISTLE.wav* 2 5 4 100 5 1 6 100 7 100 8 6 999
4 Audio\Old military\IMPACT.wav* 2 1 3 100 4 100 5 1 6 100 7 100 999
5 Audio\Old military\EXPLODE.WAV* 2 1 3 100 4 100 5 1 6 100 7 100 999
6 Audio\Old military\HGUN.wav* 0 1 1 64 2 1 3 100 4 100 5 1 6 100 7 100 8 8 999
7 Audio\Old military\WHISTLE.wav* 2 1 3 100 4 100 5 4 7 100 8 9 999
8 Audio\Old military\EXPLODE.WAV* 2 4 4 100 5 4 7 100 999
9 empty*
```

This wraps up our discussion of the user guide for the Cacophony tool. The next section examines the tool's code.

The Cacophony Project

Using Microsoft Visual Studio .NET, load the Cacophony project and use the Solution Explorer window to list the source files. With this project, we've used the programming concept of dividing it up into layers:

- The UI layer (Cacophony.cpp) deals with the user interface and flow of control.

- The second layer (DSound2DLayer.cpp) contains all the methods that use the *CSound* and *CSoundManager* objects created by the program.

- The third layer (Extended_dsutil.cpp) defines the *CSound* and *CSoundManager* classes, and provides the extended framework that communicates with the DirectSound SDK.

If the objective was performance, this would be at least one layer too many. However, since the objective is education, use this structure to remove the need for many global variables, and to make the use of the objects more obvious. If you were to write this code simply for your own use, you would probably merge DSound2DLayer.cpp into Cacophony.cpp, and do away with many of the intermediary functions.

The following sections explain the main concepts and design of Cacophony.cpp. Rather than describe every line of code, you'll see that the discussion focuses on the lower levels, where the code modifies the framework and calls the DirectSound SDK. You should also find the code comments useful.

The Cacophony.cpp and Cacophony.h Files

To begin, first open or print out the Cacophony.cpp and Cacophony.h files. The main features of 2-D sound are that mono or stereo sounds can be played, and that parameters such as volume, panning position, and frequency can be altered from their original recording. The panning position is perhaps the most exciting, providing the best option for mimicking movement.

One obvious problem with panning a sound is that it could be incompatible with a sound recorded in stereo. Although DirectSound will not fail if you try to combine these features, the panning will tend to dominate the stereo recording. Given that the movement of sound (or rather, sound effects that appear to originate from moving objects) is the most important effect that you are trying to achieve, both in 2-D and 3-D, most sounds should be recorded or converted to mono – preferably 16-bit mono.

In any event, the Cacophony tool handles both mono and stereo sounds. If you open the Cacophony.h file, and find the *cSoundEffect* class, you will see that the data members of this class match the UI.

```
class cSoundEffect
{
private:
    char        filename[MAX_PATH];
    int         setting[max_settings];
    int         status;
    DWORD       tickLength;
    DWORD       ticksElapsed;
    int         iSound;
    int         iBuffer;
```

For each sound entered in the UI, one object (in an array of 10 objects) of the *cSoundEffect* class is populated with data. The *filename* obviously contains the full path of the wave file. The settings array contains the various start and end values set using the Add or Edit Sound dialog box. Note there are nine settings, each located by a define, as shown in the following code.

```
#define     timed_start     0
#define     start_time      1
#define     start_distance  2
```

```
#define        start_position      3
#define        start_frequency     4
#define        end_distance        5
#define        end_position        6
#define        end_frequency       7
#define        on_completion       8
```

The *status* variable contains one of the four status settings (dud, loaded, playing and stopped).

The *tickLength* variable is the length of the sound sample in ticks, where each tick is one eighth of a second (therefore, a 2.5-second sound sample has a length of 20 ticks). The *ticksElapsed* variable contains a count of ticks since the sound started playing. These two variables are essential when calculating the volume, panning, or frequency change during the playing of the sound.

The *iSound* and *iBuffer* variables are indexes to the sound and the sound buffer respectively, and are used during both the analysis and playing stages. The sound index is an index into an array of *cOneSound* objects. A *cOneSound* object simply holds a repeat of the file name for convenience, the number of buffers required for it, and a Boolean flag indicating whether the wave file loaded correctly or not. The data members of this class are shown in the following code.

```
class cOneSound
{
private:
    char        filename[MAX_PATH];
    int         nBuffers;
    bool        loaded;
```

The reasoning behind having this class is that your cacophony may contain multiple instances of the same wave file, and you want to be able to combine them into one sound object with multiple buffers. This is a more efficient system than to have multiple sound objects, each containing one buffer with the identical sound loaded.

Both the *cSoundEffect* and *cOneSound* classes contain a range of methods to set and get the properties. The methods are so trivial that we defined them all in the header file, rather than give declarations in the header and definitions in a .cpp file. This follows a coding style similar to what is usually used with C# programming, and does save a lot of repetition of method prototypes. However it is just a style issue; defining and declaring the methods in separate files is much more common in C++ programming.

The only methods with any calculation going on concern the reading and writing of each sound to the cacophony file (the methods *readEffect* and *writeEffect* in the *cSoundEffect* class). The logic here is that sounds are only saved to the cacophony file if they are somewhere in the AVBook directory. This is simply so that the whole project can be moved, perhaps posted on a network for other developers, and have the cacophony files still work.

Now it's time to examine how these data classes are handled. When you open up the Cacophony.cpp file, you'll see that it is divided into two main sections, following the declarations and usual *WinMain* function. The first section deals with all the functions supporting the Add or Edit Sound dialog box, and the second part discusses those functions supporting the main Cacophony dialog box.

When the *SoundDlgProc* callback function is called, it means that the user has opened the Add or Edit Sound dialog box, where the user can change the settings for a sound. These settings are all recorded to a temporary set of variables, so the changes can be ignored if the user exits the dialog box without clicking OK. If the user does click OK, the *cSoundEffect* object, indexed by the *g_cSound* variable, is updated.

When the user clicks Play on the main dialog box, the *initCacophony* function calls the *analyzeSoundEffects* function to try and make sense of the data that was entered. Then, *initCacophony* starts the timing to set the cacophony in motion. We are not going to spend any more time on the UI code; you can easily step through what's going on with a debugger. The next section will focus on the functions in the DSound2DLayer.cpp file.

The DSound2DLayer.cpp and Extended_dsutil.cpp Files

When you open up the DSound2DLayer.cpp file, you'll see that it contains all the functions that manipulate the following two object types.

```
CSoundManager* g_pSoundManager = NULL;
CSound*        g_pSound[max_sounds];
```

Note that these are just pointers; the objects are actually created in the functions *initSound* and *loadSound* respectively. Only one sound manager object is needed, but you need one sound object for every wave file that you intend to load. Remember, of course, that one sound object can contain multiple buffers of the same sound, so that even if the Cacophony dialog box is full, the number of sound objects required can be less than or equal to ten.

The functions *initDirectSound, closeDirectSound* and *stopSound* in this file are identical to those in the High5 sample explained in the previous chapter. The first new function to examine is the *loadSound* function.

```
bool loadSound(int index, char filename[], int nBuffers)
{
    if (soundWorking)
    {
        DWORD    bufferFlags = DSBCAPS_CTRLVOLUME | DSBCAPS_CTRLPAN
                               | DSBCAPS_CTRLFREQUENCY;

        // Delete any running sound.
        stopSound(index);

        // Free any previous sound, and make a new one.
        SAFE_DELETE( g_pSound[index] );
```

```
        // Load the wave file into a DirectSound buffer.
        if (FAILED(g_pSoundManager->
            Create( &g_pSound[index] ,filename, bufferFlags,
                GUID_NULL, nBuffers )))
            return false;

        return true;
    } else
        return false;
}
```

The setting of the *bufferFlags* variable has been altered in this function (from the 0 used in the High5 sample) to enable volume, panning and frequency changes. Although the setting of the flags is straightforward, this is often forgotten in DirectSound programming, leading to hours of frustration. The only other change is that the *g_pSound* pointer requires an index, as it is now an array of ten pointers, rather than the single one used in the High5 sample.

The *playSoundBuffer* function is used to initiate the playing of one sound buffer. It takes as parameters an index into the *g_pSound* array (*iSound*) and an index into the array of buffers that the sound object might have (*iBuffer*), and the initial volume, panning position and frequency.

```
bool playSoundBuffer(int iSound, int iBuffer, int nDistance, int nPan,
        int nFreq)
{
    DWORD    dwFlags = 0L;
    long     actualVolume    = calcuateVolumeFromDistance( (float) nDistance);
    long     actualPosition  = getRelativeValue( (long) nPan, 100L,
                (long) DSBPAN_LEFT, (long) DSBPAN_RIGHT);
    DWORD    actualFrequency  = (DWORD) getRelativeValue( (long) nFreq, 100L,
                (long) 0, (long) g_pSound[iSound] -> GetRecordedFrequency() );

    if (soundWorking AND g_pSound[iSound] != NULL)
    {
        if (FAILED(g_pSound[iSound] -> PlayBuffer( iBuffer, 0, dwFlags,
                actualVolume, actualPosition, actualFrequency )))
            return false; else
            return true;
    } else
        return false;
}
```

The first thing the function does is translate the volume into units understood by DirectSound. The DirectSound SDK has definitions for *DSBVOLUME_MAX* and *DSBVOLUME_MIN*, currently set at 0 and -10,000 respectively. The units are in 100ths of a decibel, so the maximum volume means that there is zero attenuation of the recorded sound, and the minimum volume means that there is -100dB attenuation (effectively silencing the sound). The utility function *calculateVolumeFromDistance* takes the distance factor and returns the appropriate attenuation. This function is defined in the extended_dsutil.cpp file.

```
long calculateVolumeFromDistance(float distanceRatio)
{
    // Distances should always be positive and greater than the original.
    if (distanceRatio <= 1.0f)
        return DSBVOLUME_MAX;

    double hundredthsOfDeciBels = 100 * 20 * log10(distanceRatio);

    return DSBVOLUME_MAX - (long) hundredthsOfDeciBels;
}
```

Although the UI only allows integer distance factors, clearly any float value is acceptable input (for example, a value of 2.5 means that the object sounds as if it is two and a half times further away from the listener than the original recording). The actual math used to calculate the attenuation in decibels is a well-known equation in the audio business:

Attenuation (dB) = 20 * log10 (distance ratio)

The underlying logic is that if an object doubles its distance from the listener, its sound volume will drop 6.02 dB. Obviously, because we are using 100th of a decibel units, we then multiply this value by 100 to get the answer.

In the *playSoundBuffer* function, the next calculation provides the correct panning position. The *getRelativeValue* function just returns the appropriate ratio when converting a number within one range of numbers into the correct number within a second range. DirectSound provides a range from *DSBPAN_LEFT* to *DSBPAN_RIGHT*, which are -10,000 to 10,000 – which is more granularity than you will ever need. The Cacophony sample uses -50 to 50. The *getRelativeValue* function is used to convert the tool's units into DirectSound units.

The frequency calculation is very similar, except that you must first retrieve the actual recorded frequency, using the *GetRecordedFrequency* function. *GetRecordedFrequency* is a method that was added to the *CSound* class in the dsutil.cpp file provided with the DirectSound SDK, along with the *PlayBuffer* method. To view these methods, look up the Extended_dsutil.cpp file, which is provided in the Common sub-directory of the main AVBook directory.

The *GetRecordedFrequency* function is shown in the following code.

```
DWORD CSound::GetRecordedFrequency ()
{
    if( m_apDSBuffer == NULL )
        return 0;

    WAVEFORMATEX* pwfx = m_pWaveFile -> GetFormat();
    return pwfx -> nSamplesPerSec;
}
```

First, note that frequencies are recorded in double-word (*DWORD*) variables. The *CWaveFile* class, also provided in the utility code, has the *GetFormat* method, which simply returns a pointer to the *WAVEFORMATEX* structure associated with the wave file. Using this pointer, you have access to the members of this structure, from which you can conveniently return the sampling rate (which is the frequency). The *WAVEFORMA-TEX* structure will be discussed in more detail later in this chapter.

The other addition to the *CSound* class, *PlayBuffer*, is one of the core functions for 2-D sound.

```
HRESULT CSound::PlayBuffer(int iB, DWORD dwPriority, DWORD dwFlags,
                           long Volume, long Position, DWORD Frequency)
{
    HRESULT hr;
    BOOL    bRestored;

    if( m_apDSBuffer == NULL )
        return CO_E_NOTINITIALIZED;

    LPDIRECTSOUNDBUFFER pDSB = m_apDSBuffer[ iB ];

    if( pDSB == NULL )
        return DXTRACE_ERR( TEXT("PlayBuffer"), E_FAIL );

    // Restore the buffer if it was lost.
    if( FAILED( hr = RestoreBuffer( pDSB, &bRestored ) ) )
        return DXTRACE_ERR( TEXT("RestoreBuffer"), hr );

    if( bRestored )
    {
        // The buffer was restored, so you need to fill it with new data.
        if( FAILED( hr = FillBufferWithSound( pDSB, FALSE ) ) )
            return DXTRACE_ERR( TEXT("FillBufferWithSound"), hr );

        // Make DirectSound do pre-processing on sound effects.
        Reset();
    }

    hr = pDSB -> SetCurrentPosition (0);
    hr = pDSB -> SetVolume(Volume);
    hr = pDSB -> SetPan(Position);
    if (Frequency != NO_FREQUENCY_CHANGE)
        hr = pDSB -> SetFrequency(Frequency);

    hr = pDSB -> Play( 0, dwPriority, dwFlags );

    return hr;
}
```

The first portion of code concerns restoring buffers. For example, if another application running DirectSound has stolen your sound buffer, this code restores it.

The next section of code shows that the playing position is set to the start of the sound buffer, along with the required volume, panning position and frequency. Note that we provided a setting for the frequency parameter that requests that no change be made.

The *dwPriority* and *dwFlags* parameters are passed through to the *Play* method in the DirectSound SDK. The priority setting only applies if the sound buffer was created using the *DSBCAPS_LOCDEFER* flag; since that was not done, this parameter must be set to 0. See the DirectSound SDK documentation for more information about this flag. The only *dwFlags* setting that might apply is the looping flag, *DSBPLAY_LOOPING*.

Now, return to the DSound2DLayer.cpp file. Similar to the function that plays a single buffer, there is a function that tests whether a buffer has stopped playing or not *(testSoundBufferStopped)*. Again, this function calls through to a method, *IsSoundBufferPlaying*, in the *CSound* class.

```
BOOL CSound::IsSoundBufferPlaying(int iB)
{
    BOOL bIsPlaying = FALSE;

    if( m_apDSBuffer == NULL )
        return FALSE;

    if( m_apDSBuffer[iB] )
    {
        DWORD dwStatus = 0;
        m_apDSBuffer[iB] -> GetStatus( &dwStatus );
        bIsPlaying |= ( ( dwStatus & DSBSTATUS_PLAYING ) != 0 );
    }

    return bIsPlaying;
}
```

The DirectSound SDK provides the method *GetStatus*, which returns a *DWORD* with any of a number of bit flags set. The flag to test for here is *DSBSTATUS_PLAYING*, although the flag *DSBSTATUS_LOOPING* could also be set if this was a looping sound. The only other flag that could be set in this case is *DSBSTATUS_BUFFERLOST*. If the sound buffer was created with the *DSBCAPS_LOCDEFER* flag set (which was not done), then there are a few other flags that can be returned by *GetStatus*. Again, refer to the DirectSound SDK documentation for a discussion of these additional flags.

Back in the DSound2DLayer.cpp file, the next function to look at is *getPlayingTimeInSeconds*. In order to pan a sound evenly from its start to its end point, it is essential to know the length of the sound. This function calls through to the *GetPlayingTime* method that was added to the Extended_dsutil.cpp file.

```
float CSound::GetPlayingTime ()
{
    if( m_apDSBuffer == NULL )
        return 0;

    WAVEFORMATEX* pwfx = m_pWaveFile -> GetFormat();

    return (float) m_dwDSBufferSize / (float) pwfx -> nAvgBytesPerSec;
}
```

Similar to the *GetRecordedFrequency* method, this method gets a pointer to the *WAVEFORMATEX* structure and retrieves the average number of bytes per second. The *CSound* object has already recorded the buffer size in bytes, so you simply divide this size by the bytes per second value and...presto! We have a reasonable estimate for the playing time of the file.

Back for the last time in DSound2DLayer.cpp, you'll see the three functions *changeBufferVolume, changeBufferPanning* and *changeBufferFrequency*. All of these functions copy a line from *playSoundBuffer* to calculate the actual values from the numbers given through the UI, and then they call methods that we added to the *CSound* class to set these values. The three methods added to the *CSound* class, *setBufferVolume, setBufferPanPosition* and *setBufferFrequency*, are very similar. As an example, the *setBufferPanPosition* method is shown in the following code.

```
HRESULT CSound::setBufferPanPosition(int iB, long Position)
{
    HRESULT hr;

    if( m_apDSBuffer == NULL )
        return CO_E_NOTINITIALIZED;

    hr = m_apDSBuffer[ iB ] -> SetPan(Position);

    return hr;
}
```

Not much here requires explanation, except perhaps the *HRESULT* that can contain an error if the call fails. If the call returns S_OK, then all is well, otherwise, there is a whole range of potential errors. The most likely error that you will receive is *DSERR_CONTROLUNAVAIL*, which means that you did not specify the right flags for the buffer. In the *setBufferPanPosition* method, if you did not specify the *DSBCAPS_CTRLPAN* flag when creating the buffer, you will get the *DSERR_CONTROLUNAVAIL* error, rather than the desired panning effect. The correct flags should be set in the *loadSound* function, which was described earlier in this chapter.

The WAVEFORMATEX Structure

For discussion purposes, the *WAVEFORMATEX* structure is a member of, and is filled in by, a *CWaveFile* object. This structure is part of the old but still thriving Microsoft Windows MultiMedia SDK, and is not declared in Dsound.h, but in mmreg.h. You may also have come across the *WAVEFORMATEXTENSIBLE* structure, used for multi channel sound, where the number of channels exceeds two, but even then, a *WAVE-FORMATEX* structure forms the bulk of its data members. You may also come across *WAVEFORMAT* and *PCMWAVEFORMAT* in Microsoft header files – you can safely ignore these two.

The *WAVEFORMATEX* structure holds the essential recoding data for the wave file.

```
typedef struct {
  WORD  wFormatTag;
  WORD  nChannels;
  DWORD nSamplesPerSec;
  DWORD nAvgBytesPerSec;
  WORD  nBlockAlign;
  WORD  wBitsPerSample;
  WORD  cbSize;
} WAVEFORMATEX;
```

The *wFormatTag* member can take a range of values defining the audio format, but DirectSound only supports one, *WAVE_FORMAT_PCM*. This means that the audio is recorded in pulse-code modulation (PCM) data in integer format. The similar *WAVE_FORMAT_IEEE_FLOAT* format – pulse-code modulation in floating-point format – is not supported by DirectSound.

Always the easiest member to describe, *nChannels* should be 1 for mono data and 2 for stereo. As you want to apply special effects to your sounds, usually this value is set to 1.

The *nSamplesPerSec* member holds the sample rate, often referred to as the frequency, stored in samples per second (hertz). The usual values for *nSamplesPerSec* are 8.0 kHz, 11.025 kHz, 22.05 kHz, and 44.1 kHz. Note that the storage unit is in hertz rather than kilohertz, so these values are stored as 8000, 11025, 22050 and 44100 respectively.

The *nAvgBytesPerSec* member is the required average data-transfer rate, in bytes per second. This should be equal to the product of *nSamplesPerSec* and *nBlockAlign*. At first, the definition of *nBlockAlign* sounds complicated, but is actually quite simple. It holds the block alignment, in bytes, and must be equal to the product of *nChannels* and *wBitsPerSample* divided by 8 (bits per byte). So, for example, if you have a mono wave file recorded in 16-bit data (the most common format), this translates to a block alignment of (1 x 16 / 8), which equals 2. All that this means is that programs reading the data must treat a two-byte block as an indivisible chunk – obviously, because you would never want to divide one of the 16-bit audio samples in half. Perhaps the word "block" adds a bit of confusion here. Other examples are that 8-bit mono data will give a block alignment of 1, and 16-bit stereo data a block alignment of 4.

The *wBitsPerSample* member is either 8 or 16; no other value is supported by DirectSound. The *cbSize* member is ignored.

Extracting Useful Information from WAVEFORMATEX

In addition to the simple reading of the data members when they are required (for example, in the *getRecordedFrequency* method described earlier), the members can be combined to provide additional information. Note the following line from the *GetPlayingTime* method.

```
return (float) m_dwDSBufferSize / (float) pwfx -> nAvgBytesPerSec;
```

In this statement, the *m_dwDSBufferSizer* data member is held in a *CSound* object, but it is set after the inherited *CWaveFile* object reads the wave file. The *CWaveFile* class has a *GetSize* method that returns the size in bytes of the file that was just read. The previous code only provides an estimate of the playing time of the file, although an estimate is good enough for most purposes.

Summary

We have just started to explore the power of DirectSound in this chapter, with the Cacophony tool that demonstrates the effects of changing a sound's volume, panning position and frequency. As you saw, this can be valuable in an application that does not have an underlying 3-D model.

It is possible to extend 2-D sound even further than the Cacophony tool does, with the use of special effects such as distortion and echo. However, postpone going further into these effects until you have learned the basics of 3-D sound in the next chapter. A few developers may choose to run with the 2-D sound features and leave 3-D sound alone; if you are one of them, you might work the special effects code from Chapter 4 into the Cacophony tool to provide the specific effects supported by DirectSound.

The key lesson from this chapter is that the utility code can be extended to support control over individual buffers in *CSound* objects. The value of the utility code is clear from the use of the *CWaveFile* class. Although this class is part of the DirectSound framework, rather than part of the SDK, it is too valuable to just be considered a utility.

3

Moving Sounds in 3-D Space

DirectSound's most impressive abilities lie in the world of 3-D sound. Even a simple sound, such as an engine running, can wow your users if it appears to come from a moving car or plane, and especially if it appears to go over, under, or around the user to match the movement of the vehicle.

Enter the world of 3-D sound by going to the AVBook\bin directory and firing up the Rumpus 3D SFX tool. Due to the number of new concepts that this tool features, we have divided its autopsy into two chapters: this chapter covers 3-D sound, while Chapter 4 examines special and environmental effects. If you are new to 3-D sound, get ready to be impressed.

The Rumpus 3D SFX Tool

Like the Cacophony tool that flexes the 2-D sound capabilities of DirectSound, the Rumpus tool gives its 3-D capabilities a workout. There are a lot of similarities between these two tools, which are based on a very similar UI.

After you have clicked on the executable file, the dialog box shown in Figure 3.1 appears. The most notable difference between this tool and the Cacophony tool is the green grid on the Rumpus 3D SFX dialog box, which represents your 3-D world. The center of this world, marked by a white circle, is the listener. The listener is simply the location, and the direction that they are facing, of the person that is hearing the sound effects produced by DirectSound. In this sense, the 3-D features of DirectSound assume a *first person* model; it is assumed that the user of the application is playing a role within the application itself. In other words, the user is represented by the listener: they are not a spectator of the action but an integral part of it. The listener can move around in the same 3-D space as the rest of the objects in the game, although for our first few samples we will keep the listener stationary so that you can see what's going on.

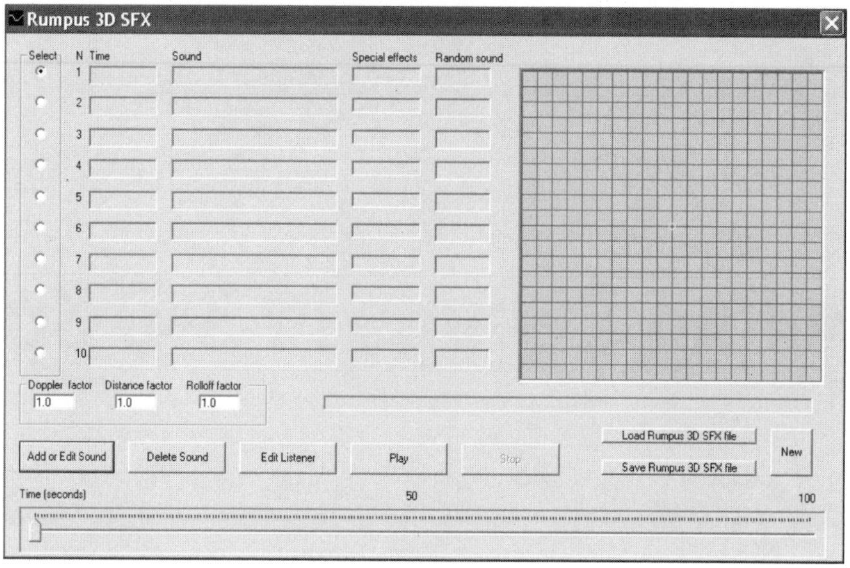

Figure 3.1 Rumpus 3-D SFX main dialog box.

As you enter sounds into your 3-D world, numbers will appear on the grid (1 through 10) that represent the stationary or moving object with which the sound is associated. The grid only shows the movement of the objects in the x- and z-coordinates (so the grid represents a flat field). The y-coordinate (height) is not represented on the grid, however, the height of the object is modeled in all the underlying code, and affects the sound output. The Rumpus tool's graphics show the movement as if it was all on a flat surface, but the sound output is full 3-D.

For your first test, click the Load Rumpus 3D SFX File button, and then select the TESTONE.rfx file. Now click Play. What you should hear is the sound of a train, first coming towards you, then passing on your left, and then variously bouncing around the 3-D world, passing both in front of and behind you. Not a bad effect for one simple wave file.

You should also see a small number 1 moving around the grid, marking the position of the sound, with the listener remaining stationary in the center.

When you are done listening to this first effect, click Stop. Now load up the Rumpus file TESTTWO.rfx. This file simply expands on the first test, with the train now more fully represented by multiple sounds (those of the locomotive, numerous train cars, and so on). This gives a more realistic effect of the various sounds that would be heard along the length of a passing train.

Now click on the TESTTHREE.rfx file. This is an identical scenario to TESTTWO.rfx, except that now the listener is on the train and traveling with it. Note that the round white circle representing the listener moves along with the numbers representing the train. By the fairly simple act of giving the listener an identical movement to the train, you get quite a different sound experience.

Also try running the CarShop.rfx file, which is an example of a file where all the sound slots are filled (see Plate 2).

Once you're done playing with these files, click Stop, and take a look at the UI. The ten time slots, the start time, the sound name, the Add or Edit Sound button, the Delete Sound button, the Play and Stop buttons, and the Load, Save and New buttons should all be familiar to you from the Cacophony tool. The Special Effects column is not used in the samples described in this chapter, but is discussed in Chapter 4. The Random Sound column shows the reference number and playing frequency of a sound that is to be triggered randomly by the initial sound. This is not a feature of DirectSound, but a feature of the Rumpus tool, and shows how effects such as claps of thunder can be generated by a consistent sound of steady rainfall. We'll discuss this in more detail during the discussion of the Add or Edit Sound dialog box later in this chapter.

The first three DirectSound parameters to look at are the Doppler factor, distance factor, and rolloff factor, currently all shown as 1.0 in the appropriate edit boxes of the main dialog box. These three factors are universal to all 3-D sounds. The value 1.0 means that the default values (those mirroring the natural world) are applied.

The Doppler Effect

The Doppler effect is certainly the most well-known audio effect, and is shown in Figure 3.2.

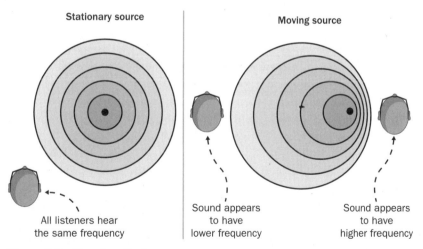

Figure 3.2   Doppler effect.

If a fast-moving object is moving towards you, it will appear to *compress* the sound waves that it is emitting, so that its sound will appear to have a *higher* frequency than it actually does. After passing you, the frequency will make a sudden change as the movement of the object away from you appears to *expand* the sound waves that the object is emitting. In this case, the object's sound appears to have a *lower* frequency than it actually does. If the object is not moving quickly, the Doppler effect is fairly unnoticeable.

Setting a value of 1.0 in the Rumpus tool for the Doppler factor applies the natural Doppler effect. If this value is increased, for example, to 2.0, then the effect is doubled, and appears to be twice as dramatic. On the other hand, if the Doppler factor is reduced, for example, to 0.5, then the effect is halved and will be less noticeable.

The theory behind providing these factors is that you can apply an exaggeration factor to overdramatize your sound effects, so typically, you would increase the Doppler factor rather than lower it. Try setting different values, and then running the OnePlane.rfx file.

The Distance Factor

The distance factor is simply the ratio of your application's modeling unit for your 3-D world to DirectSound's modeling unit of meters. A distance factor of 1.0 means that all measurements are in meters, for a 1:1 relationship. If your modeling world is in feet (this is usually determined by what you have done in D3D graphics), then change the entry in the Distance Factor edit box to 0.3048. With the value set at 1.0, the 3-D world represented by our grid is a square that measures 100 meters by 100 meters.

The Rolloff Factor

The rolloff factor determines how quickly sounds diminish as they radiate from their source. Zero is the minimum value for rolloff factor; however, if this value is set to 0, then the sounds are not attenuated at all. A value of 1.0 means that the value mirrors the natural world. A value between 0 and 1.0 means that the sounds will diminish, or attenuate, at a lesser rate than normal, for example, a value of 0.5 for Rolloff Factor means that all sounds attenuate at half the normal rate. The maximum value is 10, which will attenuate the sounds rather quickly. See the discussion later in this chapter on minimum distance to see how to adjust rolloff for individual sounds.

Note that when you save Rumpus files, the settings for Doppler Factor, Distance Factor, and Rolloff Factor are not saved. You must adjust these universal factors each time.

Now, click on the Add or Edit Sound button.

The Add or Edit Sound Dialog Box

There is very little similarity between the dialog box in Figure 3.3 and the one with the same title in the Cacophony tool. However, one identical feature is the Sound File button. Click this button to load in a wave file. Now, note the sets of sliders on the left side of the

Add or Edit Sound dialog box. The outermost set of three coordinate sliders places the object in the 3-D world. Note that the default position is dead center and at ground level (x=50, y=0, z=50). By moving these three coordinate sliders, you can place an object anywhere on the grid.

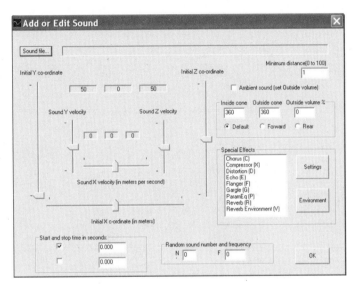

Figure 3.3   Add or Edit Sound dialog box for 3-D sounds.

The inner set of sliders gives the sound a velocity, with the default being no movement. If you have not changed the distance factor in the main dialog box, then speeds are in meters per second. Given that you cannot see height movement in the grid, try loading a sound, and then altering just the x- and z-coordinate positions and velocities. Note that a negative z velocity moves the sound farther down the grid.

You can also set the start and stop times for a sound, select the check boxes to activate one or both of these times. Like the Cacophony tool, the entire playing time is 100 seconds, but the granularity is in tenths of a second (rather than eighths), so times can be entered accordingly.

To the right of the start and stop times are the Random Sound Number (N) and the Frequency (F) boxes. If the N box is 0, then no random sound is heard. If N is a number between 1 and 10, then the sound in that numbered slot will be initiated, on average, the number of times per 100 seconds that is entered in the F box. For example, a value of 5 in the F box indicates that the random sound is fired off, on average, 5 times per 100 seconds, or once every 20 seconds. This feature is especially effective with natural effects such as adding a clap of thunder to steady rainfall, or the sound of creaks to a rocking ship, or squeaks to a moving piece of machinery.

Minimum Distance

Now look at the upper-right corner of the dialog box, at the Minimum Distance box. The theory behind this slightly confusing setting is based on the audible range of the human ear.

If the object producing this sound is within the minimum distance, measured in meters, then the sound will no longer increase in volume, but will remain at its maximum. By default, this value is 1, meaning that anywhere within one meter from the listener, the sound will be at its maximum volume. However, for very loud noises (for example, the roar of a jet engine, an explosion, or the blast of just sitting too close to the speakers at a rock concert) this distance could be 10 or 100 meters.

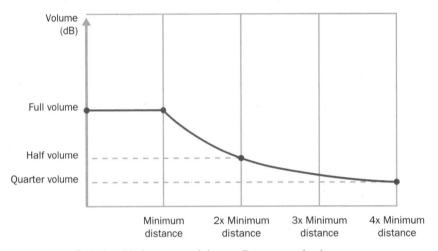

Figure 3.4 Relationship between minimum distance and volume.

Figure 3.4 shows that the minimum distance not only determines the radius around the listener within which the volume does not change, but also how the sound attenuates over distance. A value of 1 means that at 2 meters, the sound will be at half volume, and at 4 meters, at quarter volume. A value of 0.1 means that the sound will be at half volume at 0.2 meters. Similarly, a very loud object, with a minimum distance of 50 meters, will be at half volume 100 meters away, quarter volume at 200 meters, and so on. Remember that this value is combined with the global rolloff factor to give the final attenuation of a sound.

There is also a value in the DirectSound SDK that sets the maximum distance at which a sound can be heard. This turns out to not be very useful, is not represented in the Rumpus tool, and can usually be ignored.

Ambient Sounds

An ambient sound is not a 3-D sound, but a sound that is heard everywhere in the world at equal volume. Typically, this represents sounds such as rainfall, although many games implement background sounds for settings such as railyards, airports, natural environments, and so on, that work very well. One of the tricks to ambient sound is to play them at such low volumes that the human ear is incapable of determining whether it is a continuous sound or a short sample that is looping, yet is able to identify the sound as coming from a certain source.

Selecting the Ambient Sound check box disables most of the other entries in the dialog box because no 3-D positioning or movement applies. The Outside Volume setting gives an ambient sound a volume as a percentage of the recorded volume; typically, this is 100 percent.

As a piece of advice to game developers, ambient sounds and 3-D sounds work very well together.

Sound Cones

The sound cone provides an interesting set of features to DirectSound, although you should judge whether the 3-D-graphics world that your players are moving in justifies such precision in the sound output. The theory is that sounds do not emanate at equal volume from their point source, but tend to have a direction, as shown in Figure 3.5.

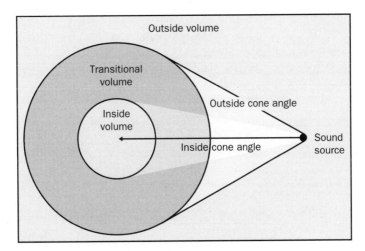

Figure 3.5 Inside and outside sound cones.

For example, when you speak, the sound is at a greater volume in front of you than behind. The Inside Cone setting gives the full diameter in degrees of the cone where full volume applies. So if this value is 90, then full volume occurs 45 degrees to either side of the direction of the sound source. The Outside Cone setting gives the full diameter of the cone outside of which the Outside Volume applies. Anywhere between the inside and outside cone settings, the sound volume is attenuated evenly. For example, if the Inside Cone is set to 90, the Outside Cone set to 180, and the Outside Volume set to 50, then the sound is at full volume up to 45 degrees from the facing of the source. The sound then attenuates evenly from full volume at 45 degrees down to half volume at 90 degrees from the facing of the source, after which the sound is at a consistent half volume.

Another feature of sound cones is that they can be made to face in any direction relative to the source object. The three radio buttons shown in Figure 3.3 provide the most obvious directional options; the first (the default) simply points the sound cone down the z-axis, so that an object placed at the top of the grid will have a cone facing towards the listener in the center of the grid (which, incidentally, has a default facing of up the z-axis).

Probably more useful are either the forward-facing or rear-facing sound cones selected by the other two radio buttons. Human speech is an example where a forward-facing cone is appropriate, while a rocket engine would require a rear-facing cone. There are also examples where a sound cone faces out to the side of an object or continuously rotates (such as an emergency vehicle's siren). The DirectSound SDK allows you to implement this (as does the Concertina framework code described in Chapter 8), but the Rumpus tool does not provide this option.

Experiment with adding sound cones to the train and plane Rumpus files to get a good idea of the concept of directional sound cones.

For now, ignore the Special Effects group box in this dialog box. We have a lot of 3-D code to dissect without making it more complicated by adding special effects. We'll examine these effects in great detail in the next two chapters.

The Rumpus tool is similar to the Cacophony tool in that clicking OK will add the sound and all the settings to the list in the main dialog box, while clicking Cancel will ignore any changes that you've made.

Now, back in the main Rumpus dialog box, click on the Edit Listener button.

The Listener

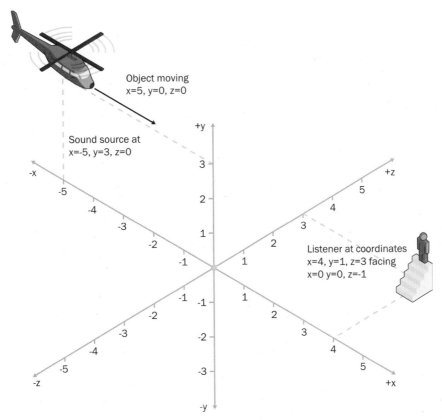

Figure 3.6   Listener in a 3-D world.

In the Rumpus tool, and also in the DirectSound SDK itself, the listener can be given a similar set of 3-D position properties to those given to sounds, as shown in Figure 3.6. After clicking on the Edit Listener button, you get the Add or Edit Sound dialog box, but with only the position and movement sliders available. By default, the listener is in the center of the grid, and not moving. However, the listener can be placed anywhere within the grid, and can be set to move, and perhaps given the same position and speed as one of the sounds. The listener is not *attached* to a sound in any way, but can simply be given identical position and movement parameters. For example, to simulate a person traveling on a train, the listener is given the same starting position and same velocity as one of the railroad cars of the train.

Any listener information that you enter is saved in a Rumpus file, along with the sounds and their settings.

The Rumpus Files

Now might be a good time to go through and play all the Rumpus files located in the Rumpus SFX files directory (except for those provided in the Special Effects sub-directory, which will be explained in the next chapter).

When saving a Rumpus file, only the non-zero sound settings are saved. Similar to the Cacophony (.cac) files, the file is saved in text format, but this time with an .rfx file name extension, so that it can conceivably be edited in Microsoft Notepad or another text file editor. However, since the .rfx files have a large number of settings, they are not as understandable as the .cac files.

Multichannel Sound

If you want a multichannel sound (for example, 5.1, 6.1, 7.1) to play using the Rumpus tool, then load it in as an ambient sound. Try loading the Rumpus file Paddling.rfx for an example of a 6.1 sound. The multichannel wave files need to be loaded as ambient (2-D) sounds because no 3-D processing can be applied to them.

Since multichannel wave files are usually very large, you will notice a considerable start latency when running the Paddling.rfx file. In order to use multichannel files effectively, you should stream them in (see Chapter 6), rather than load them into static buffers. Compare the start latency when running Paddling.rfx in the Rumpus tool with the start latency when loading PaddlingInCircles.wav into the Circular Streams sample of Chapter 6. Streaming is definitely the way to go with very large files.

If you want to create your own multichannel wave files, see Appendix B on the multichannel Audio Tool (MCAudio.exe) and use it to make 5.1 or 6.1 files. It is not an easy task to make meaningful multichannel sounds; you will probably find that you need the assistance of a good sound-editing tool.

However, perhaps a better use of multichannel output is that some audio cards will process the 3-D positioning and output the sound correctly out of the six or seven speakers.

This completes our discussion on the Rumpus user interface. Next, we'll load the Rumpus 3D SFX project, and delve into the code.

The Rumpus 3D SFX Project

When you open up this project in Microsoft Visual Studio .NET, you will see that there are five source files:

- DSound3DLayer.cpp

- Extended_dsutil.cpp

- RumpusEnvironment.cpp

- RumpusSFX.cpp

- RumpusSFXparam.cpp

There is also one header file in addition to the resource header file, RumpusSFX.h. For now, ignore RumpusEnvironment.cpp and RumpusSFX.param.cpp; these contain most of the environment and special effects code that you will examine in the next chapter.

The organization of the code is very similar to the code for the Cacophony tool. RumpusSFX.cpp controls the UI, DSound3DLayer.cpp handles the *CSound*, *CSoundManager* and 3-D buffer objects, and Extended_dsutil.cpp contains the utility code and our extensions, and also communicates with the DirectSound SDK. If performance was the issue, this is at least one layer of code too many, but dividing the code into layers helps separate the components for easier explanation.

The RumpusSFX.h File

The RumpusSFX.h header file defines two classes, *cSoundEffect* and *cOneSound*. The *cSoundEffect* class closely mirrors the UI dialog boxes, and stores all the settings that can be changed with the check boxes, edit boxes and sliders. For each slot in the main UI, one object of this class is created. Although this project has a greater number of settings than the Cacophony tool, the purpose of the first set of members in the *cSoundEffect* class is identical.

```
class cSoundEffect
{
private:
    char        filename[MAX_PATH];
    int         setting[max_settings];
    int         status;
    DWORD       tickLength;
    DWORD       ticksElapsed;
    int         iSound;
    int         iBuffer;

    D3DVECTOR   position;
    D3DVECTOR   velocity;
    D3DVECTOR   facing;

    CSoundFXData*   SoundFXData;
```

The header file contains defines for all 28 settings, one for each of the values that can be set by the UI. The final data member in this class, *SoundFXData*, is a pointer to an object containing all the special effects parameters, so we will discuss it in the next chapter. The three members that we need to explain now are the three vectors: position, velocity and facing.

The D3DVECTOR type is defined both in d3dtypes.h and dsound.h, and is a small but useful structure.

```
typedef struct _D3DVECTOR {
    float x;
    float y;
    float z;
} D3DVECTOR;
```

The three vectors obviously store the position, velocity and orientation of objects on the grid. It is easy to see why position is held as a vector. Velocities are also defined as vectors, with the values identifying the velocity in the x, y and z direction. The orientation vector similarly defines the orientation of the object in the x, y, and z directions. The advantage of holding these values all as vectors is that it becomes easy to work with all of them in a similar way. In the case of orientation, DirectSound *normalizes* the vector, so that all three values total either 1.0 or -1.0. This normalization is done for you, but it does mean that if you retrieve the values that are being used, they may not be identical to the ones that you set.

You'll need 9th-grade trigonometry and geometry to program in Direct3D, so it's back to school for some developers. To examine how vectors can be used, examine the following code for the *setConeFacing* method.

```
Void setConeFacing()
{
    switch( setting[cone_facing] )
    {
    case 0:
        facing.x    = 0.0f;
        facing.y    = 0.0f;
        facing.z    = -1.0f;
        break;
    case 1:
        facing.x    = velocity.x;
        facing.y    = velocity.y;
        facing.z    = velocity.z;
        break;
    case 2:
        facing.x    = -1.0f * velocity.x;
        facing.y    = -1.0f * velocity.y;
        facing.z    = -1.0f * velocity.z;
        break;
    }
}
```

The value of *setting[cone_facing]* can be 0 (facing down the grid), 1 (facing forwards) or 2 (facing backwards). It is fairly easy to add other orientations to this list. For example, if you wanted to add an option to direct the sound cone 90 degrees out to the right or left side of the object (at the same height of the object), we could add the two options shown in the following code.

```
case right_hand_side:
    facing.x    = velocity.z;
    facing.y    = velocity.y;
    facing.z    = -1.0 * velocity.x;
    break;
case left_hand_side:
    facing.x    = -1.0 * velocity.z;
    facing.y    = velocity.y;
    facing.z    = velocity.x;
    break;
```

If you want to do more complicated rotations than 90 degrees, you will have to use sine and cosine functions, however at 90 degrees, these conveniently turn out to be 1 and 0.

The *setInitialPositionAndVelocity* method calls the *setConeFacing* method after initializing the position according to the values in the *setting* array. Velocity is converted from meters per second to meters per tick by dividing the velocity by the number of ticks per second.

The *setInitialPosition* and *setInitialVelocity* methods take a vector as an input parameter and are used only when a random sound is being initiated by another sound, so in this case, the random sound simply inherits the vectors of the originating sound.

The next method to look at in the *cSoundEffect* class is *updatePosition*. This simply provides a reasonable bounce when the sound object strikes the edges of the grid. The object is rotated about the y-axis (so the y-coordinate is left untouched) by one radian until it is safely back on the grid again. A radian, for those of you whose memory of 9th-grade math has faded, is a measurement of an angle such that 2 * pi radians equals 360 degrees. This makes one radian equal to 57.2957795 degrees, approximately. The advantage of radians is that they make the calculations involving pi much easier, so are often used as the low-level method for storing angles, as is the case with DirectX. However, they are heinously unintuitive for humans to handle, so it is often safer on your sanity to deal with degrees or compass points when dealing with orientations, and use appropriate conversion functions when passing the angles down into an SDK. In this case, use the Windows SDK functions available in the math.h header file.

Most of the other methods in the *cSoundEffect* class simply set or retrieve data, except for the *writeEffect* and *readEffect* methods, that save and load the settings for an effect, respectively. The same format is used as for the Cacophony tool (setting number followed by value, terminated in 999), except that the special-effects parameter settings are also written out.

Now, look at the *cOneSound* class in the following code.

```
class cOneSound
{
private:
    char        filename[MAX_PATH];
    int         nBuffers;
    bool        loaded;
    bool        ambient;
```

This is a very similar class to the one of the same name in the Cacophony tool, and it has the same purpose: one object of this class is created for each wave file that is required. The new data member is the *ambient* Boolean, which is simply set to *true* if the sound is to be played everywhere at equal volume.

The methods in this class are all simple get and set methods.

These two classes are used extensively in the UI layer of the Rumpus tool, all of which is in the RumpusSFX.cpp file, which we will discuss next.

The RumpusSFX.cpp File

This source file starts with a number of global variables and tables, which we will describe later in this chapter. The first function to examine is the *WinMain* function that starts the application. The two lines added to the *WinMain* function from our previous tools (High5 and Cacophony) contain the calls *CoInitialize* and *CoUninitialize*. These two calls are only necessary if you want to enable the special effects that we address in the next chapter; for 3-D sound without special effects there is no need to call them, so they have no effect on anything discussed in this chapter. Although the calls themselves initialize and terminate much of the Component Object Model (COM), it is not necessary to know the inner workings of COM, only the situations where you need to make these calls.

Following the *WinMain* function, there is a section on functions supporting the Add or Edit Sound dialog box.

The first method, *ambientSoundSettings*, simply turns on or off a whole range of the features of the dialog box. An ambient sound does not require any 3-D settings, for obvious reasons.

The *retrieveSound* function is called when the dialog box opens up, to populate all the settings with those held in the array of *soundEffect* objects. If no sound is already loaded, then the sound name will be empty and all the settings will be at their default values.

The *OnInitSoundDialog* function does the usual initialization of a dialog box, sets the ranges for all the sliders, and initializes the special-effects edit box. It then either calls *retrieveSound,* or sets the appropriate settings for the listener, depending on whether you are editing a sound or the listener's settings. Remember that the listener is treated very similarly to a sound effect in the UI, each being given a position and velocity. Note also in this case that the words "The Listener" are entered in the file name edit box.

The *OnSoundSliderChanged* function is called when any of the position or velocity sliders are moved. The default range of a slider is zero to 100 (zero being at the left or top of a slider), but to make the UI slightly more intuitive, the code reverses this behavior for y and z positions and velocities. (Since these sliders are vertical, it seems more intuitive to have zero at the bottom of the slider, rather than at the top.) The range of the position sliders is left at 100, but the range of the velocities is set from -25 to 25.

The *ShowSoundFileDialog* function contains standard code for showing the Open File dialog box, and gives options to browse for and click on a file.

The *SoundDlgProc* function is the callback for the Add or Edit Sound dialog box. When the user sets variables, they are all stored in the temporary array *gTempSettings*, and not directly into the *soundEffect* array, simply to ensure that if the user cancels out of the dialog box, then nothing changes.

The next section of this source file deals with the functions supporting the tracking of sounds on the grid, and starts with the definition and declaration of the structure shown in the following code.

```
struct     soundTrackerStruct
{
    int     life;       // The life of the pixels in ticks.
    long    px;         // The x-coordinate on grid.
    long    pz;         // The z-coordinate on grid.
    int     color;
    bool    moving;
};
struct soundTrackerStruct soundTracker[max_tracks];
```

We need to color one pixel on the grid for every entry in the *soundTracker* array. The define *max_tracks* sets the size of this array at 1650, which is simply a number large enough to cover ten sounds plus one listener, with an average of ten pixels per shape and a lifespan of 15 ticks (so, 11 x 10 x 15 = 1650). It does not matter if the occasional pixel is missed, as the grid is constantly being updated, and since we're aiming for artistic effect rather than technical merit here.

The *numberShape* structure holds bit patterns for the numbers 1 through 10, and a circle representing the listener. If the sound is located at point x, z, then the number 1 is drawn by coloring the pixels x-1, z-3, then x, z-3, and so on. A clunky but effective way that helps represent the sounds in the table with moving points on the grid.

The first function, *cleanPoint*, sets any pixel back to its original light or dark green. Because we know that the RGB value for light green is 0x0000FF00 and the value for dark green is 0x00008000, we can hard-code these colors to avoid any complexity in having to save overwritten values.

The *findSoundTracker* function searches the entire array looking for an empty slot to insert a pixel entry, or returns the slot number if there already is an entry with the same x- and z-coordinates. This function is used by the *newSoundTrackPoint* function, which takes as input grid coordinates, the shape to draw, and a Boolean indicating whether the shape is moving or not.

The first thing that the *newSoundTrackPoint* function does is convert 3-D world coordinates to 2-D grid coordinates. Next, the color is set (hard-coded RGB values again, for white, red and black).

The main processing of this function takes each point required by the *numberShape* table, finds a slot in the *soundTracker* table for it to go into, and then populates the members of that slot with the color, coordinates, moving flag and lifespan of the pixel. The maximum life of a pixel has been set to 15 ticks.

The *drawSoundTracks* function methodically goes through the entire *soundTracker* table, setting the pixels on the grid to the appropriate color and decrementing their lifespan. When the life is reduced to 1, the pixel is cleared and the life member is set to 0 so that the slot can be recycled.

The *cleanGrid* function is called to initialize the whole process. It sets the color for each pixel in the entire grid, and then initializes the *soundTracker* structure by setting all the life members to 0.

The third section of this source file contains the functions supporting the main dialog box.

The Rumpus tool has the ability to start and stop any sound within the 100-second playing time, and these values are shown in the UI by the *setTimeBox* function.

The *displaySound* function takes the entries made in the Add or Edit Sound dialog box and displays them in the main dialog box.

The *wipeClean* function clears all the sound entries out, and is called when the user clicks New on the main dialog box just before a Rumpus file is loaded, or simply when the main dialog box is initialized by the *OnInitMainDialog* function.

OnInitMainDialog does not do anything very exciting; it simply initializes the main dialog box settings, and then calls *initDirectSound*. This function is in the DSound3DLayer.cpp source file, and as you will see in the following code, has changed since we discussed its namesake in the Cacophony tool.

The initDirectSound Function

The *initDirectSound* function, used in our previous samples, needs to be expanded for use with 3-D sounds.

```
void initDirectSound( HWND hwndDlg )
{
    int i;

    g_pSoundManager = new CSoundManager();
```

```
    for (i=0; i<max_sounds; i++)
        g_pSound[i] = NULL;

    if (g_pSoundManager != NULL)
    {
        if (FAILED(g_pSoundManager->Initialize( hwndDlg, DSSCL_PRIORITY)))
        {
            soundWorking = false;
        } else
        {
            soundWorking = true;

            if (FAILED(g_pSoundManager->
                Get3DListenerInterface( &g_pDSListener )))
                                        sound3DWorking = false; else
            {
                // Get listener parameters.
                g_dsListenerParams.dwSize = sizeof(DS3DLISTENER);
                g_pDSListener->GetAllParameters( &g_dsListenerParams );

                sound3DWorking = true;
            }
        }
    } else
        soundWorking = false;
}
```

The new code in this function is shown in bold. The *Get3DListenerInterface* call is to a method of the *CSoundManager* class, which is one of the utility classes provided originally in dsutil.cpp. This method returns a pointer to the 3-D Listener interface associated with the primary sound buffer. Having successfully retrieved this pointer, a call is made using it to the *GetAllParameters* method. This is a DirectSound SDK method that fills in a *DS3DLISTENER* structure with all the current settings for the listener. The structure is listed in the following code.

```
typedef struct {
  DWORD       dwSize;
  D3DVECTOR   vPosition;
  D3DVECTOR   vVelocity;
  D3DVECTOR   vOrientFront;
  D3DVECTOR   vOrientTop;
  D3DVALUE    flDistanceFactor;
  D3DVALUE    flRolloffFactor;
  D3DVALUE    flDopplerFactor;
} DS3DLISTENER, *LPDS3DLISTENER;
```

Notice that the global distance factor, rolloff factor, and Doppler factor are stored in this structure, along with the position, velocity and orientation of the listener. In the

Rumpus tool, we only change the position and velocity of the listener; the orientation (facing up the z-axis) is left at its default if the listener does not move. If the listener *does* move, then the *vOrientFront* vector is set to be identical to the *vVelocity* vector, which would seem to be the most obvious option (where the listener is looking in the direction that they are going). Since we do not change the *vOrientTop* vector in this tool, the listener never looks up or down.

It is a good idea to make the *GetAllParameters* call for the listener here. Not only does this allow you to examine the defaults using a debugger, which is usually a valuable thing to do, but the current settings can also be altered and sent back to the DirectSound SDK with a call to *SetAllParameters* using the same structure. Several other interfaces of DirectSound also have *GetAllParameters* and *SetAllParameters* methods that work in a very similar way.

Notice also in the *initDirectSound* code that we have added the flag *sound3DWorking*. This is simply to allow for the unlikely event of 2-D sound initializing correctly and 3-D sound failing, in which case, we do not want to deny our users the 2-D sound features of our application.

Back in the RumpusSFX.cpp file, the next function, *analyzeSoundEffects*, tries to make sense of what the user has entered using the UI. The first thing that this function does is takes each of the *soundEffect* objects and fills out a *oneSound* object for every unique wave file required. If two or more of the same wave file are referenced, then the number of buffers required for that wave file are incremented. The result is that the *oneSound* array of objects contains one entry per unique wave file.

Next, we try to load the required wave files. In this case, a test is done to see if the files are required for ambient or 3-D sounds, and then the *loadSound* or *load3DSound* functions are called. These two functions are in the DSound3DLayer.cpp file.

The *loadSound* function has not changed much since the Cacophony tool, the only difference being that the buffer flags have been set to support only volume changes (*DSBCAPS_CTRLVOLUME*), and not frequency or panning changes as we now only use this function for ambient sounds. There is a bit more to the *load3DSound* function in this tool, as shown in the following code.

```
bool load3DSound(int iS, char filename[], int nBuffers)
{
    if (sound3DWorking)
    {
        DWORD    bufferFlags    = DSBCAPS_CTRL3D | DSBCAPS_CTRLFX;

        // Delete any running sound.
        stopSound(iS);

        // Free any previous sound, and make a new one.
        SAFE_DELETE( g_pSound[iS]  );
```

```
        // Load the wave file into a DirectSound buffer.
        if (FAILED(g_pSoundManager->
                Create( &g_pSound[iS] ,filename, bufferFlags,
                        DS3DALG_HRTF_FULL, nBuffers )))
            return false;
        return true;
    } else
        return false;
}
```

The first point to notice in this method is that the buffer flags have been set to *DSBCAPS_CTRL3D | DSBCAPS_CTRLFX*, which will enable both 3-D and special effects. If you do not require special effects, then do not set the *DSBCAPS_CTRLFX* flag, as this will reduce some unnecessary processing.

Also, notice that the *Create* function has been called with the parameter *DS3DALG_HRTF_FULL*. This parameter is not nearly as interesting as it first appears. What it does is sets the 3-D algorithm DirectSound is to use if the buffer is created in software and not in hardware (that is, in virtual rather than physical memory). Most sound cards have an HRTF (head-relative transfer function) algorithm encoded onto them, which will be used by DirectSound if the buffer is created in hardware. If the buffer is created in software, then the parameter *DS3DALG_HRTF_FULL* will ensure that a full implementation of an HRTF function is applied to the buffer. The parameter can also be set to *DS3DALG_HRTF_LIGHT*, which provides less accuracy in the HRTF processing, but at less cost in CPU cycles, or *DS3DALG_NO_VIRTUALIZATION*, which provides no 3-D processing, and instead maps the sound to the normal left and right speakers.

HRTF refers to algorithms that map sounds to two speakers to mimic how a person hears sounds from the 3-D world. Most critics of the algorithms report that they perform quite well if the sound source is in front of the listener, but the results are not as good for sounds that originate above or behind the listener. Judge them for yourself.

The *Create* function of the *CSoundManager* class (in the extended_dsutil.cpp source file) is not altered by the addition of 3-D sound, however, notice the following call near the end of this function.

```
// Create the sound.
*ppSound = new CSound( apDSBuffer, dwDSBufferSize, dwNumBuffers, pWaveFile,
                dwCreationFlags );
```

This creates a new *CSound* object for the loaded wave file, and there are quite a few additions to the creation function to support 3-D sound and effects.

```
CSound::CSound( LPDIRECTSOUNDBUFFER* apDSBuffer, DWORD dwDSBufferSize,
                DWORD dwNumBuffers, CWaveFile* pWaveFile, DWORD dwCreationFlags
    )
```

(continued)

```
{
    DWORD i;

    m_apDSBuffer = new LPDIRECTSOUNDBUFFER[dwNumBuffers];

    if (m_apDSBuffer != NULL)
    {
        for( i=0; i<dwNumBuffers; i++ )
            m_apDSBuffer[i] = apDSBuffer[i];

        m_dwDSBufferSize    = dwDSBufferSize;
        m_dwNumBuffers      = dwNumBuffers;
        m_pWaveFile         = pWaveFile;
        m_dwCreationFlags   = dwCreationFlags;

        for (i = 0; i<dwNumBuffers; i++)
            FillBufferWithSound( m_apDSBuffer[i], FALSE );

        // Initializing for 3-D processing.

        m_pDS3DBuffer = new LPDIRECTSOUND3DBUFFER[dwNumBuffers];
        m_pdsBufferParams = new DS3DBUFFER[dwNumBuffers];

        for( i=0; i<dwNumBuffers; i++ )
        {
            m_pDS3DBuffer[i]    = NULL;
            m_apDSBuffer[i]-> QueryInterface(IID_IDirectSound3DBuffer,
                         (VOID**) &m_pDS3DBuffer[i] );

            m_pdsBufferParams[i].dwSize = sizeof(DS3DBUFFER);
            m_pDS3DBuffer[i] -> GetAllParameters( &m_pdsBufferParams[i] );

        }

        // Special effects.

        pFXManager = new CSoundFXManager*[dwNumBuffers];

        for( i=0; i<dwNumBuffers; i++ )
        {
            pFXManager[i] = new CSoundFXManager( );
            pFXManager[i] ->Initialize( GetBuffer(i), TRUE);
        }
    }
}
```

The first lines of code have not changed from the Cacophony tool; they first create the requested number of buffers, and then fill them in with the sound data. The new code is shown in bold.

The variable *m_pDS3DBuffer* is an array of pointers to DirectSound 3-D buffer interfaces. It is filled in with the calls to *QueryInterface* in the loop that follows. The *m_pdsBufferParams* array sets up one *DS3DBUFFER* structure for each of the sound buffers. This structure is filled in with the call to *GetAllParameters*, using the interface pointer that was just received from the *QueryInterface* call.

The important point about these *DS3DBUFFER* structures is that they are copies for your own use. DirectSound keeps its own inaccessible copy; you retrieve the current state using *GetAllParameters*, change those parameters as appropriate, and then send them back to the DirectSound SDK using the *SetAllParameters* call. There are some situations where you might want to change the defaults immediately, and call *SetAllParameters* in the creation function listed previously, so now would be a good time to examine the *DS3DBUFFER* structure.

```
typedef struct _DS3DBUFFER
{
    DWORD           dwSize;
    D3DVECTOR       vPosition;
    D3DVECTOR       vVelocity;
    DWORD           dwInsideConeAngle;
    DWORD           dwOutsideConeAngle;
    D3DVECTOR       vConeOrientation;
    LONG            lConeOutsideVolume;
    D3DVALUE        flMinDistance;
    D3DVALUE        flMaxDistance;
    DWORD           dwMode;
} DS3DBUFFER, *LPDS3DBUFFER;
```

The first parameter should be set before making any calls at all, and is always set equal to *sizeof(DS3DBUFFER)*. One reason for this data member, which you will see in many Microsoft SDK structures, is that it can make code more resilient to changes to the data structure itself (for example, the adding of a new data member to the structure).

You should recognize the rest of the data members from the previous discussions about vectors, sound cones, and minimum and maximum distances. However, the final parameter, *dwMode*, is new. You will almost always want to leave this parameter at its default of *DS3DMODE_NORMAL*, which simply means that the sound will move in the same 3-D space as the listener. However, there are two other options. One is *DS3DMODE_DISABLE*, which disables all 3-D processing so that the sound appears to originate inside the listener's head. The other option is *DS3DMODE_HEADRELATIVE*, which instructs the DirectSound SDK to interpret the position, velocity, and orientation as relative and not absolute vectors. So, in this case, the DirectSound SDK will effectively add the position, velocity, and orientation of the sound to the position, velocity, and orientation of the listener to come up with absolute values for the sound.

There may be certain special sounds that you would like to position relative to the listener (for example, an angelic voice off to the left, and a devilish one off to the right, which obviously would move completely relative to the listener). In this case, you need to add a parameter to the *Create* method of the *CSoundManager* class to instruct the Direct-Sound SDK to use head-relative positioning for this particular sound. Assuming that the parameter is a Boolean flag called *fSetHeadRelative,* then you would need to add both this parameter and the following lines of code to the *CSound* creation function after the code that calls *GetAllParameters* for the sound buffer.

```
if (fSetHeadRelative)
{
    m_pdsBufferParams[i].dwMode = DS3DMODE_HEADRELATIVE;
    m_pDS3DBuffer[i] -> SetAllParameters( &m_pdsBufferParams[i] );
}
```

Most applications do not use head-relative sounds, but perhaps there is room for some interesting effects here.

As a design note, we decided to include the 3-D interface pointers and buffer structure as members of the *CSound* class. This makes sense for the purpose of this tool, but it is possible that you may want this information to be held elsewhere in your application's data, and be attached to the *CSound* class in some other way. For example, this second method may help in avoiding duplicate copies of an object's position and velocity.

Still in the *CSound* creation function, the section of code beginning with the comment "// Special effects" initializes the special effects data. This is only necessary if you want special-effects processing, and we will go over this code in the next chapter.

This ends our discussion of the functions and methods called from the *analyzeSoundEffects* function in the RumpusSFX.cpp source file. The next function to examine in this source file is *initRumpus*, which is called when the user clicks the Play button.

The *initRumpus* function starts off by calling the *analyzeSoundEffects* and *cleanGrid* functions (which we have already described), and then starts the timer by changing *g_ticks* from -1 to 0. Then, *initRumpus* initializes the movement of the sounds on the grid with the following lines of code.

```
for (int index=0; index<max_soundsPlusListener; index++)
    soundEffect[index].setInitialPositionAndVelocity();

Set3DListenerProperties(soundEffect[the_listener].getPositionVector(),
                        soundEffect[the_listener].getVelocityVector(),false,
                        true,gDoppler,gDistance,gRolloff);
```

The first loop sets the position, velocity, and cone facing for each of the sound effects tabled in the Rumpus UI, along with the listener. The values used to do the initialization are taken from the *setting* array held for each *cSoundEffect* object (refer to the *setInitialPositionAndVelocity* method for objects of this class).

The second call extracts the information for the listener, and calls down into the DirectSound SDK to initialize the listener object.

Similar to the 3-D interface pointer and parameters structure held for each sound in the *CSound* class, we have an interface pointer and structure for the listener. However, instead of embedding it in a class, we declared them in the DSound3DLayer.cpp source file as shown in the following code.

```
LPDIRECTSOUND3DLISTENER g_pDSListener = NULL;    // 3-D listener object.
DS3DLISTENER            g_dsListenerParams;      // Listener properties.
```

It would, of course, be perfectly possible to have embedded these into the *CSound-Manager* class, which might make some design sense. However, for this sample we kept them as global variables.

With this data declared, we can call the *Set3DListenerProperties* function.

```
void Set3DListenerProperties(D3DVECTOR* pvPosition,
                             D3DVECTOR* pvVelocity,
                             bool moving,
                             bool initialize,
                             float doppler,
                             float distance,
                             float rolloff)
{
    int apply;

    if (sound3DWorking)
    {
        memcpy(&g_dsListenerParams.vPosition, pvPosition, sizeof(D3DVECTOR));
        memcpy(&g_dsListenerParams.vVelocity, pvVelocity, sizeof(D3DVECTOR));

        if (moving)
            memcpy( &g_dsListenerParams.vOrientFront, pvVelocity,
                    sizeof(D3DVECTOR) );

        if (initialize)
        {
            apply = DS3D_IMMEDIATE;

            g_dsListenerParams.flDopplerFactor    = doppler;
            g_dsListenerParams.flDistanceFactor   = distance;
            g_dsListenerParams.flRolloffFactor    = rolloff;

        } else
            apply = DS3D_DEFERRED;

        if( g_pDSListener )
            g_pDSListener -> SetAllParameters( &g_dsListenerParams, apply );
    }
}
```

The first two calls to *memcpy* faithfully copy the position and velocity vectors. The orientation of the listener is only set if the listener is moving, and therefore has a legitimate velocity vector. Remember that the Rumpus tool default simply orientates the listener so that they face up towards the top of the grid.

Although listener position and velocity are likely to change throughout an application, the Doppler factor, distance factor and rolloff factor are not, so we only set these three factors if the *initialize* flag is set. Note that our external declaration of *Set3DListenerProperties* sets defaults for these three parameters, so there is no need to set values for them to use the function.

```
extern void Set3DListenerProperties(D3DVECTOR* pvPosition,
    D3DVECTOR* pvVelocity,
    bool moving,
    bool initialize = false,
    float doppler = 1.0f,
    float distance = 1.0f,
    float rolloff = 1.0f );
```

The final call in *Set3DListenerProperties* uses the global interface pointer *g_pDSListener* to call the DirectSound SDK *SetAllParameters* method, with the *g_dsListenerParams* structure containing the new settings as the first parameter.

The story is made slightly more complicated by the second parameter for *SetAllParameters*, the requirement for a setting *DS3D_IMMEDIATE* or *DS3D_DEFERRED*. If *DS3D_IMMEDIATE* is used as the second parameter for *SetAllParameters*, then the changes come into effect immediately. In theory, this is almost always what you want, however in practice, changes to the data members of either *DS3DBUFFER* or *DS3DLISTENER* structures are costly and can result in glitches in the quality of sound output if constant changes are sent to the sound mixer that forms the engine of Direct-Sound. If the *DS3D_DEFERRED* setting is used, then none of the new data will apply until a call is made to the DirectSound SDK method *CommitDeferredSettings*. You will notice in the *Set3DListenerProperties* method that the initialization settings are applied immediately, and will not result in any glitches because no sounds are being played. However, those changes that are made during the course of play are deferred, waiting for a suitable time to commit them all.

If you look at the *OnTimer* function, you will notice a call to a wrapper function *commitAllSettings*, which occurs only after all the changes are made to each sound and the listener at the end of each tick period. This minimalizes any glitches that may occur due to the changes, and also increases the efficiency of DirectSound. The following wrapper method is only there to keep all references to the *g_pDSListener* pointer in one source file.

```
void commitAllSettings()
{
    if (g_pDSListener)
        g_pDSListener -> CommitDeferredSettings();
}
```

Although the DirectSound SDK method *CommitDeferredSettings* is made on the listener object, it actually also applies to all of the deferred settings on all of the sounds.

This ends our discussion of the *initRumpus* function. The *stopRumpus* function is fairly simple and doesn't introduce anything new. This brings us to the all-important *OnTimer* function that runs to several pages of code.

The *OnTimer* function is called once every tenth of a second in the Rumpus tool. The first short section of code deals with the situation before the Play button has been clicked.

```
for (i=0; i<max_soundsPlusListener; i++)
{
    if (soundEffect[i].getProposed3DSound() OR i == the_listener)
    {
        newSoundTrackPoint( (int) soundEffect[i].getPositionX(),
                            (int)soundEffect[i].getPositionZ(),i,false);
    }
}
```

The *getProposed3DSound* method simply returns *true* if the sound slot has been filled with a 3-D sound, as opposed to being empty or containing an ambient sound. If there are requests for 3-D sounds, then the appropriate numbers are drawn on the grid, along with the circle for the listener.

The rest of the code is run when the Play button has been clicked. We start by showing the code for the listener.

```
bool movedListener = soundEffect[the_listener].updatePosition();
newSoundTrackPoint((int)soundEffect[the_listener].getPositionX(),
                   (int)soundEffect[the_listener].getPositionZ(),
                   the_listener,movedListener);

if (movedListener)
{
Set3DListenerProperties(soundEffect[the_listener].getPositionVector(),
                        soundEffect[the_listener].getVelocityVector(),
                        movedListener);
}
```

The first line of code updates the listener's position and returns *true* if it is moving. A call is then made to the *newSoundTrackPoint* function to draw the white circle which represents the listener on the grid. If the listener is moving, then the *Set3DListenerProperties* call is made, but only with the first three parameters of the call. The fourth parameter will default to *false*, and indicate that this is not an initialization call. This is all that is needed to update the listener's properties.

We won't list all the lines of code here for playing sounds, but will concentrate on the salient calls. The first loop checks to see if any sound should be started, and if it is an ambient sound, then the following call is made.

```
playAmbientSoundBuffer( soundEffect[i].getSoundIndex(),
                        soundEffect[i].getBufferIndex(),
                        soundEffect[i].getOneSetting(outside_volume),
                        true);
```

The *playAmbientSoundBuffer* function (in the DSound3DLayer.cpp file) is as shown in the following code.

```
bool playAmbientSoundBuffer(int iS, int iB, int V, bool looping)
{
    // Ambient sounds are always centrally positioned.

    if (soundWorking AND g_pSound[iS] != NULL)
    {
        long      actualVolume   = calcuateVolumeChange(V);
        DWORD     dwFlags        = 0;

        if (looping)
            dwFlags = DSBPLAY_LOOPING;

        if (FAILED(g_pSound[iS] ->PlayBuffer( iB, 0, dwFlags,
                    actualVolume, DSBPAN_CENTER, NO_FREQUENCY_CHANGE)))
            return false; else
            return true;
    } else
        return false;
}
```

Notice that we are using a utility function, *calculateVolumeChange*, to calculate the desired volume as a percentage of the recorded volume. The definition of this function is in the extended_dsutil.cpp file, and is shown in the following code.

```
long calcuateVolumeChange(int percent)
{
    if (percent <= 0)
        return DSBVOLUME_MIN;

    if (percent > 0 && percent < 100)
    {
        double ratio = (double) percent / 100.0f;
        double hundredthsOfDeciBels = 100 * 20 * log10(ratio);

        return DSBVOLUME_MAX + (long) hundredthsOfDeciBels;
    }
    return DSBVOLUME_MAX;
}
```

This function uses the same underlying math as the *calculateVolumeFromDistance* function described in Chapter 2 (the *20 * Log10(ratio)* statement). An input percentage of 50 implies that you want the sound to appear to originate twice as far away as the original recording, so 6.02 decibels is deducted from the original volume. Note that as all the ratios will have a value less than 1, and that the *log10* function will return negative numbers for these values, then we *add* the value for *hundredthsOfDecibels* rather than subtract it to avoid the double negative.

Back in the *playAmbientSoundBuffer* function, it is usual to loop ambient sounds, so the *dwFlags* parameter is set to *DSBPLAY_LOOPING*. Then the *PlayBuffer* method of the *CSound* class is called to begin playing the sound.

Back in the *OnTimer* function, the next major call is to *Set3DSoundProperties*.

```
Set3DSoundProperties(    soundEffect[i].getSoundIndex(),
        soundEffect[i].getBufferIndex(),
        soundEffect[i].getPositionVector(),
        soundEffect[i].getVelocityVector(),
        soundEffect[i].getConeVector(),
        true,
        soundEffect[i].getOneSetting(volume_radius),
        soundEffect[i].getOneSetting(inside_cone),
        soundEffect[i].getOneSetting(outside_cone),
        soundEffect[i].getOneSetting(outside_volume));
play3DSoundBuffer(    soundEffect[i].getSoundIndex(),
        soundEffect[i].getBufferIndex(), true, rSFX, FXData);
```

The first call passes through our wrapper layer to the following method of the *CSound* class.

```
HRESULT CSound::Set3DSoundProperties(int index,
                        D3DVECTOR* pvPosition,
                        D3DVECTOR* pvVelocity,
                        D3DVECTOR* pvCone,
                        bool initialize,
                        int maxVradius,
                        int insideCone,
                        int outsideCone,
                        int outsideVolume)
{
    if (index < (int) m_dwNumBuffers)
    {
memcpy( &m_pdsBufferParams[index].vPosition, pvPosition, sizeof(D3DVECTOR) );
memcpy( &m_pdsBufferParams[index].vVelocity, pvVelocity, sizeof(D3DVECTOR) );
memcpy( &m_pdsBufferParams[index].vConeOrientation, pvCone, sizeof(D3DVECTOR) );

        if (initialize)
        {
            m_pdsBufferParams[index].flMinDistance        = (float) maxVradius;
            m_pdsBufferParams[index].dwInsideConeAngle    = insideCone;
```

(continued)

```
                m_pdsBufferParams[index].dwOutsideConeAngle    = outsideCone;
                m_pdsBufferParams[index].lConeOutsideVolume    = outsideVolume;
        }

    m_pDS3DBuffer[index] ->
            SetAllParameters( &m_pdsBufferParams[index], DS3D_DEFERRED);
        return S_OK;
    } else
        return S_FALSE;
}
```

Notice that this method is very similar to the *Set3DListenerProperties* method. The first three *memcpy* calls copy the position, velocity and orientation vectors. Only during initialization are the minimum distance and cone parameters set. Of course, it is possible to have a sound effect with a constantly varying sound cone (for example, a rotating siren), and altering our previous code to account for this would be as simple as a name change (just change the name of the *initialize* flag to something like *fResetConeParameters*).

Finally, we call the DirectSound SDK method *SetAllParameters*, with the address of the structure holding the parameters (*m_pdsBufferParams[index]*) and the *DS3D_DEFERRED* flag set. The *index*, of course, refers to the buffer index for that sound, which will often be zero as only one buffer of the sound is required. In most cases, we recommend using the *DS3D_DEFERRED* flag, which we previously explained in the section on the *Set3DListenerProperties* method. The use of this flag means that the changes are deferred and will take effect only when a call is made to *CommitAll-Settings*.

These calls change the 3-D settings for the sound, but do not actually make it start playing; that is done with the next call in the *OnTimer* function, *play3DSoundBuffer*.

```
play3DSoundBuffer( soundEffect[i].getSoundIndex(),
                    soundEffect[i].getBufferIndex(), true, rSFX, FXData);
```

For now, ignore the *rSFX* and *FXData* parameters, as these refer to special effects that we will discuss in the next chapter. If you follow the *play3DSoundBuffer* call through the DSound3DLayer.cpp code to the DirectSound SDK. You will notice that there is very little to it, since almost all of the work has already been done.

```
HRESULT CSound::Play3DBuffer(int iB, DWORD dwPriority, DWORD dwFlags )
{
    HRESULT hr;
    BOOL    bRestored;

    if( m_apDSBuffer == NULL )
        return CO_E_NOTINITIALIZED;

    LPDIRECTSOUNDBUFFER pDSB = m_apDSBuffer[ iB ];
```

```
if( pDSB == NULL )
    return DXTRACE_ERR( TEXT("Play3DBuffer"), E_FAIL );

// Restore the buffer if it was lost.
if( FAILED( hr = RestoreBuffer( pDSB, &bRestored ) ) )
    return DXTRACE_ERR( TEXT("RestoreBuffer"), hr );

if( bRestored )
{
    // The buffer was restored, so we need to fill it with new data.
    if( FAILED( hr = FillBufferWithSound( pDSB, FALSE ) ) )
        return DXTRACE_ERR( TEXT("FillBufferWithSound"), hr );

    // Make DirectSound do pre-processing on sound effects.
    Reset();
}

hr = pDSB -> Play( 0, dwPriority, dwFlags );

return hr;
}
```

Most of the code in the *Play3DBuffer* method is concerned with recovering the buffer should some other application have taken it. Otherwise, it comes down to the *Play* call. The first of the two parameters is always 0 (it is one of those reserved parameters), and the second parameter should also always be 0, unless the sound buffer was created using the *DSBCAPS_LOCDEFER* flag (which we did not do in this case). The third parameter can either be 0 or *DSBPLAY_LOOPING*.

Now go back out to the *OnTimer* function in the RumpusSFX.cpp source file, and examine the code that runs when a sound is playing. The first lines check to see if a timed stop has been set for the sound, and if so, the *stopSoundBuffer* method is called. This method, and the *testSoundBufferStopped* method, are identical to those used in the Cacophony tool and were described in Chapter 2.

The next chunk of code in the *OnTimer* function more or less repeats the previous section, but applies to sounds that are triggered at the given random frequency. Nearly at the end of the code example are the following lines of code.

```
if (soundEffect[i].getOneSetting(ambient_sound) == 0)
{
    bool movedSound = soundEffect[i].updatePosition();
    newSoundTrackPoint( (int) soundEffect[i].getPositionX(),
                        (int)soundEffect[i].getPositionZ(),i,movedSound);

    if (movedSound)
        Set3DSoundProperties( soundEffect[i].getSoundIndex(),
                              soundEffect[i].getBufferIndex(),
```

(continued)

```
                              soundEffect[i].getPositionVector(),
                              soundEffect[i].getVelocityVector(),
                              soundEffect[i].getConeVector(),
                              false );
}
```

This is very similar to the code shown earlier in this chapter for the *OnTimer* function that tests to see if the listener is moving, but in this case, the code refers to the sounds rather than to the listener. First, the sound position is updated and grid points are set, and then if the sound has moved, a shortened call to *Set3DSoundProperties* is made to pass the new position into the DirectSound SDK.

At the end of the *OnTimer* function, there is a call to *commitAllSettings*, which was discussed earlier, and then finally, a call to *drawSoundTracks* to actually render the pixels stored as sound tracker points.

The final functions of the RumpusSFX.cpp file do not need much explanation. *ShowRFXFileDialog* calls up the Open File dialog box, but with the extension .rfx to help locate Rumpus files. The *ReadRumpusFile* and *WriteRumpusFile* functions are self-explanatory, and then the main dialog box callback pulls everything together.

Summary

Even without any special effects, 3-D sounds added to an application can be impressive. This chapter, along with the Rumpus sample, explained all that you need to know to add 3-D sound to your application. Once you have grasped the concept of a listener and sound effects, each with their own position, velocity, and orientation vectors, you can see how closely 3-D sound maps to 3-D graphics. For the sake of efficiency, it is important to consider the vector requirements of 3-D sound when you are designing the classes and structures that you are going to use for your graphics objects.

The downside to creating 3-D sounds with the DirectSound SDK is the occasional tendency of DirectSound to produce sound glitches. The immediate and deferred settings are one tool that will help you to minimize this characteristic.

In just three chapters, we have already covered one-, two-, and three-dimensional sound, and examined tools that test many of the features of DirectSound. The next chapter starts to tackle the application of special effects.

4

Adding Special Effects and Environmental Reverb to 3-D Sounds

Special effects add a lot of character to a sound. A sound can be distorted, compressed, echoed and parametrically equalized, and basically used and abused until you achieve the desired effect. After playing with all the special effects that can be applied to a sound, you might think it possible to write a complex game audio engine using only a very few recorded sounds. As audio engineers refer to a pure sound as *dry*, and one with special effects applied as *wet*, look at this chapter as where we begin to get wet in our programming adventure.

This chapter describes the preset audio effects available within DirectSound, and then demonstrates them using the Rumpus tool. Go to the AVBook\bin directory, and run the Rumpus tool again. Click the Add or Edit Sound button, and then look at the Special Effects group box (see Figure 4.1).

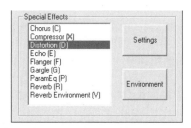

Figure 4.1 Special Effects group box.

Special Effects

In DirectSound, there are nine preset types of special effects that can be applied to a sound. The first eight effects are Chorus, Compressor, Distortion, Echo, Flanger, Gargle, ParamEq, and Reverb. These effects add some interesting character to the dry sounds that we so often hear. Because of differences in the way that it is implemented in Direct-Sound, and because we provide a more efficient alternative in Chapter 7, we are going to treat the last effect, Environmental Reverb, differently from the other eight effects.

However, the Rumpus tool demonstrates the use of all nine effects, easily enabling them to be added, combined and removed from any of the ten sound slots.

In this chapter, we'll concentrate on the coding needed to implement the special effects. The next chapter describes the audio background required to make meaningful changes to the parameters that are set for these effects. But first, start with a quick tour of the features of the Rumpus UI that we purposefully left out of the previous chapter.

Setting and Testing Effects

Back in the Rumpus tool, in the Add or Edit Sound dialog box, click the Sound File button and select the Cannon.wav sound file, leaving all the other parameters unchanged. The cannon sound will begin playing immediately. Click OK to go back to the main dialog box, and then click Play. What you'll hear is a basic cannon sound going off every few seconds.

Now, click the Select radio button for sound 2, and, in the Add or Edit Sound dialog box, load the Cannon.wav sound file in again, except this time, give it a start time of 1.5 seconds. Click OK, and then click Play in the main dialog box. You will now hear the sounds of two cannons. Alternatively, you can load the TwoCannons.rfx Rumpus file, which has two cannon sounds that do what you just did manually. Note that both cannons sound identical at this point. Now, we'll have some fun and apply special effects to the sound of the second cannon.

Although you can turn on one, any, or all of the special effects, start with one effect at a time. To turn on a special effect, simply click its name in the Add or Edit Sound dialog box so that the word takes on a blue background. To turn it off, click the effect name again. Since the second of the two cannon sounds is still selected in the main dialog box, click the Distortion effect in the Add or Edit Sound dialog box so that the name turns blue. Now click OK.

If you look at the Special Effects column in the main Rumpus dialog box, you'll see the letter D in the slot for the second cannon sound, which notes that you added the distortion effect to this sound. Each effect has its own single letter code; if multiple effects are applied, then all the relevant letters appear in the Special Effects column. The letters are listed in the Special Effects group box (see Figure 4.1) in the Add or Edit Sound dialog box.

Click Play in the Rumpus dialog box, and note the marked effect that distortion has on this cannon sound.

Now repeat the procedure, but set the Flanger special effect on one of the cannon sounds. Try it again, setting both the Flanger and Distortion effects on one of the sounds. Try the Chorus, Echo and Gargle effects too. Gargle is a bit of an odd effect, and has not always attracted favorable reviews.

The next chapter discusses the audio background of each special effect, and shows how to alter the parameters to achieve just the right effect that you want. If you click on the Settings button (in the Special Effects group box in the Add or Edit Sound dialog box), you will note that you can change a range of parameters for each of the eight special effects (see Figure 4.2). However, remember that you have to click the item in the Special Effects list box to turn that effect on or off. Note also that when you save a Rumpus file, all of the settings are recorded, regardless of whether they are set to on or off. This means that if you temporarily want to turn off, for example, the Distortion effect, all of your hard work spent getting the parameters just right is not lost.

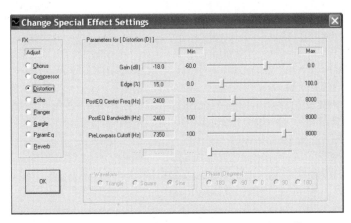

Figure 4.2   Special effects settings for the Distortion effect.

The ninth special effect, environmental reverb, is somewhat different from the other eight effects. If you click on the Environment button, the Environmental Reverb dialog box appears (see Figure 4.3), and you can select from a whole range of preset environments – from small enclosed spaces to great arenas, both man-made and natural. Probably the most humorous reverb effect is the Sewer Pipe, and other commonly used game environments include the Cave, the Hangar, and the Stone Corridor.

Figure 4.3 Environmental Reverb dialog box.

One of the main differences between the environmental reverb effect and the other special effects is that you need to create two buffers containing each wave file that you wish to process. The first buffer will be untouched by the environmental reverb effect (and so provides the main dry sound), while the second buffer will have the effect applied. This is perhaps less than ideal, and is one reason that we recommend using the EAX environmental reverb effect discussed in Chapter 7. You might, however, want to experiment with sounds with only environmental effects applied, and no dry sound.

Now, load and play the Rumpus file named CannonInPipe.rfx. This example demonstrates the environmental reverb effect of a cannon going off in a sewer pipe (clearly an essential scenario for many of today's games). Try deleting the sound without the effect applied (in slot 1), and just playing the wet sound with the environmental reverb effect. Then, load in the CannonInPipe.rfx file again and try adding another effect, such as a distortion or flanger effect, to both the dry and wet cannon sounds, and playing them again. You can get a whole range of different cannon and explosive effects simply by playing with the distortion, flanger, and environmental reverb effects.

Now, try adding an environmental effect to music. There are six preset environments designed especially for music, located at the end of the list in the Environmental Reverb dialog box, but all of the other environments can also be applied. Try playing music in various environments, for example, in an arena, in a hanger, and so on.

The Rumpus tool will help you create special-effect settings that work just right for your wave files. Along with the 3-D movement settings, we now have a useful tool working with a great deal of variable parameters. Time now to crack open the code.

The SoundFXData Class

In the *CSoundEffect* class, defined in RumpusSFX.h, the last data member, and the only one we have not described so far, is the following.

```
CSoundFXData*    SoundFXData;
```

This is a pointer to a *CSoundFXData* object, which holds special effects parameters for all nine effects.

The *CSoundFXData* class (defined in the extended_dsutil.cpp file) is declared in the extended_dsutil.h file.

```
class CSoundFXData
{
public:
    CSoundFXData( );
    ~CSoundFXData( );

    DSFXChorus              m_paramsChorus;
    DSFXCompressor          m_paramsCompressor;
    DSFXDistortion          m_paramsDistortion;
    DSFXEcho                m_paramsEcho;
    DSFXFlanger             m_paramsFlanger;
    DSFXGargle              m_paramsGargle;
    DSFXParamEq             m_paramsParamEq;
    DSFXWavesReverb         m_paramsReverb;
    DSFXI3DL2Reverb         m_paramsEnvironment;

    void CopyAllData(CSoundFXData* copyFromClass);
    void WriteBytes(FILE *fp, char* address, int nBytes);
    void WriteAllData(FILE *fp);
    void ReadBytes(FILE *fp, char* address, int nBytes);
    void ReadAllData(FILE *fp);
};
```

This class has the following constructor; notice how all the default settings are applied here.

```
CSoundFXData::CSoundFXData( )
{

    ZeroMemory( &m_paramsChorus, sizeof( DSFXChorus ) );
    ZeroMemory( &m_paramsCompressor, sizeof( DSFXCompressor ) );
    ZeroMemory( &m_paramsDistortion, sizeof( DSFXDistortion ) );
    ZeroMemory( &m_paramsFlanger, sizeof( DSFXFlanger ) );
    ZeroMemory( &m_paramsEcho, sizeof( DSFXEcho ) );
    ZeroMemory( &m_paramsGargle, sizeof( DSFXGargle ) );
    ZeroMemory( &m_paramsParamEq, sizeof( DSFXParamEq ) );
```

(continued)

```
ZeroMemory( &m_paramsReverb, sizeof( DSFXWavesReverb ) );
ZeroMemory( &m_paramsEnvironment, sizeof( DSFXI3DL2Reverb ) );

m_paramsChorus.fWetDryMix       = 50.0f;
m_paramsChorus.fDepth           = 10.0f;
m_paramsChorus.fFeedback        = 25.0f;
m_paramsChorus.fFrequency       = 1.1f;
m_paramsChorus.lWaveform        = DSFXCHORUS_WAVE_SIN;
m_paramsChorus.fDelay           = 16.0f;
m_paramsChorus.lPhase           = DSFXCHORUS_PHASE_NEG_90;

m_paramsCompressor.fGain        = 0.0f;
m_paramsCompressor.fAttack      = 10.0f;
m_paramsCompressor.fRelease     = 200.0f;
m_paramsCompressor.fThreshold   = -20.0f;
m_paramsCompressor.fRatio       = 3.0f;
m_paramsCompressor.fPredelay    = 4.0f;

m_paramsDistortion.fGain                    = -18.0f;
m_paramsDistortion.fEdge                    = 15.0f;
m_paramsDistortion.fPostEQCenterFrequency   = 2400.0f;
m_paramsDistortion.fPostEQBandwidth         = 2400.0f;
m_paramsDistortion.fPreLowpassCutoff        = 7350.0f;

m_paramsFlanger.fWetDryMix      = 50.0f;
m_paramsFlanger.fDepth          = 100.0f;
m_paramsFlanger.fFeedback       = -50.0f;
m_paramsFlanger.fFrequency      = 0.25f;
m_paramsFlanger.lWaveform       = DSFXFLANGER_WAVE_SIN;
m_paramsFlanger.fDelay          = 2.0f;
m_paramsFlanger.lPhase          = DSFXFLANGER_PHASE_ZERO;

m_paramsEcho.fWetDryMix         = 50.0f;
m_paramsEcho.fFeedback          = 50.0f;
m_paramsEcho.fLeftDelay         = 500.0f;
m_paramsEcho.fRightDelay        = 500.0f;
m_paramsEcho.lPanDelay          = DSFXECHO_PANDELAY_MIN;

m_paramsGargle.dwRateHz         = 20;
m_paramsGargle.dwWaveShape      = DSFXGARGLE_WAVE_TRIANGLE;
m_paramsParamEq.fCenter         = 7350.0f;
m_paramsParamEq.fBandwidth      = 12.0f;
m_paramsParamEq.fGain           = 0.0f;

m_paramsReverb.fInGain          = 0.0f;
m_paramsReverb.fReverbMix       = 0.0f;
m_paramsReverb.fReverbTime      = 1000.0f;
m_paramsReverb.fHighFreqRTRatio = 0.001f;
```

```
m_paramsEnvironment.lRoom                 = DSFX_I3DL2REVERB_ROOM_DEFAULT;
m_paramsEnvironment.lRoomHF               = DSFX_I3DL2REVERB_ROOMHF_DEFAULT;
m_paramsEnvironment.flRoomRolloffFactor =
                            DSFX_I3DL2REVERB_ROOMROLLOFFFACTOR_DEFAULT;
m_paramsEnvironment.flDecayTime           = DSFX_I3DL2REVERB_DECAYTIME_DEFAULT;
m_paramsEnvironment.flDecayHFRatio        = DSFX_I3DL2REVERB_DECAYHFRATIO_DEFAULT;
m_paramsEnvironment.lReflections          = DSFX_I3DL2REVERB_REFLECTIONS_DEFAULT;
m_paramsEnvironment.flReflectionsDelay =
                            DSFX_I3DL2REVERB_REFLECTIONSDELAY_DEFAULT;
m_paramsEnvironment.lReverb               = DSFX_I3DL2REVERB_REVERB_DEFAULT;
m_paramsEnvironment.flReverbDelay         = DSFX_I3DL2REVERB_REVERBDELAY_DEFAULT;
m_paramsEnvironment.flDiffusion           = DSFX_I3DL2REVERB_DIFFUSION_DEFAULT;
m_paramsEnvironment.flDensity             = DSFX_I3DL2REVERB_DENSITY_DEFAULT;
m_paramsEnvironment.flHFReference         = DSFX_I3DL2REVERB_HFREFERENCE_DEFAULT;
}
```

Chapter 5 discusses the audio background behind all of these parameters and settings.

Four of the five methods of this class only concern the reading and writing of this data out to a Rumpus (.rfx) file, and are self-explanatory. The other method, *CopyAllData*, will copy in all the parameters from a second *CSoundFXData* object. The *cSoundEffect* objects (and their associated *CSoundFXData* objects) are created when the Rumpus tool is started. All the sound effects will contain the default settings shown previously. Both the *cSoundEffect* and *CSound* classes inherit the *CSoundFXData* class. The purpose of a *cSoundEffect* object holding this information is simply to aid in changing the parameters using the UI. The copy actually used to communicate the parameters to the DirectSound SDK is held in a *CSound* object.

The CSoundFXManager Class

If you look at the creation function for a *CSound* object, you will see the following code.

```
// Special effects.
pFXManager = new CSoundFXManager*[dwNumBuffers];

for( i=0; i<dwNumBuffers; i++ )
{
    pFXManager[i] = new CSoundFXManager( );
    pFXManager[i] ->Initialize( GetBuffer(i) );
}
```

This code first creates an array of *CSoundFXManager* pointers (one for each sound buffer), creates one *CSoundFXManager* object for each member of the array, and then calls *Initialize* on that object. The *CSoundFXManager* class (also defined in the extended_dsutil.cpp file) inherits all the data and methods from the *CSoundFXData* class, and then adds functionality to support the special effect interfaces provided by the DirectSound SDK.

The declaration of this class (in the extended_dsutil.h file) follows.

```
class CSoundFXManager : public CSoundFXData
{
public:
    CSoundFXManager( );
    ~CSoundFXManager( );

    HRESULT Initialize ( LPDIRECTSOUNDBUFFER lpDSB );
    HRESULT SetFXEnable( DWORD esfxType );
    HRESULT ActivateFX( );
    HRESULT LoadCurrentFXParameters( );
    HRESULT DisableAllFX( );

    LPDIRECTSOUNDFXCHORUS8          m_lpChorus;
    LPDIRECTSOUNDFXCOMPRESSOR8      m_lpCompressor;
    LPDIRECTSOUNDFXDISTORTION8      m_lpDistortion;
    LPDIRECTSOUNDFXECHO8            m_lpEcho;
    LPDIRECTSOUNDFXFLANGER8         m_lpFlanger;
    LPDIRECTSOUNDFXGARGLE8          m_lpGargle;
    LPDIRECTSOUNDFXPARAMEQ8         m_lpParamEq;
    LPDIRECTSOUNDFXWAVESREVERB8     m_lpReverb;
    LPDIRECTSOUNDFXI3DL2REVERB8     m_lpEnvironment;
    LPDIRECTSOUNDBUFFER8            m_lpDSB8;

protected:
    DSEFFECTDESC                m_rgFxDesc[eNUM_SFX];
    const GUID *                m_rgRefGuids[eNUM_SFX];
    LPVOID *                    m_rgPtrs[eNUM_SFX];
    BOOL                        m_rgLoaded[eNUM_SFX];
    DWORD                       m_dwNumFX;

    HRESULT EnableGenericFX( GUID guidSFXClass, REFGUID rguidInterface,
                        LPVOID * ppObj );
};
```

We will start by discussing the protected data members, and then look at the protected and public methods.

The protected member *m_rgFxDesc* holds an array of buffer descriptions (held in *DSEFFECTDESC* structures) for each effect. The *DSEFFECTDESC* structure is just a small one.

```
typedef struct _DSEFFECTDESC
{
    DWORD       dwSize;
    DWORD       dwFlags;
    GUID        guidDSFXClass;
    DWORD_PTR   dwReserved1;
    DWORD_PTR   dwReserved2;
} DSEFFECTDESC, *LPDSEFFECTDESC;
```

The structure is initialized in the *EnableGenericFX* method, which we will discuss in a moment. The only member of much interest is the *guidDSFXClass* GUID. Of the other members, the size is set to the size of the structure, the flags to zero, and the reserved members are unused.

The next protected member is *m_rgRefGuids*, which holds an array of GUIDs identifying the effects to be applied. Then, *m_rgPtrs* holds the DirectSound interface pointer for each effect. There is a DirectSound interface for each of the nine effects, and they are named as follows.

```
IDirectSoundFXChorus;
IDirectSoundFXCompressor;
IDirectSoundFXDistortion;
IDirectSoundFXEcho;
IDirectSoundFXFlanger;
IDirectSoundFXGargle;
IDirectSoundFXParamEq;
IDirectSoundFXWavesReverb;
IDirectSoundFXI3DL2Reverb;
```

The only interface without an obvious name is the last one, which is the interface for environmental effects (I3DL2 stands for Interactive 3D Audio Rendering Guidelines, Level 2, and is a standard for environmental reverb).

The protected member *m_rgLoaded* simply holds a flag, set in the *SetFXEnable* method, and is simply there to prevent the effect from being initialized twice. Finally, the protected member *m_dwNumFX* holds a count of the special effects to be applied.

That covers the last of the data members, so now it's time to take a look at the methods.

The creation method of the *CSoundFXData* class simply sets all the memory locations to zero.

The *Initialize* method, called from the creation function of the *CSound* class, gets the *DirectSoundBuffer8* interface pointer (which is the DirectSound interface that supports all the special effects).

```
HRESULT CSoundFXManager::Initialize( LPDIRECTSOUNDBUFFER lpDSB )
{
    HRESULT hr;

    if( NULL == lpDSB )
        return S_FALSE;

    // Get the interface.
    if( FAILED( hr = lpDSB->
            QueryInterface( IID_IDirectSoundBuffer8, (LPVOID*) &m_lpDSB8 ) ) )
        return hr;

    return S_OK;
}
```

The next method to look at is *SetFXEnable*. This method takes one member of the enumeration *ESFXType* as a parameter. This enumeration is used here and elsewhere in the code, often to step through the nine special effects.

```
enum ESFXType
{
    eSFX_chorus = 0,
    eSFX_compressor,
    eSFX_distortion,
    eSFX_echo,
    eSFX_flanger,
    eSFX_gargle,
    eSFX_parameq,
    eSFX_reverb,
    eSFX_environment,

    // Number of enumerated effects.
    eNUM_SFX
};
```

The *SetFXEnable* method first sets the loaded flag (*m_rgLoaded*), so a subsequent call to this method will not reload anything, and then uses a switch statement to call *EnableGenericFX* for each of the special effects. The code for these two methods follows, starting with *SetFXEnable*.

```
HRESULT CSoundFXManager::SetFXEnable( DWORD esfxType )
{
    HRESULT hr;

    if( esfxType >= eNUM_SFX )
        return E_FAIL;

    if( m_rgLoaded[esfxType] )
        return S_FALSE;
    else
        m_rgLoaded[esfxType] = TRUE;

    switch ( esfxType )
    {
    case eSFX_chorus:
        hr = EnableGenericFX( GUID_DSFX_STANDARD_CHORUS,
                        IID_IDirectSoundFXChorus8,
                        (LPVOID*) &m_lpChorus );
        break;
    case eSFX_compressor:
        hr = EnableGenericFX( GUID_DSFX_STANDARD_COMPRESSOR,
                        IID_IDirectSoundFXCompressor8,
                        (LPVOID*) &m_lpCompressor );
```

```
            break;
        case eSFX_distortion:
            hr = EnableGenericFX( GUID_DSFX_STANDARD_DISTORTION,
                                  IID_IDirectSoundFXDistortion8,
                                  (LPVOID*) &m_lpDistortion );
            break;
        case eSFX_echo:
            hr = EnableGenericFX( GUID_DSFX_STANDARD_ECHO,
                                  IID_IDirectSoundFXEcho8,
                                  (LPVOID*) &m_lpEcho );
            break;
        case eSFX_flanger:
            hr = EnableGenericFX( GUID_DSFX_STANDARD_FLANGER,
                                  IID_IDirectSoundFXFlanger8,
                                  (LPVOID*) &m_lpFlanger );
            break;
        case eSFX_gargle:
            hr = EnableGenericFX( GUID_DSFX_STANDARD_GARGLE,
                                  IID_IDirectSoundFXGargle8,
                                  (LPVOID*) &m_lpGargle );
            break;
        case eSFX_parameq:
            hr = EnableGenericFX( GUID_DSFX_STANDARD_PARAMEQ,
                                  IID_IDirectSoundFXParamEq8,
                                  (LPVOID*) &m_lpParamEq );
            break;
        case eSFX_reverb:
            hr = EnableGenericFX( GUID_DSFX_WAVES_REVERB,
                                  IID_IDirectSoundFXWavesReverb8,
                                  (LPVOID*) &m_lpReverb );
            break;

        case eSFX_environment:
            hr = EnableGenericFX( GUID_DSFX_STANDARD_I3DL2REVERB,
                                  IID_IDirectSoundFXI3DL2Reverb8,
                                  (LPVOID*) &m_lpEnvironment );
            break;
        default:
            hr = E_FAIL;
            break;
    }

    return hr;
}


HRESULT CSoundFXManager::EnableGenericFX( GUID guidSFXClass,
                                          REFGUID rguidInterface,
                                          LPVOID * ppObj )
```

(continued)

```
{
    // If an effect is already allocated return S_FALSE.
    if( *ppObj )
        return S_FALSE;

    if( m_dwNumFX >= eNUM_SFX )
        return E_FAIL;

    // Set the effect to be enabled.
    ZeroMemory( &m_rgFxDesc[m_dwNumFX], sizeof(DSEFFECTDESC) );
    m_rgFxDesc[m_dwNumFX].dwSize        = sizeof(DSEFFECTDESC);
    m_rgFxDesc[m_dwNumFX].dwFlags       = 0;
    CopyMemory( &m_rgFxDesc[m_dwNumFX].guidDSFXClass, &guidSFXClass,
                sizeof(GUID) );

    m_rgRefGuids[m_dwNumFX] = &rguidInterface;
    m_rgPtrs[m_dwNumFX] = ppObj;

    m_dwNumFX++;

    return S_OK;
}
```

Note that *EnableGenericFX* is the function that initializes the buffer description structure (held in the *m_rgFxDesc* array of *DSEFFECTDESC* structures), which only copies in the GUID class, GUID and interface pointer, which are all provided as parameters. Note that the *m_rgPtrs* array contains pointers to the special effect interface pointers (such as *m_lpChorus*), which at this stage, should all be NULL.

The method that populates the interface pointers by using the *m_rgPtrs* array is *ActivateFX*. This method turns on a special effect with a call to the DirectSound SDK method *GetObjectInPath*, which changes the pointers such as *m_lpChorus* from NULL to the valid interface pointer for that effect. *ActivateFX* also provides DirectSound with the special effect information with a call to another DirectSound method, *SetFX*.

```
HRESULT CSoundFXManager::ActivateFX( )
{
    DWORD dwResults[eNUM_SFX];
    HRESULT hr;
    DWORD i;

    if( NULL == m_lpDSB8 )
        return E_FAIL;

    if( m_dwNumFX == 0 )
        return S_FALSE;

    if( FAILED( hr = m_lpDSB8->SetFX( m_dwNumFX, m_rgFxDesc, dwResults ) ) )
        return hr;
```

```
    // Get reference to the effect object.
    for( i = 0; i < m_dwNumFX; i++ )
        if( FAILED( hr = m_lpDSB8->
GetObjectInPath( m_rgFxDesc[i].guidDSFXClass, 0, *m_rgRefGuids[i],
            m_rgPtrs[i] ) ) )
            return DXTRACE_ERR( TEXT("GetObjectInPath"), hr );

    return S_OK;
}
```

Note that the DirectSound *SetFX* method takes as input parameters the number of effects to be applied and the array of buffer descriptions. It also takes, as an output parameter, the address of an array to hold the results of the loading of each effect.

Programming Tip

The Rumpus tool strictly applies the special effects in the order they appear in the Special Effects dialog box: Chorus, Compression, Distortion, Echo, Gargle, Flanger, Parameq, Reverb, and Environmental Reverb. The order in which multiple effects are applied to a sound can dramatically change the output, and that order is determined by the *SetFX* method. The order in which the array of *DSEFFECT-DESC* structures (pointed to by the *m_rgFxDesc* parameter in the sample code listed for the *ActivateFX* method) are sent to the *SetFX* method is the order that effects are applied. If your application involves the extensive use of multiple effects, you should ensure they are being applied in a meaningful order.

However, at this point, we will not take advantage of the information held in *dwResults* (there is not much that can be done if an effect fails to load, or is loaded in software rather than hardware).

Note that the *SetFX* method must be called before a call is made to the *GetObjectInPath* method.

The *DisableAllFX* method releases all the interface pointers, clears all the protected members, and then makes the following two calls.

```
// Buffer must be stopped before calling SetFx.
if( m_lpDSB8 )
    m_lpDSB8->Stop();

// This removes all effects from the buffer.
m_lpDSB8->SetFX( 0, NULL, NULL );
```

The first call stops the special effects buffer. The second call to *SetFX* with zero and NULL parameters has the effect of turning off all effects. This must be done after the sound has been stopped.

The *LoadCurrentFXParameters* method tests to see if the interface pointers for each effect are not NULL, and then makes a call to *SetAllParameters* on that interface. Each statement in this method is similar to the following code.

```
if( m_lpChorus )
        m_lpChorus->SetAllParameters( &m_paramsChorus );
```

Obviously, this takes the copy of the parameters in the *CSoundFXManager* object and provides them to the DirectSound SDK.

This completes our discussion of the *CSoundFXManager* class. Although its methods are somewhat exhausting to go through, now that we have them in place, applying special effects to the Rumpus tool will be easier.

Managing Special Effect Settings

Now, return to the RumpusSFX.cpp file. When the global variable *g_lpTempSoundFXData* is created, it is also initialized with all the default parameters for a *CSoundFXData* object that was listed previously.

```
CSoundFXData*    g_lpTempSoundFXData = new CSoundFXData;
```

However, these initial values are overwritten every time the Add or Edit Sound dialog box is called up, with the following code in the *retrieveSound* method (which, if you remember, simply loads the current wave file name and settings for that slot in the Rumpus dialog box's table of sound effects).

```
soundEffect[index].getSFXData(g_lpTempSoundFXData);
```

With this call, the *getSFXData* method fills the *g_lpTempSoundFXData* object with all the current settings for that sound effect. The code for *getSFXData* simply calls the *CopyAllData* method on the *CSoundFXData* class.

```
void getSFXData(CSoundFXData* copyFromData)
{
    copyFromData -> CopyAllData(SoundFXData);
}
```

Similarly, if the user of the tool updates the special effect parameters and clicks OK, then the *MainDlgProc* callback function will take the temporary settings back out of *g_lpTempSoundFXData*, and store the changed values in the *cSoundEffect* object with a call to the *setSFXData* method. Note the use of the *g_SFXOK* flag to prevent any updating if the user changed the values, but then clicked Cancel.

```
if (g_SFXOK)
    soundEffect[g_cSound].setSFXData(g_lpTempSoundFXData);
```

Before we delve into how these settings are passed to the DirectSound SDK, we will explain how the UI works to make it easy to change the settings.

The two source files, RumpusSFXparam.cpp and RumpusEnvironment.cpp, contain code for the UI only; no calls into the DirectSound SDK are made from within them. The code in RumpusSFXparam.cpp is based on one of the samples shipped with the DirectSound SDK, SoundFX.exe, which uses a masterly sense of control over sliders and radio buttons in order to use the same dialog box and controls for all eight special effects.

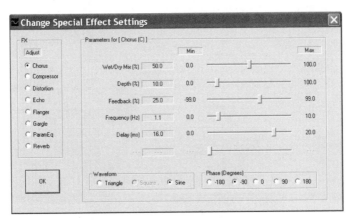

Figure 4.4   Change Special Effect Settings dialog box for the Chorus effect.

You will notice from the screen shot of the Change Special Effects Settings dialog box shown in Figure 4.4 that there are six sliders, three waveforms, and five phases. None of the special effects requires all of these parameters, but all use a subset of them. This dialog box UI enables only those parameters that apply to the special effect selected in the column of radio buttons. If you click on any one of the special effect radio buttons, you will see the range of enabled sliders, and waveform and phase buttons change appropriately.

One of the tricks used in this style of UI programming is to have consecutive ID numbers for the various settings. This makes it much easier to write code to manipulate the settings in this makeshift array form, but you do have to check by hand that the resource IDs are consecutive, as it is not a feature provided by Visual Studio. Start by looking at the *SpecialFXDlgProc* callback function, and refer to the following code snippet.

```
default:
if( LOWORD( wParam ) >= IDC_RADIO_CHORUS &&
    LOWORD( wParam ) <= IDC_RADIO_REVERB )
{
    g_dwCurrentFXType = LOWORD( wParam ) - IDC_RADIO_CHORUS;
    LoadParameterUI( hDlg, g_dwCurrentFXType );
}
```

Notice that the special effect radio buttons *IDC_RADIO_CHORUS* to *IDC_RADIO_REVERB* are consecutive, so we can write this code. The global parameter *g_dwCurrentFXType* will hold a value from 0 (chorus) to 7 (reverb), indicating which effect we are looking at, then the function *LoadParameterUI* is called to haul its current settings into the dialog box.

If you now look at the *LoadParameterUI* function, you will notice that it first clears the current UI with a call to *ResetParameterUI*, then gives the group box containing all the settings a name with the following code.

```
sprintf( tszstr, "Parameters for [ %s ]", SFXnames[dwFXType] );
SetDlgItemText( hwndDlg, IDC_FRAME, tszstr );
```

Then the *LoadParameterUI* function dives into a huge switch statement that loads up the current settings for that special effect. Look at the chorus special effect as an example.

```
case eSFX_chorus:
{
    LoadSingleParameter( hwndDlg, IDC_PARAM_NAME1,
                         TEXT( "Wet/Dry Mix (%)" ),
                         g_lpTempSoundFXData->m_paramsChorus.fWetDryMix,
                         DSFXCHORUS_WETDRYMIX_MIN,
                         DSFXCHORUS_WETDRYMIX_MAX );
    LoadSingleParameter( hwndDlg, IDC_PARAM_NAME2,
                         TEXT( "Depth (%)" ),
                         g_lpTempSoundFXData->m_paramsChorus.fDepth,
                         DSFXCHORUS_DEPTH_MIN,
                         DSFXCHORUS_DEPTH_MAX );
    LoadSingleParameter( hwndDlg, IDC_PARAM_NAME3,
                         TEXT( "Feedback (%)" ),
                         g_lpTempSoundFXData->m_paramsChorus.fFeedback,
                         DSFXCHORUS_FEEDBACK_MIN,
                         DSFXCHORUS_FEEDBACK_MAX );
    LoadSingleParameter( hwndDlg, IDC_PARAM_NAME4,
                         TEXT( "Frequency (Hz)" ),
                         g_lpTempSoundFXData->m_paramsChorus.fFrequency,
                         DSFXCHORUS_FREQUENCY_MIN,
                         DSFXCHORUS_FREQUENCY_MAX );
    LoadSingleParameter( hwndDlg, IDC_PARAM_NAME5,
                         TEXT( "Delay (ms)" ),
                         g_lpTempSoundFXData->m_paramsChorus.fDelay,
                         DSFXCHORUS_DELAY_MIN,
                         DSFXCHORUS_DELAY_MAX );
    LoadWaveformRadio( hwndDlg,
                         g_lpTempSoundFXData->m_paramsChorus.lWaveform,
                         DSFXCHORUS_WAVE_TRIANGLE, -1,
                         DSFXCHORUS_WAVE_SIN );
```

```
LoadPhaseRadio( hwndDlg,
                g_lpTempSoundFXData->m_paramsChorus.lPhase,
                DSFXCHORUS_PHASE_NEG_180,
                DSFXCHORUS_PHASE_NEG_90,
                DSFXCHORUS_PHASE_ZERO,
                DSFXCHORUS_PHASE_90,
                DSFXCHORUS_PHASE_180 );
    break;
```

Notice that there are five calls to the *LoadSingleParameter* function, which load information into the first five of the six sliders of the dialog box. The parameters for the *LoadSingleParameter* function, following the inevitable handle, are the ID of the slider, the text to describe the parameter, the current value, and then the minimum and maximum possible values. This function provides a clever way of re-using a slider for many purposes. The *LoadSingleParameter* function first calls another function, *EnableSingleParameter*, to enable the five dialog box resources for that parameter. Then, depending on the appropriate decimal precision for the range of values, it sends dialog box messages to display the current value, and the minimum and maximum values.

A call to the *LoadWaveformRadio* function has as its parameters the dialog box handle and current setting, and then the different waveform settings that apply to this effect. For the chorus effect, the triangle and sine waveforms apply, but not the square waveform (which is removed from consideration by the -1 in the parameter list).

Similarly, a call to the *LoadPhaseRadio* function indicates that wave phases apply, and the parameters supplied are the dialog box handle and the current setting. In this case, if any of the five phases are possible, all are. The call to this function seems complicated, with all five of the possible phases sent in the parameter list. However, this does mirror the define statements in dsound.h, which seem to cater for the possibility that a 90-degree phase change to one special effect may need another value than the same phase change to another effect. It perhaps would have been cleaner if all the special effects used the same definitions as well as the same values, but they do not, and this complexity makes this code look far more awkward than it should.

If you go through the rest of the *LoadParameterUI* function, you will see that for each special effect, the appropriate number of calls are made to the *LoadSingleParameter, LoadWaveformRadio* and *LoadPhaseRadio* functions.

All of the code just described is run when the user of the Rumpus tool clicks on one radio button in the column with the simple title FX.

Back in the *SpecialFXDlgProc* function, the other major thread to follow is for the function *OnEffectChanged*. The *OnEffectChanged* function is called whenever a change occurs to a slider, a waveform, or a phase radio button.

If you look at the code for *OnEffectChanged* in the RumpusSFXparam.cpp source file, you will see a long switch statement that is very similar to the one in *LoadParameterUI*. Basically, every time that a user of the tool makes any change to any setting, all of the settings are recorded back into the *g_lpTempSoundFXData* object. Again, taking the chorus effect as an example, the code is written as follows.

```
case eSFX_chorus:
{
    SaveSingleParameter( hwndDlg, IDC_PARAM_NAME1,
                         &g_lpTempSoundFXData->m_paramsChorus.fWetDryMix,
                         DSFXCHORUS_WETDRYMIX_MIN,
                         DSFXCHORUS_WETDRYMIX_MAX );
    SaveSingleParameter( hwndDlg, IDC_PARAM_NAME2,
                         &g_lpTempSoundFXData->m_paramsChorus.fDepth,
                         DSFXCHORUS_DEPTH_MIN,
                         DSFXCHORUS_DEPTH_MAX );
    SaveSingleParameter( hwndDlg, IDC_PARAM_NAME3,
                         &g_lpTempSoundFXData->m_paramsChorus.fFeedback,
                         DSFXCHORUS_FEEDBACK_MIN,
                         DSFXCHORUS_FEEDBACK_MAX );
    SaveSingleParameter( hwndDlg, IDC_PARAM_NAME4,
                         &g_lpTempSoundFXData->m_paramsChorus.fFrequency,
                         DSFXCHORUS_FREQUENCY_MIN,
                         DSFXCHORUS_FREQUENCY_MAX );
    SaveSingleParameter( hwndDlg, IDC_PARAM_NAME5,
                         &g_lpTempSoundFXData->m_paramsChorus.fDelay,
                         DSFXCHORUS_DELAY_MIN,
                         DSFXCHORUS_DELAY_MAX );

    if( IsDlgButtonChecked( hwndDlg, IDC_RADIO_TRIANGLE ) == BST_CHECKED )
        g_lpTempSoundFXData->
                    m_paramsChorus.lWaveform = DSFXCHORUS_WAVE_TRIANGLE;
    else
        g_lpTempSoundFXData->m_paramsChorus.lWaveform = DSFXCHORUS_WAVE_SIN;

    if( IsDlgButtonChecked( hwndDlg, IDC_RADIO_NEG_180 )==BST_CHECKED )
        g_lpTempSoundFXData->m_paramsChorus.lPhase = DSFXCHORUS_PHASE_NEG_180;
    else if( IsDlgButtonChecked( hwndDlg, IDC_RADIO_NEG_90 ) == BST_CHECKED )
        g_lpTempSoundFXData->m_paramsChorus.lPhase = DSFXCHORUS_PHASE_NEG_90;
    else if( IsDlgButtonChecked( hwndDlg, IDC_RADIO_ZERO ) == BST_CHECKED )
        g_lpTempSoundFXData->m_paramsChorus.lPhase = DSFXCHORUS_PHASE_ZERO;
    else if( IsDlgButtonChecked( hwndDlg, IDC_RADIO_90 )==BST_CHECKED )
        g_lpTempSoundFXData->m_paramsChorus.lPhase = DSFXCHORUS_PHASE_90;
    else
        g_lpTempSoundFXData->m_paramsChorus.lPhase = DSFXCHORUS_PHASE_180;

        break;
```

Clearly, the *SaveSingleParameter* function performs more or less the opposite of *LoadSingleParameter,* with the following code calculating the value.

```
FLOAT percent = ( FLOAT ) ( pos - DEFAULT_SLIDER_MIN ) /
                ( FLOAT ) ( DEFAULT_SLIDER_MAX - DEFAULT_SLIDER_MIN );
*val = percent * ( max - min ) + min;
```

The *percent* value receives the position of the slider as a percentage of its range from left to right. The resulting value is used to calculate the actual parameter from the minimum and maximum possible which are supplied to the function in the *min* and *max* parameters.

The **val* parameter points to the *g_lpTempSoundFXData* object.

This time, the waveform and phase radio buttons do not require an additional function, a simple set of if statements step through the radio buttons, and if the radio button is checked, the waveform or phase value is updated.

That wraps up the purpose and coding of the RumpusSFXparam.cpp file.

The other source file handling only UI, RumpusEnvironment.cpp, is comparatively trivial. There is very little to say about it, other than the selected environment number is loaded into the *g_Environment* global variable.

Now, back to the main RumpusSFX.cpp file, to learn how to actually attach special effects to a sound buffer.

Playing Special Effects

Here we finally address how special effects are applied to wave files.

In the description of the *OnTimer* function in the last chapter, we left out the following two calls that come before the function *Set3DSoundProperties*.

```
soundEffect[i].getSpecialEffectsArray(rSFX);
FXData = soundEffect[i].getSpecialEffectsData();

Set3DSoundProperties(…….);
play3DSoundBuffer(soundEffect[i].getSoundIndex(),
                  soundEffect[i].getBufferIndex(),
                  true, rSFX, FXData);
```

The *getSpecialEffectsArray* method simply returns an array of ones or zeros (flags) indicating whether a special effect is to be applied or not. The code for this method is written as follows.

```
void getSpecialEffectsArray(int rSFX[max_specialeffects])
{
    int i;
    for (i=sfx_chorus; i< sfx_chorus + max_specialeffects; i++)
    {
        rSFX[ i - sfx_chorus ] = setting[i];
    }
}
```

The *rSFX* array has nine elements, so it includes a flag for the environmental effect. The defines starting with *sfx_chorus* are the positions of these flags in the *settings* array of the *cSoundEffect* class (for example, *sfx_chorus* is 16). However, in the *rSFX* array, the *ESFXType* enumeration is used to determine the location of the flags.

Following the retrieval of this array of flags is the retrieval of the parameter data itself, with the following line.

```
FXData = soundEffect[i].getSpecialEffectsData();
```

The *getSpecialEffectData* method treats the environmental flag differently from the rest, because the Rumpus tool supports all the preset environmental locations but does not adjust the parameters for these locations (this task is left as an exercise for the reader).

```
CSoundFXData*    getSpecialEffectsData()
{
    // Load in environmental data if required.
    if (setting[sfx_environment] == 1)
    {
        CopyMemory( &SoundFXData -> m_paramsEnvironment,
                    &envValues[ setting[sfx_enviroReverb] ],
                    sizeof(DSFXI3DL2Reverb));
    }
    return SoundFXData;
}
```

The parameters for a *CopyMemory* call are *destination*, *source*, and then the number of bytes to copy. The *envValues* structure has been defined in order to make it easy for you to add your own environment, which we will do later in this chapter. For the moment, this structure supports the environments that are pre-defined in DirectSound.

```
struct   _DSFXI3DL2Reverb envValues[max_environments] =
{
    I3DL2_ENVIRONMENT_PRESET_DEFAULT,
    I3DL2_ENVIRONMENT_PRESET_GENERIC,
    I3DL2_ENVIRONMENT_PRESET_PADDEDCELL,
    I3DL2_ENVIRONMENT_PRESET_ROOM,
    I3DL2_ENVIRONMENT_PRESET_BATHROOM,
    I3DL2_ENVIRONMENT_PRESET_LIVINGROOM,
    I3DL2_ENVIRONMENT_PRESET_STONEROOM,
    I3DL2_ENVIRONMENT_PRESET_AUDITORIUM,
    I3DL2_ENVIRONMENT_PRESET_CONCERTHALL,
    I3DL2_ENVIRONMENT_PRESET_CAVE,
    I3DL2_ENVIRONMENT_PRESET_ARENA,
    I3DL2_ENVIRONMENT_PRESET_HANGAR,
    I3DL2_ENVIRONMENT_PRESET_CARPETEDHALLWAY,
    I3DL2_ENVIRONMENT_PRESET_HALLWAY,
    I3DL2_ENVIRONMENT_PRESET_STONECORRIDOR,
    I3DL2_ENVIRONMENT_PRESET_ALLEY,
```

```
        I3DL2_ENVIRONMENT_PRESET_FOREST,
        I3DL2_ENVIRONMENT_PRESET_CITY,
        I3DL2_ENVIRONMENT_PRESET_MOUNTAINS,
        I3DL2_ENVIRONMENT_PRESET_QUARRY,
        I3DL2_ENVIRONMENT_PRESET_PLAIN,
        I3DL2_ENVIRONMENT_PRESET_PARKINGLOT,
        I3DL2_ENVIRONMENT_PRESET_SEWERPIPE,
        I3DL2_ENVIRONMENT_PRESET_UNDERWATER,
        I3DL2_ENVIRONMENT_PRESET_SMALLROOM,
        I3DL2_ENVIRONMENT_PRESET_MEDIUMROOM,
        I3DL2_ENVIRONMENT_PRESET_LARGEROOM,
        I3DL2_ENVIRONMENT_PRESET_MEDIUMHALL,
        I3DL2_ENVIRONMENT_PRESET_LARGEHALL,
        I3DL2_ENVIRONMENT_PRESET_PLATE
};
```

You will find the definition of these defines in dsound.h; as an example, here is the definition for the underwater environment.

```
#define I3DL2_ENVIRONMENT_PRESET_UNDERWATER -1000,-4000, 0.0f, 1.49f, 0.10f,
        -449, 0.007f, 1700, 0.011f, 100.0f, 100.0f, 5000.0f
```

Note how the preset is simply a list of values, each corresponding to one data member of a *DSFXI3DL2Reverb* structure. This structure is listed here with its range of allowable values and defaults given as comments.

```
typedef struct _DSFXI3DL2Reverb
{
    LONG    lRoom;               // [-10000, 0]      default: -1000 mB
    LONG    lRoomHF;             // [-10000, 0]      default: 0 mB
    FLOAT   flRoomRolloffFactor;// [0.0, 10.0]      default: 0.0
    FLOAT   flDecayTime;         // [0.1, 20.0]      default: 1.49s
    FLOAT   flDecayHFRatio;      // [0.1, 2.0]       default: 0.83
    LONG    lReflections;        // [-10000, 1000]   default: -2602 mB
    FLOAT   flReflectionsDelay;  // [0.0, 0.3]       default: 0.007 s
    LONG    lReverb;             // [-10000, 2000]   default: 200 mB
    FLOAT   flReverbDelay;       // [0.0, 0.1]       default: 0.011 s
    FLOAT   flDiffusion;         // [0.0, 100.0]     default: 100.0 %
    FLOAT   flDensity;           // [0.0, 100.0]     default: 100.0 %
    FLOAT   flHFReference;       // [20.0, 20000.0]  default: 5000.0 Hz
} DSFXI3DL2Reverb, *LPDSFXI3DL2Reverb;
```

We will come back to the use of these define statements when we explain how to add your own environment. Also, the individual data members (*lRoom*, for example) are discussed in detail in Chapter 7. For now, however, the *getSpecialEffectData* method adds the environmental values to the *SoundFXData* object, and then returns a pointer to that object.

All that happens next in the *OnTimer* function is that this information is passed to the *Play3DSoundBuffer* function.

```
play3DSoundBuffer(soundEffect[i].getSoundIndex(),
                  soundEffect[i].getBufferIndex(),
                  true, rSFX, FXData);
```

Note that both the array of flags and the *FXData* object containing all the parameter settings are passed in. *Play3DSoundBuffer* then makes the following call.

```
g_pSound[iS] -> activateSFX(iB, rSFX, FXData);
```

The code for the *activateSFX* method first checks to see if any special effects have been set, and if so, calls the *SetFXEnable* method on the *CSoundFXManager* object that is created for each *CSound* object.

```
HRESULT CSound::activateSFX( int iB, int rSFX[max_specialeffects],
                             CSoundFXData* FXData)
{
    int i;
    int anyFX = false;

    for (i=0; i<max_specialeffects; i++)
    {
        if (rSFX[i] == 1)
        {
            pFXManager[iB] -> SetFXEnable(i);
            anyFX = true;
        }
    }
    if (anyFX)
    {
        pFXManager[iB] -> ActivateFX();
        pFXManager[iB] -> CopyAllData(FXData);
        pFXManager[iB] -> LoadCurrentFXParameters();
    }

    return true;
}
```

Note that the *SetFXEnable* call is made for each special effect that applies; if any apply, then one call is made to the *ActivateFX*, *CopyAllData* and *LoadCurrentFXParameter* methods, which are also methods of the *CSoundFXManager* class.

That's all you need to do. The special effects should now be loaded, ready to edit, and ready to run.

Defining an Environmental Effect

In this section, we'll show how to add a new environmental reverb effect to the pre-defined list. This new effect will be for the environment inside of a submarine.

The Submarine Project

There are very few steps needed to add a new environment. The first is perhaps the most difficult, in that you must come up with a define that matches the *DSFXI3DL2Reverb* structure listed previously. In dsound.h, you will find a list of these defines for the preset environments, as shown in the following example.

```
#define I3DL2_ENVIRONMENT_PRESET_SEWERPIPE -1000,-1000, 0.0f, 2.81f, 0.14f,
        429, 0.014f, 648, 0.021f, 80.0f, 60.0f, 5000.0f
```

Follow these steps to create a submarine environment:

1. Create an I3DL2 definition for the environment. Chapter 5 and 7 will give you a lot of insight on these values, but for now, we will simply copy the sewer pipe environment and make it a submarine one. Add the following lines before the code for the *envValues* structure in RumpusSFX.cpp.

   ```
   // Custom environment definitions.
   #define I3DL2_ENVIRONMENT_SUBMARINE -1000,-1000, 0.0f, 2.81f, 0.14f,
           429, 0.014f, 648, 0.021f, 80.0f, 60.0f, 5000.0f2
   ```

2. At the end of the *envValues* structure, add the define name into the structure.

   ```
   I3DL2_ENVIRONMENT_PRESET_SMALLROOM,
   I3DL2_ENVIRONMENT_PRESET_MEDIUMROOM,
   I3DL2_ENVIRONMENT_PRESET_LARGEROOM,
   I3DL2_ENVIRONMENT_PRESET_MEDIUMHALL,
   I3DL2_ENVIRONMENT_PRESET_LARGEHALL,
   I3DL2_ENVIRONMENT_PRESET_PLATE,
   I3DL2_ENVIRONMENT_SUBMARINE
   ```

3. Change the value for *max_environments* in RumpusSFX.h from 30 to 31.

4. Add the "submarine" name to the end of the *Enames* structure in RumpusEnvironment.cpp.

   ```
   "Small room (music)",
   "Medium room (music)",
   "Large room (music)",
   "Medium hall (music)",
   "Large hall (music)",
   "Plate (music)",
   "Submarine"
   ```

5.   Compile and test the code. If there are any errors, double-check the previous steps.

You can add any number of new environments this way, since there is no limit.

Design Considerations

The classes and program design described previously are tailored towards editing parameters of special effects using a UI, and demonstrating each one of the special effects.

DirectSound does not limit the number of special effects that can be applied to a sound buffer. For example, it is typical for a professional audio-editing system to have three or even five parametric equalizers. There may also be situations when you might want multiple chorus, echo or compressor effects. Any number of these effects can be applied to a DirectSound buffer by filling out a *DSEFFECTDESC* structure, and then making calls to *SetFX* and *GetObjectInPath*.

The same is true for environmental effects – more than one environmental reverb effect can be applied to one sound buffer, although clearly there are diminishing returns in applying more and more effects to a single sound.

We are not crazy about the implementation of I3DL2 in DirectSound. As only the wet reverb sound is the output, you might need to add a second buffer playing the dry sound. Apart from the performance issue of having two buffers, the DirectSound SDK does not provide any means of synchronizing buffers, so you cannot be sure that tiny reverb delays are going to be distinguishable (not to mention unwanted phase effects). In fact, you cannot even be sure that the two buffers will have the same latency each time that the application is run. See Chapter 7 for the recommended technique for applying environmental effects.

Summary

Much of the coding in this chapter described how to add special effects to the Rumpus tool, and how to develop a user interface to manipulate the parameters of special effects. Environmental Reverb is treated slightly differently than the other effects, and although the Rumpus tool does not allow you to define your own environmental reverb effect, it does provide thirty preset environments. We also demonstrated how to add your own environment by adapting a preset environment, and then adding just a few lines of code to the project.

This concludes the hard-core coding for the moment. In order to be able to define your own environments, or meaningfully adjust the parameters of the other eight special effects, you need to understand the audio background for these parameters. The next chapter delves deeply into this topic.

5

Understanding Audio Special Effects

In Chapter 4, you learned how to programmatically create audio special effects by using DirectSound. This chapter provides more information about when to use the various audio effects, what the individual settings mean, and how to tweak the settings to create various effects that you might want to add to sounds. This chapter won't introduce any new code; you'll simply use the Rumpus sample to learn about creating the audio effects that you want.

This chapter also provides some basic information about the nature of sound in order to aid the discussion of the various audio special effects.

Why Use Audio Effects?

There was a time when the soundtracks that accompanied computer games consisted of a cacophony of beeps and monophonic tones. Around the same time, the types of media available to consumers, such as videotapes for viewing movies or compact cassettes for music listening, provided varying levels of quality. Consumers willing to spend large sums of money could enjoy video and music that delivered relatively high fidelity, but this was no guarantee that the content originators would make the investment in creating source material that delivered a great experience. After all, if most viewers or listeners didn't have the equipment to reproduce a presentation with stunning realism, why spend the time and money to implement the required technologies during the production phase?

Things have changed drastically since those days. Compact disc (CD) audio has become the standard for music playback, delivering noise-free, high-fidelity playback for everyone. Digital video disc (DVD) technology has brought the same kind of audio and video quality into homes at a price point that most can afford. Multichannel surround-sound systems are becoming more common in homes, providing consumers with an experience to rival the best movie theater presentations, and Hollywood is providing the soundtrack content to deliver an immersive audio experience.

The audio technology available for personal computers has advanced in the same way. Modern sound cards are a far cry from the tone generators of the past; they can create the same high-fidelity experience that consumers have come to expect from Hollywood motion pictures. Manufacturers who used to create speaker systems solely for the audiophile market now sell multichannel, surround-sound speaker systems designed exclusively for personal computers. In fact, many consumers use personal computers as DVD playback systems. Game developers can now expect that players have the equipment they need to faithfully reproduce a soundtrack. Indeed, a game that fails to deliver a convincing audio experience may disappoint today's savvy player.

The difference between a soundtrack that pulls the player into the virtual world of the computer game and a soundtrack that sounds flat and unconvincing can be the intelligent use (or lack) of audio special effects. Audio special effects can enhance sound in many ways, including the following:

- Make a sound recorded in one type of space sound like it is occurring in a completely different environment.

- Make several sounds recorded separately seem like they are occurring in the same environment simultaneously.

- Create an environment that does not exist in the real world.

- Create a sound that does not occur naturally.

- Enhance musical performances.

- Compensate for inconsistencies between various soundtrack elements.

The remainder of this chapter explores the audio effects available to you when using DirectSound.

Types of Audio Effects

In general, audio effects fit into three categories, or *domains*:

- Time
- Frequency
- Amplitude

Time Domain Effects

Time-domain effects simulate the reflections that occur when sound waves strike surfaces in the physical world. If you have ever shouted into a canyon and heard your own voice echo back to you some seconds later, you have experienced a very obvious, time-domain effect. However, many of the reflections that you hear from day to day are not as obvious or discrete as the canyon echo. When you have a conversation with a colleague in an office, many reflections occur as your voices careen off the various surfaces in the room. Because the distances between these surfaces (the walls, the desk, the floor) tend to be relatively short, you don't perceive the reflected sounds as echoes. Nevertheless, these reflections are short, attenuated echoes that combine to color your perception of your colleague's voice, and to provide your brain with subtle cues about the size and composition of the space around you.

Now, imagine having the same conversation in a school gymnasium. In this space, some of the surfaces are fairly close to you, such as the floor. Others, like the walls, are farther away (although not nearly as far as the opposite wall of a canyon). As you speak, the sound waves produced by your voice create short echoes that you hear almost immediately. The sound waves also create a large number of longer echoes that occur over different periods of time. The paths followed by these sound waves occur rather randomly as the sound reflects first off a nearby wall, then the ceiling, then off another wall, and finally, off the floor before reaching your ear. As some of these multiple reflective paths cause sound waves to reach your listening position at various intervals, you experience the time domain effect called reverberation, or *reverb*. If you closed your eyes, you certainly could guess that you were no longer standing in an office, and you could probably estimate the size and composition of the space.

You can use digital algorithms to recreate real-world, time domain effects, like those that occur in canyons, offices, and gymnasiums. You can also use digital technology to create effects that don't occur naturally.

DirectSound provides the following time-domain audio-effect algorithms to create special effects:

- Echo
- Reverb
- Chorus
- Flanger

Frequency Domain Effects

Sound waves occur in a periodic manner. The number of times that one cycle of a wave repeats during a given time interval is called the frequency of the wave. For sound waves, frequency is measured in cycles per second, or *hertz* (Hz).

Sound frequency is analogous to pitch; the higher the frequency, the higher the perceived pitch. The generally accepted range for audible frequencies is from 20 Hz to 20,000 Hz (20 kHz).

Complex sound waveforms, like the human voice or a piano note, are actually composed of a *fundamental* sine wave and a number of additional sine waves, called *harmonics*. The fundamental and the harmonics each occur at different frequencies, with the harmonics occurring at successively higher multiples of the fundamental frequency. When you hear a note played on a piano, the pitch that you perceive for the note is the pitch of the fundamental frequency. It is the combination of the fundamental and the harmonics that give the piano its unique character, or *timbre*.

Figure 5.1 shows an example of output from a *spectrum analyzer,* which shows the amplitude of a signal at various frequencies. In the figure, you can see the amplitude of the fundamental tone, followed by the amplitudes of six harmonic tones.

Spectrum Analyzers

Spectrum analyzers for audio come in a variety of forms. Analog spectrum analyzers use a series of electronic filters to isolate the various frequency bands to be measured. Digital spectrum analyzers use a digital algorithm called a fast Fourier transform, or *FFT*. FFT algorithms take advantage of Fourier's Theorem (after Baron Jean Baptiste Joseph Fourier). Simply put, Fourier's Theorem states that a complex waveform can be represented by a series of sine and cosine waves. FFT algorithms recursively devolve a complex waveform into its component waves, and then output the amplitude for each frequency.

Spectrum analyzers are available as hardware devices, software programs, and as combination hardware/software packages. Some audio-editing software includes spectrum analysis as a feature.

Windows Media Player uses an FFT algorithm to provide amplitude and frequency data for visualization code. You can see two different views of spectrum analysis by watching the visualizations named Bars and Scope that come with Windows Media Player 9 Series. You can inspect the code for these two visualizations by creating a sample visualization project using the Windows Media Player plug-in wizard, which is a feature of the Windows Media Player 9 Series SDK.

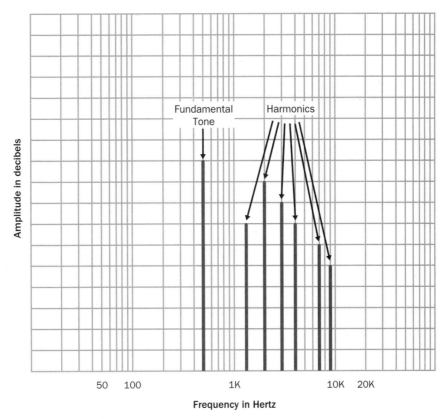

Figure 5.1   Spectrum analysis showing a fundamental tone and its harmonics.

Frequency domain effects change the relationship between the various components of a complex waveform by changing the amplitude within a given frequency range. This process is commonly called *equalization*, and the devices (real or virtual) that create this effect are called equalizers. The most common equalizers are the bass and treble controls that can be found on most home stereo equipment. DirectSound provides one frequency domain effect, ParamEq, to enable you to apply equalization to your sound.

Amplitude Domain Effects

Amplitude domain effects process sound volume. The unit of measurement for sound volume is the *decibel* (dB). The decibel represents the logarithm of a ratio, usually a power ratio or a voltage ratio. By itself, the decibel has little meaning; it is meaningful only when referenced to some standard level. Therefore, it is not useful to say, "The volume of the sound is 85 dB," unless it is understood to mean that the sound is 85 dB louder than the threshold of hearing. It is useful, and common, to use positive values to refer to volume increases above some reference level, and to use negative values to refer to volume decreases below the reference. Therefore, it is useful to say, "The threshold level is set at -50 dB," if, for instance, it is understood to mean that the threshold is 50 dB below some predetermined level, like *digital full scale*.

The range of possible volumes that can be represented by a given system, analog or digital, is called the *dynamic range*. For digital systems, each doubling of the level yields a 6 dB increase in volume. Conversely, each halving of the level yields a 6 dB decrease in volume. Given that each binary digit corresponds to a doubling of available values, a 16-bit representation of audio can effectively represent a 96 dB dynamic range (16 x 6 = 96). A particular sound or soundtrack can have its own dynamic range as well, which clearly must be less than or equal to the available dynamic range of the system. Figure 5.2 shows the relationship between the dynamic ranges of human hearing and 16-bit digital audio.

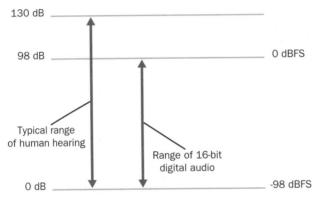

Figure 5.2 Dynamic range of human hearing compared to 16-bit digital audio.

Amplitude domain effects give you the means to manipulate the dynamic range of your audio content.

DirectSound provides the following amplitude domain effects:

- Gargle
- Distortion
- Compressor

Parameters of Audio Effects

Each audio effect has a set of parameters that you can change to alter the way the effect processes sound. The Rumpus 3D SFX sample maps each of these parameters to a control in the Change Special Effect Settings window to enable you to easily adjust the value so you can hear the result during playback. The following sections discuss the parameters for each effect, and provide some relevant background information.

Time Domain Effects

The following sections describe the time domain effects and their parameters:

- Echo

- Reverb

- Chorus

- Flanger

Echo Effect

It makes sense to begin the discussion of time domain effects with the echo effect because it is the most basic of the time domain effects. In its simplest form, the echo effect is like shouting into a canyon: the original sound occurs and, at some time in the future, it repeats (see Plate 3). When it repeats, the echo is perceived as being a completely separate instance of the sound.

Of course, this effect isn't unique to canyons. An empty soccer stadium or even an empty city street might give this effect. A large reflective surface must be far enough away from the source so that the sound takes a perceptible amount of time to travel to the surface and then reflect directly back to the listener.

The echo effect exposes the following parameters:

- Left delay and right delay

- Wet/dry mix

- Feedback

- Pan delay

Left Delay and Right Delay Parameters

The term *delay* refers to the time elapsed between when the original sound occurs and when the effect occurs. Delay is measured in milliseconds (ms). Sound travels through air at a rate of 1130 feet per second (at sea level when the temperature is 59 degrees Fahrenheit). This means that you can assume a delay of about 1 ms per foot of sound propagation. For example, to simulate an echo from a stadium wall 250 feet away, you could use a delay time of 565 ms (282.5 ms to the wall plus 282.5 ms from the wall).

The DirectSound echo effect is actually a stereo effect — you can adjust the delay value separately for the left and right audio channels. This can be particularly useful to create a more realistic sense of space by using a slightly different delay time for each channel, which more closely approximates the way an echo would arrive at the listening position in the physical world.

Wet/Dry Mix Parameter

When discussing audio effects, the term *dry* always refers to the original signal, and the term *wet* always refers to the processed signal. For the echo effect, the wet/dry mix parameter enables you to adjust the balance between the volume of the original signal and the volume of the echo. This is useful because in the physical world, echoes always occur at a decreased volume relative to the original sound, the natural result of the sound wave traveling some distance to and from the reflective surface. The wave loses energy as it travels through air, and when the sound reflects off a surface, some energy is actually absorbed by the surface. How much energy is lost in this process varies by a number of factors, not the least of which is the material of which the reflective surface is made.

The wet/dry mix (*fWetDryMix*) parameter actually represents the percentage of processed signal in the final output. For example, a value of 30 means that 30 percent of the output signal is echo and 70 percent of the output signal is the original input signal. Figure 5.3 shows how signals are mixed by the DirectSound when you specify a value for the wet/dry mix parameter.

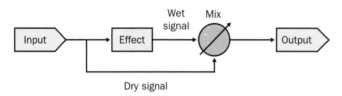

Figure 5.3   Block diagram of wet/dry mix functionality.

Feedback Parameter

When you see the term *feedback*, you might be inclined to think of the annoying squeal that happens when a performer points a microphone toward a speaker. Happily, the feedback parameter creates no such effect. Rather, this parameter mixes some of the processed signal back into the input buffer for the effect. The result is one of echoes creating echoes in a trailing, repetitive manner. Used carefully, feedback can make the canyon effect even more realistic. Lots of feedback can even make for an eerie, outer space-like effect.

The feedback (*fFeedback*) parameter represents the percentage of processed signal mixed back into the input. Figure 5.4 show how DirectSound feeds the output signal back into the input when you specify a value for the feedback parameter.

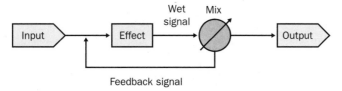

Figure 5.4 Block diagram of feedback functionality.

Pan Delay Parameter

The pan delay (*lPanDelay*) parameter enables you to specify whether the left delay and right delay values alternate, or swap, with each successive echo. If you create an effect with vastly different values for left delay and right delay, the pan delay effect can create a sense of motion as the echoes seem to move from speaker to speaker.

Reverb Effect

Reverb is a commonly used effect because enclosed spaces are always reverberant to some degree. This means that reverb is something people are accustomed to hearing as a natural occurrence, and when it is missing, sounds can seem quite unnatural. In the music industry, reverb is used extensively to enhance the sounds of vocalists and musical instruments because, used judiciously, it can add a sense of spaciousness and even help to gloss over flaws in the performance.

The reverb effect sounds more like a gymnasium or concert hall than like a canyon. The echoes that create this effect are not perceived as discrete events; they blend together to create an effect that builds quickly and then slowly fades away. It is the way that this effect waxes and wanes that gives each space its unique characteristics. The parameters enable you to adjust this behavior somewhat to create the space you desire.

There are two ways to create the reverb effect using DirectSound:

- Waves reverb (*DSFXWavesReverb*)
- Environmental reverb (*DSFXI3DL2Reverb*)

Waves Reverb

The Rumpus 3D SFX sample uses this type of reverb effect, which enables you to adjust the following parameters:

- Reverb time
- Reverb mix
- High-frequency reverb time ratio
- Input gain

Reverb Time Parameter

The reverb time (*fReverbTime*) parameter enables you to specify, in milliseconds, the amount of time it takes for the reverberation to fade by 60 dB after the input signal has ceased. This time is often referred to as the *decay* time. You can use this parameter to adjust the apparent size and composition of the space you are creating. Longer reverb times correspond to larger, more reverberant spaces.

Reverb Mix Parameter

Once again, imagine you are standing in a gymnasium. Imagine that you are standing at the foul line on the basketball court, and your friend is standing on the opposite foul line, facing you. Your friend shouts to you. What you hear is a mixture of direct sound, which arrives in a straight path from your friend's mouth to your ears, and reverberant sound, which arrives in a myriad of reflections. In fact, if your friend faces the other way, you hear only reverberant sound.

Now imagine that you and your friend are both standing at center court, having a conversation. What you hear is still a mixture of direct sound and reverberation, but now the vast majority of that sound comes directly from your friend's mouth to your ears.

The reverb mix (*fReverbMix*) parameter enables you to adjust this balance between direct and reflected sound. This can help you to simulate the placement of the listener in the space relative to the source of the sound. The parameter value is specified in decibels below maximum level, which means the value is always zero or some negative number. At zero, the output signal is 100 percent processed, at -96 dB, the output signal is basically dry.

High-Frequency Reverb Time Ratio Parameter

Suppose that instead of standing in a gymnasium, you and your friend are standing in an empty movie theater. The walls are covered with drapes, part of the floor is carpeted, the ceiling is made of acoustical tile, and there are hundreds of upholstered seats. You can still stand a great distance apart, or even very close together, and there is still reverberation happening in this very large room. Yet, the sound of the reverberation is nothing like that in the gymnasium, because the surfaces in the theater are made of very different materials from the surfaces in the gymnasium. The surfaces in the gymnasium are mostly hard, made of concrete, oak, aluminum, and glass, and have a high degree of reflectivity. Because these types of surfaces reflect sound well, they also tend to reflect a wider spectrum of frequencies. Surfaces like drapes and carpeting still permit reflection to occur from the hard surfaces beneath, but the upper range of the frequency spectrum tends to be absorbed.

The high-frequency reverb time ratio (*fHighFreqRTRatio*) parameter enables you to simulate the effects of softer, less reflective surfaces within a space. This value represents a multiplier that scales the rate at which high-frequency energy in the processed signal fades, or decays. A value of 1.0 creates the impression of the hardest surfaces and gives the reverb a bright character. As you use successively smaller values for this parameter, you can hear the character of the reverb change, creating the impression of a space that contains fewer hard surfaces.

Input Gain Parameter

When the original signal and the processed signal for the reverb effect are summed, it is possible for the resulting signal to exceed the available dynamic range. When this happens, the result is audible distortion, called *clipping*. The name clipping comes from the idea that a visual representation of an audio waveform usually looks something like a mountain range, having many peaks and valleys. When the height of one of the peaks exceeds the maximum value that can be represented by the system, whether analog or digital, the top of the waveform looks like it has been cut off, or clipped.

If you experience clipping, you can use the input gain (*flnGain*) parameter to reduce the input level. Reducing the input level before applying the effect creates *headroom* to allow for the additional signal level. Figure 5.5 shows how a sine wave changes shape when clipped.

Original signal

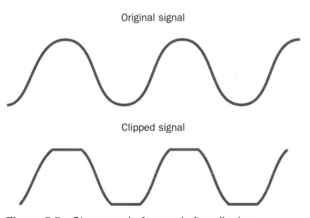

Clipped signal

Figure 5.5   Sine wave before and after clipping.

Environmental Reverb Effects

The environmental reverb effect offers a greater amount of flexibility and control than the waves reverb effect when creating virtual reverberant spaces. The Rumpus 3D SFX sample exposes this as a group of preset reverb environments. In the physical world, reverberation consists of not only the late-arriving echoes that create the more obvious effect, but also much shorter reflection paths that arrive very soon after the source sound. These shorter echoes are called *early reflections*. The environmental reverb effect provides parameters that let you specify how these early reflections behave.

Environmental reverb also provides parameters for adjusting the following properties:

- The diffusion and density of the late echoes, which allows you to imitate more closely the character of real-world rooms.

- Rolloff factor, which represents the rate at which the volume level of reflections decreases, or rolls off, as distance increases.

- The interaction between early reflections and late reverberation, called room effect.

- Longer reverb decay times than with the waves reverb effect.

Note that environmental reverb does not include the direct, unprocessed sound. You must play the direct sound in a separate buffer, and adjust the levels of the direct sound buffer and the reverb buffer individually to create the desired wet/dry mix.

DirectSound provides 24 default environmental-reverb settings. You may find that these meet your needs. The presets simulate a range of spaces, including a living room, a bathroom, a concert hall, and a parking lot. If you want to experiment with creating your own environmental reverb, you should begin by listening closely to the preset effects using the Rumpus 3D SFX sample. Then review the values associated with the presets by inspecting the definitions for the various constants in the dsound.h header file. Choose a preset that sounds close to the effect that you desire, and use the values from that preset as a starting point when creating your own environmental reverb.

For more information about environmental reverb, see Chapter 7.

Chorus Effect

The chorus effect is aptly named, because the goal of the effect is to create copies of the original sound in a way that tricks the listener into believing that he or she is hearing many sounds in unison—a chorus. The effect is achieved by creating a duplicate of the source using a short delay, and then modulating the delay time. By modulating the delay time, an impression can be created that many sounds are being created at the same time. Modulating the delay time also introduces slight variations in pitch, which adds complexity to the effect. The effect is not convincing in every instance, but it can make ensemble sounds seem bigger. It can be a pleasing effect on musical instruments like acoustic guitars, and can be an interesting special effect when used to create unnatural sounds.

The modulation effect is achieved by using a low-frequency oscillator (LFO). The LFO creates a fundamental waveform—in this case, a sine wave or a triangle wave. At a given instant in time, the phase of the LFO is used as a factor to determine the delay time. The frequency and shape of the LFO waveform help to determine the character of the chorus effect.

The DirectSound chorus effect exposes the following parameters:

- Delay
- Depth

- Frequency

- Waveform

- Phase

- Wet/dry mix

- Feedback

Delay Parameter

The delay (*fDelay*) parameter represents the baseline time for the echo—the delay time without LFO modulation. The range of possible values for this parameter falls into the category of doubling echo. This means that the time is too short for humans to perceive the echo as a discrete occurrence (the default delay is 16 ms); rather, it sounds like a doubling of the original signal. Shorter delay times make the doubling effect less obvious.

Depth Parameter

The depth (*fDepth*) parameter enables you to adjust the range of variance from the baseline delay time. You can think of this as a level control for the LFO. The greater the depth value, the greater the range of delay times created by the LFO. Depth is specified as a percentage value, with 100 percent yielding the greatest variation in the delay time.

When creating chorus effects for musical instruments, you should use the depth parameter judiciously. High depth values tend to make the modulation effect of the LFO very obvious, which may be desirable for special effects, but can make a musical instrument effect sound unnatural.

Frequency Parameter

You can adjust the rate at which the LFO modulates the delay time by specifying a value for the frequency (*fFrequency*) parameter. The available frequencies are relatively low, between 0 Hz and 10.0 Hz. Specifying lower values for frequency makes the delay modulation occur more slowly, making the effect of the LFO less obvious; higher values can sound like an obvious vibration.

Waveform Parameter

You can alter the shape of the LFO waveform by specifying a value for the waveform (*lWaveform*) parameter. Changing the shape of the LFO waveform enables you to vary the way that the LFO modulates the delay over time. Figure 5.6 shows what the waveform shapes look like. Applying a sine wave shape to the LFO creates a series of delay times that rise and fall gradually. Applying a triangle wave shape to the LFO creates a series of delay times that rise and fall sharply. Which one you choose is a matter of taste and application. You should experiment with each waveform shape to hear for yourself the effect that it creates.

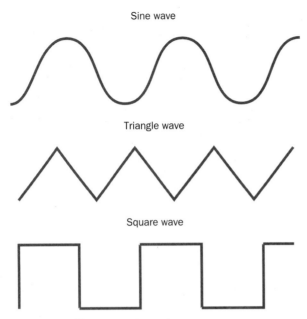

Sine wave

Triangle wave

Square wave

Figure 5.6 Three waveform shapes.

Phase Parameter

The DirectSound chorus effect uses separate LFOs for the left and right channels. The phase (*lPhase*) parameter enables you to adjust how the waveforms for the two LFOs relate to one another in time. When you set this value to zero, the waveforms created by the left and right LFOs match exactly; they are said to be *in phase*. The result is that the effects for both the left and right channels sound exactly alike.

When you choose a value of 180 or -180, the waveforms become mirror images of each other; they are said to be 180 degrees *out of phase*. The result is that the left and right channels sound different because, at any given moment, the delay time created by the LFO in each channel is different. (The notable exception is when the waveforms for both LFOs cross the zero point simultaneously.)

Choosing a value of 90 or -90 creates a similar effect, except that the waveforms are not exactly mirror images of each other; they are said to be 90 degrees out of phase or in *quadrature phase*. Figure 5.7 shows the relationship between two sine waves in quadrature phase.

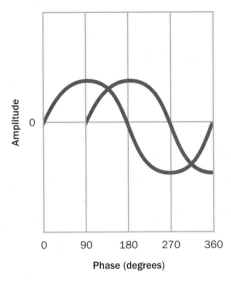

Figure 5.7   Two sine waves in quadrature phase.

The differences created between the left and right channels can create some interesting complexities that give the chorus effect a wider stereo image. This is a parameter that requires some experimentation because the effect is not entirely predictable and varies depending on the source material.

Wet/Dry Mix Parameter

The wet/dry mix (*fWetDryMix*) parameter represents the percentage of processed signal in the final output. Typically, you will want to add some percentage of the processed signal to the original signal to achieve the desired effect, rather than using 100 percent of the processed signal.

Feedback Parameter

As with the echo effect, the feedback (*fFeedback*) parameter represents the percentage of the output signal mixed back into the input buffer. Unlike the echo effect, the chorus effect lets you use a negative value for feedback. When you specify a negative value, the parameter represents the percentage of processed signal subtracted from the input. In either case, the goal is to add to the complexity of the chorus effect by compounding the processing.

Large amounts of positive or negative feedback can drastically change the character of the original sound, because phase interactions introduce frequency-dependent cancellations and reinforcements to the original signal. This can add interesting coloration ranging from hollow to metallic or strangely electronic-sounding. While this type of destructive alteration of the source material might not be appropriate for standard musical fare, it might be just the effect that you want for an alien sound.

Flanger Effect

The flanger effect has a unique sound that is reminiscent of the Doppler effect that you hear when a jet airplane passes overhead. The effect is achieved in an identical fashion to the chorus effect, but the range of delay times used is shorter. When two identical signals that are separated by a very short delay time combine, some audio frequencies cancel each other, while others are reinforced. As the delay time changes, the frequencies at which cancellation and reinforcement occurs also changes. In fact, this is exactly what happens during the Doppler effect. The difference is that the Doppler effect occurs twice (once while the airplane is approaching and again as it moves away), while the flanger effect occurs continuously for as long as the LFO varies the delay time.

The flanger effect has the same parameters as the chorus effect. For details about each parameter, refer to the chorus effect section.

The History of Flanging

Legend has it that the flanging effect was discovered by accident. In the early days of rock-and-roll recording, time domain effects were achieved by using two synchronized, open-reel tape decks. Each machine received the identical input signal, and then the output signals were combined. During a session that used this technique, someone rubbed up against one of the tape reels, which caused the tape to slow down slightly. The resulting effect sounded interesting. With some experimentation, it was discovered that lightly touching one's finger against the tape reel on one machine and then the other consistently produced the desired effect.

The flat side of a tape reel is called a *flange*, which is why the effect is named "flanging" and a device that simulates the effect is called a "flanger."

Frequency Domain Effects

The one frequency domain effect provided by DirectSound is ParamEq. This section describes the ParamEq effect and its parameters.

ParamEq Effect

A *parametric equalizer* is representative of a class of devices, named equalizers, which alter the frequency response of a signal.

Other devices and filter types include:

■ **Graphic equalizer** This device commonly uses a row of vertically oriented slider controls. Each slider controls a filter that can boost or cut the amplitude of a fixed frequency. The name graphic equalizer comes from the notion that the positions of the sliders give a graphical representation of the change to the frequency response that the device creates. In reality, this isn't true because the combination of the bell-shaped filters results in a change far more complex than the slider positions convey. Graphic equalizers typically can adjust between 5 and 31 bands, depending on the configuration.

- **Notch filter**   This filter type creates a sharp attenuation within a very narrow frequency bandwidth. Sometimes this type of filter is used to remove a specific noise from the signal, such as hum or buzz.

- **High-pass filter**   This filter type is an equalizer that attenuates all frequencies below a specified cutoff frequency, leaving only the higher-frequency content in the signal.

- **Low-pass filter**   This filter type is an equalizer that attenuates all frequencies above a specified cutoff frequency, leaving only the lower-frequency content in the signal.

- **Band-pass filter**   This filter type is an equalizer that attenuates all frequencies, above and below specified cutoff frequencies, leaving only mid-range frequencies in the signal. You can think of this type of filter as a combination of a high-pass filter with a low-pass filter.

The parametric equalizer is the most flexible type of equalizer. To a great extent, it can do the job of any of the other types of equalizers and filters, simply by altering its settings. This ability to "dial in" the required settings, or *parameters,* gives the parametric equalizer its name.

The ParamEq effect can be used as a single effect or as a chain of effects. In the world of electronics, parametric equalizers typically have between two and five bands. This enables you to dedicate one equalizer to a specific part of the audio spectrum, while using another equalizer for another part. For example, you might want to boost some low frequencies to accentuate the bass while attenuating part of the high-frequency range to eliminate noise such as hiss.

It is not a good idea to depend on the ParamEq effect as a way to compensate for problems with your audio source material. Using this effect to fix problems would be far too time-consuming, especially since it is much easier to simply load the sound into commercially available audio-editing software to make changes. The ParamEq effect is a good way for you to provide the user with control over the sound.

The ParamEq effect exposes the following parameters:

- Bandwidth

- Center

- Gain

Bandwidth Parameter

When the ParamEq effect changes the frequency response of the signal, it does so by simultaneously boosting or attenuating a range of frequencies. However, all frequencies are not changed by the same amount. Rather, the frequency response is altered along a bell-shaped curve, with the greatest amount of change occurring at the peak of the curve. This behavior closely matches the way the filter circuits affect the audio signal in an electronic parametric equalizer. Because of the shape of the filter response, this type of equalization is called *peaking equalization*.

The bandwidth (*fBandwidth*) parameter enables you to adjust the width of the bell-shaped curve. Larger values create a wider curve. The value is given in *semitones*; in music, 12 semitones equal one *octave*. Each semitone corresponds to a unique note name, such as C, G-sharp, E-flat, and so on.

Figure 5.8 shows a graphical representation of peaking equalization. Notice that for each of the three equalization curves shown, the center frequency remains constant, while the range of frequencies affected changes as the bandwidth value changes.

To understand how musical semitones relate to equalization, you first need to know that audible frequencies behave logarithmically with regard to pitch. Each doubling of the frequency results in pitch unison, or one octave. For instance, on a piano keyboard, the A note below middle C has a fundamental frequency of 440 Hz. The A note above middle C has a higher pitch, but sounds like the same note. It has a fundamental frequency of 880 Hz.

It is common to express equalization in terms of fractions of an octave (one-third octave, one-half octave, and so forth). For instance, if you wanted to present the user with a software user interface that imitates a one-third-octave equalizer device, you would create 31 slider controls. Each slider would control a ParamEq effect with a bandwidth of 4 semitones (12 semitones divided by 3).

Center Parameter

The center (*fCenter*) parameter enables you to specify the frequency, in hertz, at which maximum boost or attenuation occurs. Put another way, this is the frequency at which the peak occurs. The range of frequencies available for your use depends on the content in the DirectSound buffer. The maximum frequency permitted cannot exceed one-third the sampling rate. This prevents the ParamEq effect from attempting to process frequencies outside the available range in the content.

For your one-third octave equalizer, each slider control would represent a ParamEq effect with a different value for *fCenter*. In electronic devices, these are standard frequency values designated by the International Organization for Standardization (ISO).

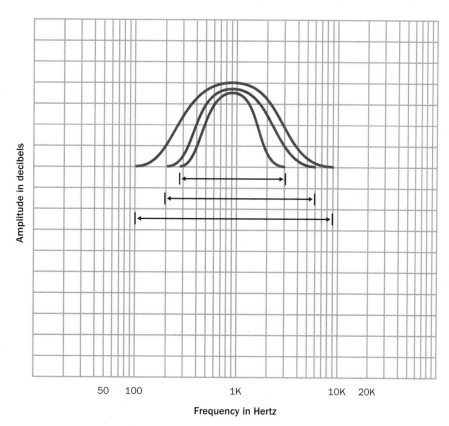

Figure 5.8   Peaking equalization showing three different bandwidths at the same center frequency.

Gain Parameter

The gain (*fGain*) parameter enables you to specify, in decibels, the amount of boost or attenuation at the center frequency, or *peak*. The available range is from 15 decibels of boost (+15 dB) to 15 decibels of attenuation (-15 dB). Specifying a value of zero means that the equalizer has no effect.

For your one-third octave equalizer, each slider control would vary the *fGain* value of the ParamEq effect. If the user moves the slider all the way up, *fGain* equals 15. When the user moves the slider all the way down, *fGain* equals -15. When the user moves the slider to the center, *fGain* equals zero.

Amplitude Domain Effects

The following sections describe the following amplitude domain effects and their parameters:

■ Gargle

■ Distortion

■ Compressor

Gargle Effect

The simplest amplitude domain effect is the gargle effect. As you can imagine, this effect causes the audio material to sound like gargling, by using an LFO to modulate the amplitude of the sound.

The Gargle effect exposes the following parameters:

■ Rate

■ Waveform

Rate Parameter

The rate (*dwRateHz*) parameter enables you to specify the frequency of the LFO that creates the effect. Higher values for *dwRateHz* yield faster-sounding gargle effects.

Waveform Parameter

The waveform (*dwWaveShape*) parameter enables you to specify the type of waveform created by the LFO. Applying a triangle wave shape to the LFO creates a gargle effect with a sharp character. Applying a square wave shape to the LFO creates a gargle effect with an even more abrupt modulation. Which one you choose is a matter of taste and application. You should experiment with each waveform shape to hear for yourself the effect that it creates.

Distortion Effect

Distortion (specifically, harmonic distortion) is a change in the sound that happens when the amplitude of the signal exceeds the available range. The result is that additional harmonic artifacts are created as the shape of the waveform is changed, or "clipped". You have probably heard distortion before; it is that fuzzy sound that happens when, for instance, a speaker is damaged.

Usually, distortion is something that audio engineers seek to avoid because it changes the sound in unwanted ways. However, sometimes distortion is a desirable effect, most frequently used in electric guitar amplifiers. The signal that an electric guitar creates tends to have a clean, pure sound. Deliberately adding some distortion to the signal can make the sound more interesting. The DirectSound distortion effect is designed to create this kind of sound.

Of course, you don't have to use the distortion effect strictly to enhance musical instruments. You might use it to create a special effect for your game. For example, this effect can create the impression of a noisy radio transmission.

The distortion effect exposes the following parameters:

- Edge

- Post-EQ center frequency

- Post-EQ bandwidth

- Pre-lowpass cutoff

- Gain

Edge Parameter

The edge (*fEdge*) parameter enables you to specify the intensity of distortion in the output signal. (Distortion is often characterized as having an "edgy" sound.) Values close to 100 percent tend to make the output signal sound unintelligible, so usually you will want to use values less than 50 percent.

Post-EQ Center Frequency Parameter

Although the distortion effect is classified as an amplitude domain effect, the extra harmonics that make the sound distorted are created in the frequency domain. This means that frequency-domain processing like equalization can have a profound impact on the sound of the distortion effect. The DirectSound distortion effect provides a single band of peaking equalization that you can use to accentuate the effect. The equalization provides a fixed amount of boost, but you can adjust the center frequency and the bandwidth.

The post-EQ center frequency (*fPostEQCenterFrequency*) parameter enables you to specify the peak frequency for the equalizer.

Post-EQ Bandwidth Parameter

The post-EQ bandwidth (*fPostEQBandwidth*) parameter lets you adjust the range of frequencies (relative to the center frequency) that are boosted. You specify this range in hertz. Wider-range values result in more harmonics being generated, thereby resulting in denser-sounding distortion.

Pre-lowpass Cutoff Parameter

Because the harmonics that make up the audible distortion signal are higher multiples of fundamental frequencies, it is useful to filter out high-frequency content from the original signal before creating distortion. To enable this, the distortion effect provides the pre-lowpass cutoff (*fPreLowpassCutoff*) parameter. This value represents the frequency above which all frequencies are attenuated.

Gain Parameter

The gain (*fGain*) parameter lets you adjust the volume of the output of the effect. The default value is -18 dB. Specifying values higher than the default (closer to 0 dB) provides an increase in volume; lower values provide a decrease in volume.

Compressor Effect

Dynamic compression is the process of reducing the dynamic range of a signal in response to changes in signal level. In the analog world, this is accomplished by using an amplifier with an output gain that varies in response to the input level. When the amplifier's input exceeds a predetermined level, called the *threshold*, the circuitry reduces the output gain by a predetermined amount. The amount of gain is usually expressed as a ratio. For example, a 3-to-1 ratio means that for every 3 dB by which the input signal exceeds the threshold, only 1 dB of gain occurs at the output.

Dynamic compression can be used for several purposes. First, it is useful to help prevent an input signal from exceeding the dynamic range of the medium. For instance, if you were to record a source with a 110 dB dynamic range as a 16-bit digital signal, you would need to compress the dynamic range by about 14 dB because 16-bit digital audio has a 96 dB dynamic range. To be absolutely sure that the signal never exceeds the dynamic range, you can use a very high compression ratio with a threshold close to the limit of the medium. This type of compression is called *limiting*.

Dynamic compression is also used as an effect. A little bit of compression can help make a musical performance sound better. For instance, if a particular vocalist is inconsistent with his or her microphone usage, a compressor can even out the dynamics. If the vocalist is performing with a loud band, the compression can ensure that each syllable of each word can be heard and understood. Keep this idea in mind when mixing sounds for your game soundtrack, because the compressor effect might be able to fix problems in the source sounds.

The compressor effect exposes the following parameters:

- Threshold

- Ratio

- Pre-delay

- Attack

- Release

- Gain

Threshold Parameter

You can set the threshold for the compressor effect by specifying a value for the threshold (*fThreshold*) parameter. This parameter lets you set the volume level at which the compression effect engages. This parameter has a maximum value of zero, which represents digital full scale. Other values are specified in decibels below full scale.

The dotted line in Figure 5.9 represents the threshold. Notice how the output level with compression is consistently lower above the threshold than with no compression.

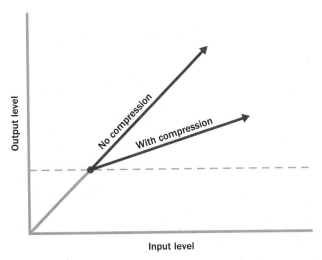

Figure 5.9   Signal amplitude before and after compression.

The value that you choose for this parameter depends on the dynamics of the source material and the effect you are trying to achieve. If you set the threshold higher than the maximum signal level, no compression will occur. If you set it too low, you risk limiting the dynamics of the source material, which can make the audio turn "dark" or muddy sounding.

Ratio Parameter

The ratio (*fRatio*) parameter lets you specify how much gain reduction occurs when the threshold level is exceeded. For instance, a value of 3 represents a 3-to-1 compression ratio.

Again, the value you choose for this parameter depends on the content. High values (greater than 10) make the effect behave like a hard limiter. This can be useful if you want to ensure that the volume of the material doesn't ever exceed some particular level. The range between 2 and 10 represents the most commonly used settings. In this range, the effect can be more subtle, less noticeable, while still helping to smooth out the dynamics of the content.

Pre-delay Parameter

Some sounds start with a sharp part, called the *attack*, followed by a lower-level sustained portion, which is then followed by a decaying portion, called the *release*. For example, think of a piano note. When you press a piano key, a hammer inside the piano momentarily strikes a taut wire. The hammer strike creates the attack portion of the sound. Once the hammer moves away from the wire, the note sustains and decays for as long as the piano key is depressed.

Now, suppose you want to apply some compression to a piano soundtrack. You want to help even out the dynamics of the performance to keep it audible, but you also need to maintain the relationship between the hammer strikes and the sustaining notes. In other words, you don't want the compressor effect to engage every time that a hammer strikes a wire, because this would change the very nature of how the piano sounds.

You can prevent the compressor effect from functioning too soon by specifying a value for the pre-delay (*fPredelay*) parameter. Pre-delay introduces a very short hesitation before the compressor effect engages after the compression threshold is exceeded. This is an ideal way to prevent compression of the attack portion of a sound.

Attack Parameter

The attack (*fAttack*) parameter enables you to specify how long it takes for compression to reach the specified ratio. For instance, suppose you set a ratio of 10 to 1. If the compressor effect reduces the volume by that ratio instantly each time the level exceeds the threshold, the result can be a "pumping" effect when the volume changes introduced by compression become obvious. Specifying a longer attack time causes the effect to ease in more gradually. Conversely, if you want the compression to happen right away, specify a very short time for the attack parameter.

Release Parameter

Like the attack parameter, the release (*fRelease*) parameter affects the way the compressor effect behaves over time. When the level drops below the threshold, the compression takes some amount of time to disengage, or release. How suddenly this happens depends on the time that you specify for the release parameter.

Gain Parameter

The gain (*fGain*) parameter allows you to change the output level of the effect. Typically, this is most useful for "make-up gain." Often, the end result of applying the compressor effect is that the average volume of the program material lowers. By adding some gain after the compression, you can restore the apparent volume level of the material after reducing the overall dynamic range. This helps to make the softer portions sound louder.

Summary

This chapter discussed the various audio special effects available for your use, and described each parameter. Use this information by experimenting with the various effects. Spend some time trying out different types of effects with different types of sounds. Use the Rumpus sample to adjust the various parameters and listen to the results. With a little practice, you can become an expert at crafting your own sound effects for your game programming.

6

Streaming Sounds into Circular Buffers

Streaming is a good word to describe the flow of audio data from a hard disk into a buffer at just the right rate to keep it playing smoothly. The main advantage of streaming a sound from a hard disk (or CD) is that the buffer used to play the sound can be much shorter than the length of the sound file. As always, there are issues. The main issue that stands out is the obvious additional complexity imposed by having two methods of playing a file, streaming and non-streaming.

In addition, there are several ways of handling streaming; unfortunately, one of the most publicized ways of handling streaming uses Windows notifications, which is not the model recommended by developers at Microsoft. However, the only sample that ships with the DirectSound SDK uses notifications, and the *CStreamingSound* class that is an integral part of the utility code (dsutil.cpp) only supports the notifications model.

The recommended model of handling streaming is to use a polling system, tracking the play cursor and topping up a circular buffer as the sound is being played. The reasons why this model is preferred are numerous although not obvious, and center around the reported unreliability of notifications when used with certain types of audio hardware. In other words, you may well (as we did) get your notification sample to work well on your new development system, but somewhere out there in the world some of your customers will get a glitch-ridden experience. Other advantages of the polling system include that you can create hardware buffers and apply special effects, whereas the notification-based system should be created in software to avoid glitching, which noticeably affects performance if special effects are applied.

This chapter describes two samples; the Circular Streams sample, which uses the recommended model of polling, and, for the sake of comparison, the Three Streams sample, which uses notifications. Both have identical UIs so you can compare and test their performance. Start by loading and running the Circular Streams sample, located in the AVBook\bin directory.

The Circular Streams Sample

After running Circular Streams.exe, you'll notice that there are slots for three sounds, each with its own Play and Stop buttons (see Figure 6.1). To make the first test easy, we have added the Load Presets button, which will select three appropriate files (musical tracks in this case) and load them in with a single click. Click Play for one of the sounds, and then for the other two. As you randomly click Play and Stop, you should hear the music tracks smoothly start and stop without interfering with each other and without any sound glitches.

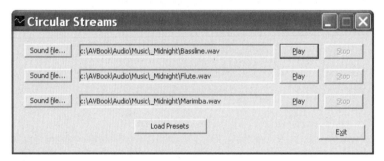

Figure 6.1   Circular Streams dialog box.

Use the Sound File button to load in alternative sounds, and test the sample again. Again, note the smooth starting, stopping, and looping of tracks.

Behind the scenes, what is happening is that each of the three slots in the UI matches a one-second buffer. Each time that you press Play, the first second of a track is loaded and begins playing. This buffer is topped up from the file on the hard disk around every tenth of a second. If all three streams are playing, then this topping up is going on for all three of them. This was the main design goal of this sample, to demonstrate multiple streams working together, and not tripping each other up.

If you have a small number of sounds in your project, you will want to have them in static (non-streaming) buffers, to maximize performance and simplify the coding. However, there are several situations where you might want to consider using streaming buffers. These include music and speech, because they are probably long files and perhaps are sounds where you do not want to apply special effects or 3-D processing to the audio data. However, you may also want to use streaming when you have a very large number of sound effects, which is typical of many games, and want to maximize the performance (that is, minimize latency and glitching) of all of them.

To summarize, we suggest the use of streaming buffers in the following specific cases:

- If you have music tracks, then set up a single streaming buffer for each to play the music smoothly regardless of the length of the files.

- If you want to be more adventurous, try the idea of separating your music tracks into bass, percussion, sax, drums and so on, and then play one or more of these tracks together to create a certain atmosphere. At certain times during your game, you can turn on or off one or more of the tracks that make up the theme music of your game to add a different feel to the music. This requires multiple software buffers similar to the Circular Streams sample. However, note that it is not possible to synchronize the playing of any buffers exactly using DirectSound, so compose your music accordingly.

- For human (or even non-human) dialog that is lengthy (more than a few seconds long), consider setting up one stream per speaker.

- Use streaming when your application requires a very large number of sounds, and you want most or all of them to be created using hardware buffers. You should be careful not to create very small streaming buffers, because there are a number of impenetrable issues that lead to glitching if the buffers are too small (the recommended minimum is 100ms for a streaming buffer).

So with these specific applications in mind, we'll crack open the code.

The Circular Streams Project

Before we can make any progress in writing a polling-based streaming sample, we need to define a new class supporting this technique, similar to *CStreamingSound*, which we have called *CCircularSound*. If you open the extended_dsutil.h file, you will see the declaration of this class.

```
class CCircularSound : public CSound
{
protected:
    long m_lWritePosition;
    long circularDistance(long lValue);
public:
    CCircularSound( LPDIRECTSOUNDBUFFER pDSBuffer, DWORD dwDSBufferSize,
                    CWaveFile* pWaveFile );
    ~CCircularSound();
    HRESULT TopUpBuffer(DWORD index);
    HRESULT Reset();
};
```

The declaration is noticeably simpler than the *CStreamingSound* class, with just a single protected variable, *lWritePosition*, which acts as a cursor pointing to the byte at which the next write should start. The creation function does nothing more than set *lWritePosition* to 0, and call the creation function for the *CSound* class.

```
CCircularSound::CCircularSound( LPDIRECTSOUNDBUFFER pDSBuffer,
                        DWORD dwDSBufferSize, CWaveFile* pWaveFile )
                : CSound( &pDSBuffer, dwDSBufferSize, 1, pWaveFile, 0 )
{
    m_lWritePosition = 0;
}
```

The short protected method, *circularDistance*, simply ensures that the given value lies within the boundaries of the buffer. For example, the call *circularDistance(dwBufferSize)* will return the value 0, as the boundaries of the buffer are from 0 to *dwBufferSize* − 1.

```
long CCircularSound::circularDistance(long lValue)
{
    if (lValue < 0)
        return lValue + m_dwDSBufferSize;
    if (lValue >= (long) m_dwDSBufferSize)
        return lValue - m_dwDSBufferSize;
    return lValue;
}
```

All the serious processing in the class is encapsulated in one method, *TopUpBuffer*, which does all the polling and topping up of a sound buffer.

```
HRESULT CCircularSound::TopUpBuffer(DWORD index)
{
    DWORD    dwCurrentPlay;      // Current play cursor.
    DWORD    dwCurrentWrite;     // Current safe write cursor
                                 // (not used in this sample).
    long     lSafeWriteTo;       // Upper safe-writing limit.
    long     lCurrentPlay;       // Signed copy of play cursor.
    long     actualRead;         // Actual number of bytes written.
    BOOL     fEOF;               // End of File flag.

    if( m_apDSBuffer[0] == NULL || m_pWaveFile == NULL )
        return CO_E_NOTINITIALIZED;

    // Retrieve the current play position.
    m_apDSBuffer[0] ->GetCurrentPosition(&dwCurrentPlay,&dwCurrentWrite);

    // Make sure calculations work with negative numbers.
    lCurrentPlay = (long) dwCurrentPlay;

    // Ensure a 32-byte safety margin (some cards
    // mis-report their play position).
    if (circularDistance(lCurrentPlay - m_lWritePosition) > 32)
    {
```

```
        lSafeWriteTo = circularDistance(lCurrentPlay - 32);

        // Do not top up the buffer if less than 10% of the buffer
        // size would be written.
        if (circularDistance(lSafeWriteTo -
                m_lWritePosition) > (long) m_dwDSBufferSize/ 10)
        {
            // Test to see if the block to write is contiguous.
            if (lSafeWriteTo > m_lWritePosition)
            {
                // Top up the buffer.
                actualRead = PartFillBufferWithSound(0, m_lWritePosition,
                                          lSafeWriteTo, &fEOF);

                // Update the write position depending on the number
                // of bytes actually written.
                m_lWritePosition = circularDistance(m_lWritePosition
                               + actualRead);
            } else
            {
                // Wrap around case.
                // First top up the end of the buffer.
                actualRead = PartFillBufferWithSound(0, m_lWritePosition,
                                     (long)m_dwDSBufferSize - 1, &fEOF);

                if (fEOF == false)
                {
                    // Second top up the beginning of the buffer.
                    actualRead = PartFillBufferWithSound(0, 0L, lSafeWriteTo,
                             &fEOF);
                    m_lWritePosition = actualRead;
                } else
                    m_lWritePosition = circularDistance(m_lWritePosition
                                   + actualRead);
            }
            // End of file reached so reset the read pointer into the wave file
            // back to the start.
            if (fEOF)
                m_pWaveFile ->ResetFile();
        }
    }
    return S_OK;
}
```

After the usual checks to see that we have valid parameters, the *TopUpBuffer* method calls the DirectSound SDK method, *GetCurrentPosition*. The *GetCurrentPosition* method takes two DWORDs as parameters, and fills in the current play position and the safe-write position for the buffer. The current play position is what we want, which is the cursor position pointing to where the sound buffer is currently being played from. The next statement in our method simply changes this to a long value, so it is signed as we need to do some calculation that may involve negative numbers. Unfortunately, not all sound cards report the play position very accurately, and some are known to misreport it by up to 32 bytes. Because of this, we subtract 32 bytes from the current play position to get a safe limit for writing. Notice how we use the *circularDistance* method to ensure that the calculation works when the pointers are wrapping around the buffer.

Polling Models

As a matter of interest, we do not use the *dwCurrentWrite* value returned by the *GetCurrentPosition* call. This is a pointer to where it is safe to write to the buffer ahead of the play cursor. This can be used in a different style of polling model called After-Write-Cursor, where the buffer is topped up in advance of the play cursor to a certain number of milliseconds of playing time.

In practice, though, this model tends to have very low latency (which is good) but at the expense of having more glitches. The technique that we are using to top up the buffer is called Before-Play-Cursor, which tends to result in slightly higher latency than After-Write-Cursor, but with fewer glitches. However, because the After-Write-Cursor model is appropriate to use where audio data is being generated on the fly, which is not the case for almost all applications, the Before-Play-Cursor model is usually the appropriate polling model.

It doesn't make sense to top up the buffer when only a trivial amount of data would be written. For this sample, we have simply defined a trivial amount to be less than ten percent of the length of the buffer. The recommended minimum (sometimes referred to as the *wake-up* time) is 10ms.

If our calculations tell us that it is time to top up the buffer, the next thing we do is check whether we have the simple case of filling a contiguous block of memory in the buffer. The more complex case would involve having to fill some data at the top of the buffer, and then wrap around and start filling from the beginning of the buffer.

In the former case, we make one call to the *PartFillBufferWithSound* method, which we have added to the *CSound* class. In the latter case, where a wraparound occurs, we make two calls to the *PartFillBufferWithSound* method, first filling to the top of the buffer, and then filling from the beginning. However, in both of these cases there is one important check to make: we need to know if the end of the wave file has been reached. If the end-of-file condition is true, we have to call *ResetFile* for the wave file, obviously to reset its read pointer back to the beginning of the file. Note that when we increment the *m_lWritePosition* cursor, it is always by the amount of bytes actually written, to take into account the end-of-file situation.

The *TopUpBuffer* method is nice and simple. However, before we can use it, we should examine the *PartFillBufferWithSound* method of the *CSound* class, and also the *CreateCircular* method of the *CSoundManager* class.

```
DWORD CSound::PartFillBufferWithSound(int index, long lFrom, long lTo,
                                      BOOL *fEOF )
{
    HRESULT hr;
    VOID*   pDSLockedBuffer = NULL;   // Pointer to locked buffer memory.
    DWORD   dwDSLockedBufferSize = 0; // Size of the locked DirectSound buffer.
    DWORD   dwWavDataRead        = 0; // Amount of data read from
                                      // the wave file.

    if( m_apDSBuffer[index] == NULL )
        return CO_E_NOTINITIALIZED;

    // Make sure we have focus, and didn't just switch in from
    // an application which had a DirectSound device.
    if( FAILED( hr = RestoreBuffer( m_apDSBuffer[index], NULL ) ) )
        return DXTRACE_ERR( TEXT("RestoreBuffer"), hr );

    // Lock the buffer down.
    if( FAILED( hr = m_apDSBuffer[index]->Lock( 0, m_dwDSBufferSize,
                &pDSLockedBuffer, &dwDSLockedBufferSize, NULL, NULL, 0L ) ) )
        return DXTRACE_ERR( TEXT("Lock"), hr );

    // Read data into the section of the buffer identified by lFrom and lTo.
    if( FAILED( hr = m_pWaveFile->Read( (BYTE*) pDSLockedBuffer + lFrom,
                lTo - lFrom + 1, &dwWavDataRead ) ) )
        return DXTRACE_ERR( TEXT("Read"), hr );

    // Unlock the buffer because we don't need it anymore.
    m_apDSBuffer[index]->
                    Unlock( pDSLockedBuffer, dwDSLockedBufferSize, NULL, 0 );

    // Return true if the end of the file has been reached.
    if (dwWavDataRead == lTo - lFrom + 1)
        *fEOF = false; else
        *fEOF = true;
    return dwWavDataRead;
}
```

The *PartFillBufferWithSound* method takes as parameters the index of the buffer to be written to (always 0 in this sample), two pointers identifying the range of bytes to write to, and a flag to be set if the end of the file has been reached. The process of this method is to lock the buffer, read in the appropriate amount of bytes, and then unlock the buffer.

Note that we do not have to alter the *Read* method of the *CWaveFile* class; it already does what we want (reads in a section of the wave file) without modification.

In order to create an object of the *CCircularSound* class, the following method is added to the *CSoundManager* class.

```
HRESULT CSoundManager::CreateCircular( CCircularSound** ppCircularSound,
                                       LPTSTR strWaveFileName,
                                       DWORD dwCreationFlags,
                                       GUID guid3DAlgorithm,
                                       DWORD dwRequestedSize )
{
    HRESULT hr;

    if( m_pDS == NULL )
        return CO_E_NOTINITIALIZED;
    if( strWaveFileName == NULL || ppCircularSound == NULL )
        return E_INVALIDARG;

    LPDIRECTSOUNDBUFFER pDSBuffer      = NULL;
    CWaveFile*          pWaveFile      = NULL;

    pWaveFile = new CWaveFile();
    if( pWaveFile == NULL )
        return E_OUTOFMEMORY;
    pWaveFile->Open( strWaveFileName, NULL, WAVEFILE_READ );

    // Set up the DirectSound buffer, and note that the flag
    // DSBCAPS_GETCURRENTPOSITION2 is required.
    DSBUFFERDESC dsbd;
    ZeroMemory( &dsbd, sizeof(DSBUFFERDESC) );
    dsbd.dwSize           = sizeof(DSBUFFERDESC);
    dsbd.dwFlags          = dwCreationFlags |
                            DSBCAPS_GETCURRENTPOSITION2;
    dsbd.dwBufferBytes    = dwRequestedSize;
    dsbd.guid3DAlgorithm  = guid3DAlgorithm;
    dsbd.lpwfxFormat      = pWaveFile->m_pwfx;

    if( FAILED( hr = m_pDS->CreateSoundBuffer( &dsbd, &pDSBuffer, NULL ) ) )
    {
        return DXTRACE_ERR( TEXT("CreateSoundBuffer"), hr );
    }

    // Create the sound.
    *ppCircularSound = new CCircularSound( pDSBuffer, dwRequestedSize,
                                           pWaveFile );

    return S_OK;
}
```

The process here is to set up the DirectSound buffer structure, call *CreateSoundBuffer* with the address of the structure as input and a DirectSound buffer pointer as output, and finally call the creation function for the *CCircularSound* class. All nice and straightforward. Notice in particular that we must set the *DSBCAPS_GETCURRENTPOSITION2* creation flag to enable the DirectSound SDK *GetCurrentPosition* method to work. Notice also that this is the only flag we have to set; although volume, frequency, panning, 3-D, and special effect flags could also be set for the buffer, none are required for this sample.

The Circular Streams.cpp File

Having added all the low-level functionality to implement a polling-based streaming class, we can examine the high-level code that takes advantage of it.

The only global variables we need are in the following code.

```
#define     nStreams    3
#define     AllStreams  (streamNumber=0;streamNumber<nStreams;streamNumber++)
#define     NUM_SECONDS 1                    // Size of circular buffers.
HINSTANCE           g_hInst             = NULL;
CSoundManager*      g_pSoundManager     = NULL;
CCircularSound*     g_pCircularSound[nStreams] = { NULL, NULL, NULL };
TCHAR               g_soundDir[MAX_PATH];   // AVBook directory path.
```

Notice how we are using the *AllStreams* macro as a lazy way of stepping through the streams. The *NUM_SECONDS* define provides the size of the circular buffers in seconds (it is only used once, in the *LoadWaveAndCreateBuffer* function).

The *WinMain*, *MainDlgProc*, *OnOpenSoundFile* and *OnInitDialog* functions should by now be very familiar to you, so we will not list them here. The only point of interest that is particular to polling is that we set a Windows timer going, ticking every 50ms, in the *OnInitDialog* function. If you are using buffers much smaller than 1 second, say the recommended minimum of 100ms, the timer should be set to tick every 10ms. Each time the timer ticks, the *OnTimer* function is called.

```
VOID OnTimer( HWND hwndDlg )
{
    int streamNumber;

    for AllStreams
    {
        if (g_pCircularSound[streamNumber] != NULL)
        {
            if (g_pCircularSound[streamNumber] ->IsSoundBufferPlaying(0))
            {
                g_pCircularSound[streamNumber] -> TopUpBuffer(0);
            }
        }
    }
}
```

The *OnTimer* function is certainly simple; for each stream that is actually playing, a call is made to the *TopUpBuffer* method. This is all that's needed. The *OnOpenSoundFile* function calls the *LoadWaveAndCreateBuffer* function, which is the function that creates a *CCircularSound* object.

```
VOID LoadWaveAndCreateBuffer( HWND hDlg, TCHAR* strFileName, int streamNumber )
{
    HRESULT   hr;
    CWaveFile waveFile;
    DWORD     dwCircularSize;

    // Load the wave file.
    if( FAILED( hr = waveFile.Open( strFileName, NULL, WAVEFILE_READ ) ) )
    {
        waveFile.Close();
        SetDlgItemText( hDlg, IDC_FILENAME1 + streamNumber,
                        TEXT("Bad wave file.") );
        return;
    }

    if( waveFile.GetSize() == 0 )
    {
        waveFile.Close();
        SetDlgItemText( hDlg, IDC_FILENAME1 + streamNumber,
                        TEXT("Wave file blank.") );
        return;
    }

    // The wave file is valid, and waveFile.m_pwfx is the wave's format
    // so we are done with the reader.
    waveFile.Close();

    // Determine the dwCircularSize.
    // It should be an integer multiple of nBlockAlign.
    DWORD nBlockAlign = (DWORD)waveFile.m_pwfx->nBlockAlign;
    INT nSamplesPerSec = waveFile.m_pwfx->nSamplesPerSec;
    dwCircularSize = nSamplesPerSec * NUM_SECONDS * nBlockAlign;
    dwCircularSize -= dwCircularSize % nBlockAlign;

    // Create a new sound.
    SAFE_DELETE( g_pCircularSound[streamNumber] );

    // Set up the DirectSound buffer.
    if( FAILED( hr = g_pSoundManager->
                CreateCircular( &g_pCircularSound[streamNumber],
                strFileName, 0, GUID_NULL, dwCircularSize )))
```

```
    {
        SetDlgItemText( hDlg, IDC_FILENAME1 + streamNumber,
                        TEXT("Could not support the file's audio format.") );
        return;
    }

    // Update the UI controls to show the sound as the file is loaded.
    EnablePlayUI( hDlg, TRUE, streamNumber );
    SetDlgItemText( hDlg, IDC_FILENAME1 + streamNumber, strFileName );
}
```

After performing a few checks on the validity of the wave file, notice the calculation of the buffer size using the sampling rate, block alignment (1 or 2 bytes), and the *NUM_SECONDS* define.

Following this, any existing sound is deleted, and then a call made to *CreateCircular* to create the new circular sound buffer. Finally, the circular sound can be played with a call to the *PlayCircularBuffer* function.

```
HRESULT PlayCircularBuffer( BOOL bLooped, int streamNumber )
{
    HRESULT hr;

    if( NULL == g_pCircularSound[streamNumber] )
        return E_FAIL; // Sanity check

    if( FAILED( hr = g_pCircularSound[streamNumber]->Reset() ) )
        return E_FAIL;

    // Fill the entire buffer with wave data. If the wave file is small,
    // repeat the wave file if the user wants to loop the file,
    // otherwise fill in silence.
    LPDIRECTSOUNDBUFFER pDSB = g_pCircularSound[streamNumber]->GetBuffer( 0 );
    if( FAILED( hr = g_pCircularSound[streamNumber]->
            FillBufferWithSound( pDSB, bLooped ) ) )
        return E_FAIL;

    // Always play with the LOOPING flag since the streaming buffer
    // wraps around before the entire wave file is played.
    if( FAILED( hr = g_pCircularSound[streamNumber] ->
            PlayBuffer(0, 0, DSBPLAY_LOOPING, DSBVOLUME_MAX,
                        DSBPAN_CENTER, NO_FREQUENCY_CHANGE ) ) )
        return E_FAIL;

    return S_OK;
}
```

The *PlayCircularBuffer* function is notable in that it calls *FillBufferWithSound,* a *CSound* method that it was not necessary to modify for the polling sample, which fills the one-second buffer up completely to start with. The *PlayBuffer* call sets the sound going.

That completes our examination of the polling model for streaming sounds. This is the recommended method, but for comparison purposes, the next section discusses the Three Streams sample.

The Three Streams Sample

The Three Streams.exe has a nearly identical UI to the Circular Streams sample, (see Figure 6.2), but uses the notifications rather than the polling model of managing the streaming.

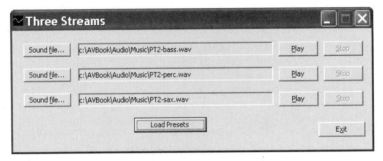

Figure 6.2   Three Streams dialog box.

Behind the scenes, what is happening is that each of the three slots in the UI matches a three-second buffer. Each time that you press Play, the first three seconds of a track are loaded and begin playing. This buffer is refilled from the file on the hard disk every fifth of a second; if the three tracks are playing together, this constant refilling of each buffer goes on in a different thread for each track.

Using notifications, the streaming buffers must be set up in software, so there is a high cost of applying special effects or 3-D processing in those cases. The reason for this oddity is that Windows notifications require the refilling of each stream to be handled by a separate thread, and audio hardware does not work well with a program that is multi-threaded and sending notifications to more than one of these threads. For this reason, we are suggesting the use of notification-based streaming buffers only in a few specific cases:

■   Playing one or more music tracks.

■   For human dialog, consider setting up one stream per speaker.

Three Streams Project

The Three Streams.cpp file is the only source file unique to this sample, and is relatively short, only about eight pages long. The basis of the sample, however, is the *CStreaming-Sound* class declared in extended_dsutil.cpp. We have not amended this class from its original form in the dsutil.cpp file (but note that it inherits the *CSound* class, which has been extensively amended).

The key data and definitions for the sample follow.

```
#define    nStreams    3
#define    AllStreams    (streamNumber=0;streamNumber<nStreams;streamNumber++)
#define    NUM_PLAY_NOTIFICATIONS  15
#define    NUM_SECONDS  3
CSoundManager*      g_pSoundManager              = NULL;
CStreamingSound*    g_pStreamingSound[nStreams]  = { NULL, NULL, NULL };
HANDLE             g_hNotificationEvent[nStreams] = { NULL, NULL, NULL };
DWORD              g_dwNotifyThreadID[nStreams]  = { 0, 0, 0 };
HANDLE             g_hNotifyThread[nStreams]     = { NULL, NULL, NULL };
```

The number of streams was arbitrarily chosen to be three (held by the *nStreams* define) and the *AllStreams* definition simply provides us with a macro to step through each of the streams (it assumes that *streamNumber* has been declared as a variable within the method that the macro is being used in).

The definition *NUM_SECONDS* sets the length of the streaming buffers, obviously to 3 seconds in this case. Note that the actual size of the three buffers in bytes will only be equal if their sampling rates are also identical.

The *NUM_PLAY_NOTIFICATIONS* define sets the number of times that a Windows notification event is sent for the length of the streaming buffer. For example, with this define set at 15 and the length of the buffer set at three seconds, an event is sent off to refill the buffer every fifth of a second. Setting *NUM_PLAY_NOTIFICATIONS* to be too big or too small might affect the performance of the audio if you have a large number of streaming buffers. Trial and error seems to be the method of choice in determining what combinations of buffer size and notification frequency work best.

Next you will see that we need one sound manager object, with one streaming sound object per stream. Note that an object created from the *CStreamingSound* class handles a single streaming buffer. This differs from objects created from the *CSound* class, which can handle multiple buffers per wave file.

The next three declarations handle the multithreaded nature of this sample. Each stream, and therefore each thread, requires its own handle, as well as a notification event handle and ID. All these variables are initialized to zero or *NULL* for the sake of code safety, although in some cases, this is unnecessary.

If you have not attempted multithreaded programming before, then this sample is a good place to start. It is not as intimidating as you might think; most of the work, as is often the case, is in initializing everything correctly. Starting with the essential *WinMain* function:

```
INT APIENTRY WinMain( HINSTANCE hInst, HINSTANCE hPrevInst, LPSTR pCmdLine,
                      INT nCmdShow )
{
int streamNumber;
   g_hInst = hInst;

   GetCurrentDirectory(MAX_PATH, g_soundDir);
   g_soundDir[2] = 0;// Delete all but the drive.
   strcat(g_soundDir,"\\AVBook\\Audio\\Music");

   for AllStreams
     g_hNotificationEvent[streamNumber] = CreateEvent( NULL, FALSE, FALSE,
                                                       NULL );

   DialogBox( hInst, MAKEINTRESOURCE(IDD_MAIN), NULL, MainDlgProc );

   for AllStreams
     CloseHandle( g_hNotificationEvent[streamNumber] );

   return TRUE;
}
```

After storing the music sound directory in a global string variable, note the three calls to the Windows *CreateEvent* function. The four parameters are for event attributes, whether a manual reset is enabled, the initial state, and an optional event name. We do not need any variations on the default for this function, so the four parameters are all set to NULL or FALSE appropriately.

After you close the Three Streams dialog box, there are three calls to the Windows *CloseHandle* function to shut down the three events that we have created.

The next function in the code is one of the core functions for multithreaded event-driven programming, *NotificationProc*. This is the function, which runs in its own thread.

```
DWORD WINAPI NotificationProc( LPVOID lpParameter )
{
    HRESULT hr;
    MSG     msg;
    DWORD   dwResult = 0;
    BOOL    bDone = FALSE;
    BOOL    bLooped = TRUE;
    int     streamNumber = (int) lpParameter;
```

```
while( !bDone )
{
    dwResult = MsgWaitForMultipleObjects( 1,
                &g_hNotificationEvent[streamNumber],
                FALSE, INFINITE, QS_POSTMESSAGE );
    switch( dwResult )
    {
        case WAIT_OBJECT_0 + 0:
            if (g_pStreamingSound[streamNumber] != NULL)
            {
                if( FAILED( hr = g_pStreamingSound[streamNumber] ->
                        HandleWaveStreamNotification( bLooped ) ) )
                    bDone = TRUE;
            } else
                bDone = TRUE;
            break;

        case WAIT_OBJECT_0 + 1:
            while( PeekMessage( &msg, NULL, 0, 0, PM_REMOVE ) )
            {
                if( msg.message == WM_QUIT )
                    bDone = TRUE;
            }
            break;
    }
}

return 0;
}
```

With three threads, we will have three different versions of this procedure running simultaneously. Also, any functions called by *NotificationProc* will run separately and independently in each of the three threads.

The *lpParameter* parameter provided in this code is used to identify which stream is being serviced (note the conversion to an *int* and its assignment to *streamNumber*). Typically, *lpParameter* is used to point to an array or a structure, if more information beyond just a single value needs to be sent to the thread. In this case, our use of global data keeps things simple.

Once initiated, the *NotificationProc* function will run continuously in its thread until it receives a *WM_QUIT* message, which only occurs when the Three Streams sample is closed. The *NotificationProc* function basically loops, picking up posted *WAIT_OBJECT* events after they are sent. The *MsgWaitForMultipleObjects* function is used to pick up the events, and takes a number of parameters. The "1" indicates that we are waiting for one object, the handle indicates which notification event (and therefore which thread and stream) we are waiting for, and the next parameter is only relevant if we are waiting for multiple objects, so we set it to *FALSE*. The *INFINITE* setting indicates that we do not want the waiting to be timed out.

Note that although we are sending events every fifth of a second when a stream is playing, we are not sending events if the stream has been stopped; however, we want to keep the thread open and running in case Play is pressed again. The final parameter (*QS_POSTMESSAGE*) simply indicates which kind of event we are waiting for, which in this case is posted messages, rather than say, timer events, mouse movements and so on.

The only two messages that will be received are *WAIT_OBJECT_0* and *WAIT_OBJECT_0 + 1*. There is a convention in notification coding to add the redundant "+ 0" to the first message to highlight the fact that no offset is being added. If the first of these messages is received, we check that the streaming sound pointer is not erroneously set to *NULL* (which should not happen if we have coded things correctly). Then, we call the *HandleWaveStreamNotification* method of the streaming sound object. For the Three Streams sample, the tracks are always looped, which is the only parameter to this method.

The next few functions of the Three Streams.cpp file mostly concern the UI, which we won't discuss here in any depth. However, we do need to point out a few issues.

In *MainDlgProc*, notice that when one of the Stop buttons is pressed, a call is made to the *Stop* and then *Reset* methods of the streaming sound object. In this case, the *Stop* method is inherited from the *CSound* class, but the *Reset* method is specific to the *CStreamingSound* class.

Also in *MailDlgProc*, when the final *WM_DESTROY* message is received, note the sending of the *WM_QUIT* message to all three threads. When the word is received that the thread has closed down, the handles are closed too.

In the *OnInitDialog* function, the last few lines of code create the three threads that we need, one for each stream.

```
for AllStreams
{
    g_hNotifyThread[streamNumber] = CreateThread( NULL, 0, NotificationProc,
            (LPVOID) streamNumber, 0,&g_dwNotifyThreadID[streamNumber] );
}
```

The first two parameters of the *CreateThread* function refer to attributes and stack size, which we won't go into here except to point out that they should be NULL and 0, respectively. Then, we send the all-important address of the *NotificationProc* function, followed by the stream number cast into an LPVOID, even though it is not a pointer. Remember that we stated that it is often convenient to send the address of an array or structure if more than one value needs to be sent to the notification procedure, which is why an LPVOID is used here. As we are sending just one value to the notification function, simply casting it as an *LPVOID* works just fine. The zero that follows the *streamNumber* parameter indicates that we are setting no specific creation flags for the thread. Finally, we pass in the address of the array holding the thread IDs. These IDs are filled in by this call.

Moving on to the *OnOpenSoundFile* function, note that it first stops and resets any stream that is currently playing in the buffer, and then finally calls *LoadWaveAndCreate-Buffer* to load in a new wave file. This function is another important one for streaming buffers.

```
VOID LoadWaveAndCreateBuffer( HWND hDlg, TCHAR* strFileName, int streamNumber )
{
    HRESULT    hr;
    CWaveFile  waveFile;
    DWORD      dwNotifySize;

    if( FAILED( hr = waveFile.Open( strFileName, NULL, WAVEFILE_READ ) ) )
    {
        waveFile.Close();
        SetDlgItemText( hDlg, IDC_FILENAME1 + streamNumber,
                        TEXT("Bad wave file.") );
        return;
    }

    if( waveFile.GetSize() == 0 )
    {
        waveFile.Close();
        SetDlgItemText( hDlg, IDC_FILENAME1 + streamNumber,
                        TEXT("Wave file blank.") );
        return;
    }

    waveFile.Close();

    DWORD nBlockAlign = (DWORD)waveFile.m_pwfx->nBlockAlign;
    INT nSamplesPerSec = waveFile.m_pwfx->nSamplesPerSec;
    dwNotifySize = nSamplesPerSec * NUM_SECONDS * nBlockAlign /
                   NUM_PLAY_NOTIFICATIONS;
    dwNotifySize -= dwNotifySize % nBlockAlign;

    SAFE_DELETE( g_pStreamingSound[streamNumber] );

    if( FAILED( hr = g_pSoundManager->CreateStreaming(
                &g_pStreamingSound[streamNumber], strFileName,
                DSBCAPS_LOCSOFTWARE, GUID_NULL, NUM_PLAY_NOTIFICATIONS,
                dwNotifySize, g_hNotificationEvent[streamNumber] ) ) )
```

(continued)

```
    {
        SetDlgItemText( hDlg, IDC_FILENAME1 + streamNumber,
                        TEXT("Could not support the file's audio format.") );
        return;
    }

    EnablePlayUI( hDlg, TRUE, streamNumber );
    SetDlgItemText( hDlg, IDC_FILENAME1 + streamNumber, strFileName );
}
```

The *LoadWaveAndCreateBuffer* function first checks that the wave file is valid, and is not of zero length. The next statements calculate *dwNotifySize*, which is basically the number of samples per second multiplied by the number of seconds multiplied by the block alignment (usually one or two bytes), then divided by the number of notifications. The final subtraction is just to make sure that the notification size is an integer multiple of the block alignment (so if the block alignment is two bytes, the notification size is a multiple of two).

Following the calculation of *dwNotifySize*, any existing sound is deleted, and a new streaming sound object is created with a call to *CreateStreaming* (a method on the sound manager object). The parameters to *CreateStreaming* are as follows:

- A pointer to the streaming sound object to be created.

- The full path of the wave file.

- Any creation flags in addition to those enforced by the *CreateStreaming* method (so, as we have three streams, we set the *DSBCAPS_LOC-SOFT-WARE* flag).

- A 3-D GUID algorithm which we have set to GUID_NULL as we do not want 3-D effects to be applied.

- The number of notifications.

- The notification size.

- The notification event handle.

If all of this works, the function successfully updates the Three Streams UI. The *PlayStreamingBuffer* function is called when a Play button is pressed for that stream.

```
HRESULT PlayStreamingBuffer( BOOL bLooped, int streamNumber )
{
    HRESULT hr;

    if( NULL == g_pStreamingSound[streamNumber] )
        return E_FAIL; // Sanity check.
```

```
if( FAILED( hr = g_pStreamingSound[streamNumber]->Reset() ) )
    return E_FAIL;
LPDIRECTSOUNDBUFFER pDSB = g_pStreamingSound[streamNumber]->GetBuffer( 0 );
if( FAILED( hr = g_pStreamingSound[streamNumber]->
            FillBufferWithSound( pDSB, bLooped ) ) )
    return E_FAIL;

if( FAILED( hr = g_pStreamingSound[streamNumber]->
            PlayBuffer(0, 0, DSBPLAY_LOOPING, DSBVOLUME_MAX, DSBPAN_CENTER,
                       NO_FREQUENCY_CHANGE ) ) )
    return E_FAIL;

return S_OK;
}
```

The last call in *PlayStreamingBuffer*, to the *PlayBuffer* method of the streaming sound object, can be used to set volume, panning and frequency changes. However, these will not work unless you also set the appropriate creation flags in the call to *CreateStreaming* mentioned previously. In this case, one or more of the following flags should be set in this call:

■   DSBCAPS_CTRLFREQUENCY

■   DSBCAPS_CTRLPAN

■   DSBCAPS_CTRLVOLUME

We will show an example of how to do this, enabling a change of volume, in Chapter 8.

You will notice that there is a small latency problem in the Three Streams sample if you try to play all three tracks exactly in sync, as the *PlayStreamingBuffer* function first fills a buffer and then starts the sound playing. Better synchronization is achieved by filling all the buffers first, and then setting the tracks to play together. This is also addressed in the coding for the Concertina framework in Chapter 8.

The final function of Three Streams.cpp, *EnablePlayUI*, just sets the Play and Stop buttons appropriately.

The CStreamingSound Class

There are only four methods in the *CStreamingSound* class: the creation function, the destructor (which is empty), and the two methods mentioned previously, *HandleWaveStreamNotification* and *Reset*. All the other methods needed to set and get information on an object created from the *CStreamingSound* class are identical to those in the *CSound* class, and therefore are available to the streaming sound object as *CStreamingSound* inherits *CSound*.

However, first we should look at the *CreateStreaming* method of the *CSoundManager* object.

```
HRESULT CSoundManager::CreateStreaming( CStreamingSound**
                                        ppStreamingSound,
                                        LPTSTR strWaveFileName,
                                        DWORD dwCreationFlags,
                                        GUID guid3DAlgorithm,
                                        DWORD dwNotifyCount,
                                        DWORD dwNotifySize,
                                        HANDLE hNotifyEvent )
{
    HRESULT hr;

    if( m_pDS == NULL )
        return CO_E_NOTINITIALIZED;
    if( strWaveFileName == NULL || ppStreamingSound == NULL ||
                    hNotifyEvent == NULL )
        return E_INVALIDARG;

    LPDIRECTSOUNDBUFFER pDSBuffer      = NULL;
    DWORD               dwDSBufferSize = NULL;
    CWaveFile*          pWaveFile      = NULL;
    DSBPOSITIONNOTIFY*  aPosNotify     = NULL;
    LPDIRECTSOUNDNOTIFY pDSNotify      = NULL;

    pWaveFile = new CWaveFile();
    if( pWaveFile == NULL )
        return E_OUTOFMEMORY;
    pWaveFile->Open( strWaveFileName, NULL, WAVEFILE_READ );

    dwDSBufferSize = dwNotifySize * dwNotifyCount;

    DSBUFFERDESC dsbd;
    ZeroMemory( &dsbd, sizeof(DSBUFFERDESC) );
    dsbd.dwSize          = sizeof(DSBUFFERDESC);
    dsbd.dwFlags         = dwCreationFlags |
                           DSBCAPS_CTRLPOSITIONNOTIFY |
                           DSBCAPS_GETCURRENTPOSITION2;
    dsbd.dwBufferBytes   = dwDSBufferSize;
    dsbd.guid3DAlgorithm = guid3DAlgorithm;
    dsbd.lpwfxFormat     = pWaveFile->m_pwfx;

    if( FAILED( hr = m_pDS->CreateSoundBuffer( &dsbd, &pDSBuffer, NULL ) ) )
    {
        if( hr == DSERR_BADFORMAT || hr == E_INVALIDARG )
            return DXTRACE_ERR( TEXT("CreateSoundBuffer"), hr );
```

```
        return DXTRACE_ERR( TEXT("CreateSoundBuffer"), hr );
    }

    if( FAILED( hr = pDSBuffer->QueryInterface( IID_IDirectSoundNotify,
                                        (VOID**)&pDSNotify ) ) )
    {
        SAFE_DELETE_ARRAY( aPosNotify );
        return DXTRACE_ERR( TEXT("QueryInterface"), hr );
    }

    aPosNotify = new DSBPOSITIONNOTIFY[ dwNotifyCount ];
    if( aPosNotify == NULL )
        return E_OUTOFMEMORY;

    for( DWORD i = 0; i < dwNotifyCount; i++ )
    {
        aPosNotify[i].dwOffset      = (dwNotifySize * i) + dwNotifySize - 1;
        aPosNotify[i].hEventNotify = hNotifyEvent;
    }

    if( FAILED( hr = pDSNotify->SetNotificationPositions( dwNotifyCount,
                                            aPosNotify ) ) )
    {
        SAFE_RELEASE( pDSNotify );
        SAFE_DELETE_ARRAY( aPosNotify );
        return DXTRACE_ERR( TEXT("SetNotificationPositions"), hr );
    }

    SAFE_RELEASE( pDSNotify );
    SAFE_DELETE_ARRAY( aPosNotify );

    *ppStreamingSound = new CStreamingSound( pDSBuffer, dwDSBufferSize,
                                        pWaveFile, dwNotifySize );

    return S_OK;
}
```

The *CreateStreaming* method first checks the sense of its input parameters, and then initializes most of its data members to NULL. Then it opens the appropriate wave file. Note the calculation of the buffer size with the following statement.

```
dwDSBufferSize = dwNotifySize * dwNotifyCount;
```

Following this, a buffer description is prepared, and then a call is made to create a single sound buffer. Then note the call to *QueryInterface* to get a notification interface pointer and store it in the *pDSNotify* data member.

```
hr = pDSBuffer->QueryInterface( IID_IDirectSoundNotify,
                        (VOID**)&pDSNotify )
```

The next statement creates new *DSBPOSITIONNOTIFY* structures for each of the required notifications. This structure is declared in dsound.h and is defined as follows.

```
typedef struct _DSBPOSITIONNOTIFY
{
    DWORD           dwOffset;
    HANDLE          hEventNotify;
} DSBPOSITIONNOTIFY, *LPDSBPOSITIONNOTIFY;
```

The loop that follows the creation of these *DSBPOSITIONNOTIFY* structures populates the two data members of each structure. These structures are used as input parameters to the call to *SetNotificationPositions*, using the *pDSNotify* pointer to the *IDirectSoundNotify* interface. A call to the creation function for a streaming sound ends the *CreateStreaming* method (of the *CSoundManager* class).

```
CStreamingSound::CStreamingSound( LPDIRECTSOUNDBUFFER pDSBuffer,
                                  DWORD dwDSBufferSize,
                                  CWaveFile* pWaveFile, DWORD dwNotifySize )
                : CSound( &pDSBuffer, dwDSBufferSize, 1, pWaveFile, 0 )

{
    m_dwLastPlayPos     = 0;
    m_dwPlayProgress    = 0;
    m_dwNotifySize      = dwNotifySize;
    m_dwNextWriteOffset = 0;
    m_bFillNextNotificationWithSilence = FALSE;
}
```

In the *CStreamingSound* class, the *HandleWaveStreamNotification* method is easily the most complex method.

```
HRESULT CStreamingSound::HandleWaveStreamNotification( BOOL bLoopedPlay )
{
    HRESULT hr;
    DWORD   dwCurrentPlayPos;
    DWORD   dwPlayDelta;
    DWORD   dwBytesWrittenToBuffer;
    VOID*   pDSLockedBuffer = NULL;
    VOID*   pDSLockedBuffer2 = NULL;
    DWORD   dwDSLockedBufferSize;
    DWORD   dwDSLockedBufferSize2;

    if( m_apDSBuffer == NULL || m_pWaveFile == NULL )
        return CO_E_NOTINITIALIZED;

    // Restore the buffer if it was lost.
    BOOL bRestored;
    if( FAILED( hr = RestoreBuffer( m_apDSBuffer[0], &bRestored ) ) )
        return DXTRACE_ERR( TEXT("RestoreBuffer"), hr );
```

```
    if( bRestored )
    {
        // The buffer was restored, so we need to fill it with new data.
        if( FAILED( hr = FillBufferWithSound( m_apDSBuffer[0], FALSE ) ) )
            return DXTRACE_ERR( TEXT("FillBufferWithSound"), hr );
        return S_OK;
    }


    // Lock the DirectSound buffer.
    if( FAILED( hr = m_apDSBuffer[0]->
                Lock( m_dwNextWriteOffset, m_dwNotifySize,
                &pDSLockedBuffer, &dwDSLockedBufferSize,
                &pDSLockedBuffer2, &dwDSLockedBufferSize2, 0L ) ) )
        return DXTRACE_ERR( TEXT("Lock"), hr );


    if( pDSLockedBuffer2 != NULL )
        return E_UNEXPECTED;


    if( !m_bFillNextNotificationWithSilence )
    {
        // Fill the DirectSound buffer with wave data.
        if( FAILED( hr = m_pWaveFile->Read( (BYTE*) pDSLockedBuffer,
                                             dwDSLockedBufferSize,
                                             &dwBytesWrittenToBuffer ) ) )

            return DXTRACE_ERR( TEXT("Read"), hr );
    }
    else
    {
        // Fill the DirectSound buffer with silence.
        FillMemory( pDSLockedBuffer, dwDSLockedBufferSize,
                    (BYTE)( m_pWaveFile->m_pwfx->
                    wBitsPerSample == 8 ? 128 : 0 ) );
        dwBytesWrittenToBuffer = dwDSLockedBufferSize;
    }


    // If the number of bytes written is less than the
    // amount we requested, we have a short file.
    if( dwBytesWrittenToBuffer < dwDSLockedBufferSize )
    {
        if( !bLoopedPlay )
        {
            // Fill in silence for the rest of the buffer.
            FillMemory( (BYTE*) pDSLockedBuffer + dwBytesWrittenToBuffer,
                        dwDSLockedBufferSize - dwBytesWrittenToBuffer,
                        (BYTE)(m_pWaveFile->m_pwfx->
                        wBitsPerSample == 8 ? 128 : 0 ) );
```

(continued)

```
            // Any future notifications should just fill the
            // buffer with silence.
            m_bFillNextNotificationWithSilence = TRUE;
        }
        else
        {
            // We are looping, so reset the file and fill the
            // buffer with wave data.
            DWORD dwReadSoFar = dwBytesWrittenToBuffer;
            // From previous call above.
            while( dwReadSoFar < dwDSLockedBufferSize )
            {
                // This will keep reading in until the buffer is full
                // (for very short files).
                if( FAILED( hr = m_pWaveFile->ResetFile() ) )
                    return DXTRACE_ERR( TEXT("ResetFile"), hr );

                if( FAILED( hr = m_pWaveFile
                    ->Read( (BYTE*)pDSLockedBuffer + dwReadSoFar,
                                dwDSLockedBufferSize - dwReadSoFar,
                                &dwBytesWrittenToBuffer ) ) )
                    return DXTRACE_ERR( TEXT("Read"), hr );

                dwReadSoFar += dwBytesWrittenToBuffer;
            }
        }
    }
}

// Unlock the DirectSound buffer.
m_apDSBuffer[0]->Unlock( pDSLockedBuffer, dwDSLockedBufferSize, NULL, 0 );

// Figure out how much data has been played so far. When we have played
// past the end of the file, we will either need to start filling the
// buffer with silence or starting reading from the beginning of the file,
// depending on whether the user wants to loop the sound.
if( FAILED( hr = m_apDSBuffer[0]->
    GetCurrentPosition( &dwCurrentPlayPos, NULL ) ) )
    return DXTRACE_ERR( TEXT("GetCurrentPosition"), hr );

// Check to see if the position counter looped.
if( dwCurrentPlayPos < m_dwLastPlayPos )
    dwPlayDelta = ( m_dwDSBufferSize - m_dwLastPlayPos )
                    + dwCurrentPlayPos;
else
    dwPlayDelta = dwCurrentPlayPos - m_dwLastPlayPos;

m_dwPlayProgress += dwPlayDelta;
m_dwLastPlayPos = dwCurrentPlayPos;
```

```
    // If we are now filling the buffer with silence, we have found the end,
    // so  check to see if the entire sound has played.
    // If it has, then stop the buffer.
    if( m_bFillNextNotificationWithSilence )
    {
        // We don't want to cut off the sound before it's done playing.
        if( m_dwPlayProgress >= m_pWaveFile->GetSize() )
        {
            m_apDSBuffer[0]->Stop();
        }
    }

    // Update where the buffer will lock (for next time).
    m_dwNextWriteOffset += dwDSLockedBufferSize;
    m_dwNextWriteOffset %= m_dwDSBufferSize; // Circular buffer.

    return S_OK;
}
```

The first thing that the *HandleWaveStreamNotification* method does is restore the contents of the buffer if it was lost to another process. After this, the main thing to note is that the buffer is locked while work is being done on it, preventing any other process from gaining access to it. The buffer is filled from the file, taking into account whether the file should be looped, or any extra space filled with silence, before it is unlocked. Finally, a number of pointers and counts are updated.

The *Reset* method for this class differs from the much simpler method in the *CSound* class, largely because of the need to reset various counts and also reset the file.

```
HRESULT CStreamingSound::Reset()
{
    HRESULT hr;

    if( m_apDSBuffer[0] == NULL || m_pWaveFile == NULL )
        return CO_E_NOTINITIALIZED;

    m_dwLastPlayPos    = 0;
    m_dwPlayProgress   = 0;
    m_dwNextWriteOffset = 0;
    m_bFillNextNotificationWithSilence = FALSE;

    // Restore the buffer if it was lost.
    BOOL bRestored;
    if( FAILED( hr = RestoreBuffer( m_apDSBuffer[0], &bRestored ) ) )
        return DXTRACE_ERR( TEXT("RestoreBuffer"), hr );

    if( bRestored )
    {
```

(continued)

```
    // The buffer was restored, so we need to fill it with new data.
    if( FAILED( hr = FillBufferWithSound( m_apDSBuffer[0], FALSE ) ) )
        return DXTRACE_ERR( TEXT("FillBufferWithSound"), hr );
}

m_pWaveFile->ResetFile();

return m_apDSBuffer[0]->SetCurrentPosition( 0L );
}
```

You will probably not need to amend any methods in the *CStreamingSound* class, but it is useful to know the process that each of them is working through.

Summary

In this chapter, we have demonstrated and described the Circular Streams and Three Streams samples. Unless you have already made an investment in the Windows notifications-based method of streaming (the Three Streams sample) *and* it is working well for you, then it is highly recommended that you base your work on the polling method (the Circular Streams sample).

In order to get the polling method to work, we needed to define a new class, *CCircularSound*, which inherits from the *CSound* class. The *TopUpBuffer* method of the *CCircularSound* class is the key to getting streaming to work well.

Many games developers should work with the *CCircularSound* class to get the best audio performance for their game, because it has the reliability across many different systems that is absent from the Windows notifications method. Although we have not shown an example of applying effects to streaming buffers, they can be applied without any significant difference in performance from applying effects to static buffers.

7

Driving Hardware with Property Sets

If a manufacturer adds a feature to its sound cards that is not supported by the Direct-Sound SDK, the manufacturer can make the feature available to the programmer through the use of *property sets*. Property sets provide a way to write code more or less directly to the hardware. This may seem intimidating, but using property sets is in fact as easy, and in some cases easier, than programming for the SDK.

This chapter will focus on how to use Environmental Audio Extensions (EAX), which are the property set extensions most widely supported in sound cards.

The Property Values Sample

The Property Values sample demonstrates the 26 preset audio environments of EAX 2.0 (from Padded cell to Psychotic) and includes an example of obstruction and occlusion.

In this context, obstruction means that although there is an airway from the source of a sound to the listener, that airway is blocked in some way. For example, a pillar or vehicle or large piece of furniture can obstruct the airway. Occlusion occurs when there is no airway from the source to the listener, and the sound has to pass through an object – usually a wall or window (see Figure 7.1).

Run the PropertyValues.exe that is found in the AVBook\bin directory. This sample takes just one sound file as input. Load in a simple sound such as cannon.wav, and press Play. The sound will loop and play until you press Stop or Exit. Try clicking on the radio buttons for different environments and listening to the reverb effects that are produced. Environments with very noticeable reverb effects include the Hangar, Sewer Pipe, Underwater, Bathroom, and the weird but wonderful collection of Drugged, Dizzy, and

Psychotic. The 26 environments available in this sample are all those that are predefined for EAX 2.0 (see Figure 7.2).

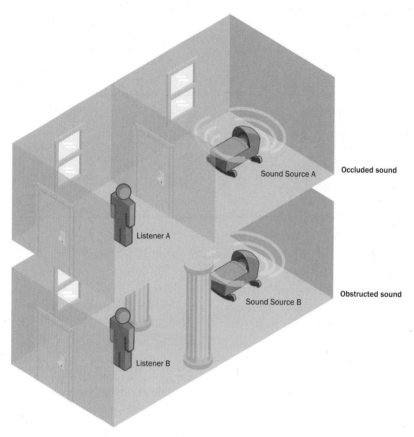

Figure 7.1 Examples of occluded and obstructed sound.

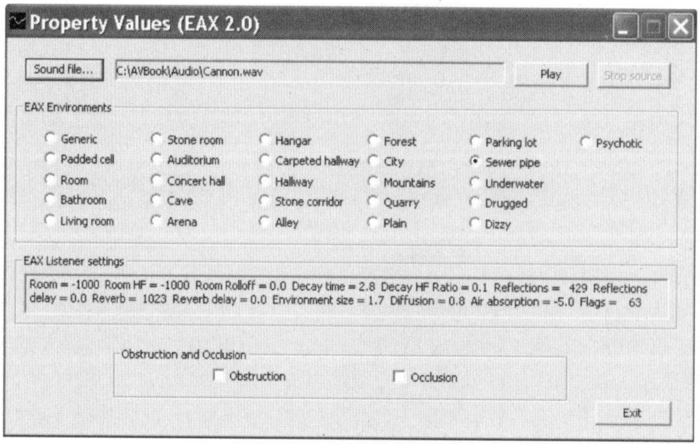

Figure 7.2 Property Values dialog box.

Notice that if you press Stop Source, only the source sound stops; the reverb effects continue until they are silent. This gives you a good method of checking out the reverb. Click Play, and then (after listening to it loop a few times), just when the sound is at its loudest, click Stop Source, and then listen to the reverb sound until it dies off.

The Obstruction and Occlusion check boxes enable you to hear the sound as if it was blocked by a pillar and in another room, respectively. You can select both boxes, although not much additional sensory value will be achieved.

Along with selecting or clearing the Obstruction and Occlusion check boxes, you can also change the environment mid-sound, and the sound will immediately reflect your changes.

Load in different kinds of sounds, and then change the settings to evaluate how the different environments affect the sound that you hear. Try experimenting with high- or low-frequency sound, or some music.

Clearly, this sample will only work if you have a sound card that supports the EAX standard. However, because most sound cards do support the EAX 2.0 standard, it is recommended that you incorporate these extensions into your program.

Before examining the code for the sample, we'll compare the EAX 2.0 environment with the I3DL2 environment that we introduced in Chapter 4.

EAX 2.0 and I3DL2 Environments

The EAX 2.0 and I3DL2 environments are both audio standards. The I3DL2 (Interactive 3D Audio Rendering Guidelines, Level 2) environments are supported in software by DirectSound, and are implemented in the Rumpus 3D SFX sample. The I3DL2 environment is not widely supported in hardware, which gives EAX 2.0 the obvious advantage of performance. The standards themselves are very similar; the following sections describe the environmental effects settings that are used in both.

Room Property

The Room property determines the master volume for reflected sound. It is expressed in both standards as units of hundredths of a decibel in the range -10,000 (-100 dB, the minimum value, indicating no reflections) to 0 (0 dB, the maximum value).

Both standards also use an identical default value of -1,000 (-10 dB).

Room HF Property

The Room HF (Room High Frequency) property is similar to the Room property, but it only applies to high-frequency sound, attenuating it differently from the low frequencies for that room.

Again both standards use the same range (-10,000 to 0) and units, with the default for I3DL2 being 0 (0 dB) and for EAX -10 (-1 dB).

One difference between EAX and I3DL2 in our implementation is that these values can be applied to both the source and listener in EAX (see the EAX Source Buffer section later in this chapter), but just to the source in I3DL2.

Room Rolloff Factor Property

The Room Rolloff Factor property has a very similar effect to the global rolloff factor that you can define in DirectSound (see Chapter 3), in that it determines how a sound attenuates over distance, but in this case applies to reflected sound.

A value of 0 indicates that the sound does not attenuate. A value of 1 indicates that the volume will decrease by 6 dB (in other words, by half) when the distance from the source doubles. See the description of rolloff and minimum distance in Chapter 3 for the effect that will happen when the values are less than or greater than 1.

Both standards use a range of 0 to 10, and both have a default of 0.

Decay Time Property

The Decay Time property sets the time that it takes for the reverberation to decay, in seconds. Both standards set ranges from a minimum of 0.1 seconds to a maximum of 20 seconds, with a default of 1.49 seconds.

Confined spaces containing sound-deadening material will have a very short decay time, whereas large rooms with reflective surfaces will have long decay times.

Decay HF Ratio Property

The Decay HF Ratio property provides a ratio that is used to determine how quickly high-frequency sounds decay relative to other sounds. A value of 1.0 for this ratio means that both decay at the same rate. A value of less than 1.0 indicates that high-frequency sound decays faster than other sounds, and a value of greater than 1.0 indicates that high-frequency sound decays at a slower rate.

Both standards use a range of 0.1 (the minimum setting, indicating that high frequencies decay ten times faster than other frequencies) to 2.0 (the maximum setting, indicating that high frequencies decay at half the rate of other frequencies), with a default setting of 0.83.

Reflections Property

The Reflections property sets the amount of early reflections for an environment. This is much higher with hard reflective surfaces than with softer absorbing ones. Both standards set the range from -10,000 (-100 dB, the minimum setting indicating no early reflections) to 1,000 (10 dB, the maximum setting). This property is used along with the initial Room property to set the final output of early reflections. Both standards set the default at -2,602 (-26.02 dB).

Reflections Delay Property

While the Reflections property sets the amount of early reflections, the Reflections Delay property sets the timing of those reflections. The time here is obviously the delay in seconds, and ranges from 0.0 (indicating no delay) to 0.3 (indicating a delay of three tenths of a second).

To simulate the audio properties of a narrow passageway, the Reflections property will be set high, and the delay very short. A wide open field, on the other hand, will have a very low Reflections setting, and a much longer delay. Both standards set the default for the Reflections Delay property at 0.007 seconds.

Reverb Property

The Reverb and Reverb Delay properties are very similar to the Reflections and Reflections Delay properties, except that they apply to late reverberations instead of early reflections. Again, the Room setting is used in conjunction with these properties to come up with a final output of late reverberations.

Both the EAX and I3DL2 standards use a minimum setting of -10,000 (-100 dB, indicating no late reverberations at all) to a maximum of 2,000 (20 dB). Note that the maximum level for late reverberations is double that for early reflections. Both standards set a default of 200 (2 dB).

Reverb Delay Property

The Reverb Delay property obviously sets the delay time for the late reverberations, and the important point here is that this time is relative to the Reflections Delay property time described previously. Reverb Delay can be set in the range 0.0 (indicating no addition to the Reflections Delay time) to 0.1 (indicating that one tenth of a second is added to the Reflections Delay value to give the start time for late reverberations). Both standards use the default setting of 0.011 (11 hundredths of a second added to the Reflections Delay).

Very metallic surfaces, such as the sewer pipe environment (see Figure 7.3), will have high levels of late reverberation. Natural settings will often have none at all.

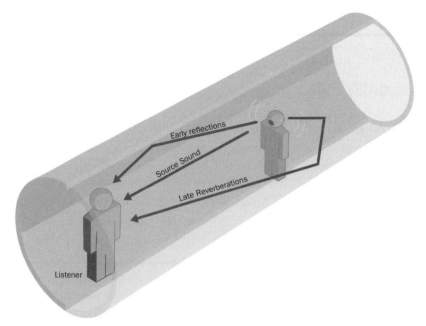

Figure 7.3   Sewer pipe environment.

Diffusion Property

The Diffusion property is slightly more complicated to explain. It refers to the density of the sound in the reverberations. A high value here makes the echoes of reverberation sound most solid, and a low value will give a grainy effect closer to a series of distinct echoes. In the I3DL2 standard, the range for this setting is given as a percentage (from 0.0 to 100.0), with the default set at 100 percent. For EAX, the property is called Environment Diffusion, and the range is from 0.0 to 1.0. So an I3DL2 setting of 50.0 corresponds to an EAX setting of 0.5. The EAX default is 1.0 (so is identical to the I3DL2 default of 100 percent).

An appropriate use of diffusion settings below the default would be for percussive sound sources such as drums, or perhaps public address systems.

Environment Size Property

The Environment Size property is unique to EAX, and sets the apparent size of the environment in meters. This value can range from 1.0 to 100.0, with the default set at 7.5 meters. By default, varying this property scales several of the other properties to match, including the Reflections, Reflections Delay, Reverb, Reverb Delay and Decay Time properties. This default effect can be prevented by setting some of the flags in the EAX Flags property described later in this chapter.

Air Absorption HF Property

The Air Absorption HF property is unique to EAX. It provides a setting to adjust the medium that the sound is traveling through, to simulate humid, foggy, or other air conditions. Its units are in hundredths of a decibel per meter, and the range is from -100 (-1 dB) to 0 (0 dB, no deduction). The default value is set at -0.05 dB, so there is this small attenuation of both the source and reflected sound. This setting should be lowered if the air is humid, or raised if the air is very dry.

Density Property

The Density property is unique to the I3DL2 standard. It refers to the number of resonances per hertz in late reverberations. The range for this is a percentage (from 0.0 to 100.0), with the default at 100 percent. Typically, you might set lower densities in smaller rooms to produce more hollow sounds.

HF Reference Property

The High Frequency (HF) Reference property is unique to the I3DL2 standard, and simply provides a setting for what is considered high-frequency sound. The units are in Hz and the range is from 20.0 to 20000.0. The default value is set at 5000.0 Hz. In the EAX standard, the definition of high frequency is fixed at 5000 Hz.

EAX Flags

There are six flags that can be set for EAX environments, all of which are set to true by default. The first five, if set to true, indicate that a change to the Environment Size property will have a proportional effect on the property identified by the flag, or, if false, that a change in Environment Size will have no effect. The flags are:

EAXLISTENERFLAGS_DECAYTIMESCALE
EAXLISTENERFLAGS_REFLECTIONSSCALE
EAXLISTENERFLAGS_REFLECTIONSDELAYSCALE
EAXLISTENERFLAGS_REVERBSCALE
EAXLISTENERFLAGS_REVERBDELAYSCALE

The final flag helps limit unnaturally long decay times of high-frequency sounds by forcing a limit to the decay time to be calculated from the Air Absorption HF value:

EAXLISTENERFLAGS_DECAYHFLIMIT

EAX Source Buffer

EAX also allows a range of settings to be applied to sound sources. They are less important than listener settings because they only apply to the one sound, rather than all sounds. In our sample we use these settings to apply obstruction and occlusion effects only, but they can be used to add some reverberation settings only for that sound source. The full description of the source and listener settings is available in a document entitled "Environmental Audio Extensions: EAX 2.0," which can be downloaded from *http://developer.creative.com*.

Obstruction Property

The Obstruction property is in the range of -10,000 (-100 dB, indicating that no direct sound gets through) to 0 (0 dB, indicating that all direct sound gets through). The lower this value is below zero, the greater the muffling effect of the obstruction.

Remember that an obstructed sound source is one where the direct path to the listener is blocked, but where there is a clear airway to the listener, so that early and late reflections and reverberations are not affected by the obstruction (see Figure 7.1).

Obstruction LF Ratio Property

The Obstruction LF Ratio property is a ratio that sets how low-frequency sound is attenuated relative to high-frequency sound. If the value is 0.0, there is no attenuation for low-frequency sound (it all gets through). If the value is 1.0 (the maximum), it is attenuated at the same rate as high-frequency sound.

Occlusion Property

The values and ranges for the Occlusion and Occlusion LF Ratio properties have a very similar effect as those for obstruction. A value of -10,000 (-100 dB) for Occlusion indicates full occlusion (no sound gets through), and any value above this indicates that some source sound gets through.

Remember that occlusion occurs when there is no direct airway from the sound source to the listener. An example of occlusion occurs when you are in a room with the doors and windows closed, but can still hear noises from outside (see Figure 7.1).

Occlusion LF Ratio Property

The Occlusion LF Ratio property determines the ratio of how the occlusion muffling of low-frequency sound compares to high-frequency sound. A fully occluded listener (indicated by an occlusion setting of -10,000) will still be able to hear plenty of low-frequency sound if Occlusion LF Ratio is set between 0.0 and 0.5 (0.25 is the default).

Occlusion Room Ratio Property

The Occlusion Room Ratio property applies only to early reflections and late reverberations; it does not apply to the source sound. It applies an additional attenuation factor for these sounds. The value ranges from 0.0 (indicating no additional attenuation) up to 10 (indicating ten times the attenuation). The default value is 0.5.

The characteristics of an occlusion depend on the type of material creating the occlusion; in other words, the material that stands between the sound source and the listener (for example, a metal door, a glass window, a stone wall, or a wooden floor). The eax.h header file includes some presets to give you an idea of the occlusion properties of different materials.

Implementation of EAX Properties

All the EAX 2.0 properties previously described are supported by property sets, and many are implemented both in the Property Values sample described in this chapter, and in the Concertina framework in the following chapter.

With all this theory now out of the way, we'll start by looking at the code for the sample.

The Property Values Project

In order to do any development work on the Property Values sample, you will need to download the EAX 2.0 development package from the Creative Labs Web site: *http://developer.creative.com.*

After you download the EAX 2.0 package, copy the eax.h header into the Property Values project. You can then compile the project. You will also receive the eax.lib library in the download, which you will need to place in an appropriate directory for the linker to find. The PropertyValues.exe program will run if you do not download the EAX 2.0 package. The download is only necessary to examine the eax.h file, and to compile and link the sample after you have made any changes to it.

Other than the eax.h header file, there is one other unique file for the Property Values project, PropertyValues.cpp. In addition, the extended_dsutil.cpp and extended_dsutil.h files also form part of the project.

PropertyValues.cpp

One difference between this project and the other projects in this book is the following definition.

```
#define INITGUID
```

This is necessary to prevent obscure link errors relating to GUIDs. This is because GUID constants are generally used across multiple source files, but each constant can only be initialized once, otherwise it appears in multiple object files and the linker throws up errors. To make this easier to manage, the *DEFINE_GUID* macro is used to declare GUID constants. If *INITGUID* is not defined, *DEFINE_GUID* resolves to the following code.

```
extern const GUID name;
```

However, if *INITGUID* is defined, *DEFINE_GUID* resolves as follows.

```
extern const GUID name = { <guid data> };
```

So if you declare your GUIDs in a header file that might be included multiple times, use the define *INITGUID* statement. One and only one source file must define *INITGUID*, and it should be defined before including any header files.

The global variables that are unique to this project are as follows.

```
LPKSPROPERTYSET         lpPropertySet = NULL; // Property Set Interface.
LPDIRECTSOUND3DBUFFER   lpDS3DBuffer;
int                     g_Environment = -1;   // Environment number.
EAXBUFFERPROPERTIES     EAXBufferProperties;  // Structure to hold
                                              // default values.
Long                    lObstruction = -4000; // Sample obstruction value.
Float                   fObstructionLFRatio = 0.2f;
Long                    lOcclusion = -1500;   // Sample occlusion value.
float                   fOcclusionLFRatio = 0.2f;
```

The *lpPropertySet* value is the most important global variable. It is through a property set interface that you gain access to all the listener and source buffer properties that you want to use. In this sample, we have only one property set pointer (corresponding to our one sound). In a full application, you would need one for every sound buffer that you want to apply the source buffer effects to, and at least one in order to apply the listener environmental effects. Although the listener properties are accessed through a property set for one individual sound buffer, they in fact apply to all sounds.

The DirectSound 3-D pointer (*lpDS3DBuffer*) is needed for an interim stage in gaining access to the property set. The *EAXBufferProperties* structure is used in this sample simply to hold the default values of a source buffer, so we can restore them when obstruction or occlusion is turned off. The four obstruction and occlusion values were chosen to provide the appropriate example effects to the sample.

Most of the code in this sample will be familiar to you from our previous samples, so we will concentrate only on the new requirements of property sets.

The first function to look at is *initDirectSound*. Note the call to *CoInitialize* with a NULL parameter. This call is necessary to initialize COM, which is required for the property sets to work. It is also necessary for DirectSound special effects to work. However, this call is not necessary for 3-D positioning and for the playback of 2-D or 3-D sounds.

The code for the *load3DEAXSound* function should be examined in full.

```
bool load3DEAXSound(char filename[])
{
   HRESULT hr;
   unsigned long bytesReturned;
   DWORD bufferFlags = DSBCAPS_CTRL3D;
   if (g_pSound)
   {
      g_pSound ->Stop();
      SAFE_DELETE( g_pSound  );
   }
   if (SUCCEEDED(g_pSoundManager->Create( &g_pSound ,filename,
              bufferFlags, DS3DALG_HRTF_FULL, 1 )))
   {
      lpDS3DBuffer = g_pSound -> Get3DInterface(0);
      if (lpDS3DBuffer != NULL)
      {
         if(SUCCEEDED(lpDS3DBuffer->QueryInterface(IID_IKsPropertySet,
                                              (void**)&lpPropertySet)))
         {
            // Check for EAX 2.0 support.
            if (SUCCEEDED(hr = lpPropertySet->QuerySupport(
                            DSPROPSETID_EAX20_ListenerProperties,
                            DSPROPERTY_EAXLISTENER_ALLPARAMETERS,
                            &ulSupport)))
            {
               // Record the default buffer properties settings.
               hr = lpPropertySet->Get(DSPROPSETID_EAX_BufferProperties,
                              DSPROPERTY_EAXBUFFER_ALLPARAMETERS,
                              NULL, 0, &EAXBufferProperties,
                              sizeof(EAXBufferProperties),
                              &bytesReturned);
               return true;
            }
         }
      }
   }
   return false;
}
```

In this function, the *bufferFlags* variable is set to *DSBCAPS_CTRL3D*. We set this flag because a 3-D buffer is required in order to retrieve a property set interface.

Next we test to see if the sound already exists. If it does, we first stop it, and then we delete it.

To create the sound buffer, we call the *Create* method of the *CSoundManager* object. The *bufferFlags* parameter of the *Create* method indicates that we need a 3-D buffer. The next step is to retrieve a pointer to that 3-D buffer, using the *get3DInterface* method that we added to the *CSound* class just for this purpose.

Performance Tip

To apply environmental effects to 2-D sounds, set up the buffers for 3-D sounds using the *DSBCAPS_CTRL3D* flag, and then make the following DirectSound SDK call to disable the actual 3-D processing for the buffer.

```
SetMode(DS3DMODE_DISABLE, DS3D_IMMEDIATE);
```

Then comes the critical call to *QueryInterface* to retrieve a property set interface using the *IID_IKsPropertySet GUID*.

Next we check whether the hardware supports EAX 2.0 properties. This is done by using the *QuerySupport* call on the *lpPropertySet* interface pointer. The three arguments are: a GUID that identifies the properties we are looking for, in this case *DSPROPSET-ID_EAX20_ListenerProperties*; an identifier for the properties we want to use, in this case *DSPROPERTY_EAXLISTENER_ALLPARAMETERS*; and the address of a DWORD (or unsigned long) that will contain certain additional flags that can be used beyond the success or failure of the call. Nothing further is tested here; the success of the call gives us enough information.

That is all that is essential in this function. However, for the purposes of the sample we also retrieve the current settings (the default settings in this case) for the source buffer properties. This is done using the *Get* method of a property set object.

Get Method

Notice that the first parameter to the *Get* method is a GUID, *DSPROPSET-ID_EAX_BufferProperties*, which is defined in eax.h. The second parameter is a member of an enumeration, *DSPROPERTY_EAXBUFFER_ALL-PARAMETERS*, also defined in eax.h. The third and fourth parameters should be set to *NULL* and 0 respectively (we do not need these to get and set properties). The fifth parameter is the address of where the *Get* call is to store its findings – in this case an *EAXBUFFERPROPERTIES* structure, also defined in eax.h but declared as global data in the PropertyValues.cpp file. The sixth parameter provides the *Get* call with the size of the object passed to it (in this case a structure, but it is often a float or a long). Finally, we add the address of a DWORD to record the actual amount of data copied to the location provided. We do not use this last parameter in our code, but if you get errors, it may be useful to check that it does equal the buffer size that is passed in.

There are a number of methods of a property set interface, but we are mainly interested in three of them: *Get*, *Set*, and *QuerySupport*. The other three are the ubiquitous COM methods: *QueryInterface*, *AddRef* and *Release*. The *QuerySupport* method is used once in our sample to test for the correct hardware support.

We use another *Get* call in the *showEAXSettings* function to help display all the listener settings in an edit box of the Property Values dialog box. This is provided so you can easily see which listener parameters change with the environment setting.

Finally, in the main callback function *MainDlgProc*, we actually make some *Set* calls.

Starting with the easy example of the 26 radio buttons, clicking any one of these initiates the following code.

```
case IDC_RADIO1:
case IDC_RADIO26:
        g_Environment = LOWORD(wParam) - IDC_RADIO1;
        hr = lpPropertySet ->Set(DSPROPSETID_EAX_ListenerProperties,
                         DSPROPERTY_EAXLISTENER_ENVIRONMENT,
                         NULL,0,&g_Environment,sizeof(int));
        showEAXSettings( hDlg );
    break;
```

The *g_Environment* parameter simply holds an integer value from 0 to 25, indicating which of the 26 preset environments to apply. All that is necessary to set a preset environment is to call *Set* with this integer and the *DSPROPERTY_EAX-LISTENER_ENVIRONMENT* property. Note that the *Set* call uses the identical first six parameters to the *Get* call (see the discussion of the *Get* method earlier in this section).

After selecting an environment by using the radio buttons, the user might press the Play button. This will run the following code.

```
case IDC_PLAY:
    if (g_Environment == -1)
    {
        g_Environment = EAX_ENVIRONMENT_GENERIC;
        hr = lpPropertySet ->Set(DSPROPSETID_EAX_ListenerProperties,
                         DSPROPERTY_EAXLISTENER_ENVIRONMENT,
                         NULL,0,&g_Environment,sizeof(int));
        showEAXSettings( hDlg );
    }
    if(!play3DEAXSoundBuffer(true) )
    {
        EndDialog( hDlg, IDABORT );
    }
    EnablePlayUI( hDlg, FALSE );
    break;
```

This code first sets the preset generic environment if none has yet been set, then calls the *play3DEAXSoundBuffer* function. This function does nothing special; all the work to activate the environment and sound source property sets has already been done.

```
bool play3DEAXSoundBuffer(bool loopit)
{   DWORD   dwFlags;
    if (g_pSound != NULL)
    (
        if (loopit)
            dwFlags = DSBPLAY_LOOPING; else
            dwFlags = 0;
        if (SUCCEEDED(g_pSound ->Play3DBuffer( 0, 0, dwFlags )))
            return true;
    }
    return false;
}
```

Finally, the following code is run when the occlusion check box is selected. This code snippet shows an example of occlusion, although the code is almost identical for obstruction.

```
case IDC_OCCLUSION:
    if ( IsDlgButtonChecked( hDlg, IDC_OCCLUSION )   == BST_CHECKED )
    {
        hr = lpPropertySet->Set(DSPROPSETID_EAX_BufferProperties,
                            DSPROPERTY_EAXBUFFER_OCCLUSION,
                            NULL, 0, &lOcclusion, sizeof(long));
        hr = lpPropertySet->Set(DSPROPSETID_EAX_BufferProperties,
                            DSPROPERTY_EAXBUFFER_OCCLUSIONLFRATIO,
                            NULL, 0, &fOcclusionLFRatio,sizeof(float));
        hr = lpPropertySet->Set(DSPROPSETID_EAX_BufferProperties,
                            DSPROPERTY_EAXBUFFER_OCCLUSIONROOMRATIO,
                            NULL, 0, &fOcclusionLFRatio, sizeof(float));
    } else
    {
        hr = lpPropertySet->Set(DSPROPSETID_EAX_BufferProperties,
                            DSPROPERTY_EAXBUFFER_OCCLUSION,
                            NULL, 0, &EAXBufferProperties.lOcclusion,
                            sizeof(long));
        hr = lpPropertySet->Set(DSPROPSETID_EAX_BufferProperties,
                            DSPROPERTY_EAXBUFFER_OCCLUSIONLFRATIO,
                            NULL, 0,
                            &EAXBufferProperties.flOcclusionLFRatio,
                            sizeof(float));
        hr = lpPropertySet->Set(DSPROPSETID_EAX_BufferProperties,
                            DSPROPERTY_EAXBUFFER_OCCLUSIONROOMRATIO,
                            NULL, 0,
                            &EAXBufferProperties.flOcclusionLFRatio,
                            sizeof(float));
    }
    break;
```

The first block of code is run if the Occlusion check box is selected. Notice that there are three *Set* calls, setting the three source buffer properties:

DSPROPERTY_EAXBUFFER_OCCLUSION

DSPROPERTY_EAXBUFFER_OCCLUSIONLFRATIO

DSPROPERTY_EAXBUFFER_OCCLUSIONROOMRATIO

These properties are set to the global values that we defined at the top of the source file. For simplicity, we set the low-frequency ratio and room ratio to be identical.

The second block of code is run if the Occlusion check box is cleared. In this case, the three properties are set back to their defaults – remember that the *load3DEAXSound* function stored a copy of all the source buffer settings in an *EAXBufferProperties* structure, precisely for this purpose. When coding your application, you might also want to get the default listener properties and store them in a similar structure.

We have not shown how to set individual environment properties in this sample, only the environment presets. However, the procedure for setting individual environment properties is very similar to the setting of individual properties on the source buffer, as shown earlier for occlusion and obstruction.

Resources

To download the header files, libraries, and documentation for EAX 2.0, go to:

http://eax.creative.com/developers/

The I3DL2 standard was created by the Interactive Audio Special Interest Group (IA-SIG). For more information go to:

http://www.iasig.org/wg/closed/3dwg/3dl2v1a.pdf

To utilize the SDK for 3-D audio by Sensaura, which offers some property set-based features in addition to EAX 2.0, go to:

http://www.sensauradeveloper.com/

Creative Labs and Sensaura are not the only companies to provide property-set access to their hardware. NVidea, C-Media, Yamaha, Philips, Crystal Semiconductors, and no doubt others have also enabled property sets covering EAX, I3DL2 or other voice-management functions for their sound cards.

Summary

In this chapter, we described a sample that demonstrates the EAX 2.0 environmental sound settings. The sample demonstrated how to use a property set interface to set one of the predefined environments, and individual settings for obstruction and occlusion. Driving the hardware directly with property sets can create convincing atmosphere and sound effects with very little performance cost.

Coding property sets is fairly easy and, given the high-quality results, is the recommended way to get great environmental sound effects.

8

Building an Application with the Concertina Framework

The Concertina framework is a header file that combines the functionality of the audio samples that you have seen, and presents it all in an SDK format. So if you accept the design decisions that we have made in designing this framework, you need do no more than include the headers and sources in your project, amend the tables of wave files to match those that you require, and you're ready to go. Of course, you will probably want to tailor the code to suit your particular application, but as a framework that wraps all the complexity of DirectSound and presents the programmer with a powerful, flexible, and obvious set of calls, it's not bad.

The purpose of the Concertina framework is to provide the kind of layer that simply involves calls to methods whose names and functions match the movement of objects around a 3-D world, or the playing of background music or ambient sounds.

The Concertina.exe program is a small sample showing how to call into the framework (see Figure 8.1). It only has Play Game, Stop Game and Exit buttons, with text telling you what is going on in our mock 3-D world. Run this program now, which is located in the AVBook\bin directory.

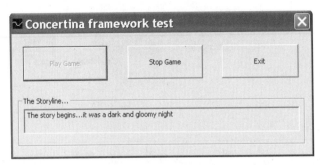

Figure 8.1   Concertina framework test dialog box.

This chapter describes the design philosophy behind the framework, how to initialize it for your own project, and finally, all the methods that it implements.

Design Philosophy

The main assumption in the design is that you have created a 3-D world, with objects moving around within that world. These objects make a variety of noises: there are environmental effects, there is atmospheric music, and there are some ambient and random sounds. With this scenario, you do not know exactly how many times any one sound will need to be played, and in particular, how many buffers of the same sound that might need to be played at once.

For this reason, the Concertina framework operates using a table of best guesses at how many buffers you need for each sound, but includes an overflow set of buffers that can be used when your guess is wrong. It also prints out a report at the end of the program letting you know the actual requirement for sound buffers. The idea is that you can improve your best guesses with the testing of your game, but that you need never get it exactly right as the overflow area will take care of most of the excesses as they occur.

Another design decision is that there are a small number of streaming buffers to handle the music that may be required. We have not enabled applying 3-D or special effects processing to the streaming buffers, although you could amend the code to do this.

Of course another design decision is that you want the full range of 3-D and special effects that have been demonstrated in the Cacophony, Rumpus and Circular Streams samples.

To include the Concertina framework in your own project, go through the following steps.

Step 1

Perhaps a good way to start is to copy all the files of the Concertina project to a new Visual Studio project, get the same code as the Concertina.exe working to test the process, and then delete the contents of Concertina.cpp and replace it with code for your own game.

Alternatively, set up a Visual Studio project, and include the following headers and source files: Concertina.h, extended_dsutil.h, and extended_dsutil.cpp. You will also need any of the headers that these files reference, such as dxutil.h. Remember that the samples assume that the extended_dsutil source and header are in the AVBook\Common directory, so you may need to adjust the include statements, depending on how you set up your project.

Step 2

Next go into the Concertina.h file, locate the *bestGuessAudio* structure and replace the wave file names and associated settings with your own. For example, if your game is a simulation of four-wheel-drive vehicles, and you have wave files for engine sounds, squeaky wheels, gear changes, exploding engines, collisions, and breaking glass, along with ambient rain and thunder sounds, then your *soundIDenum* enumeration and *bestGuessAudio* structure might look like the following code.

```
enum soundIDenum{
    ID_engine = 0,
    ID_squeakyWheel,
    ID_gearChange,
    ID_explodingEngine,
    ID_collision,
    ID_breakingGlass,
    ID_rain,
    ID_thunder,
    // Terminate this enumeration with these values.
    ID_end,
    eNUM_fixedSounds = ID_end,
    eNUM_allSounds = ID_end + Max_overflow_buffers
};

struct bestGuessAudioStruct bestGuessAudio[] = {
// ID file name 3-D Buffers (min 1, max 16).
    {   ID_engine,              "engine.wav",           1,   4   },
    {   ID_squeakyWheel,        "squeaky wheel.wav",    1,   16  },
    {   ID_gearChange,          "gear change.wav",      1,   4   },
    {   ID_explodingEngine,     "exploding engine.wav", 1,   1   },
    {   ID_collision,           "collision.wav",        1,   1   },
```

(continued)

```
{   ID_breakingGlass,      "breaking glass.wav",   1,   1   },
{   ID_rain,               "rain.wav",             0,   1   },
{   ID_thunder,            "thunder.wav",          0,   1   },
// Must have ID_end to terminate table.
{   ID_end,                "end"   }
};
```

When you have completed this table, make sure that the order of the members of *soundIDenum* matches their order in the *bestGuessAudio* structure.

Performance Tip

Always create the sound buffers that are used most often, or are of greatest importance, first. This is because if you are using hardware acceleration, with each buffer you are consuming hardware resources, and eventually these resources will run out. If you do run out of resources, but buffers requiring hardware acceleration are continually requested, DirectSound will try to make a best guess, based on such things as distance from the listener, the time that a sound has been playing, and other criteria, to juggle the hardware resources available.

Note that the IDs are given names that match the wave files, but only to make it easy to understand, because there is no need here for an exact copy. The number that follows the wave file name is a flag set to either 1 (for sounds requiring 3-D effects), or 0 (for ambient sounds), and the last number is a best guess at the number of buffers required for each sound. The values that we entered in the previous code represent a game where up to four four-wheel-drive vehicles can be active at any one moment.

Notice that there is only one exploding engine sound. If you want to have more (for example, you want two engines exploding so close in time to each other that both cannot share the same buffer), then the overflow area should easily accommodate the second buffer. However, for engine sounds, you might be able to hear all four at once, and so should declare four buffers to make sure that all can be played simultaneously.

It is perfectly alright for you to enter zero for the number of buffers required. This means that the sound will only be played in the overflow area, and no buffers will be reserved for it. This is more efficient if you know that the sound will be rarely played.

Note that the *bestGuessAudio* structure assumes the wave files are all in the AVBook/Audio directory. If they are in a sub-directory of Audio, then that directory name should be added to the previous code, for example, if the sub-directory was called FWD, then enter all the wave file names preceded by "FWD//".

Step 3

Amend the table of streaming sounds to exactly what you want. Say you have four music tracks, stored in a Music sub-directory of your Audio directory, that capture the sound of individual instruments, then you would set up the *streamingIDenum* and *streamingAudio* structure as follows.

```
enum streamingIDenum{
    ID_bass = 0,
    ID_perc,
    ID_drums,
    ID_sax,
// Terminate this enumeration with these values.
    eNUM_streams,
    dud_stream = -1,
};
struct streamingStruct StreamingAudio[] = {
    { ID_bass,  "Music\\PT2-Bass.wav" },
    { ID_perc,  "Music\\PT2-Perc.wav" },
    { ID_drums, "Music\\PT2-Drums.wav" },
    { ID_sax,   "Music\\PT2-Sax.wav" },
// Terminate the structure with this entry.
    { eNUM_streams, "end"}
};
```

Step 4

Now you need to come up with the special effects settings that you will apply to the sounds throughout the game. The concept of the design here is to make it simple to attach special effects to a sound buffer. As with the other initialization procedures, you need to prepare an enumeration and a structure, which in this case are called *SFXID* and *presetSpecialEffect*, respectively. The enumeration provides IDs that call up any one of the effects, and the structure has a string format making it easy to enter values.

```
enum SFXID{
    SFXID_environment1 = 0,
    SFXID_environment2,
    SFXID_chorus1,
    SFXID_chorus2,
    SFXID_compressor1,
    SFXID_distortion1,
    SFXID_echo1,
    SFXID_flanger1,
    SFXID_gargle1,
    SFXID_parameq1,
```

(continued)

```
    SFXID_parameq2,
    SFXID_reverb1,
// Terminate the enumeration with this value.
    SFXID_end
};
```

You can define as many special effects of one type that you want. The definition is provided in a *genericSoundEffectStruct* structure. Refer to this structure in the Concertina.h file, and use the following entry for an echo effect as an example.

```
//                          wetdry feedback leftdelay rightdelay pan
{   SFXID_echo1,   eSFX_echo,   "50.0f   50.0f   500.0f   500.0f   0"},
```

Note that the first entry is the ID from the *SFXID* enumeration, and the second is the type of effect from the *ESFXType* enumeration that we used extensively with the Rumpus 3D SFX tool (defined in the extended_dsutil.h file and described in Chapter 4). We have these two values because you may want to define a range of echo effects (*SFXID_echo1* to *SFXID_echo10*, for example), but each will have an identical *type* with a different *ID*.

The main use of the structure is in the easy entry of values in the form of a string. All floating point values should be entered with an ending *f*, and all integers entered just as they appear. This makes it easy to scan the string and enter the values. The purpose of this string is ease-of-use; you can enter as many effects as you like into the structure and enumeration by copying the format of the strings that are already provided.

The goal is pain-free special-effect attachment. You are not limited to using the special effects as defined, but the methods provided in the framework make it very easy to attach one of these predefined effects to a buffer.

Hopefully, you have used the Rumpus tool, and referred to the chapters on special effects settings to create precisely the settings that you prefer.

One limitation of our implementation is that each sound buffer can only have one of each type of effect applied. If this turns out to be a problem, as it would be if you want to attach two echo effects, or three parametric equalizers, to one sound buffer, then you will have to adapt the code. Step 11 describes the methods used to attach special effects to a buffer, and discusses how to use effects that are not defined in the preset table.

Step 5

For now, leave the Concertina.h file alone and declare the *Concertina* object in your own program.

```
CConcertina    Concertina;    // Create one Concertina object.
```

Now place the *initConcertina* and *endConcertina* calls into your own game's initialization and termination functions.

```
bool initConcertina(HWND hDlg);
```

The only input parameter is the Windows handle. The *initConcertina* method basically takes the tables you have previously filled out, and creates a suitable sound environment.

```
void endConcertina(bool fPrintReport = false);
```

This method cleans up everything. Set the optional parameter to true for a printed report, which will be sent to the file Concertina Log.txt in the current directory (see Step 12).

Step 6

Because the first sounds that you may want to play are the title music tracks, let's start with the methods that you have at your disposal.

```
bool PlayStreamingBuffers(int nBuffers, streamingIDenum sN0,
                          streamingIDenum sN1 = dud_stream,
                          streamingIDenum sN2 = dud_stream,
                          streamingIDenum sN3 = dud_stream,
                          streamingIDenum sN4 = dud_stream );
```

This method will start between one and five streaming tracks in sync (more or less). The *PlayStreamingBuffers* method could easily be extended to play more than five sounds. Note the use of the *dud_stream* enumeration member as a default. The call to play just one track is as follows.

```
PlayStreamingBuffers(1,ID_drums);
```

Or to play four of the tracks, use the following.

```
PlayStreamingBuffers(4,ID_bass,ID_perc,ID_drums,ID_sax);
```

These IDs can be listed in any order. If you want to vary the volume of the music, use the following function.

```
bool SetStreamingBuffersVolume(float distanceRatio, int nBuffers,
                               streamingIDenum sN0,
                               streamingIDenum sN1 = dud_stream,
                               streamingIDenum sN2 = dud_stream,
                               streamingIDenum sN3 = dud_stream,
                               streamingIDenum sN4 = dud_stream );
```

The following statement sets the volume for the drums track to sound as if it were two and a half times the distance that the audio recorder was when it recorded the sound.

```
SetStreamingBuffersVolume(2.5f,1,ID_drums);
```

To fade music in and out, this method can be called repeatedly from your timer function.

The method to stop streaming tracks follows the same syntax design.

```
bool StopStreamingBuffers(int nBuffers, streamingIDenum sN0,
                    streamingIDenum sN1 = dud_stream,
                    streamingIDenum sN2 = dud_stream,
                    streamingIDenum sN3 = dud_stream,
                    streamingIDenum sN4 = dud_stream );
```

You can stop any of the tracks without any hindrance to the others, using the following code.

```
StopStreamingBuffers(2,ID_drums,ID_sax);
```

Step 7

Now things get a bit more complicated. You will want to attach sound buffers to the objects in your game world, and to do this you need to call the *getSoundID* method. However, first you need to become familiar with *soundBufferRef*, which is a fairly simple structure.

```
struct soundBufferRef {
    WORD iSound;  // Sound index.
    BYTE iBuffer; // Buffer index.
};
```

Each object in your game that you want to attach a sound to must have a *soundBufferRef* structure. You do not do anything with the values within the structure, because the Concertina framework will fill it in with a call to *getSoundID*, and then use it in most of the other playing methods.

For example, if you were writing a tank simulation, and had a class containing all the methods and data for a tank, you could add the following array into that class.

```
soundBufferRef  soundReference[eNUM_tanksounds];
```

Where *eNUM_tanksounds* comes from an enumeration like the following.

```
Enum tankSounds {
    Engine_sound = 0,
    Tracks_sound,
    Turrent_rotating_sound,
    Main_gun_firing_sound,
    Machine_gun_firing_sound,
    Squeaky_tracks_sound,
    eNUM_tanksounds
};
```

Also, you must have set up the *bestGuessAudio* structure and its associated enumerations with appropriate tank noises.

Then, to fill in the *soundReference* array, add the following loop.

```
For (int sound=0; sound< eNUM_tanksounds; sound++)
{
   if (getSoundID(sound,&soundReference[sound]) == false)
   {
      // Handle the failure condition here if necessary, but do nothing yet.
      // Failure to play will be recorded in the Rejections which
      // you can view later.
   }
}
```

The *soundBufferRef* structure is the only one you need from the Concertina.h source file in your own code.

The actual syntax of *getSoundID* is as follows.

```
bool getSoundID(soundIDenum ID,soundBufferRef* sID);
```

Note that it takes a sound ID (such as *ID_prop1* or *ID_rain*) as its first parameter, although it might be more efficient to use an integer for this parameter and get the sound IDs in a loop (as in the previous tank example).

The purpose of getting a sound ID is that you can then be sure that your sound will play, as a buffer has been secured for it. This would obviously be important in the tank in which the game player is riding, as you would want to be sure they could hear the sounds of their own tank. However, it may be less critical if a tank somewhere else on the battlefield was unable to secure a sound ID, and you may not know when writing the game exactly how many tanks you will have on the battlefield at once.

For this reason, secure the sound IDs for the most important objects first.

```
bool clearSoundBuffer(soundBufferRef* sID);
```

This is used to return the sound buffer to the pool, so it (and obviously its associated buffers) can be used later in the program. For example, this would happen if a tank was destroyed, or left the battlefield for any other reason.

Call the *clearSoundBuffer* function whenever you are sure that the object will not need to make that noise again.

Finally, there are two housekeeping commands, one to stop a sound buffer from playing, and the other to stop all sounds from playing.

```
bool stopSoundBuffer(soundBufferRef* sID);
void stopAllSounds();
```

Step 8

It is simple to play ambient sounds. The only essential new method needed is the following.

```
bool playAmbientSound(soundBufferRef* sID, bool fLooping, int percentVolume,
                bool fFreeOnCompletion = false);
```

So the complete code needed to play background rain is the following.

```
soundBufferRef sIDRain;
if (Concertina.getSoundID(ID_rain,&sIDRain))
    Concertina.playAmbientSound(&sIDRain,true,100);
```

The first statement declares the *soundBufferRef* structure, the second fills in that structure, and the third plays it looping at 100 percent of its recorded volume.

Note the optional *fFreeOnCompletion* flag at the end of the *playAmbientSound* call. If you leave this at false, then the sound buffer will be attached until the end of the program, or a call to *clearSoundBuffer*, whichever comes sooner. However, if you set it to true, then the sound buffer will be returned to the pool as soon as the sound stops playing. As most ambient sounds are looping, this will occur when you make a specific call to stop the sound.

It is also possible to change the volume of any sound, ambient or 3-D, using the following method.

```
bool setBufferVolume(soundBufferRef* sID, float distanceRatio);
```

The *distanceRatio* is the relative distance of the listener from the sound source, compared with the distance of the audio recorder from the sound source when the wave file was recorded. So a value of 1.0 will give the maximum volume, values less than 1.0 are not allowed, and a value of 3.0 will give a volume that sounds as if the object is three times further away than when the wave file was recorded.

When a sound buffer is playing, this call can be made repeatedly to gradually (or dramatically) increase or decrease the volume.

Step 9

To play 3-D sounds, the first thing that you may want to do is place the 3-D listener. The listener object has been created by the call to *initConcertina*, and all you have to do is provide the 3-D vectors containing their position, velocity and orientation.

The syntax for the call to set listener properties is shown.

```
void Set3DListenerProperties(D3DVECTOR* pvPosition,
    D3DVECTOR* pvVelocity,
    D3DVECTOR* pvOrient,
    bool fInitialize = false,
```

```
float Doppler = 1.0f,
float distance = 1.0f,
float rolloff = 1.0f);
```

The first call to this function enables the Doppler factor, distance factor and rolloff factor to be changed from their defaults. For more details, see Chapter 3.

You could embed the following three structures in a listener class of your own.

```
D3DVECTOR vListenerPosition;
D3DVECTOR vListenerVelocity;
D3DVECTOR vListenerOrient;
```

These should be initialized with appropriate real-world coordinates (see the Concertina.cpp file for an example), and if we wanted to exaggerate the Doppler effect, the first call to *Set3DListenerProperties* should be the following.

```
Concertina.Set3DListenerProperties(&vListenerPosition,&vListenerVelocity,
          &vListenerOrient,true,2.0f);
```

Note that the *fInitialize* flag is set to true, and the 2.0f value will double the Doppler effect; however, the defaults for distance factor and rolloff factor are not changed. All future calls to change the listener's position can drop any reference to the flag, as its default is to be set to false.

You would have a similar set of vectors for all your moving objects in the game, and initialize those properties with a call to *Set3DSoundProperties*.

```
bool Set3DSoundProperties(soundBufferRef* sID,
    D3DVECTOR* pvPosition,
    D3DVECTOR* pvVelocity,
    D3DVECTOR* pvCone,
    bool fChangeCone = false,
    int maxVradius = 1.0f,
    int insideCone = 360,
    int outsideCone = 360,
    int outsideVolume = 100);
```

For example, for a snowmobile class, that class might have the following three data members.

```
D3DVECTOR vSnowPosition;
D3DVECTOR vSnowVelocity;
D3DVECTOR vSnowOrientation;
```

The orientation vector is the orientation of the sound cone, so if you wanted a rear-facing cone, then this vector would be the opposite vector to the velocity. We are assuming that the sound cone is unlikely to change very often, so the *fChangeCone* flag should be set to true if you need to change the volume radius or the sound cone angles.

Set up the 3-D properties before calling *play3DSoundBuffer*, and then again at any time after that to change them.

```
bool play3DSoundBuffer(soundBufferRef* sID, bool loopit = false,
                       bool fFreeOnCompletion = false);
```

This method obviously sets off a 3-D sound, taking the address of the *soundBuffer-Ref* structure, and optional looping and free-on-completion flags.

To create the sound of a running engine, set the looping flag to true and the *fFreeOnCompletion* flag to false. However, for a breaking glass sound, the reverse is probably true, since you don't want it to loop but you do want the buffer to become free after it has played. For example, say we have a snowmobile with a *soundBufferRef* structure for its engine and another for wind noise.

```
// Place the snowmobile engine and wind noise correctly.
Set3DSoundProperties(&sIDengine, vSnowPosition, vSnowVelocity,
                     vSnowOrientation);
Set3DSoundProperties(&sIDwindNoise, vSnowPosition, vSnowVelocity,
                     vSnowOrientation);
// Start playing the sounds.
play3DSoundBuffer(&sIDengine,true);
play3DSoundBuffer(&sIDwindNoise,true);
// Add the sound of the snowmobile colliding with a tree.
play3DSoundBuffer(&sIDcollision,false,true);
// Stop the snowmobile's engine.
stopSoundBuffer(&sIDengine);
```

You would obviously want to add code to change the frequency or volume of the engine and wind noise, depending on factors like the snowmobile's speed and exposure to the wind. This could be done by frequency and volume changes, or by adding special effects. The previous example shows that while many 3-D sounds loop, some do not (like the collision) so the *fFreeOnCompletion* flag should usually be set to true in the case of occasional non-looping sounds. Unless, of course, you plan to have a lot of collisions, and don't want to risk losing the sound buffer to another snowmobile driver.

The call to change volume is the same as for ambient sounds (see the *setBufferVolume* method in Step 8). To change frequency, use the following method.

```
bool set3DBufferFrequency(soundBufferRef* sID, DWORD dwFrequency);
```

Most frequency changes are likely to be multiplications or divisions of the recorded frequency, so you will need to get and store the recorded frequency before making any calls to change it, using the following call.

```
DWORD getSoundFrequency(soundBufferRef* sID);
```

For example, use the following to increase the frequency of a snowmobile engine sound referenced by *snowID*.

```
DWORD snowFrequency = getSoundFrequency(&snowID);
Set3DBufferFrequency(&snowed, snowFrequency * 1.5f);
```

Note that the *getSoundFrequency* method always returns the original recorded frequency, not the frequency to which it may have been subsequently changed. It is possible to set different frequencies on different buffers containing the same sound.

Before any changes to 3-D sounds will take effect, you must call the following method.

```
void commitAllSettings();
```

Typically, this call would be at the end of your timing function. For an example, see the *OnTimer* function in the Concertina.cpp file.

Performance Tip

If a sound no longer requires 3-D processing, it is a good idea to turn off this processing. An example might be where a player in an adventure game picks up an object emitting a sound. The object is then no longer moving in relation to the listener, and the listener is within the minimum distance for the sound produced by that object. To turn off 3-D processing, use the DirectSound *SetMode* method for a sound buffer, with the *DS3DMODE_DISABLE* flag as its first parameter. You may want to add a method to the Concertina framework that does this.

Step 10

There is one call needed to add randomly generated sounds to your game. These random sounds are attached to other sounds with the following call.

```
bool addRandomSound(soundIDenum ID_random, soundBufferRef* sIDMain, bool f3D,
                 int playsPer100Seconds);
```

A good example is adding random thunder to the ambient sound of rain. Remember that in Step 8, the following code started the rain.

```
soundBufferRef sIDRain;
if (Concertina.getSoundID(ID_rain,&sIDRain))
    Concertina.playAmbientSound(&sIDRain,true,100);
```

Then, to add a clap of thunder, occurring on average five times per 100 seconds of rain time, use the following call.

```
Concertina.addRandomSound(ID_thunder,&sIDRain,false,5);
```

The first parameter identifies the random sound that we want, the second the ID of the sound to attach it to, the third should be true if we want a 3-D sound, and the last is the number of times per 100 seconds that it should be played.

There is no need to call *getSoundID* for a random sound; once you have made this one call, the framework takes care of the buffer references for you. However you must call *commitAllSettings* for your random sounds to take effect (see Step 9), as this is the call that actually fires off the random sounds. If you have one or more random sounds, call *commitAllSettings*, even if you have no 3-D sounds.

Stopping the main sound will automatically stop any random sounds that are attached to it.

If, on analysis of the printed log at the end of the game, you find that random sounds are being rejected too often, increase their maximum number by increasing the value for *Max_random_sounds* in Concertina.h.

Step 11

Playing a special effect on a sound buffer is a two-stage process. First, the effect is attached to the sound, and then that effect is activated. The theory is that you may want to attach a number of effects to a sound, but only turn on certain ones for a particular rendition of that sound buffer.

You can use two different options to attach a special effect, using one overloaded method.

```
bool attachSpecialEffect (soundBufferRef* sID, SFXID fxID);
bool attachSpecialEffect (soundBufferRef* sID, ESFXType type,
                          char paramString[]);
```

The first option is simple; enter the ID of the sound buffer and the ID of the preset special effect. For example, the following two lines of code attach a preset distortion and flanger effect to an engine sound identified by *sIDEngine*.

```
Concertina.attachSpecialEffect(&sIDEngine,SFXID_distortion1);
Concertina.attachSpecialEffect(&sIDEngine,SFXID_flanger1);
```

Here is an alternative method of attaching a special effect, using distortion as an example.

```
Concertina.attachSpecialEffect(&sIDEngine, eSFX_distortion,
            "0.0f  15.0f  2400.0f   2400.0f   7350.0f");
```

In this case, we identify that it is a distortion effect by the *eSFX_distortion* enumeration member, and then enter a string of text matching the required parameters for this effect. It might be helpful to add a comment preceding a line of code like this, identifying each entry.

```
Concertina.attachSpecialEffect(&sIDEngine, eSFX_distortion,
//            gain  edge   frequency  bandwidth  cutoff
            "0.0f  15.0f  2400.0f    2400.0f    7350.0f");
```

You can attach one of each special effect type to any one sound buffer. You can play a sound buffer with any number of these types activated. To activate a range of special effects, call the following method.

```
bool activateSpecialEffects(soundBufferRef* sID, ESFXType e1,
                            ESFXType e2 = eSFX_dud,
                            ESFXType e3 = eSFX_dud,
                            ESFXType e4 = eSFX_dud,
                            ESFXType e5 = eSFX_dud);
```

This method will allow you to activate up to five special effects. You could redefine it with more parameters if there are cases where more than five need to be activated for one playing (or simply call this method twice).

To call this method to activate a distortion effect, use the following code.

```
Concertina.activateSpecialEffects(&sIDEngine,eSFX_distortion);
```

Or, use the following to activate an echo and a flanger effect.

```
Concertina.activateSpecialEffects(&sIDEngine,eSFX_echo,eSFX_flanger);
```

The call to *activateSpecialEffects* must be made before the sound buffer starts playing. Typically, you would keep the two lines of code together.

```
Concertina.activateSpecialEffects(&sIDEngine eSFX_distortion);
Concertina.play3DSoundBuffer(&sIDEngine true);
```

To summarize, the process of adding special effects has been reduced to three steps by the Concertina framework, defining the special effect parameters in the form of an enumeration and text string, attaching one or more effects to a sound, and then activating some or all of the attached special effects before playing that sound.

Step 12

If you want your program to support EAX 2.0 environmental settings, set the following global definition at the beginning of your source code, before the Concertina.h header is included (see this code at the beginning of the Concertina.cpp file).

```
#define EAX   1
```

If you do not wish to support EAX, then comment this line out (or delete it altogether).

If you set the EAX define to 1, then the header file eax.h is included by Concertina.h, and a range of methods becomes available to you to drive the EAX hardware, if the user has it available (see Chapter 7 on using property sets and EAX 2.0 extensions). The initialization of property set interfaces is not dependent on either EAX hardware or the inclusion of the header, so this is always completed by the initialization process. These property set interfaces could, of course, be used for implementations other than EAX, if you were to add the methods to the *Concertina* class. We have implemented EAX as the one that you will probably most want to include in your application.

The first method simply sets one of the preset EAX 2.0 environments.

```
bool SetEAXPresetEnvironment(int envNumber);
```

For example, to set the Psychotic environmental reverb on all sounds in your game, use this simple call.

```
SetEAXPresetEnvironment(PSEAX_ENVIRONMENT_PSYCHOTIC);
```

If you want to define some of your own EAX environments, add them to the following enumeration and structure in Concertina.h.

```
enum EAX_ENVIRONMENT_ID {
    EAXID_submarine,
    EAXID_canyon,
// Terminate the enumeration with this value.
    EAXID_end
};
struct eaxEnvironmentStruct eaxEnvironment[] = {
{
    EAXID_submarine, {-1000, -1000, 0.0f, 2.8f, 0.1f, 429, 0.0f, 1023, 0.0f,
                    EAX_ENVIRONMENT_SEWERPIPE, 1.7f, 0.8f, -5.0f, 63},
    EAXID_canyon, {-1000, -698, 0.0f, 7.2f,0.3f,-1166, 0.0f, 16, 0.0f,
                    EAX_ENVIRONMENT_AUDITORIUM, 36.2f, 1.0f, -5.0f, 63},
// Terminate this structure with the end value.
EAXID_end
};
```

Note that in this case, unlike the string used to provide settings for the special effects, we are filling in an *EAXLISTENERPROPERTIES* structure. (For example, the values listed for the submarine are in the correct order for the *EAXLISTENERPROPERTIES* structure). There are code comments in Concertina.h that make this easier. This way, you can add as many of your own environments as you want, and then the call to set these environments is very simple.

```
bool SetEAXAllListenerProperties(EAX_ENVIRONMENT_ID eax_ID);
```

Here is an example.

```
SetEAXALLListenerProperties(EAXID_canyon);
```

If you wish to change just a few of the properties of EAX listener, there are two methods that you can use. The first method sets new flags.

```
bool SetEAXListenerFlags(DWORD newFlags);
```

To turn off all flags except *EAXLISTENERFLAGS_DECAYHFLIMIT*, which limits high-frequency decay time according to air absorption, make the following call.

```
SetEAXListenerFlags(EAXLISTENERFLAGS_DECAYHFLIMIT);
```

The second method allows you to set from one to seven of the properties of the EAX listener at once. Note that to enter long properties, the value should be entered as a float.

```
void SetEAXListenerProperties(DSPROPERTY_EAX_LISTENERPROPERTY p0, float v0,
    DSPROPERTY_EAX_LISTENERPROPERTY p1 = DSPROPERTY_EAXLISTENER_NONE,
            float v1 = 0.0f,
    DSPROPERTY_EAX_LISTENERPROPERTY p2 = DSPROPERTY_EAXLISTENER_NONE,
            float v2 = 0.0f,
    DSPROPERTY_EAX_LISTENERPROPERTY p3 = DSPROPERTY_EAXLISTENER_NONE,
            float v3 = 0.0f,
    DSPROPERTY_EAX_LISTENERPROPERTY p4 = DSPROPERTY_EAXLISTENER_NONE,
            float v4 = 0.0f,
    DSPROPERTY_EAX_LISTENERPROPERTY p5 = DSPROPERTY_EAXLISTENER_NONE,
            float v5 = 0.0f,
    DSPROPERTY_EAX_LISTENERPROPERTY p6 = DSPROPERTY_EAXLISTENER_NONE,
            float v6 = 0.0f,
    DSPROPERTY_EAX_LISTENERPROPERTY p7 = DSPROPERTY_EAXLISTENER_NONE,
            float v7 = 0.0f);
```

A typical call to this method would set a range of the listener properties.

```
SetEAXListenerProperties(DSPROPERTY_EAXLISTENER_ENVIRONMENTSIZE, 50.0f,
    DSPROPERTY_EAXLISTENER_ENVIRONMENTDIFFUSION, 0.9f,
    DSPROPERTY_EAXLISTENER_AIRABSORPTIONHF, -10.0f);
```

There is nothing magic about having a maximum of seven properties; you could extend this method to take more if necessary. Or if you required, say, nine properties to change, simply make two calls, one for seven properties and one for two.

The range of methods for setting source buffer properties is similar, except of course we have to pass in a sound ID, as we are only setting the properties for the sound source, and not for all sounds. Again, the following method to change source properties can affect up to seven elements.

```
void SetEAXSourceProperties(soundBufferRef* sID,
    DSPROPERTY_EAX_BUFFERPROPERTY p0, float v0,
    DSPROPERTY_EAX_BUFFERPROPERTY p1 = DSPROPERTY_EAXBUFFER_NONE,
            float v1 = 0.0f,
```

(continued)

```
DSPROPERTY_EAX_BUFFERPROPERTY p2 = DSPROPERTY_EAXBUFFER_NONE,
            float v2 = 0.0f,
DSPROPERTY_EAX_BUFFERPROPERTY p3 = DSPROPERTY_EAXBUFFER_NONE,
            float v3 = 0.0f,
DSPROPERTY_EAX_BUFFERPROPERTY p4 = DSPROPERTY_EAXBUFFER_NONE,
            float v4 = 0.0f
);
```

A typical use of this would be to set obstruction or occlusion properties. Assuming that you had a sound ID for an engine, and the vehicle was about to pass behind an obstruction, you could use the following code.

```
SetEAXSourceProperties(&sIDEngine,
    DSPROPERTY_EAXBUFFER_OBSTRUCTION, -2000.0f,
    DSPROPERTY_EAXBUFFER_OBSTRUCTIONLFRATIO, 0.5f);
```

Typically, a call like this would be preceded by a call to reset the source buffer defaults, eliminating any leftover settings from previous obstructions or occlusions. Use the following call to reset the defaults.

```
bool ResetEAXSourceDefault(soundBufferRef* sID);
```

So, to reset our engine source buffer settings, use this call.

```
ResetEAXSourceDefault(&sIDEngine);
```

Finally, there is a call to change the source buffer flags.

```
bool SetEAXSourceFlags(soundBufferRef* sID, DWORD newFlags);
```

This is simply shown here for completeness, as in most cases, you want the flags to remain at their defaults. See Chapter 7 for details on how to obtain the EAX 2.0 documentation.

Step 13

Play the game and examine the report. If you set the *fPrintReport* flag to true in the *end-Concertina* method, it will produce a report in a file called Concertina Log.txt (written to the current directory).

The output of the file will look like the following example from a successful run of Concertina.exe.

```
Concertina Log file
=====================
```

Wave file	Fixed Area	Overflow Area	Rejected
Prop.wav	1	0	0
TurboProp.wav	1	0	0
Rain.wav	1	0	0
Thunder.wav	0	1	0 - overflow area only

This will tell you how often an attempt to get a sound ID for the wave file succeeded from the fixed area, how often the request was sent to the overflow area, and finally, how often an attempt to get the ID failed. Failure can be when all the fixed and overflow buffers are full. You might want to increase or decrease the number of fixed buffers for a wave file, depending on the results. No overflow indicates that you might want to reduce the number of buffers, while some rejected plays along with a high number of normal and overflow plays indicates you might consider increasing the number of fixed buffers. If all plays are rejected, then probably something else is wrong, such as the file could not be found, or was in the wrong format (in these cases an error will follow the entry for that wave file in the log).

The number of fixed buffers is specified in the *bestGuessAudio* structure.

Summary

In this chapter, you saw the features described in the previous chapters wrapped up into one header file and one class that you can include in your own application. The Concertina framework provides an extensive range of methods to support 3-D sounds, streaming sounds, ambient and random sounds, and EAX 2.0 extensions. The framework makes defining new special effects and I3DL2 or EAX environments a simple issue; you just add the list of settings and an enumeration that identifies them.

One of the main features of the framework is a system that allows you to take a best guess at the number of buffers needed for each sound, and then prints out a report at the end of the program that indicates the actual number of buffers utilized. Each 3-D sound is given an ID, and an overflow area is provided to support those cases where more buffers are required than you guessed. This gives the framework a lot of flexibility.

The framework was tested using a contrived story and a very simple dialog, in order to make the story consist almost entirely of audio output. Although your application may not suit the assumptions that we made in creating this sample code, hopefully it should help you put together your own framework.

The Concertina framework is as far as we are going to take the output of sound in this book, although we cover how to optimize the quality of recorded sound in the third section (see Part Three, Production Quality).

We now leave the world of audio to dive into the realms of video rendering and special effects.

Part II

Video

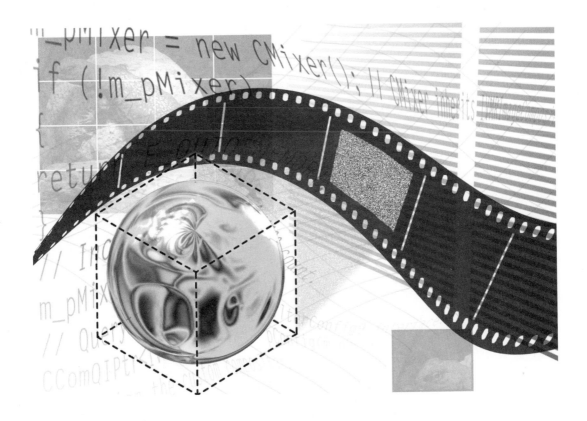

Introducing DirectShow and Video Rendering

In the past few years, truly incredible advances have been made in 3-D graphics. The advances in digital video on the computer have been no less impressive. It was not so long ago that a jerky, thumbnail-sized image represented the state of the art in computer video. Today full-motion, high-resolution video is commonplace, and consumers can watch television, DVDs, and DV video on relatively low-end machines.

In many ways, 3-D graphics and video are complementary technologies. With 3-D graphics, you can create imaginary worlds that never existed, and explore and interact with them. The tricky part is making it look realistic, and that's where the ingenuity of programmers and artists comes in. Video, although it is two-dimensional and is not inherently interactive, captures the real world in all of its complicated and beautiful detail.

Yet, inside the computer, these two technologies have more in common than it might appear. Consider how a 3-D object is rendered. The object begins as a set of points (vertices), which are mathematically transformed into 2-D screen coordinates. The object's surface details — for example, the pattern of bricks on a building — are stored in a bitmap image (a texture), which in effect is "pasted" onto the sides of the object.

Now consider how a video is rendered on a computer screen. A certain area of the screen is designated to display the video. This might be a rectangle inside a window, or the entire screen. In any case, the area is defined by a set of screen coordinates that form a *destination rectangle*. Each video frame is a bitmap that gets stretched to fit the destination rectangle. Starting to sound familiar? These are the very same steps used to draw the 3-D object. Of course, there are important differences. For example, the destination rectangle for video is usually defined in screen coordinates, rather than using transformed 3-D vertices. Also, in video, the bitmap is updated many times a second, whereas most 3-D models use static textures. But the final step when the image gets rendered is the same in both cases.

In fact, for many years DirectX has been the underlying technology used to render video in Windows. Unfortunately, for various historical reasons, it was difficult to combine video seamlessly with 3-D graphics. That changed with DirectX 9.0. Now DirectShow uses the latest Direct3D APIs to render video, and 3-D graphics applications can take full advantage of these capabilities. In this section of this book, you'll learn how to do that. You'll draw 3-D objects on top of video cut scenes, draw video on the sides of 3-D objects, create sliding tile puzzles with full-motion video, and generally push the boundaries of what video can do. Our motto is, "Why be flat?"

In this chapter, we begin with a quick introduction to the DirectShow architecture, which is necessary for understanding the material that follows. However, we won't delve too deeply into the inner workings of DirectShow — there is plenty of SDK documentation that you can read for that. Also in this chapter, we explore some of the powerful video-mixing capabilities that are provided in DirectX 9.0.

In Chapter 10, we put DirectShow to work in a Direct3D sample application. Before you read that section, you should have a basic understanding of Direct3D programming. You should know how to create a Direct3D device; enable lighting and texturing; set the world, view, and projection transforms; and draw 3-D primitives and meshes. If you have worked through the tutorials in the Direct3D SDK, you'll be able to follow this material with no problem.

In Chapter 11, we show how to create some interesting video-mixing effects. For example, we'll show how to create circular regions of transparency in a video image, using alpha maps. Chapter 12 is the "odd and ends" chapter, and includes miscellaneous topics that didn't fit anywhere else.

Our focus in these chapters is video playback. DirectShow is a large SDK, and some of the features that we will *not* cover include video capture, DVD navigation, MPEG-2, and television tuners, among others. If you'd like a more general introduction to everything that DirectShow offers, an excellent place to start is *Programming Microsoft DirectShow for Digital Video and Television,* by Mark Pesce (Microsoft Press).

Video Playback in DirectShow

We start with an overview of the DirectShow archicture. We'll introduce some terminology that we'll be using extensively throughout the next few chapters, then we'll walk through some basic code to play a video file. After that, we'll explore some of the sophisticated video-mixing features that are provided in DirectShow "out of the box." With minimal coding, you can mix and alpha-blend multiple videos, creating fades, zooms, picture-in-picture effects, "fly-in" effects, and so forth. These effects look impressive enough on a 2-D window — embedded in a 3-D environment, they look even better. But that's a subject for Chapter 10.

The Five-Minute Introduction to DirectShow

If you're already familiar with DirectShow programming, you can skip this section. Otherwise, please stick with it! Some of what follows may seem a bit dry and abstract, but it's important for understanding everything that comes later.

DirectShow was designed to process streams of data — typically these are audio and video streams, but the architecture is sufficiently general that a stream can hold any other kind of data, such as text, MIDI, or network packets. In any case, to accomplish a given task, DirectShow divides the task into smaller subtasks. For example, a typical task is "play an AVI file."

This task can be broken down into the following subtasks:

1.   Pull data from the AVI file as a stream of bytes.

2.   Parse the byte stream to extract the audio samples and video frames.

3.   If the audio samples are compressed, send them to an audio decoder. The decoder outputs uncompressed audio.

4.   If the video frames are compressed, send them to a video decoder, which outputs uncompressed video frames.

5.   Send the uncompressed audio to the sound card.

6.   Draw the uncompressed video frames on the screen. This step must be carefully timed to maintain the correct frame rate, and to make sure the video stays in sync with the audio.

For each of these subtasks, DirectShow provides a software component called a *filter*. Filters are COM objects that expose a defined set of interfaces.

To continue our example, the following filters are used in AVI file playback:

■   **Async File Source filter.**   This filter reads data from the file as a stream of bytes, without parsing the data in any way.

■   **AVI Splitter filter.**   This filter reads the AVI file headers and index, and parses the AVI file structure. It pulls data from the Async File Source filter.

■   **Audio decoder filter.**   Numerous audio decoders exist, and the specific filter that must be used depends on the type of audio compression in the file. The audio decoder receives compressed audio samples from the AVI Splitter and outputs uncompressed PCM audio. If the audio in the file is not compressed to begin with, the audio decoder is not needed.

■   **Video decoder filter.**   Again, there are many video decoders, and the specific decoder filter depends on the type of compression used in the file. The video decoder receives compressed video frames from the AVI Splitter and outputs uncompressed video frames.

- **DirectSound Renderer filter.**   This filter sends the uncompressed audio samples to the sound card, using DirectSound.

- **Video renderer filter.**   This filter draws uncompressed video frames onto the screen, using DirectX Graphics. In case DirectX is not available, GDI is available as a fallback. For reasons that will be explained shortly, DirectShow provides several distinct video renderer filters, each with its own feature set.

Figure 9.1 shows how these six DirectShow filters would be assembled by an application to play an AVI file. The entire configuration shown in this diagram is called a *filter graph,* a term that really just means "a collection of filters that work together." (When the context is clear, we'll often shorten the phrase "filter graph" to simply call it a "graph.")

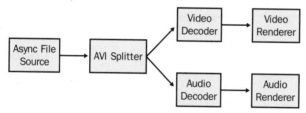

Figure 9.1   DirectShow filter graph for AVI file playback.

As you can see from the diagram, the filters in the graph are connected to each other, and the arrows in the diagram indicate the direction of data flow. For example, by tracing the arrows, you can follow the life cycle of a video frame from unparsed bytes in the file to a rendered image on the screen. Audio samples follow a different route to the sound card. The AVI Splitter has the job of sending the video and audio data down the correct paths.

The points where the filters connect are called *pins.* Pins, which are also COM objects, provide the mechanism for filters to move data through the graph. Each pin has a defined direction, either input or output. The audio and video data always travels from output pin to input pin. At any given time, several buffers of data might be traveling across different pin connections. While the video renderer is drawing a frame on the screen, the decoder may be decoding a new frame, and the AVI splitter may be parsing the file. This helps to ensure that there are no gaps during playback.

One nice feature of the DirectShow architecture is that filters are implemented as separate modules, so they can be used independently of one another. You've already seen that various decoder filters might be used in the AVI playback graph, depending on the compression format. Similarly, to play some other file type, such as ASF or MP3, you can simply substitute a different parser filter in place of the AVI Splitter. Also, because filters use a set of well-defined COM interfaces to communicate with each other, you can write your own custom filters that do specialized processing tasks.

Media Types and Data Flow

We've described how data moves through the filter graph across pin connections. Because filters modify the data that moves through them, the format of the data can change from one filter to the next. We alluded to this earlier when we described how the AVI Splitter takes an unparsed byte stream, and outputs video frames and audio samples. Filters therefore need a way to describe the format of the data at each pin connection. This is done by using a structure called a *media type*. The media type can be used to describe audio formats, video formats, or any other kind of data format.

Filters have a built-in logic that enables them to negotiate the media type for each pin connection. For example, a video decoder has a list of all the uncompressed video formats that it is capable of outputting. Similarly, a video renderer has a list of all the video formats that it can render to the screen. In both filters, the exact list of supported formats may change depending on various factors — such as the incoming data on the decoder or the user's current display setting. When the decoder connects to the video renderer, the two filters are able to select a common format. This process happens automatically when the application connects the filters.

Filters also manage the flow of data through the graph. The application does not have to push each individual video frame or audio sample from one pin to the next. As you'll see, the application simply gives "run" and "stop" commands. Streaming then occurs on worker threads, which are created and managed by the filters. This means an application can block — for example, while waiting for user input — without interrupting playback.

The Filter Graph Manager

Another important object in DirectShow is the Filter Graph Manager. As its name suggests, its role is to mediate between the filters and the application. It assembles the filter graph (with help from the application), sends run and stop commands to the filters, returns event messages to the application, and performs other housekeeping tasks. It is possible to write a DirectShow application that communicates exclusively with the Filter Graph Manager and never deals directly with filters. More often, an application will interact with both layers, sometimes calling methods on the Filter Graph Manager, and sometimes calling methods directly on filters. Figure 9.2 shows these relationships.

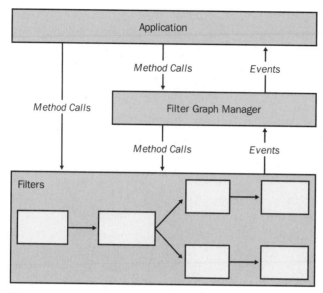

Figure 9.2   Filter Graph Manager.

Using GraphEdit to Explore DirectShow

The quickest way to see DirectShow in action is to play around with the GraphEdit utility. This utility, which is installed as part of the DirectX SDK, gives you a way to visualize what happens inside a DirectShow application. With GraphEdit, you'll get an intuitive feel for filters and filter graphs.

Launch GraphEdit from the Start menu. Under Programs, click Microsoft DirectX 9.0 SDK, then DirectX Utilities, and then GraphEdit. Figure 9.3 shows the GraphEdit window after startup.

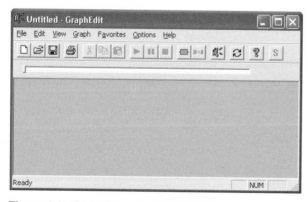

Figure 9.3   DirectShow GraphEdit utility.

To see how GraphEdit works, trying using it to play a video file. From the File menu, click Render Media File. From the Open File dialog box that appears, select an AVI file on your local machine and click Open. At this point, a bunch of rectangles and arrows will appear in the GraphEdit window. The rectangles represent DirectShow filters, and the arrows represent pin connections. Figure 9.4 shows the result if you open Ruby.avi, one of the sample media files provided in the DirectX SDK. If you select a different video file, a different set of filters might be selected.

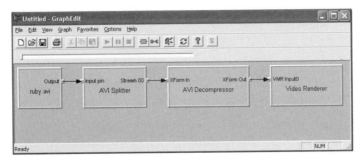

Figure 9.4   AVI file playback in GraphEdit.

Next click the Play button in the toolbar, or click Play from the Graph menu. The video will begin to play inside a pop-up window entitled ActiveMovie Window. You can stop playback by clicking the Stop button, or pause playback by clicking the Pause button. While the video is paused, the most recent frame is displayed in the window. If you pause before starting playback, the first frame in the file is displayed. You can seek by dragging the slider bar.

Now we'll describe the same steps in terms of the DirectShow architecture. When you select Render Media File, GraphEdit calls a DirectShow method that instructs the Filter Graph Manager to build a filter graph for file playback.

In very broad terms, the graph-building process works as follows:

■   The Filter Graph Manager first determines the file format. Based on this information, it selects a source filter and adds it to the filter graph.

■   Next, the Filter Graph Manager goes through a recursive process of adding more filters to the graph. At each step, it queries the most recent filter for a list of possible media types. Then it looks for filters installed on the user's computer that can accept any of those media types as input. (This information is stored in the system registry.) If it finds a match, it adds that filter to the graph and attempts to connect it to the previous filter.

■   This process continues until every stream terminates with a renderer filter.

Once the process completes, the filter graph is ready to begin playback. When you click the Play button in GraphEdit, the Filter Graph Manager sets the graph in motion by sending "run" commands to all the filters. At that point, data begins to stream through the graph and is rendered as audio and video.

Your First DirectShow Application

GraphEdit is particularly useful because its UI commands correspond almost exactly to DirectShow method calls. The following code listing is a complete console application that plays a video file.

```
#include "dshow.h"      // DirectShow header file.
#include "atlbase.h"    // ATL smart pointers.
#pragma comment(lib, "strmiids")    // Link to DirectShow GUIDs.

void main(void)
{
    // Initialize the COM library.
    HRESULT hr = CoInitialize(NULL);
    if (FAILED(hr))
    {
        printf("Could not initialize the COM library.\n");
        return;
    }

    {   // Scope for smart pointers.

        // Create the Filter Graph Manager.
        CComPtr<IGraphBuilder> pGraph;
        hr = pGraph.CoCreateInstance(CLSID_FilterGraph);
        if (FAILED(hr))
        {
            printf("Could not create the Filter Graph Manager.\n");
            return;
        }
        // Query for interfaces.
        CComQIPtr<IMediaControl> pControl(pGraph);
        CComQIPtr<IMediaEventEx> pEvent(pGraph);

        // Build the graph. (Make sure to use a real file name!)
        hr = pGraph->RenderFile(L"C:\\Example.avi", NULL);
        if (FAILED(hr))
        {
            printf("Could not build the graph.\n");
            return;
        }
```

```
    // Run the graph.
    hr = pControl->Run();
    if (FAILED(hr))
    {
        printf("Could not build the graph.\n");
        return;
    }

    // Wait for playback to complete.
    long evCode;
    pEvent->WaitForCompletion(INFINITE, &evCode);
    }
    CoUninitialize();
}
```

This application uses ATL smart pointers to manage reference counts on COM interfaces. In case you've never used the ATL smart pointer classes before, they are the *CComPtr* and *CComQIPtr* variables in the code.

```
CComPtr<IGraphBuilder> pGraph;
```

The basic idea behind smart pointers is that they automatically call *AddRef* and *Release* as needed — well, almost automatically. You can find more information about them in Appendix A. We'll be using smart pointers extensively in the next few chapters.

The application begins by initializing COM. Then it creates a new instance of the Filter Graph Manager by calling *CoCreateInstance* with the Filter Graph Manager's class identifier (CLSID), which is *CLSID_FilterGraph*. The call returns a pointer to the *IGraph-Builder* interface, which has methods for building the filter graph. We'll need two other interfaces on the Filter Graph Manager as well, so we query for them right away: *IMedia-Control* has methods for starting and stopping playback, and *IMediaEventEx* has methods for listening to events from the graph.

Next, the *IGraphBuilder::RenderFile* method assembles a filter graph to play the specified file. This method is equivalent to the Render Media File command in GraphEdit. If the method succeeds, we now have a functioning filter graph. (If the method fails, it usually means that DirectShow does not support the file type, assuming you passed in a valid file name.) The *IMediaControl::Run* method starts playback, and is equivalent to the Play button in GraphEdit. This is the point when the video window is displayed.

(Incidentally, if you're wondering why the title bar on the video window says ActiveMovie Window, this is a holdover from the days when DirectShow was named ActiveMovie. The title bar hasn't changed since 1996! In practice, end users will never see it, because you will display the video inside your own application window.)

The *IMediaEventEx::WaitForCompletion* method blocks until playback completes. Normally you wouldn't do this in a real application, because it blocks for the duration of the video, or until the user closes the window. It works as a quick example, but you'll see a better approach later in this chapter. After *WaitForCompletion* returns, we can release all of our interfaces (which occurs automatically when the ATL smart pointers go out of scope) and call *CoUninitialize* to clean up. And that's it — video playback in about a dozen lines of code. The next step is to mix two video streams and display the result inside the application window, instead of using the ActiveMovie window.

Comparing the Video Renderer Filters

So far, we've been glossing over the fact that DirectShow has more than one video rendering filter. In our filter graph diagram, we just labeled one of the boxes "video renderer" and left it at that. However, for historical reasons, and because each release of DirectShow needed to remain backward-compatible, there are no fewer than five distinct video renderer filters to choose from:

- The video renderer that first shipped in DirectShow was named, appropriately, the Video Renderer filter. It is still the default video renderer on operating systems earlier than Windows XP. Whenever possible, the Video Renderer uses DirectDraw to draw the video frames onto the screen. Otherwise, it uses GDI, which is slower than DirectDraw but is actually not bad on newer computers. Unfortunately for our purposes, the Video Renderer uses very old versions of the DirectDraw interfaces. These work perfectly well for ordinary playback, but they don't give us the features that we need for 3-D graphics.

- On computers running Windows XP, the default video renderer is the Video Mixing Renderer 7 (VMR-7). This filter uses DirectDraw 7 interfaces and has lots of cool features, such as alpha-blending multiple videos. However, the VMR-7 is not available on earlier platforms, and it does not use the latest Direct3D interfaces.

- The newest video renderer is the Video Mixing Renderer 9 (VMR-9), introduced in DirectX 9.0. It is available for all versions of Windows that are supported by DirectX 9.0 or later. Its capabilities are similar to those of the VMR-7, but it uses Direct3D surfaces instead of DirectDraw surfaces, and it always uses the version 9 interfaces. The only catch is that the VMR-9 is not the default video renderer on any platform. This is because it has higher hardware requirements than the older Video Renderer filter. If it were the default renderer, it might break existing applications on some computers.

- The Overlay Mixer filter, although now considered obsolete, was designed for destination color keying (for example, to display DVD subpicture data) and to support hardware overlay.

- The Full Screen Renderer filter was designed for displaying full-screen video on older graphics cards. To avoid stretching the video, it would switch the display to a very low resolution. Modern graphics cards don't have any problems stretching video to full-screen, so this filter is obsolete.

All the video applications in this book use the VMR-9, because it has the features needed to combine video and 3-D graphics. By default, however, the *RenderFile* method will always use either the old Video Renderer filter or the VMR-7. To use the VMR-9, therefore, an application must explicitly select it. You'll learn how to do that shortly.

> **Note**   When we refer to the "VMR" in this book, we always mean the VMR-9 unless we specify the VMR-7. The two filters use different COM interfaces and have somewhat different capabilities. However, much of the information in this book can be applied to the VMR-7 as well.

VMR Rendering Modes

The VMR runs in one of three distinct modes, depending on how the application configures it at run time:

- In windowed mode, the VMR creates its own window where it draws the video. This mode exists only for backward-compatibility with the old Video Renderer filter. Unless you're retrofitting an existing application to use the VMR-9, there is no particular reason to use windowed mode, and we will not use it in this book.

- In windowless mode, the VMR does not create its own video window. Instead, it draws the video directly onto the application's window. The application specifies a rectangular clipping region within its client area, and the VMR automatically draws the video inside that region. Don't be misled by the term "windowless" — the application still uses a window. The name simply refers to the fact that the VMR does not create its own separate window, which distinguishes this mode from windowed mode.

- In renderless mode, the application takes over responsibility for two important tasks: allocating Direct3D surfaces to hold the video frames, and rendering those surfaces onto the screen. This mode enables applications to use video inside a Direct3D application.

We'll use renderless mode extensively in the next chapter, but first we'll describe how an application uses windowless mode. This will give you an opportunity to play around with the VMR's video mixing capabilities, and also to get a feel for VMR programming, before we throw Direct3D into the mix.

Mixing Video Streams in Windowless Mode

Run the Mangler sample, which is included in the AVBook/bin directory. This application plays two video files at once, alpha-blending them in the same window. The application window also has several controls that can be used to change the video-mixing parameters (see Plate 5).

> **Note**   Make sure that hardware acceleration is enabled in the DirectX control panel before you run the application. The VMR-9 requires hardware acceleration.

The two sliders labeled Stream 1 and Stream 2 change the width, height, and position of the two video streams, independently of each other. (Stream 1 is the dog, Stream 2 is the car.) The sliders labeled Video Source control the portion of the final image that appears in the application window. If you reduce the width of the video source, it has the effect of stretching the image horizontally, because a smaller portion of the image fills the same area of the window. Reducing the height causes the image to stretch vertically.

The check box labeled Switch Z Order flips the order of the images — the stream on top moves to the bottom, and vice versa. At startup, the application sets the alpha value of both video streams to 0.8 (where 0.0 is translucent and 1.0 is opaque), so that the video on the bottom layer shows through the video on the top layer.

The check box labeled Preserve Aspect Ratio controls whether the VMR-9 letterboxes the video. If this box is checked, the VMR-9 maintains the correct aspect ratio. If the box is unchecked, the image is stretched to fill the entire destination area.

Most of the code in the Mangler application is Microsoft Win32 code for the UI, which we can ignore. We'll jump right into the DirectShow code, starting with building the filter graph.

Building the Filter Graph and Configuring the VMR

In our previous DirectShow application, we called *RenderFile*, which built the entire filter graph all at once. However, as we noted earlier, *RenderFile* does not select the VMR-9. Therefore, we need to place the VMR-9 into the graph ourselves and tell the Filter Graph Manager to use it. This also gives us a chance to configure the VMR for windowless mode, which must be done before the VMR is connected to any other filters.

The following code adds the VMR to the filter graph and initializes the VMR for windowless mode.

```
CComPtr<IGraphBuilder> m_pGraph;   // Filter Graph Manager.
CComPtr<IBaseFilter> m_pVMR;       // VMR-9 filter.

// Create the Filter Graph Manager.
hr = m_pGraph.CoCreateInstance(CLSID_FilterGraph);

// Add the VMR-9 filter to the graph.
hr = AddFilterByCLSID(m_pGraph, CLSID_VideoMixingRenderer9, &m_pVMR);

// Configure the VMR for windowless mode before we connect
// any video streams to it.
CComQIPtr<IVMRFilterConfig9> pConfig(m_pVMR);
hr = pConfig->SetRenderingMode(VMR9Mode_Windowless);

// Set the window where we want the VMR to paint the video.
CComQIPtr<IVMRWindowlessControl9> pWC(m_pVMR);
pWC->SetVideoClippingWindow(hVidWin);
```

To make the code more readable, some error-checking has been left out. Also, some code has been re-arranged to make the procedures more linear. The actual Mangler source code is organized into several C++ classes.

As in the previous application, the first step is to create the Filter Graph Manager. Then we create the VMR-9 and add it to the graph by calling an application-defined helper function, *AddFilterByCLISD*. We'll describe this function in a moment.

To set up windowless mode, query the VMR filter for the *IVMRFilterConfig9* interface and call *IVMRFilterConfig9::SetRenderingMode* with the flag *VMR9Mode_Windowless*. After windowless mode is established, we need to tell the VMR about the application window where it should draw the video. Query the VMR for the *IVMRWindowlessControl9* interface, and call *IVMRWindowlessControl9::SetVideoClippingWindow* with the handle of the window. In the Mangler application, the video-clipping window is a static rectangle control that belongs to the dialog box.

The order of these method calls is important, because the VMR does not expose the *IVMRWindowlessControl9* interface until you specify windowless mode. Before you do that, calling *QueryInterface* for *IVMRWindowlessControl9* will fail.

Although it is not required in the Mangler application, at this point you may want to set the number of video streams. In both windowed mode and windowless mode, the VMR-9 defaults to four input pins, meaning you can render and mix four video streams simultaneously. If you want to mix more than that, call *IVMRFilterConfig9::SetNumberOf-Streams* and specify the number of streams that you want, up to 16. If you plan to mix fewer than four streams, you can leave the default value — there won't be a performance penalty for having extra unconnected pins. When we get to renderless mode in the next chapter, we'll see that video mixing works somewhat differently in that mode.

(Unlike the VMR-9, the VMR-7 creates only one input pin by default. If you are using the VMR-7 to mix multiple video streams, you must call *IVMRFilterConfig::SetNumberOfStreams.*)

The code for the *AddFilterByCLISD* function is shown in the following code. It calls *CoCreateInstance* to create the filter, and then calls *IGraphBuilder::AddFilter* on the Filter Graph Manager to insert the filter into the graph. (Creating a filter does not automatically add it to the graph.) The function returns the filter's *IBaseFilter* interface.

AddFilterByCLSID

```
// Function to add a filter to the filter graph.
HRESULT AddFilterByCLSID(
    IGraphBuilder *pGraph,    // Pointer to the Filter Graph Manager.
    const GUID& clsid,        // CLSID of the filter to create.
    IBaseFilter **ppF)        // Receives a pointer to the filter.
{
    if (!pGraph || ! ppF)
    {
        return E_POINTER;
    }
    *ppF = 0;
    CComPtr<IBaseFilter> pF;
    HRESULT hr = pF.CoCreateInstance(clsid);
    if (SUCCEEDED(hr))
    {
        hr = pGraph->AddFilter(pF, NULL);
        if (SUCCEEDED(hr))
        {
            // Return the IBaseFilter pointer to the caller.
            // The caller must release it.
            *ppF = pF.Detach();
        }
    }
    return hr;
}
```

Now that the VMR is set up for windowless mode, we can load the video files and render the streams.

```
WCHAR *wsFileName; // File name.
// Initialize wsFileName with the file name (not shown).
// Add a source filter for the source file.
CComPtr<IBaseFilter> pSource; // Source filter.
hr = m_pGraph->AddSourceFilter(wsFileName, L"Source Filter",
    &pSource);

// Collect all the source filter's output pins into a list.
PinList pins;
hr = GetPinList(pSource, PINDIR_OUTPUT, pins);

// Try to render each pin, using only the renderers in the graph.
CComQIPtr<IFilterGraph2> pGraph2(m_pGraph);
for (PinIterator iter = pins.begin(); iter != pins.end(); ++iter)
{
    // If any pin succeeds, treat it as a global success. Some pins
    // may output non-video media types, so it's OK if they fail.
    HRESULT hrTmp;
    hrTmp = pGraph2->RenderEx(*iter,
        AM_RENDEREX_RENDERTOEXISTINGRENDERERS, 0);
    if (SUCCEEDED(hrTmp))
    {
        hr = S_OK;
    }
}
// Release wsFileName (not shown).
```

We start by calling *IGraphBuilder::AddSourceFilter* to add a source filter for the video file. The first parameter is the file name, and the second parameter is a name for the filter. (The filter name is useful for debugging but otherwise won't be used.) The *AddSourceFilter* method returns a pointer to the source filter's *IBaseFilter* interface in the third parameter.

Next we hook up the source filter to the video renderer. For reasons that will become clear in a moment, we need to get a list of the source filter's output pins. The *Get-PinList* function finds all of the pins on a filter that match a specified direction — in this case, the output pins — and collects them into an STL *list* object. We'll describe the code for *GetPinList* later in this section.

Finally, we iterate through the list of pins and call *IFilterGraph2::RenderEx* with each pin. The *RenderEx* method takes a pointer to an output pin's *IPin* interface. The *AM_RENDEREX_RENDERTOEXISTINGRENDERERS* flag tells the Filter Graph Manager to connect the pin to a renderer filter, using only the renderer filters that are already in the graph. DirectShow may add other intermediate filters to the graph, such as splitters or decoders, but it will not add any new renderers. This prevents DirectShow from using one of the other video renderer filters that we mentioned earlier. When the *for* loop exits, the source filter is connected to the VMR-9 through some number of intermediate filters. The resulting filter graph is shown in Figure 9.5.

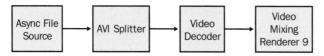

Figure 9.5   AVI file playback using the VMR-9.

The source filter shown in this diagram has only one output pin, and this will be true in general for AVI files. So why go through the trouble of building a list of pins? The reason is that some source filters have multiple output pins — for example, the source filter used to render Windows Media files creates one output pin per stream in the file.

Also, note that we did not put an audio renderer into the graph beforehand. Therefore, even if the video file has an audio stream, the audio won't be rendered, because we specified the *AM_RENDEREX_RENDERTOEXISTINGRENDERERS* flag. If you want to render the audio, you need to add the audio renderer to the graph first, as we did with the VMR. The CLSID for the audio renderer filter is *CLSID_DSoundRender* — so named because it uses DirectSound to play the audio. You can easily modify the code in the Mangler application to include audio playback.

Here is the code for the *GetPinList* function.

GetPinList

```
typedef CComPtr<IPin> PinPtr;
typedef std::list<PinPtr> PinList;
typedef PinList::iterator PinIterator;

HRESULT GetPinList(
    IBaseFilter *pFilter,    // Pointer to the filter.
    PIN_DIRECTION Direction, // The pin direction to search for.
    PinList& list            // A list to collect the pins.
)
{
    if (!pFilter)
    {
        return E_POINTER;
    }
    CComPtr<IEnumPins> pEnum;
    HRESULT hr = pFilter->EnumPins(&pEnum);
```

```
if (FAILED(hr))
{
    return hr;
}
CComPtr<IPin> pPin;
while (S_OK == pEnum->Next(1, &pPin, NULL))
{
    PIN_DIRECTION ThisDirection;
    hr = pPin->QueryDirection(&ThisDirection);
    if (FAILED(hr))
    {
        return hr;
    }
    if (ThisDirection == Direction)
    {
        list.push_back(pPin);
    }
    pPin.Release();
}
return S_OK;
}
```

To enumerate a filter's pins, we use the *IEnumPins* interface, which we get by calling *IBaseFilter::EnumPins* on the filter. To iterate through all of the pins, call *IEnumPins::Next* until the return value is something other than *S_OK*. (Don't use the *SUCCEEDED* macro, because in this case *S_FALSE* does not mean the same thing as *S_OK*.) The *Next* method returns an *IPin* pointer for the pin.

For each pin, the *GetPinList* function calls *IPin::QueryDirection* to find the direction of the pin, either input or output. If the pin direction matches the *Direction* parameter, the *IPin* pointer is stored in the list. The STL *push_back* function makes a copy of the *CComPtr* object, which calls *AddRef* on the raw *IPin* pointer, so the reference count remains correct.

Setting the Video Mixing Preferences

Once the graph is built, we can configure how it mixes the video streams. The VMR gives you a lot of control over the mixing process. Some mixing properties are global to the VMR, and some are applied individually to each stream. Figure 9.6 shows the relationships among those settings that affect the positions of the video streams.

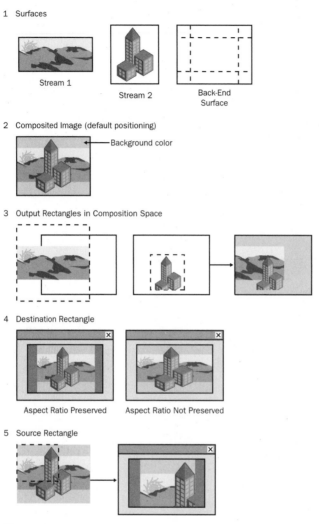

Figure 9.6   Video-mixing preferences in the VMR-9.

Output Rectangles

Each stream has an *output rectangle*. The output rectangles control how the video streams are positioned relative to each other.

Internally, the VMR creates a Direct3D surface where is mixes the videos. This surface is called the *back-end surface*. The size of this surface in each dimension is equal to the maximum size of all the source images in that dimension. For example, if the first video stream is 200 × 400 pixels, and the second video stream is 400 × 200 pixels, the back-end surface will be 400 × 400 pixels.

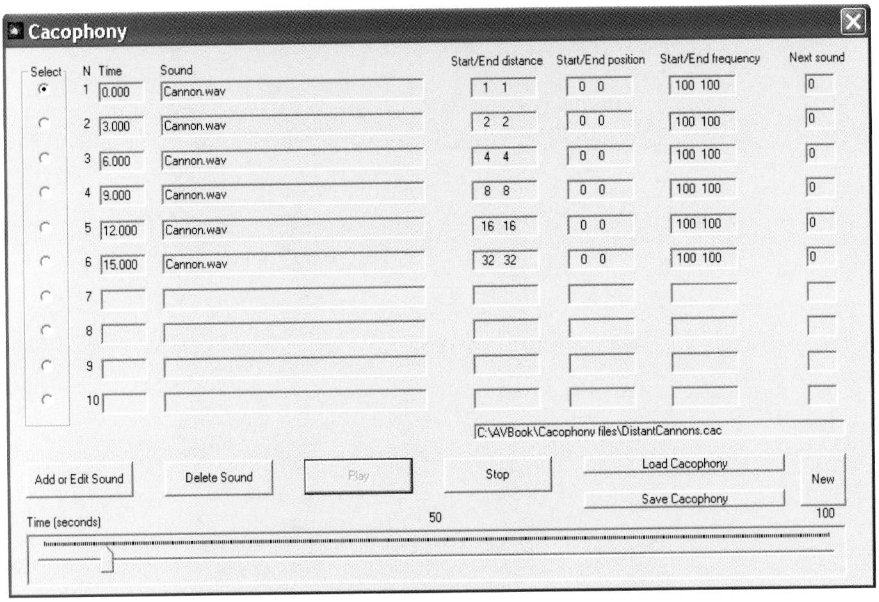

Color Plate 1   Cacophony tool running the DistantCannons file.

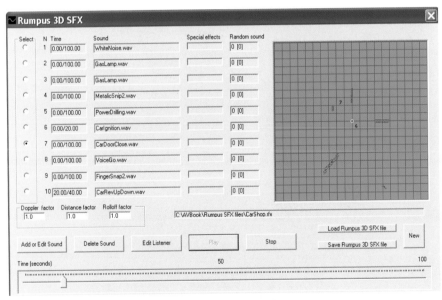

Color Plate 2   Rumpus tool running the CarShop file.

Color Plate 3   To calculate echo delays use the formula: echo delay (ms) = 6 * distance to cliff in meters.

Color Plate 4   The natural world provides great inspiration for audio occlusion and obstruction effects.

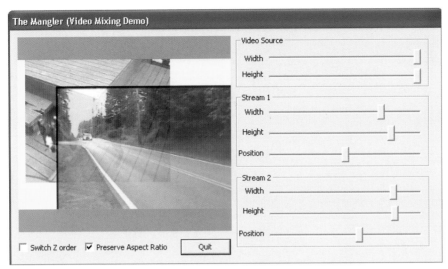

Color Plate 5 Mixing two video streams in DirectShow with the VMR-9 filter.

Color Plate 6 3-D mesh rendered on top of a video cut scene.

Color Plate 7 Video texture applied to a 3-D scene.

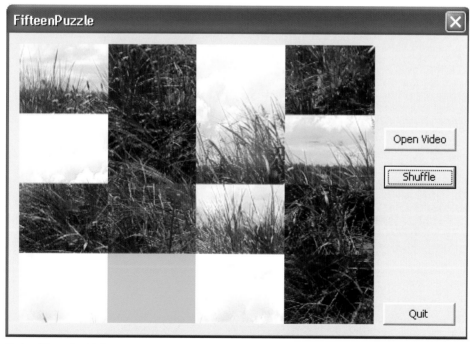

Color Plate 8 Using custom video mixing to create a 15 puzzle.

Color Plate 9 Two videos blended with an alpha map.

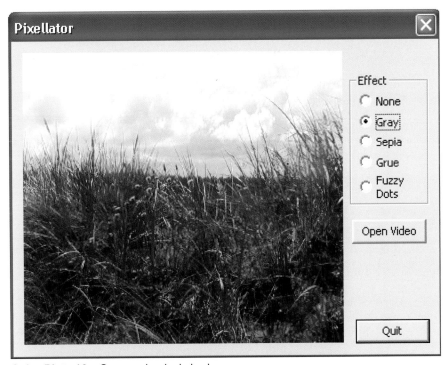

Color Plate 10 Gray scale pixel shader.

Color Plate 11 Sepia tone pixel shader.

Color Plate 12 "Grue" (green-blue) pixel shader.

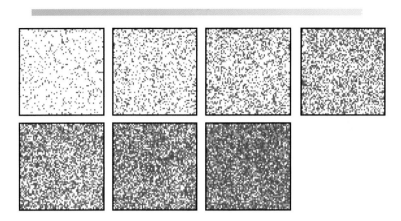

Color Plate 13 Texture bitmaps used in the Pixellator sample.

Color Plate 14 "Fuzzy dots" pixel shader, using a volumetric texture lookup.

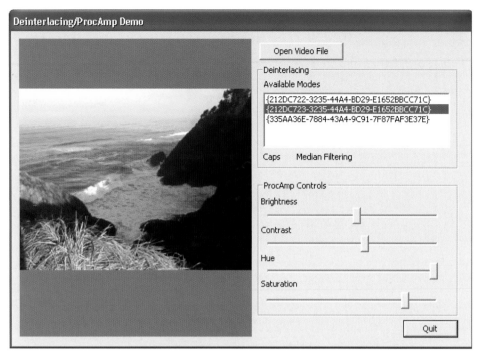

Color Plate 15 ProcAmp controls for brightness, contrast, hue, and saturation.

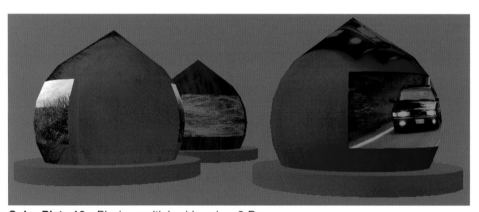

Color Plate 16 Playing multiple videos in a 3-D scene.

By default, the VMR positions each video in the center of the surface, so that it fills the entire surface along one dimension, while preserving the video aspect ratio in the other dimension. You can re-position a stream by changing the output rectangle for that stream. The coordinates of the output rectangle are defined so that the upper-left corner of the back-end surface has coordinates (0.0, 0.0) and the lower-right corner of the surface has coordinates (1.0, 1.0).

The output rectangle is measured relative to these coordinates, so the default position of each stream is {0.0, 0.0, 1.0, 1.0}. To place the image in the upper-left quadrant, you would set the output rectangle to {0.0, 0.0, 0.5, 0.5}. This also has the effect of shrinking the video to fit the smaller rectangle.

You are not limited to the range [0.0 ... 1.0]. Any part of the image that falls outside of this range is simply clipped, and does not get rendered. You can use this feature to create *fly-in effects*. For example, you could set the initial output rectangle to {-1.0, -1.0, 0.0, 0.0}, which is outside the visible area, and gradually update the rectangle to {0.0, 0.0, 1.0, 1.0} so that the video slides diagonally into the application window.

To set the output rectangle for a stream, call *IVMRMixerControl::SetOutputRect*.

```
DWORD deStreamId = 0; // First video stream.
VMR9NormalizedRect rect;
// Set the rectangle boundaries to {0,0,1,1}.
rect.left = rect.top = 0.0f;
rect.right = rect.bottom = 1.0f;
m_pMixer->SetOutputRect(dwStreamId, &rect);
```

The first parameter (*dwStreamId*) specifies the video stream, indexed from zero. The index number is determined by the order in which the VMR pins are connected. The first pin to be connected is stream 0, the second is stream 1, and so on. In the Mangler application, this corresponds to the order in which the application's *RenderVideoStream* function is called.

Alpha

You can apply a per-stream alpha value to make a video stream transparent. The alpha can range from 0.0, which is completely transparent, to 1.0, which is completely opaque. Set the alpha value for a stream with the *IVMRMixerControl::SetAlpha* method.

```
m_pMixer->SetAlpha(dwStreamId, 0.5f); // Semi-transparent (50% alpha).
```

The value is applied to the entire image area for that stream.

Background Color

In the places where the video images do not cover the back-end surface, the surface is filled with a solid background color. This color is also visible behind the image, if the image is transparent. Set the background color with the *IVMRMixerControl::SetBackgroundClr* method, which takes a *COLORREF* value. The default color is black.

```
m_pMixer->SetBackgroundClr(RGB(0xFF, 0xFF, 0xC0)); // Pale yellow.
```

Z-Order

The z-order specifies the order in which the streams are composited onto the back-end surface. Higher z-orders are farther back — in other words, the highest z-order is rendered first. If the stream's alpha is set to 1.0, the image obscures anything below it. Otherwise, the image is alpha-blended with layer below it. Set the z-order with the *IVMRMixerControl::SetZOrder* method.

```
m_pMixer->SetZOrder(dwStreamId, 0); // Move this stream to the front.
```

In the Mangler application, the Switch Z Order check box sets the z-order of stream number 1, switching it between the values 0 and 2. Stream number 0 is kept at z-order 1.

Source and Destination Rectangles

The *source rectangle* is a subrectangle within the back-end surface, and the *destination rectangle* is a subrectangle within the application window's client area. After the VMR composites the video streams to the back-end surface, it stretches the surface's source rectangle onto the window's destination rectangle. Thus if you reduce the destination rectangle, the video occupies a smaller portion of the application window. If you reduce the source rectangle, the VMR stretches a smaller portion of the composited image into the destination rectangle, with the effect of magnifying a section of the composited image. If the source rectangle is equal to the entire back-end surface, the entire image is displayed in the destination rectangle.

To set the source and destination rectangles, call *IVMRWindowlessControl9::SetVideoPosition*. To find the actual size of the back-end surface, call *IVMRWindowlessControl9::GetNativeVideoSize*. Always set the value of the source and destination rectangles before playback starts, or the video will not be visible, because both rectangles default to {0, 0, 0, 0}. The following code sets the source rectangle equal to the entire back-end surface and the destination rectangle equal to the entire window client area.

```
RECT rcSource;
RECT rcDest;
// Find the size of the composited video image.
ZeroMemory(&rcSource, sizeof(RECT));
m_pWC->GetNativeVideoSize(
    &rcSource.right,   // Width.
    &rcSource.bottom,  // Height.
    NULL, NULL         // Aspect ratio X and Y (optional).
    );

// Use the entire client area for the destination rectangle.
GetClientArea(hwnd, &rcDest);
m_pWC->SetVideoPosition(&rcSource, &m_rcDest);
```

Letterbox Mode

By default, the VMR does not preserve the aspect ratio of the image when it stretches the source rectangle to the destination rectangle. To preserve the aspect ratio, call *IVMRWindowlessControl9::SetAspectRatioMode* with the flag *VMR9ARMode_LetterBox*.

```
m_pWC->SetAspectRatioMode(VMR9ARMode_LetterBox);
```

Note that letterbox mode controls how the VMR stretches the back-end surface to the window, not how it draws the video streams onto the back-end surface.

Border Color

If you enable letterbox mode, you can define the color of the border where the video is letterboxed. To do so, call *IVMRWindowlessControl9::SetBorderColor* with a *COLORREF* value. The Mangler application sets the border color to orange, which is quite ugly, but makes the effect very obvious.

```
m_pWC->SetBorderColor(RGB(0xFF, 0x80, 0x00)); // Orange.
```

The border color is not the same as the background color mentioned earlier. The background color is used to fill the areas of the back-end surface where the video does not appear, while the border color is used to fill the letterboxed edges of the client window, in letterbox mode only. The default border color is black.

Miscellaneous VMR Features

The VMR has some additional features that are not demonstrated in the Mangler application:

- You can alpha-blend a static bitmap onto the video. For example, you could use this to put a logo onto the video window. Call *IVMRMixerBitmap9::SetAlphaBitmap*.

- You can grab a copy of the most recent video frame, in the form of a device-independent bitmap (DIB). Call *IVMRWindowlessControl::GetCurrentImage*.

- If the graphics hardware supports it, the VMR can perform hardware-accelerated deinterlacing and image adjustment. This feature is described in detail in Chapter 12.

Running the Filter Graph

With our initial mixing preferences established, we are ready to start video playback by calling *IMediaControl::Run* on the Filter Graph Manager.

```
m_pControl->Run();
```

While the graph is running, each decoder in the graph delivers video frames to the VMR. The VMR runs a worker thread that picks up the decoded frames, mixes them onto the back-end surface, and stretches the composited image onto the application window. The application does not have to take any actions while this is happening — it is all managed automatically by the VMR. However, because the VMR does not own the video window, the application must inform it whenever certain events occur:

- **Repaints.**   When the application receives a *WM_PAINT* message, call *IVMRWindowlessControl::RepaintVideo* to inform the VMR to repaint the video window. Note that you do not have to call *RepaintVideo* just to get the VMR to draw each frame while the video plays; that happens automatically. The purpose of calling *RepaintVideo* is to make sure the VMR repaints the most recent frame after the application window is invalidated. This could happen between frames while the graph is running, or while the graph is paused.

- **Window size changes.**   When the application receives a *WM_SIZE* message, you may need to recalculate the source and destination rectangles and call *SetVideoPosition* again. You can skip this call if you don't need to adjust the video position after the resize — it will depend on your application. The Mangler application uses a non-resizable window, so it's not a issue.

- **Display changes.**   When the application receives a *WM_DISPLAY-CHANGE* message, call *IVMRWindowlessControl::DisplayModeChanged*. This tells the VMR to take whatever actions are needed to respond to the display change.

As the Mangler application demonstrates, you can change any of the mixer settings while the video is playing, and thereby achieve interesting animation effects. The VMR automatically applies the new settings to the next frame that it renders.

Handling Filter Graph Events

DirectShow has an event mechanism that lets the Filter Graph Manager inform your application when interesting things happen inside the graph — for example, when playback reaches the end of the file. In our first application, back at the start of this chapter, we waited for the end of the file by calling *WaitForCompletion* with a timeout value of *INFINITE*. That's not a good practice for a real-world application, because you don't want your application to block while the file is playing. The Mangler application shows how to perform proper event handling.

At startup, we ask the Filter Graph Manager to notify our application whenever there is a new event. It will do so by posting a message to the application's message loop. We define a private Windows message for this purpose.

```
static const long WM_GRAPH_EVENT = WM_APP + 1;
```

To set up the notification, call *IMediaEventEx::SetNotifyWindow.*

```
m_pEvent->SetNotifyWindow((OAHWND)hwnd, WM_GRAPH_EVENT, 0);
```

The first argument is the window handle, cast to an *OAHWND* type. The second argument is the Windows message, and the third argument is an optional value that will be returned to the application in the *lParam* parameter of the message. The *lParam* value is not used in the Mangler application, but you could use it to track events from multiple filter graphs. Whenever the Filter Graph Manager queues a new event, the designated window receives the *WM_GRAPH_EVENT* message (defined as *WM_APP + 1*). In your message loop, respond to the message by calling *IMediaEvent::GetEvent.*

```
LRESULT CALLBACK WindowProc(HWND hwnd, UINT msg,
    WPARAM wParam, LPARAM lParam)
{
    long EventCode, param1, param2; // Event parameters.
    switch (msg)
    {
    case WM_GRAPH_EVENT:
        // Loop until no messages are left in the queue.
        while (SUCCEEDED(hr = m_pEvent->GetEvent(&EventCode, &param1,
            &param2, 0)))
        {
            // Decide what to do based on the event code.
            switch (EventCode)
            {
            case EC_COMPLETE:  // End of file.
                // Handle the event (not shown).
                break;
            }
        }

        // Release any resources allocated for the event parameters.
        m_pEvent->FreeEventParams(EventCode, param1, param2);
    break;

    // Handle other Windows messages as usual (not shown).
    }
}
```

The *GetEvent* method returns an event code and two event parameters. The event code defines what kind of event happened. For example, the end of the file is signalled by the *EC_COMPLETE* event. The event parameters are similar to the *lParam* and *wParam* values in a Windows message — they contain additional information whose meaning depends on the event type. Sometimes you may need to cast the event parameters to another data type, such as a COM pointer. The DirectShow SDK documentation has a complete list of all the events and their parameters. After you get the event and respond to it, always call *IMediaEvent::FreeEventParams*. This tells the Filter Graph Manager to release any memory it may have allocated for the event parameters.

You may have noticed in the previous code example that we called *GetEvent* and *FreeEventParams* inside a *while* loop, which repeats for as long as *GetEvent* succeeds. This is done because several events might be queued by the time the application receives the *WM_GRAPH_EVENT* message and responds to it. Using a loop ensures that we get all the pending events.

Seeking to the Start of the File

When the Mangler application receives the *EC_COMPLETE* event, it stops the graph and seeks to the start of the file.

```
m_pControl->Stop();
LONGLONG rtPosition = 0;
m_pSeek->SetPositions(
    &rtPosition, AM_SEEKING_AbsolutePositioning,  // Current position.
    NULL, AM_SEEKING_NoPositioning  // Stop position (no change).
);
m_pControl->Run();
```

Seeking is performed by calling *IMediaSeeking::SetPositions* on the Filter Graph Manager. The first parameter is the time to seek to. The units are 100 nanoseconds (10^{-7} seconds), so 1 second is 10,000,000 units. The *AM_SEEKING_AbsolutePositioning* flag means the seek time is expressed relative to the start of the file, as opposed to being relative to the current playback position. The third parameter specifies a stop time. In this case, *NULL* is used because we do not want to modify the stop time, as indicated by the *AM_SEEKING_NoPositioning* flag.

When the VMR mixes multiple video streams, it has limited support for seeking. You can stop the graph and seek all the streams back to the beginning, but you cannot seek around in the file during playback. In Chapter 12, we'll show a way to get around this limitation by using several VMR instances in the same application.

Summary

This chapter provided an overview of DirectShow and demonstrated some of the possibilities that the VMR-9 offers for mixing video. With this foundation, you're ready for the next step — taking video out of the window and into the third dimension.

10

Taking Video to the Third Dimension

In this chapter, we take video out of the window and move it into the world of 3-D. The key feature of the VMR that makes this possible is renderless mode, which gives us near complete control over how we present the video frames.

Video Cut Scene

In games, a common use for video is to create *cut scenes* — short, full-screen video clips. You might use a cut scene as a title sequence, a segue between levels, or in the closing credits. Cut scenes can give your game a dramatic, cinematic feel. The first sample application in this chapter shows how to render a cut scene that combines video with 3-D elements.

Build and run the Ducky sample that is located in the AVBook\bin directory. The Ducky sample plays a video of waves crashing against rocks, while a 3-D model of a duck rotates in front of the video. (See Plate 6. We're not sure what kind of game would use this cut scene, we just liked the duck.) You can use the arrow keys to move the camera around the duck. Press the Escape key to quit the sample.

Keyboard control	Camera movement
Left/right arrow	Rotate left/right (yaw)
Shift + left/right arrow	Slide left/right
Up/down arrow	Slide forward/backward
Shift + up/down arrow	Rotate up/down (pitch)

About the 3-D Framework

All of the Direct3D sample applications in this book are built on the same framework, which handles common tasks such as setting up Direct3D, rendering the scene, and so on. If you're curious and want to see the framework without any of the DirectShow code, look at the D3DApp_Basic sample that is located in the AVBook\bin directory. The framework was designed to make the code easy to follow, so it's not necessarily very efficient, and it's certainly not a full-fledged game engine. For example, there is no collision detection, so the camera can move freely through meshes, which produces a rather disconcerting effect.

The following table lists all the C++ classes defined in the base framework. We won't describe all of the code in these classes, but the source files are well commented.

Class	Description
CCamera	Defines the camera, which is used to set the view matrix.
CClock	Simple timer for controlling the frame rate of the 3-D scene.
CD3D	Manages the *IDirect3D9* interface.
CDevice	Manages the Direct3D device.
CDisplayModes	Helper class to enumerate the available display modes.
CFrame	Hierarchical frame class, used to build the scene graph.
CGame	Manages the entire rendering process. This class contains the device, clock, camera, keyboard, and scene objects.
CKeyboard	Manages keyboard input, using DirectInput.
CMatrixStack	Manages a matrix stack, used to store local world transforms when the scene graph is rendered. This class is a simple wrapper for the *ID3DXMatrixStack* interface, which is part of the Direct3D utility library.
CMesh	Manages a 3-D mesh. This class is a simple wrapper for the *ID3DXMesh* interface from the Direct3D utility library.
CRefCountedObject	Base class that implements reference counting using the *AddRef* and *Release* methods (but not *QueryInterface*). This class is defined so that reference counting can be applied to objects that do not have COM interfaces.
CScene	Abstract class for managing a Direct3D scene. Each Direct3D sample application in this book defines its own subclass that derives from *CScene*, whose purpose is to load the scene and render it. The subclass contains the scene graph, meshes, and other scene objects.

VMR Plug-In Components

In the previous chapter, we used the VMR filter "as is," but the VMR has two plug-in components, shown in Figure 10.1, that you can replace with your own custom components:

Allocator-presenter

■   This component creates Direct3D surfaces (allocation) and draws video frames on the screen (presentation).

Compositor

■   This component mixes the incoming video streams.

The filter itself manages everything else: pin connections, format negotiation with the decoders, and all the other DirectShow overhead.

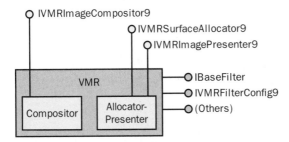

Figure 10.1   VMR plug-in components.

By replacing the allocator-presenter or the compositor with your own custom versions, you can control those portions of the rendering process. The allocator-presenter can be replaced when the VMR is in renderless mode (in fact, this is the definition of renderless mode), while the compositor can be replaced in any mode. In this chapter, we focus on the allocator-presenter. In the next chapter, we show how to write a custom compositor.

Mixing Mode versus Pass-Through Mode

In order for the VMR to mix two or more video streams, it must load the compositor into memory. The VMR's default compositor also performs several other useful functions besides mixing. For example, it automatically deinterlaces the source video when needed. Therefore, it can be useful to have the compositor loaded even if you are rendering a single video stream. Whether the compositor is loaded also affects the operations of the allocator-presenter.

When the VMR loads the compositor, it is said to be operating in *mixing* mode. Otherwise, it is in *pass-through* mode. Which of these two modes the VMR selects by default depends on the rendering mode, and also on which version of the VMR you are using. The following table lists the default behavior of both VMR versions.

Version	Rendering mode	Default behavior
VMR-7	Windowed	Pass-through
	Windowless	Pass-through
	Renderless (custom allocator-presenter)	Pass-through
VMR-9	Windowed	Mixing
	Windowless	Mixing
	Renderless	Pass-through

As the previous table shows, the VMR-7 always defaults to pass-through mode. The VMR-9 defaults to mixing mode when it's in windowed mode or windowless mode, but it defaults to pass-through mode when it's in renderless mode. You can always activate mixing mode by *calling IVMRFilterConfig::SetNumberOfStreams* on the VMR-7, or *IVMRFilterConfig9::SetNumberOfStreams* on the VMR-9. This method must be called before you connect any of the VMR's input pins.

Why is all this important? Because the VMR behaves differently in mixing mode and pass-through mode, and these differences will affect your custom allocator-presentor.

The VMR Rendering Process: Mixing Mode

In mixing mode, shown in Figure 10.2, the VMR composites the incoming video streams onto a single Direct3D surface, called the *back-end surface*. The video decoders do not touch the back-end surface; instead, the VMR assigns each decoder its own pool of surfaces. The allocator-presenter creates the back-end surface and the VMR creates the decoder surfaces.

Whenever a decoder generates a new video frame, the VMR collects the most recent frame from each decoder and passes them all to the compositor, which mixes them onto the back-end surface. At that point, the VMR calls into the allocator-presenter to present the back-end surface to the screen. The allocator-presenter might do something as simple as call *StretchRect*, or it might perform a complex texture operation. The VMR's default allocator-presenter uses a flipping chain that is associated with the video window.

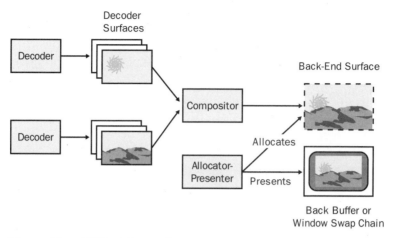

Figure 10.2   VMR mixing mode.

The VMR Rendering Process: Pass-Through Mode

In pass-through mode, shown in Figure 10.3, the VMR performs no video mixing. Therefore, only one video stream is allowed. Nor does the VMR create a back-end surface: The video frames are presented as they come out of the decoder, without any modification by the compositor. The allocator-presenter creates the decoder surfaces and presents the decoded video frames. The compositor is not loaded, so it is not involved in the process at all.

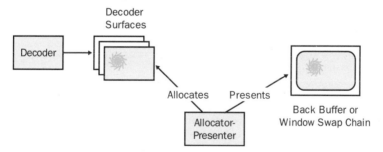

Figure 10.3   VMR pass-through mode.

In the Ducky sample, we use pass-through mode, because it keeps things slightly simpler than mixing mode. However, mixing mode is more powerful, as the next sample application will demonstrate.

Writing a Custom Allocator-Presenter

An allocator-presenter must implement two COM interfaces: *IVMRSurfaceAllocator9*, which defines methods for allocating surfaces, and *IVMRImagePresenter9*, which defines methods for presenting surfaces. These two interfaces provide a consistent way for the VMR to communicate with any allocator-presenter.

The allocator-presenter receives its allocation requirements from the VMR, based on the video format and the mixing mode. The VMR also tells the allocator-presenter when to present each video frame. The Direct3D device is created either by the allocator-presenter or directly by the application. Either way, the VMR must be notified of the device pointer.

On the application side, the application must configure the VMR for renderless mode and hook up the custom allocator-presenter. As far as building and running the filter graph, we can reuse most of the code from the previous chapter.

Outline of the Ducky Sample

The Ducky sample adds some new C++ classes to the D3DApp_Basic framework.

Class	Description
CAllocator	Implements the custom allocator-presenter.
CCriticalSection	Thin wrapper for a Windows *CRITICAL_SECTION* structure.
CGraph	Manages the DirectShow filter graph.
CGraphEventHandler	Defines a callback for handling filter graph events.
CLock	Locks a critical section before entering a code path, and automatically unlocks the critical section on exit.
CVmrGame	Derives from *CGame* but adds video functionality.

The *CGraph* and *CGraphEventHandler* classes are adapted from the Mangler sample in Chapter 9, with minor modifications to handle the VMR in renderless mode.

Here's the overall sequence of events when the Ducky sample runs:

Initialization

1. Initialize COM.

2. Create the application window.

3. Create the Direct3D object and the Direct3D device.

4. Initialize DirectInput for keyboard input.

5. Load the scene: Load meshes, set up lights, set the render states, and build the scene graph hierarchy. Set the initial camera position and the projection matrix.

6. Initialize DirectShow: Configure the VMR for renderless mode, build the filter graph, and set up the custom allocator-presenter.

Rendering

1. Show the application window.

2. Start the DirectShow filter graph.

Clean up

1. Stop the filter graph.

2. Release everything.

3. Shut down COM.

While the filter graph is running, the VMR notifies the allocator-presenter whenever a new video frame should be rendered. This happens on a callback function, so the message loop of the sample application does not do very much. Most of the code in the Ducky sample is generic Windows programming or Direct3D setup code, and will not be covered in detail.

Building the Filter Graph

The code to build the filter graph is quite similar to the Mangler sample from the previous chapter, except the VMR must be configured for renderless mode instead of windowless mode. We define a new function for this purpose, *InitVMR_RenderlessMode*, which replaces the *InitVMR_WindowlessMode* function that was used in the Mangler sample.

```
HRESULT CGraph::InitVMR_RenderlessMode(
    IVMRSurfaceAllocatorNotify9 **ppAlloc)
{
    // Create the Filter Manager.
    HRESULT hr = m_pGraph.CoCreateInstance(CLSID_FilterGraph);
    m_pGraph.QueryInterface(&m_pControl);
    m_pGraph.QueryInterface(&m_pEvent);

    // Create the VMR-9 and add it to the graph.
    hr = AddFilterByCLSID(m_pGraph, CLSID_VideoMixingRenderer9, &m_pVMR);

    // Set the VMR-9 to renderless mode.
    CComQIPtr<IVMRFilterConfig9> pConfig(m_pVMR);
    hr = pConfig->SetRenderingMode(VMR9Mode_Renderless);

    // Return the IVMRSurfaceAllocatorNotify9 interface pointer
    // to the caller.
    return m_pVMR.QueryInterface(ppAlloc);
}
```

Again, we've left out some *HRESULT* tests, in the interest of making the code examples shorter. To establish renderless mode, we call the *IVMRFilterConfig9::SetRenderingMode* method with the *VMR9Mode_Renderless* flag. Then we query the VMR for the *IVMRSurfaceAllocatorNotify9* interface, which controls the VMR in renderless mode — analogous to the role of the *IVMRWindowlessControl9* interface in windowless mode. As in the Mangler sample, the order of these method calls is important, because the VMR does not expose the *IVMRSurfaceAllocatorNotify9* interface until the application has specified renderless mode.

The *InitVMR_RenderlessMode* function is called from the *CVmrGame::InitializeVMR* function, which initializes the VMR and the allocator-presenter.

```
HRESULT CVmrGame::InitializeVMR(
    HWND hwnd, WindowMode mode, CScene *pScene)
{
    // Set up the VMR for renderless mode.
    HRESULT hr = m_Graph.InitVMR_RenderlessMode(&m_pVmrNotify);

    // Tell the VMR about the Direct3D device and the monitor.
    HMONITOR hMonitor = g_d3d->GetAdapterMonitor(D3DADAPTER_DEFAULT);
    hr = m_pVmrNotify->SetD3DDevice(m_pDevice, hMonitor);

    // Hook up the VMR and the allocator-presenter.
    hr = m_pVmrNotify->AdviseSurfaceAllocator(0, m_pAlloc);
    hr = m_pAlloc->AdviseNotify(m_pVmrNotify);

    return hr;
}
```

The application gives the VMR a pointer to the Direct3D device by calling *IVMRSurfaceAllocatorNotify9::SetD3DDevice*. This method also specifies the monitor that we are using, which is easily obtained by calling *IDirect3D9::GetAdapterMonitor*. The Ducky sample always uses the primary display adapter.

> **Note**   When you create the Direct3D device, set the device type to *D3DDEVTYPE_HAL*. Otherwise the *SetD3DDevice* method will fail, because the VMR requires hardware acceleration. Also set the *D3DCREATE_MULTITHREADED* flag.

The *IVMRSurfaceAllocatorNotify9::AdviseSurfaceAllocator* method informs the VMR about the custom allocator-presenter. It takes a pointer to the allocator-presenter's *IVMRSurfaceAllocator9* interface, represented by the *m_pAlloc* variable. The *IVMR-*

SurfaceAllocator9::AdviseNotify method does the reverse — it tells the allocator-presenter about the VMR. Together, these two methods establish the necessary link between the VMR and the allocator-presenter. (We'll see how *AdviseNotify* is implemented shortly.)

Now we can build the rest of the filter graph by loading the video file and connecting it to the VMR. This code is exactly the same as the code in the previous chapter.

```
hr = m_Graph.RenderVideoStream(wszVideoFile);
```

Note that a second call to *RenderVideoStream* would fail in this case, because the VMR is in pass-through mode and cannot mix a second video stream.

That covers the graph-building side of things. Next we'll look at the code for the allocator-presenter, and then we'll show how the sample application renders the 3-D scene.

Implementing the Allocator-Presenter

Here is the declaration of the *CAllocator* class, which implements our custom allocator-presenter.

```
class CAllocator :
    public IVMRSurfaceAllocator9, public IVMRImagePresenter9
{
    friend class CVmrGame;
public:
    CAllocator(CVmrGame *pGame);
    virtual ~CAllocator();
    HRESULT SetDevice(IDirect3DDevice9 *pDevice);

    // IUnknown methods.
    STDMETHODIMP_(ULONG) AddRef();
    STDMETHODIMP_(ULONG) Release();
    STDMETHODIMP QueryInterface(REFIID riid, void **ppv);

    // IVMRSurfaceAllocator9 methods.
    STDMETHODIMP AdviseNotify(IVMRSurfaceAllocatorNotify9* pNotify);
    STDMETHODIMP GetSurface(DWORD_PTR dwUserID, DWORD SurfaceIndex,
        DWORD SurfaceFlags, IDirect3DSurface9** ppSurface);
    STDMETHODIMP InitializeDevice(DWORD_PTR dwUserID,
        VMR9AllocationInfo* pAllocInfo, DWORD* pNumBuffers);
    STDMETHODIMP TerminateDevice(DWORD_PTR  dwID);

    // IVMRImagePresenter9 methods.
    STDMETHODIMP PresentImage(DWORD_PTR dwUserID,
        VMR9PresentationInfo* pPresInfo);
    STDMETHODIMP StartPresenting(DWORD_PTR dwUserID) { return S_OK; }
    STDMETHODIMP StopPresenting(DWORD_PTR dwUserID) { return S_OK; }
protected:
```

(continued)

```
        IDirect3DSurface9 *m_pVideoSurf;
private:
    void ReleaseSurfaces();

    long m_nRefCount;              // Our reference count.
    CCriticalSection m_CritSec;    // Critical section object.
    CVmrGame* m_pGame;             // Parent game object.

    // VMR interface pointers.
    CComPtr<IVMRFilterConfig9> m_pConfig;
    CComPtr<IVMRSurfaceAllocatorNotify9> m_pNotify;

    // D3D interface pointers.
    CComPtr<IDirect3DDevice9> m_pDevice;

    // Surfaces.
    IDirect3DSurface9 **m_pSurf;   // Surfaces we provide to the VMR.
    DWORD m_dwNumSurfaces;         // The number of surfaces.
};
```

The *CAllocator* class inherits both of the COM interfaces that it supports. The public declaration section begins with three functions that are specific to this class, and are not part of the COM interfaces: the constructor, the destructor, and the *SetDevice* method. These are followed by declarations of *IVMRSurfaceAllocator9* and *IVMRImagePresenter9*, plus the *IUnknown* methods, which are inherited from the other two interfaces.

Implementing the IUnknown Methods

Because the allocator-presenter exposes two COM interfaces, it must implement the methods in *IUnknown*. Fortunately, unless you're doing something complicated, you can use boilerplate code for all of your *IUnknown* implementations. Here is the code for *AddRef* and *Release*.

```
STDMETHODIMP_(ULONG) CAllocator::AddRef()
{
    return InterlockedIncrement(&m_nRefCount);
}


STDMETHODIMP_(ULONG) CAllocator::Release()
{
    assert(m_nRefCount >= 0);
    ULONG uCount = InterlockedDecrement(&m_nRefCount);
    if (uCount == 0)
    {
        delete this;
    }
    // For thread safety, return the temporary variable, not the
    // class member variable.
```

```
        return uCount;
}
```

The reference count is stored in the *m_nRefCount* variable. The *InterlockedIncrement* and *InterlockedDecrement* functions increase and decrease the reference count by one. Both of these functions are thread-safe. It's crucial that we make the *CAllocator* object safe for multithreaded use, because the allocator-presenter is called from at least two threads, the sample application thread and the DirectShow streaming thread. When the reference count goes to zero in the *Release* method, the object deletes itself.

Here is the code for *QueryInterface*.

```
STDMETHODIMP CAllocator::QueryInterface(REFIID iid, void **ppv)
{
    if (ppv == NULL)
    {
        return E_POINTER;
    }
    if (iid == __uuidof(IUnknown))
    {
        *ppv = static_cast<IUnknown*>(
            static_cast<IVMRSurfaceAllocator9*>(this));
    }
    else if (iid == __uuidof(IVMRSurfaceAllocator9))
    {
        *ppv = static_cast<IVMRSurfaceAllocator9*>(this);
    }
    else if (iid == __uuidof(IVMRImagePresenter9))
    {
        *ppv = static_cast<IVMRImagePresenter9*>(this);
    }
    else
    {
        return E_NOINTERFACE;
    }
    AddRef();
    return S_OK;
}
```

In C++ implementations of COM objects, an interface pointer is really just a pointer to the class that exposes the interface. You can think of the interface as a window into the class — the client can "see" only those class methods defined in the interface. The class provides the implementation, while the interface provides the type definition. The client knows about the interface, but nothing about the class, so the class pointer must be coerced to an interface pointer. The static cast operation is valid here because the class inherits the interface.

You might notice the double cast operation when the *IUnknown* interface is requested. This unusual construct is needed because *CAllocator* inherits *IUnknown* twice, once from *IVMRSurfaceAllocator9* and once from *IVMRImagePresenter9*. Therefore, casting the *this* pointer directly to an *IUnknown* pointer is ambiguous as far as the compiler is concerned. To disambiguate, we must cast the pointer first to an *IVMRSurfaceAllocator9* or *IVMRImagePresenter9* pointer (the choice is arbitrary), and from there to an *IUnknown* pointer. Just one of the minor obscure mysteries of COM.

Before returning the interface pointer, the object increments its own reference count. The client will later call *Release* on the interface pointer, for a net change of zero.

Note Some people prefer to use ATL to implement COM objects. If you're familiar with the ATL COM wizards and are comfortable with them, by all means use them. Our personal feeling is that ATL is great for doing anything more complicated than what we've done here — for example, if your COM object needs a class factory, a type library, or (shudder) a proxy/stub DLL, then ATL is definitely the way to go. But for a simple *IUnknown* implementation, we find it's easier just to cut and paste the code that we've shown.

Implementing the IVMRSurfaceAllocator9 Methods

The *IVMRSurfaceAllocator9* interface controls how the allocator-presenter creates Direct3D surfaces. The interface contains four methods. We'll discuss them in the order that they are typically called.

Advise Notify

This method should be called by your application to inform the allocator-presenter about the VMR, as we saw in the *CVmrGame::InitializeVMR* method.

```
HRESULT AdviseNotify(
  IVMRSurfaceAllocatorNotify9* pNotify
);
```

The *pNotify* parameter is a pointer to the VMR-9 filter's *IVMRSurface-AllocatorNotify9* interface. The allocator-presenter needs to store the pointer; it will be used later to call methods on the VMR. Here is the *CAllocator* implementation.

```
HRESULT CAllocator::AdviseNotify(IVMRSurfaceAllocatorNotify9* pNotify)
{
    CLock lock(&m_CritSec); // Hold the critical section.
    if (!pNotify)
    {
        return E_POINTER;
```

```
    }
    m_pNotify = pNotify;
    return S_OK;
}
```

Note the use of the *CLock* object, declared in the first line. This object holds the critical section of the allocator-presenter until the *lock* variable goes out of scope. Holding the critical section protects the allocator-presenter's instance data from being modified by another thread until the critical section is released. You'll see this paradigm throughout the *CAllocator* code.

InitializeDevice

The VMR calls this method whenever it needs the allocator-presenter to create one or more Direct3D surfaces. The method might be called several times as the VMR negotiates different formats with the decoder.

```
HRESULT InitializeDevice(
    DWORD_PTR  dwUserID,
    VMR9AllocationInfo* pAllocInfo,
    DWORD*  pNumBuffers
);
```

The *dwUserID* parameter contains whatever value the sample application used for *dwUserID* when it called *IVMRSurfaceAllocatorNotify9::AdviseSurfaceAllocator*. If your sample application connects several instances of the VMR filter to the same allocator-presenter object, you can use this value to identify which filter instance is calling the allocator-presenter. Because the Ducky sample uses only one VMR instance, we can ignore this parameter. (In Chapter 12, we'll see a sample that uses more than one VMR instance.)

The *pAllocInfo* parameter is a pointer to a *VMR9AllocationInfo* structure. The VMR fills in this structure with information about the Direct3D surfaces that it needs. We'll examine the structure fields in a moment.

The *pNumBuffers* parameter is a pointer to a *DWORD* value. When the VMR calls *InitializeDevice*, it sets the value equal to the maximum number of surfaces that it requires. Before the method exits, the allocator-presenter should set the value equal to the actual number of surfaces that were created.

Here is the definition of the *VMR9AllocationInfo* structure.

```
typedef struct VMR9AllocationInfo {
    DWORD     dwFlags;
    DWORD     dwWidth;
    DWORD     dwHeight;
    D3DFORMAT Format;
    D3DPOOL   Pool;
    DWORD     MinBuffers;
    SIZE      szAspectRatio;
    SIZE      szNativeSize;
};
```

The structure members describes the allocation requirements:

- The *dwFlags* field indicates what type of surface to create. For example, the VMR may request an offscreen surface or a texture. The valid flags are defined by the *VMR9SurfaceAllocationFlags* enumeration.

- The *dwWidth* and *dwHeight* fields define the size of the surface.

- The *Format* field defines the surface format. The format could be just about any Direct3D surface format. If the value is *D3DFMT_UNKNOWN*, it means you can use any format compatible with the current display mode. (Generally, you should pick one that has the same color depth as the display mode.) In mixing mode, this field refers to the format for the back-end surface. In pass-through mode, it refers to the format requested by the video decoder. Often this is a YUV format, but it depends entirely on the output formats supported by the decoder. If the source file contains uncompressed video, there won't be a video decoder for that stream. In that case, the requested format might be the native video format — probably an RGB type — or else DirectShow might insert a color converter filter into the stream, in order to match the display mode. For example, if the source is 24-bit RGB and the display mode is 32-bit RGB, the source might be converted up to 32-bit RGB.

- The *Pool* field indicates which Direct3D memory pool to use.

- The *MinBuffers* field gives the minimum number of surfaces to create. Usually this value is the same as *pNumBuffers,* but it could be less. The actual number of surfaces that the allocator-presenter creates should be *MinBuffers* <= N <= *pNumBuffers*. If you always use N = *pNumBuffers*, you'll be safe.

- The *szAspectRatio* field gives the aspect ratio of the video, and *szNativeSize* gives the size of the original video source. These may not be the same value — for example, DV video is natively 720 × 480 pixels, but should be displayed at a 4:3 aspect ratio (640 × 480).

Given all of these parameters, it can be tricky to allocate the surfaces correctly. Luckily, the VMR-9 provides a helper function, *IVMRSurfaceAllocatorNotify9::AllocateSurfaceHelper*, that does the allocation for us. This might seem kind of strange — supposedly we're writing code to allocate Direct3D surfaces for the VMR, but then we call a method on the VMR that does the allocating. Even so, the *InitializeDevice* method gives us a lot of control over the allocation process, even if we use *AllocateSurfaceHelper* to create the surfaces.

For example, the Ducky sample uses *IDirect3DDevice9::StretchRect* to stretch the video onto the back-end surface. Depending on the video driver, there may be limitations as to which formats are supported for *StretchRect* operations. We can therefore use the *InitializeDevice* method to check the proposed format and verify whether the driver supports the format conversion. Also, drivers earlier than DirectX 9.0 cannot stretch a texture surface, so to be safe we can reject any requests for texture surfaces. The *CAllocator* class performs both of these tests before allocating the surfaces.

```cpp
STDMETHODIMP CAllocator::InitializeDevice(DWORD_PTR dwUserID,
    VMR9AllocationInfo* pAllocInfo, DWORD* pNumBuffers)
{
    CLock lock(&m_CritSec);

    // Because we are using StretchRect, we do not want a texture surface.
    if (pAllocInfo->dwFlags & VMR9AllocFlag_TextureSurface)
    {
        return E_FAIL;
    }

    // See if we can stretch this format to the back buffer.
    D3DDISPLAYMODE dm;
    ZeroMemory(&dm, sizeof(D3DDISPLAYMODE));
    HRESULT hr = g_d3d->GetAdapterDisplayMode(D3DADAPTER_DEFAULT, &dm);
    if (FAILED(hr))
    {
        return hr;
    }
    hr = g_d3d->CheckDeviceFormatConversion(D3DADAPTER_DEFAULT,
        D3DDEVTYPE_HAL, pAllocInfo->Format, dm.Format);
    if (FAILED(hr))
    {
        // This format cannot be converted, so we should reject it.
        return VFW_E_INVALIDMEDIATYPE;
    }

    // Free existing surfaces and create a new array of surface pointers.
    ReleaseSurfaces();
    m_pSurf = new IDirect3DSurface9* [*pNumBuffers];
    if (m_pSurf == NULL)
    {
        return E_OUTOFMEMORY;
    }

    // Let the VMR-9 do the surface allocation.
    hr = m_pNotify->AllocateSurfaceHelper(pAllocInfo,
        pNumBuffers, m_pSurf);
    m_dwNumSurfaces = *pNumBuffers;
    if (FAILED(hr))
    {
        ReleaseSurfaces();
        *pNumBuffers = 0;
    }
    return hr;
}
```

First, we hold the critical section with a *CLock* object. Then we check whether the VMR is requesting a texture surface, indicated by the *VMR9AllocFlag_TextureSurface* flag in the *dwFlags* field. If so, we reject the request by returning an error code. Next, we call *IDirect3D9::CheckDeviceFormatConversion* to test whether the proposed surface format can be converted to the display format.

Assuming we get past those hurdles, we create an array of size **pNumBuffers* to hold the *IDirect3DSurface9* pointers. Then we call *AllocateSurfaceHelper* on the VMR, passing in the allocation information plus the address of our array. If all goes well, we update *pNumBuffers* with the number of surfaces. The VMR checks this value when the method returns.

GetSurface

The VMR calls this method to retrieve a surface pointer. It will not call this method until the allocator-presenter has finished creating the surfaces.

```
HRESULT GetSurface(
    DWORD_PTR  dwUserID,
    DWORD  SurfaceIndex,
    DWORD  dwReserved  // Not used.
    IDirect3DSurface9** ppSurface
);
```

The *dwUserID* parameter identifies the VMR instance, as before. The *SurfaceIndex* parameter is an index into the array *of IDirect3DSurface9* pointers. The *GetSurface* method should copy the pointer at that index into the *ppSurface* parameter. The code for this method is straightforward.

```
STDMETHODIMP CAllocator::GetSurface(DWORD_PTR dwUserID, DWORD SurfaceIndex,
    DWORD SurfaceFlags, IDirect3DSurface9** ppSurface)
{
    CLock lock(&m_CritSec);
    if (!ppSurface)
    {
        return E_POINTER;
    }
    if (SurfaceIndex >= m_dwNumSurfaces)
    {
        return E_INVALIDARG;
    }
    assert (m_pSurf != NULL);
    *ppSurface = m_pSurf[SurfaceIndex];
    (*ppSurface)->AddRef();
    return S_OK;
}
```

Note that we have to *AddRef* the pointer before handing it to the VMR. The VMR will call *Release* when it's done with the pointer, as per the rules of COM.

TerminateDevice

The VMR calls this method when it's done using the allocator-presenter.

```
HRESULT TerminateDevice(
    DWORD_PTR  dwUserID
);
```

The only thing we need to do inside this method is release all the surfaces.

```
STDMETHODIMP CAllocator::TerminateDevice(DWORD_PTR  dwID)
{
    CLock lock(&m_CritSec);
    ReleaseSurfaces();
    return S_OK;
}
void CAllocator::ReleaseSurfaces()
{
    // Private method. The caller should hold the critical section.
    for (DWORD i = 0; i < m_dwNumSurfaces; i++)
    {
        SAFE_RELEASE(m_pSurf[i]);
    }
    SAFE_ARRAY_DELETE(m_pSurf);
    m_dwNumSurfaces = 0;
}
```

We noted earlier that the VMR calls the allocator-presenter from a separate thread. It also keeps a reference count on the allocator-presenter. Therefore, the application cannot decide when to release the surfaces, because the VMR might still be using them to decode and mix the video. Even if you stop the filter graph and release all of your Direct-Show interface pointers, a race condition could still occur in which you release a surface that the VMR is still using, causing a run-time exception. Instead, the allocator-presenter must wait until *TerminateDevice* is called before releasing any surfaces.

Implementing the IVMRImagePresenter9 Methods

The *IVMRImagePresenter9* interface controls how the allocator-presenter draws the video frames onto the back buffer. The interface has three methods, but two of them don't need any code. (Well, hardly any code.)

StartPresenting

This method is called right before the graph runs. It is just a notification from the VMR — there's nothing in particular that the allocator-presenter needs to do in this method. But we do need to implement it, because it's part of a COM interface. Therefore, we simply return *S_OK*.

```
STDMETHODIMP CAllocator::StartPresenting(DWORD_PTR dwUserID)
{
    return S_OK;
}
```

StopPresenting

This method is called right after the graph stops. Again, we don't have to do anything inside this method, so we just return *S_OK*.

```
STDMETHODIMP CAllocator::StopPresenting(DWORD_PTR dwUserID)
{
    return S_OK;
}
```

PresentImage

The VMR calls this method whenever it has a new video frame for the allocator-presenter. (You should be aware that this method can be called before the first call to *StartPresenting* or after the last call to *StopPresenting*. For example, if the application pauses the filter graph while the graph is stopped, the VMR calls *PresentImage* to draw one video frame.)

```
HRESULT PresentImage(
    DWORD_PTR   dwUserID
    VMR9PresentationInfo* pPresInfo
);
```

The *pPresInfo* parameter is a pointer to the *VMR9PresentationInfo* structure. This structure holds a pointer to a Direct3D surface containing the video image, plus some additional information such as the presentation time, the duration of the frame, and the correct aspect ratio. For the Ducky sample, we use the surface but ignore the other fields.

```
STDMETHODIMP CAllocator::PresentImage(DWORD_PTR dwUserID,
    VMR9PresentationInfo* pPresInfo)
{
    CLock lock(&m_CritSec);

    // Store the surface pointer in a temporary variable.
    m_pVideoSurf = pPresInfo->lpSurf;

    // Render one frame.
    m_pGame->DoGameLoop();

    // Clear the pointer.
    m_pVideoSurf = NULL;
    return S_OK;
}
```

To draw the scene, the allocator-presenter calls the *DoGameLoop* method on its parent *CVmrGame* class. This method renders one frame in the 3-D scene, including processing the user input from the keyboard, updating the camera and model positions, and so on. Eventually, it results in a call to the *CVmrGame::Render* method, which does the rendering.

```
HRESULT CVmrGame::Render()
{
    CComPtr<IDirect3DSurface9> pRenderTarget;
    m_pDevice->GetRenderTarget(0, &pRenderTarget);

    // Clear the render target.
    m_Device.Clear(0x00);
    // Note: If the video completely overwrites the back buffer,
    // you do not have to clear it. In this case, we need to clear
    // the depth/stencil buffer so the duck gets rendered correctly.

    HRESULT hr = m_pDevice->BeginScene();
    if (FAILED(hr))
    {
        return hr;
    }
    // Stretch the video surface onto the back buffer.
    hr = m_pDevice->StretchRect(m_pAlloc->m_pVideoSurf, NULL,
        pRenderTarget, NULL, D3DTEXF_NONE);
    if (m_pScene)
    {
        m_pScene->Render(m_pDevice);  // Render the scene meshes.
    }
    m_pDevice->EndScene();
    hr = m_pDevice->Present(NULL, NULL, NULL, NULL);
    return hr;
}
```

In this method, we use *IDirect3DDevice9::StretchRect* to stretch the video surface onto the back buffer. The scene object's *Render* method then draws the duck mesh over the video. The *IDirect3DDevice9::Present* method presents the back buffer. And that's it! Next we look at a sample application that uses video on a texture surface.

Video Textures

The Ducky sample is interesting, but it has a number of limitations. For one thing, it uses a plain offscreen surface instead of a texture, and there's a limit to what you can do with ordinary surfaces. Textures offer much more interesting possibilities.

A second limitation is that the Ducky sample renders a frame whenever the VMR tells it to, so the frame rate of the 3D scene is driven by the frame rate of the video. In some situations, this may be what you want. Letting the VMR drive the frame rate will certainly produce the smoothest video playback, so for cut scenes that is probably the best approach. However, you might prefer that the sample controls the frame rate instead.

A third limitation is that the Ducky sample uses the VMR in pass-through mode. Pass-through mode has several drawbacks compared with mixing mode. First, there is no video mixing, and the VMR can only render one video stream. Second, you get the video frames exactly as the decoder outputs them, with no massaging by the VMR. For example, there is no automatic deinterlacing. If you watch the Ducky video carefully, you can see horizontal jagged lines ("jaggies") in the image, especially when the camera pans. This is because the source file is interlaced DV video. The video frames from the decoder contain two fields interleaved together, causing jagged lines in the image. (See the Deinterlacing sidebar.) In mixing mode, the VMR automatically deinterlaces the frame.

The next sample application that we'll describe addresses both of these issues. Run the TeeVee sample that is located in the AVBook\bin directory. This sample renders a 3-D scene of a room with a television set on the floor (see Plate 7). Video plays on the back wall of the room, and the same video plays on the television screen. To achieve this effect, a texture surface is used for the video. When the scene is rendered, the texture is applied twice — once to the back wall of the room mesh, and once to the television mesh. If you move the camera, you can see that the television screen is convex, causing a slight "fish-eye" effect. The television screen also has a specular component, which simulates the effect of light reflecting from the glass. These are only some of the possibilities offered by video textures.

A lot of the code in the TeeVee sample is identical to the Ducky sample, so in the following sections we'll focus on the differences.

What is Deinterlacing?

A television draws an image by moving an electron beam across the surface of the glass. The glass is coated with phosphor, which emits light when struck by the beam. However, the beam does not draw every horizontal scan line on each pass; instead, it skips alternate lines on one pass and draws the missing lines on the next pass. For example, on the first pass it might draw lines 0, 2, 4, 6, and so on. On the next pass it draws lines 1, 3, 5, 7, and so on. Each set of alternating scan lines is called a *field*. Two fields make up one frame, so the effective frame rate is half the number of fields per second. For example, 60 fields per second gives a frame rate of 30 frames per second. This type of video display, shown in Figure 10.4, is called *interlaced* video. Analog television broadcasts are one source of interlaced video, and DV camcorders are another.

Unlike television sets, most computer monitors are *progressive* displays, which means the monitor draws every scan line on each pass instead of skipping lines. To display interlaced video on a progressive monitor, you must *deinterlace* the video by constructing frames that contain all of the scan lines. The problem is that the second field occurs slightly later than the first field. If there is a lot of motion in the scene, there may be obvious differences between the two fields.

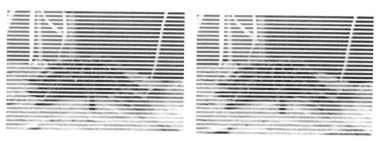

Figure 10.4   Two fields of interlaced video.

The two simplest techniques for deinterlacing video are *bob* and *weave*, shown in Figure 10.5. In bob mode, the fields are displayed sequentially. To fill in the missing lines, each scan line is stretched to twice its height. In weave mode, both fields are combined into a single frame by interleaving the scan lines.

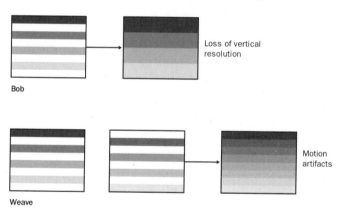

Figure 10.5   Bob and weave modes.

Both techniques have drawbacks. Bob mode reduces the vertical resolution of the image, and weave mode can result in motion artifacts, because two sequential fields are displayed at the same time. More sophisticated deinterlacing techniques use interpolation to fill in the missing information. These techniques can often be implemented very efficiently by the graphics hardware. The DirectShow DV decoder filter outputs each DV frame as two interleaved fields, so in effect, it implements weave mode. When the VMR is in mixing mode, a more advanced deinterlacing technique may be applied before the frame is rendered. (In Chapter 12, we'll see how an application can set deinterlacing preferences.) The Ducky sample uses the VMR in pass-through mode, so the only deinterlacing is the DV decoder's weave, which results in the characteristic jagged lines.

Setting the VMR to Use Mixing Mode

The TeeVee sample uses mixing mode instead of pass-through mode. As we mentioned earlier, pass-through mode is the default setting for the VMR-9 in renderless mode. To enable mixing mode, call *IVMRFilterConfig9::SetNumberOfStreams* before you connect any of the video streams, and specify the maximum number of video streams that you plan to connect. This value can be 1 if you don't plan to mix multiple streams but still want the VMR to load the compositor. To support mixing mode, the TeeVee sample adds a new member variable, *m_dwNumStreams*, to the *CGraph* class. If the value of *m_dwNumStreams* is more than zero, the *InitVMR_RenderlessMode* function calls *SetNumberOfStreams* with the specified value. The new code is shown in bold type.

```
HRESULT CGraph::InitVMR_RenderlessMode(
    IVMRSurfaceAllocatorNotify9 **ppAlloc)
{
    ....
    /* The rest of this function does not change. */
    ....

    if (m_dwNumStreams > 0)
    {
        hr = pConfig->SetNumberOfStreams(m_dwNumStreams);
    }
    return m_pVMR.QueryInterface(ppAlloc);
}
```

The *CVmrGame* class sets the value of *m_dwNumStreams* to 1 before calling *InitVMR_RenderlessMode*.

Restoring the Render Target

In mixing mode, the VMR switches the render target while you're not looking. The reason for this behavior is that the VMR uses Direct3D to composite the video frames onto the back-end surface, and it needs to set this surface as the render target. However, it doesn't restore the original render target when it's done, so we have to restore it before we draw our scene.

In the *CAllocator::SetDevice* method, we call *IDirect3DDevice9::GetRenderTarget* to get a pointer to the current render target, and we store this pointer in a new member variable, *m_pRenderTarget*. (Recall that *SetDevice* is a custom method on our allocator-presenter, and is not part of the COM interfaces.) Here is the new code.

```
HRESULT CAllocator::SetDevice(IDirect3DDevice9 *pDevice)
{
    if (!pDevice)
    {
        return E_POINTER;
    }
```

```
    m_pDevice = pDevice;
    m_pRenderTarget.Release(); // Release the old pointer, if any.
    m_pDevice->GetRenderTarget(0, &m_pRenderTarget);
    return S_OK;
}
```

Now we can restore the render target in the *PresentImage* method:

```
STDMETHODIMP CAllocator::PresentImage(DWORD_PTR dwUserID,
    VMR9PresentationInfo* pPresInfo)
{
    CLock lock(&m_CritSec);

    // Restore the original render target.
    m_pDevice->SetRenderTarget(0, m_pRenderTarget);

    ....

    return hr;
}
```

Creating a Texture Surface

To create a texture surface in the *InitializeDevice* method, we add the *VMR9-AllocFlag_TextureSurface* flag to the *dwFlags* field in the *VMR9AllocationInfo* structure. Also, we get rid of the code from the Ducky sample that calls *CheckDeviceFormatConversion*, which was needed to test for *StretchRect* support. The new code is shown in bold.

```
STDMETHODIMP CAllocator::InitializeDevice(DWORD_PTR dwUserID,
    VMR9AllocationInfo* pAllocInfo, DWORD* pNumBuffers)
{
    CLock lock(&m_CritSec);
    if (!pAllocInfo || !pNumBuffers)
    {
        return E_POINTER;
    }

    // We want a texture surface.
    pAllocInfo->dwFlags |= VMR9AllocFlag_TextureSurface;

    ....
    // Create the array of surface pointers, and allocate the surfaces.
    // This code is identical to the Ducky sample.

}
```

Not all video drivers support texture surfaces with non-power-of-2 sizes. For now, we'll simply gloss over this issue and assume that the video driver supports them. However, this is a complication that we do need to consider, and we'll come back to it at the end of this chapter.

Rendering the Scene

When it is time to render a frame, the VMR calls *PresentImage*. First we restore the render target, as shown earlier. Then we retrieve a pointer to the surface's texture by calling *IDirect3DSurface9::GetContainer*. (The VMR always gives us a pointer to the surface, not the texture.) The *CVmrGame* class will use this texture when it renders the scene.

```
STDMETHODIMP CAllocator::PresentImage(DWORD_PTR dwUserID,
    VMR9PresentationInfo* pPresInfo)
{
    CLock lock(&m_CritSec);

    // Restore the original render target.
    m_pDevice->SetRenderTarget(0, m_pRenderTarget );

    // Get the parent texture from the surface pointer.
    pPresInfo->lpSurf->GetContainer(IID_IDirect3DTexture9,
        (void**)&m_pVideoTex);

    // Render the frame.
    m_pGame->DoGameLoop();

    // Release the texture.
    m_pVideoTex.Release();
    return S_OK;
}
```

Some changes are also needed in the code that renders the scene. Obviously, the scene objects themselves are different, as reflected in how the *CMyScene* class loads the meshes. But we also need to associate the video texture surface with the scene objects. Here is the new code.

```
HRESULT CVmrGame::Render()
{
    // Restore rendering settings that the VMR may have changed.
    RestoreRenderSettings();
    m_Device.Clear(0x00);
    HRESULT hr = m_pDevice->BeginScene();
    if (FAILED(hr))
    {
        return hr;
    }
```

```
// Get the video texture pointer from the allocator.
IDirect3DTexture9 *pTex = m_pAlloc->m_pVideoTex;
if (m_pScene)
{
    // Set the video texture on the scene meshes.
    CMesh *p1 = m_pScene->m_MeshList[ROOM_MESH];
    CMesh *p2 = m_pScene->m_MeshList[TV_MESH];

    p1->SetTexture(ROOM_MESH_BACKWALL, pTex);
    p2->SetTexture(TV_MESH_SCREEN, pTex);

    m_pScene->Render(m_pDevice);  // Render the scene meshes.

    // Clear the texture, because pTex will become invalid
    // after this method returns.
    p1->SetTexture(ROOM_MESH_BACKWALL, NULL);
    p2->SetTexture(TV_MESH_SCREEN, NULL);
}
m_pDevice->EndScene();
hr = m_pDevice->Present(NULL, NULL, NULL, NULL);
return hr;
}
```

The *RestoreRenderSettings* method restores some render settings that the VMR may have changed when it mixed the video. We'll explain that code in a moment. Next, we call a method on our custom *CMesh* class to associate the video texture with a particular subset of the mesh, overriding whatever texture was defined in the original model. For the TeeVee sample, we place the video texture on the back wall of the room and on the television screen. The indices of the mesh subsets are hard-coded using *define* constants, based on the models that we loaded. Here is the code for the *CMesh::SetTexture* method.

```
HRESULT CMesh::SetTexure(DWORD iSubset, IDirect3DTexture9 *pTexture)
{
    if (iSubset >= m_dwNumMaterials)
    {
        return E_INVALIDARG;
    }
    SAFE_RELEASE(m_ppTextures[iSubset]);
    m_ppTextures[iSubset] = pTexture;
    if (pTexture)
    {
        pTexture->AddRef();
    }
    return S_OK;
}
```

Switching textures is relatively costly in the rendering pipeline, so a good optimization is to sort your meshes by texture — unlike the code here, which was designed mainly for ease of implementation.

VMR Render States in Mixing Mode

In mixing mode, the VMR changes some of the Direct3D render states so that it can mix the video streams onto the back-end surface. Therefore, we set them back in the *Restore-RenderSettings* function. Of course, your own application may use different settings than the ones shown here.

```
void CVmrGame::RestoreRenderSettings()
{
    m_pDevice->SetRenderState(D3DRS_CULLMODE, D3DCULL_CCW);
    m_pDevice->SetRenderState(D3DRS_LIGHTING, TRUE);
    m_pDevice->SetRenderState(D3DRS_AMBIENT, m_AmbientLightColor);
    m_pDevice->SetRenderState(D3DRS_ALPHABLENDENABLE, FALSE);
    m_pDevice->SetRenderState(D3DRS_ALPHATESTENABLE, FALSE);
    m_pDevice->SetRenderState(D3DRS_SRCBLEND, D3DBLEND_ONE);
    m_pDevice->SetRenderState(D3DRS_DESTBLEND, D3DBLEND_ZERO);

    m_pDevice->SetTextureStageState(0, D3DTSS_COLOROP, D3DTOP_MODULATE);
    m_pDevice->SetTextureStageState(0, D3DTSS_COLORARG1, D3DTA_TEXTURE);
    m_pDevice->SetTextureStageState(0, D3DTSS_COLORARG2, D3DTA_CURRENT);

    m_pDevice->SetSamplerState(0, D3DSAMP_ADDRESSU, D3DTADDRESS_CLAMP);
    m_pDevice->SetSamplerState(0, D3DSAMP_ADDRESSV, D3DTADDRESS_CLAMP);

    m_pDevice->SetSamplerState(0, D3DSAMP_MAGFILTER, D3DTEXF_LINEAR);
    m_pDevice->SetSamplerState(0, D3DSAMP_MINFILTER, D3DTEXF_LINEAR);
    m_pDevice->SetSamplerState(0, D3DSAMP_MIPFILTER, D3DTEXF_LINEAR);

}
```

The following tables list the settings that the VMR uses in mixing mode.

Render state	Setting	Description
D3DRS_CULLMODE	D3DCULL_NONE	Do not cull back faces.
D3DRS_LIGHTING	FALSE	Disable lighting.
D3DRS_ALPHABLENDENABLE	TRUE	Enable alpha blending.
D3DRS_SRCBLEND	D3DBLEND_SRCALPHA	Blend the source's alpha value.
D3DRS_DESTBLEND	D3DBLEND_INVSRCALPHA	Blend the inverse of the destination's alpha value (1 - alpha).

Texture stage 0	Setting	Description
D3DTSS_COLOROP	D3DTOP_SELECTARG1	Use the first color argument, unmodulated.
D3DTSS_COLORARG1	D3DTA_TEXTURE	Use the texture color.
D3DTSS_ALPHAARG1	D3DTA_DIFFUSE	Use the diffuse vertex color for the alpha.

Sampler state	Setting	Description
D3DSAMP_ADDRESSU	D3DTADDRESS_CLAMP	Clamp texture along the u-axis.
D3DSAMP_ADDRESSV	D3DTADDRESS_CLAMP	Clamp texture along the v-axis.
D3DSAMP_MAGFILTER	Depends on the value set in *IVMRMixerControl9::SetMixingPrefs*. Defaults to point filtering (D3DTEXF_POINT).	
D3DSAMP_MINFILTER		
D3DSAMP_MIPFILTER		

The flexible vertex format (FVF) is set to *D3DFVF_XYZRHW | D3DFVF_DIFFUSE | D3DFVF_TEX1*. The diffuse vertex color is white (0xFFFFFF) and lighting is disabled, so no Gouraud shading is performed on the pixels in the frame.

For each stream, if the media type has a valid alpha channel (which is not common), the VMR sets the following render states.

Render state	Setting	Description
D3DRS_ALPHATESTENABLE	TRUE	Enable per-pixel alpha testing.
D3DRS_ALPHAFUNC	D3DCMP_GREATER	Write only pixels that exceed the reference alpha.
D3DRS_ALPHAREF	0x10	Reference alpha.

Texture stage 0	Setting	Description
D3DTSS_ALPHAOP	D3DTOP_MODULATE	Modulate the two alpha arguments.
D3DTSS_ALPHAARG1	D3DTA_TEXTURE	Use the texture color for argument 1.
D3DTSS_ALPHAARG2	D3DTA_DIFFUSE	Use the diffuse vertex color for argument 2.

These settings enable per-pixel alpha testing. Otherwise, if the media type does not contain a valid alpha channel, the VMR sets the following values.

Render state	Setting	Description
D3DRS_ALPHATESTENABLE	FALSE	Disable per-pixel alpha testing.

Texture stage 0	Setting	Description
D3DTSS_ALPHAOP	D3DTOP_SELECTARG1	Use the first alpha argument, unmodulated.
D3DTSS_ALPHAARG1	D3DTA_DIFFUSE	Use the diffuse vertex color.

Note that even when the incoming video does not contain alpha information, the video frame as a whole may have an alpha value set by the sample application, as part of the mixing preferences.

Handling Non-Power-of-2 Textures

The graphics driver may not support textures with non-power-of-2 dimensions. The dimensions of your video source are not likely to be even powers of 2, so if the driver requires power-of-2 textures, we need to adjust the size of the texture inside the *InitializeDevice* method.

To check for driver support, call *IDirect3DDevice9::GetDeviceCaps* and examine the *TextureCaps* field. The *D3DPTEXTURECAPS_POW2* flag means the driver does not provide general support for non-power-of-2 textures. This flag might be combined with the *D3DPTEXTURECAPS_NONPOW2CONDITIONAL* flag, which means the driver supports certain kinds of non-power-of-2 textures, but with various restrictions. Depending on your sample application, you may want to check for that flag or simply ignore it. (In our experience, it's safer to ignore the flag and always create power-of-2 textures if the *D3DPTEXTURECAPS_POW2* flag is present.) Also check for the *D3DPTEXTURECAPS_SQUAREONLY* flag, which means the driver requires square textures.

If you determine that a power-of-2 texture is required, simply scale up the width and height to the next power of 2 before calling *AllocateSurfaceHelper*. If a square texture is required, take the maximum of both dimensions. To handle these various permutations, the TeeVee sample adds the following helper function, *AdjustTextureSize*, to the *CAllocator* class.

```
void CAllocator::AdjustTextureSize(VMR9AllocationInfo* pAllocInfo)
{
    D3DCAPS9 caps;
    m_pDevice->GetDeviceCaps( &caps );
    if (caps.TextureCaps & D3DPTEXTURECAPS_POW2)
    {
        DWORD dwWidth = 1;
        DWORD dwHeight = 1;
        // Multiply each dimension by 2 until it is large enough.
        while( dwWidth < pAllocInfo->dwWidth )
        {
            dwWidth = dwWidth << 1;
        }
        while( dwHeight < pAllocInfo->dwHeight )
        {
            dwHeight = dwHeight << 1;
        }
        // Check whether square textures are required.
        if (caps.TextureCaps & D3DPTEXTURECAPS_SQUAREONLY)
        {
            dwHeight = dwWidth = max(dwWidth, dwHeight);
        }
        // Calculate the scaling factor for the texel coordinates.
        m_fTU = (float)(pAllocInfo->dwWidth) / (float)(dwWidth);
        m_fTV = (float)(pAllocInfo->dwHeight) / (float)(dwHeight);
        // Set the new dimensions.
        pAllocInfo->dwWidth = dwWidth;
        pAllocInfo->dwHeight = dwHeight;
    }
}
```

If the texture surface is scaled up, you don't want the extra area of the texture to show. (It will be filled with the background color specified by the mixing preferences of the application, with black as the default color.) The *m_fTU* and *m_fTV* variables in the *AdjustTextureSize* function are used to calculate a scaling factor for the texels in each dimension. Both variables are initialized to 1.0, so if the driver does support non-power-of-2 textures, the entire texture is applied to the model. Otherwise, a smaller portion of the texture is applied. The following function sets the appropriate scaling transform on the first texture stage.

```
HRESULT CAllocator::ScaleVideoTexture()
{
    CLock lock(&m_CritSec);
    HRESULT hr = S_OK;
    if ((m_fTU != 1.0f) || (m_fTV != 1.0f))
    {
        D3DXMATRIX  mat;
        D3DXMatrixIdentity(&mat);
        D3DXMatrixScaling(&mat, m_fTU, m_fTV, 1.0f);
        hr = m_pDevice->SetTransform(D3DTS_TEXTURE0, &mat);
        if (SUCCEEDED(hr))
        {
            hr = m_pDevice->SetTextureStageState(0,
                D3DTSS_TEXTURETRANSFORMFLAGS, D3DTTFF_COUNT2);
        }
    }
    return hr;
}
```

In the TeeVee sample, the other textures in the scene are just patterns, so it doesn't matter if they get scaled. Therefore, we just call *ScaleVideoTexture* once, and the same texture transform remains in place throughout the rendering process. With more complicated models, you probably want to remove the scaling transform when you apply the other textures in the scene, or else use two texture stages.

Oversized Textures

If the video image is larger than the back buffer, Direct3D will complain (via the debug output) that your depth-stencil buffer is smaller than your render target, and it won't render the video.

This is unlikely to happen in full-screen mode. But suppose your application renders DV video (640 x 480) in windowed mode, using power-of-2 textures. The resulting video texture will be 1024 x 512 pixels, which could easily be larger than the application window. In that case, you need to replace the default depth buffer with a larger one. (This assumes that you set *EnableAutoDepthStencil* to *TRUE* when you first created the Direct3D device.) Create a new depth buffer by calling *IDirect3DDevice9::CreateDepthStencilSurface*. Then call *IDirect3DDevice9::SetDepthStencilSurface* to set the new buffer. The *CAllocator::FixDepthBuffer* function encapsulates this process.

```
HRESULT CAllocator::FixDepthBuffer(VMR9Alloca tionInfo* pAllocInfo)
{
    // Private method. The caller should hold the critical section.
    HRESULT hr = S_OK;
    // Check if the video size is larger than the back buffer.
    if ((pAllocInfo->dwWidth > m_pGame->m_Device.GetWidth()) ||
        (pAllocInfo->dwHeight > m_pGame->m_Device.GetHeight()))
    {
        // Create a new depth buffer.
        CComPtr<IDirect3DSurface9> pDepth;
        hr = m_pDevice->CreateDepthStencilSurface(
            pAllocInfo->dwWidth,  // Width
            pAllocInfo->dwHeight, // Height
            m_pGame->m_Device.GetDepthStencilFormat(),  // Same format.
            D3DMULTISAMPLE_NONE,  // No multisampling
            0,                    // Multisample quality
            FALSE,                // Disable z-buffer discarding.
            &pDepth,
            NULL);
        if (SUCCEEDED(hr))
        {
            hr = m_pDevice->SetDepthStencilSurface(pDepth);
        }
    }
    return hr;
}
```

Frame Stepping

We mentioned earlier that you might want the application, rather than the VMR, to control the frame rate. Unfortunately there's no elegant solution to this problem. The fundamental difficulty is that DirectShow works on a "push" model — the AVI Splitter filter pushes samples to the decoder as quickly as possible, and the VMR controls the flow of data by holding frames until it is time for them to be rendered. Ideally, we would want a "pull" model, in which the application requests frames one at a time. DirectShow does not provide this ability directly, but we can get almost the same effect by using a technique called *frame stepping*. Frame stepping enables the VMR to step through the video one frame at a time.

First, we must deactivate the filter graph's clock. Normally, the Filter Graph Manager automatically selects a clock for the entire graph, called the *reference clock*. The reference clock enables the renderer filters to schedule when they render samples, based on the presentation time of each sample. It is also used to keep audio and video streams in sync. Because we're using frame stepping, we don't want the VMR to schedule the rendering. Therefore, we disable the reference clock by calling the Filter Graph Manager's *IMFMediaFilter::SetSyncSource* method with the value *NULL*.

```
CComQIPtr<IMediaFilter> pMF(m_pGraph);
pMF->SetSyncSource(NULL);
```

Next, instead of running the filter graph by calling *Run*, we call *IVideoFrame-Step::Step* to step forward by one frame.

```
CComPtr<IVideoFrameStep>    m_pFrameStep;
m_pGraph.QueryInterface(&m_pFrameStep);
hr = m_pFrameStep->CanStep(1, NULL);
if (SUCCEEDED(hr))
{
    m_pFrameStep->Step(1, NULL);
}
```

The *IVideoFrameStep* interface is exposed by the Filter Graph Manager, but the frame-stepping mechanism is implemented, in this case, by the VMR filter. If no filter in the graph supports frame stepping, the *CanStep* method returns an error code. That shouldn't happen, because we know that the VMR supports frame stepping, but it doesn't hurt to check. The first parameter to the *Step* and *CanStep* methods is the number of frames to step. For example, you could step forward 2 frames at a time, skipping every other frame. Even if you skip frames, however, the decoder still decodes the frames that you skip, because the VMR is doing the stepping, not the decoder. (In any case, with many kinds of video compression, it is not possible for the decoder to skip frames arbitrarily, because the previous frames are needed to decode the current frame.)

The *Step* method is asynchronous, so it returns immediately. When the VMR has a new frame ready, it calls the *Present* method of the allocator-presenter on the DirectShow streaming thread, as before. When the frame has been rendered, the Filter Graph Manager sends an *EC_STEP_COMPLETE* event to the application. This signals that you can call *Step* again to step forward another frame. We add this logic to the event handling code in the *CVmrGame* class.

```
void CVmrGame::OnGraphEvent(long lEvent, long lParam1, long lParam2)
{
    if (lEvent == EC_STEP_COMPLETE)
    {
        m_Graph.FrameStep();
    }
    else if (lEvent == EC_COMPLETE)
    {
        m_Graph.Stop();
        m_Graph.Seek(0);
        m_Graph.FrameStep();
    }
}
```

Now the graph will run as fast as the decoder can run, or as fast as the application allows. If you set the Direct3D presentation interval to *D3DPRESENT_INTER-VAL_DEFAULT*, rendering will also be gated by the monitor refresh rate.

Using Surface Copies for Independent Frame Rates

We've shown two different ways to get video frames from the VMR. In the Ducky sample, the video is rendered on a DirectShow streaming thread and the VMR tells the sample when to present a new frame. In the TeeVee sample, the sample requests a new frame and the VMR notifies it when the frame is available. In both cases, the 3-D scene is drawn once for every video frame. A third option is to make a private copy of the video frame and always draw from the private copy. With this approach, you can draw the 3-D scene at any frame rate, independent of the video frame rate. Just make sure to hold a critical section for any code paths that access the surface. The drawback is the extra copy required. Also, this approach can only work in pass-through mode. In mixing mode, the VMR uses the Direct3D device to composite the video. As a result, the only time it's safe for the application to make *BeginScene* and *EndScene* calls is inside the *PresentImage* method of the allocator-presenter.

Summary

This chapter showed how you can integrate video into your 3-D scene. Hopefully the Ducky and TeeVee samples sparked your imagination and gave you some ideas of how you can incorporate video in your own games. In the next chapter, we take control over the video-mixing process.

11

Customizing Compositors

In Chapter 10, you learned how to write an allocator-presenter that renders video from the Video Mixing Renderer (VMR) onto a Direct3D scene of your choice. As you saw, the allocator-presenter is not involved in the video mixing process. Instead, another component, the compositor, mixes the input streams, and the VMR passes the result to the allocator-presenter.

The VMR's default compositor gives you a fair amount of control over the mixing process, through the *IVMRMixerControl9* interface (see Chapter 9). You can position and resize the input streams relative to each other, set the transparency and z-order, and so forth — but none of the mixing settings goes beyond your basic video inside a rectangle. We want circular video, fragmented video, false-color video — in short, *weird-looking* video — and we can do that by writing our own compositors.

Implementing a Compositor

A compositor must implement the *IVMRImageCompositor9* interface. We'll give a quick overview of the methods in this interface before we look at some implementations.

InitCompositionDevice

This method is called when the VMR selects a new render target.

```
HRESULT InitCompositionDevice(
  IUnknown* pD3DDevice
);
```

The *pD3DDevice* parameter is a pointer to the *IUnknown* interface of the Direct3D device. You can query this pointer for the *IDirect3DDevice9* interface. Typically, a compositor will cache this pointer so that it can call methods on the device later. You could also use the *InitCompositionDevice* method to perform other initializations. For example, you might attach a depth/stencil buffer to the render target, or create any resources that you'll need later.

SetStreamMediaType

This method is called whenever the format changes on an input stream.

```
HRESULT SetStreamMediaType(
    DWORD  dwStrmID,
    AM_MEDIA_TYPE*  pmt,
    BOOL  fTexture
);
```

The *dwStrmID* parameter identifies the input stream. This number corresponds to the index of input pin on the VMR that receives the video stream. The first pin is stream 0, the second is stream 1, and so on. During mixing, the VMR sorts the video frames according to their z-order. As a result, the stream identifier does not always correspond to the mixing order. For example, the compositor may be asked to render stream 2 on the bottom, stream 0 in the middle, and stream 1 on the top. The application sets the z-order by calling *IVMRMixerControl9::SetZOrder*, as described in Chapter 9. The range of stream identifiers is fixed at 0 through 15.

The *pmt* parameter is a pointer to the *AM_MEDIA_TYPE* structure. This structure, called a *media type*, is used in DirectShow to describe any kind of media format. In this case, the *pmt* parameter describes the format of the video stream. The pointer may also be *NULL* to clear the media type for that stream. We'll have more to say about media types later in this chapter.

The *fTexture* flag is *TRUE* if the decoder surface is a texture, or *FALSE* otherwise. This information is useful if you want to use textures in your compositor. If the flag is *FALSE*, you'll need to create a private texture and copy the video surface to that texture.

If your compositor refers to the media type and the texture flag during rendering, copy this information into an array that is indexed by stream identifier. If *pmt* is *NULL*, clear the array entry. Be aware that *SetStreamMediaType* can be called multiple times for each stream, with both *NULL* and non-*NULL* pointers assigned to *pmt*, seemingly at random. (Of course, it's not really random; it's all part of the DirectShow filter connection process.)

CompositeImage

This method is used to mix the video frames, so it's where most of the work is done in a compositor.

```
HRESULT CompositeImage(
    IUnknown*  pD3DDevice,
    IDirect3DSurface9*  pRenderTarget,
```

```
    AM_MEDIA_TYPE* pmtRenderTarget,
    REFERENCE_TIME rtStart,
    REFERENCE_TIME rtEnd,
    D3DCOLOR dwClrBkGnd,
    VMR9VideoStreamInfo* pVideoStreamInfo,
    UINT cStreams
);
```

The parameters to this method contain all of the information needed to mix the video streams:

■   *pD3DDevice* is a pointer to the device's *IUnknown* interface.

■   *pRenderTarget* is a pointer to the render target where the video frames should be drawn. The compositor does not have to set the render target on the device. The VMR automatically sets the render target before calling *CompositeImage*.

■   *pmtRenderTarget* is a media structure that describes the format of the render target.

■   *rtStart* and *rtEnd* contain the start and end times of the final composited image. These values are useful if your compositor does any kind of transition between videos. You can use the start and end times to calculate how far along you are in the transition.

■   *dwClrBkGnd* is the background color for the render target surface. The application sets this value by calling *IVMRMixerControl9::SetBackgroundClr*. If any part of the render target does not contain composited video, or if the video is transparent, the background should be filled with this color.

■   *pVideoStreamInfo* is a pointer to an array of *VMR9VideoStreamInfo* structures that contain additional information about each stream. The size of the array is given in *cStreams*. The array is sorted by z-order, from back to front. That means you can loop through the array in order, draw each frame, and the resulting image will have the correct z-ordering.

Here is the definition of the VMR9VideoStreamInfo structure.

```
typedef struct VMR9VideoStreamInfo {
    IDirect3DSurface9* pddsVideoSurface;
    DWORD              dwWidth;
    DWORD              dwHeight;
    DWORD              dwStrmID;
    FLOAT              fAlpha;
    VMR9NormalizedRect rNormal;
    REFERENCE_TIME     rtStart;
    REFERENCE_TIME     rtEnd;
    VMR9_SampleFormat  SampleFormat;
};
```

This structure contains the following members:

- *pddsVideoSurface* is a pointer to the surface that contains the decoded video frame.

- *dwWidth* and *dwHeight* are the width and height of the video surface.

- *dwStrmID* is the stream identifier.

- *fAlpha* is the stream's alpha value. The application sets this value by calling *IVMRMixerControl9::SetAlpha*. You should apply this value to the entire video surface.

- *rNormal* specifies the normalized rectangle where the video should appear. If you recall from Chapter 9, the render target is defined as having coordinates that range from (0.0, 0.0) to (1.0, 1.0). Anything that falls outside this range is clipped. Each stream is positioned relative to these coordinates. The application sets the normalized rectangle by calling *IVMRMixerControl9::SetOutputRect*.

- *rtStart* and *rtEnd* are the start and end times of the frame. These values do not necessarily match the *rtStart* and *rtEnd* parameters for the composited image, because the various input streams can have different frame rates.

- For interlaced video, the *SampleFormat* flag indicates how a particular frame is interlaced. For progressive frames, the value is *VMR9_SampleProgressiveFrame*.

Keep in mind that your own custom compositor can ignore any of the mixing settings that are defined by the *IVMRMixerControl9* interface. For example, you may not care about the placement of the video streams in composition space, in which case you can ignore the values for *rNormal*. It all depends on what effect you are trying to achieve. Also, remember that the compositor does not present the final image — that's the responsibility of the allocator-presenter.

TermCompositionDevice

This method is called when the VMR-9 has finished mixing. Use it to free resources, if needed.

```
HRESULT TermCompositionDevice(
    IUnknown* pD3DDevice
);
```

Again, the *pD3DDevice* parameter is a pointer to the device's *IUnknown* interface.

A Note about Compositors and Deinterlacing

One significant drawback of custom compositors should be noted, which is the lack of hardware-accelerated deinterlacing. The compositor is responsible for deinterlacing any interlaced video content that it receives. The default compositor of the VMR performs hardware-accelerated deinterlacing when the graphics card supports it. Unfortunately, there is no way for a user-mode component to use the same functionality. To perform deinterlacing in a compositor, therefore, you would have to implement the deinterlacing routines in software — which is not a trivial task. With no deinterlacing support, it's effectively impossible to write a general-purpose compositor. In the context of game programming, however, you can assume that you control the authored content, so you can side-step the whole problem by not using interlaced video.

Setting the Compositor on the VMR

Once the compositor has been implemented, attaching it to the VMR is easy. Just call *IVMRFilterConfig9::SetImageCompositor* with a pointer to the compositor's *IVMRImage-Compositor9* interface.

```
// Create a new instance of the compositor.
m_pMixer = new CMixer();  // CMixer inherits IVMRImageCompositor9.
if (!m_pMixer)
{
    return E_OUTOFMEMORY;
}
// Increment the reference count.
m_pMixer->AddRef();

// Query the VMR for the IVMRFilterConfig9 interface.
CComQIPtr<IVMRFilterConfig9> pConfig(m_pWC);

// Assign the custom compositor.
pConfig->SetImageCompositor(pMix);
```

One minor point to keep in mind is that the VMR does not automatically load the compositor when you call *SetImageCompositor*. Instead, it merely stores a copy of the *IVMRImageCompositor9* pointer. It will load the compositor if it switches to mixing mode, but not if it remains in pass-through mode. So if video starts playing but the VMR never calls any methods on your compositor, check to make sure that your application calls *IVMRFilterConfig9::SetNumberOfStreams* to activate mixing mode.

Video 15 Puzzle

Now that you have seen the general outlines of writing a compositor, it's time for some specific examples. For our first example, we'll write a video 15 puzzle.

A 15 puzzle, also called a *slide puzzle*, is a set of 15 tiles placed in a square frame, with an empty slot where the 16th tile would be. The tiles can be shuffled by sliding them horizontally or vertically, the object being to return the tiles to their original configuration. Typically, there is a picture on the tiles; when you solve the puzzle, you get to see the completed picture. Using the VMR, we can add a modern twist to an old game by putting video on the tiles instead of a static image. All we need is a compositor that divides the video into rectangles and draws them on the puzzle tiles. To see the video 15 puzzle in action, run the FifteenPuzzle sample that is in the AVBook\bin directory. (See Plate 8.)

The UI portion of the FifteenPuzzle application is essentially the same as the Mangler application from Chapter 9, minus the controls for setting the mixing preferences (because our compositor will ignore them anyway). The graph-building code is almost the same as well, except that we call *IVMRFilterConfig9::SetImageCompositor* to set the compositor, as described in the previous section. The compositor is an instance of the *CPuzzleMixer* class, declared as follows.

```
class CPuzzleMixer : public IVMRImageCompositor9
{
public:
    CPuzzleMixer(void);
    ~CPuzzleMixer(void);
    void HandleMouseClick(POINT &pt);
    void ShufflePuzzle() { m_puzzle.Shuffle(); }

    // IUnknown methods (not listed).
    // IVMRImageCompositor9 methods (not listed).

private:
    long m_nRefCount;         // Reference count.
    CCriticalSection m_CritSec; // Critical section.
    CPuzzle m_puzzle;         // Manages the puzzle.
    ScaledRect m_SrcRect;     // Scales the source rectangle.
    ScaledRect m_DestRect;    // Scales the destination rectangle.
};
```

The *CPuzzle* object (declared as the *m_puzzle* variable) manages the state of the puzzle. This class contains an abstract representation of the puzzle tiles — it knows nothing about the video surfaces that are drawn on the tiles. Tile coordinates, as defined by this class, range from 0 to 1. The *m_SrcRect* and *m_DestRect* variables, which are both instances of the *ScaledRect* class, are used to map the tile coordinates to pixels. For example, if the destination rectangle is 320 pixels wide, then tile coordinate 1.0 maps to pixel 320, as shown in Figure 11.1.

Each tile has a starting position and a current position. The starting position is the tile's location before the puzzle is shuffled. The current position reflects the tile's location as the puzzle is shuffled and tiles are moved around by the user. For example, in a 4 × 4 puzzle, the tile in the upper-left corner has a starting position of (0, 0). If the user slides that tile one square to the right, the tile's new position becomes (0.25, 0). The tiles are animated: when the user clicks on a tile, the tile is given a velocity and a target position. The tile's current position is updated each frame until the tile reaches the target position.

The image on a tile is always calculated relative to its starting position, which never changes. This position is used to derive the source rectangle on the video surface when the mixer draws that particular tile. The tile's placement within the application window is determined by the tile's current position.

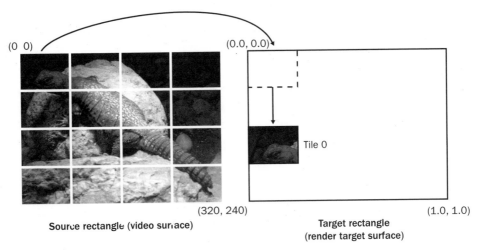

Figure 11.1   Source and target rectangles in the video 15 puzzle.

The compositor for this application is reasonably simple, so we can do all of the work inside the *CompositeImage* method. The other *IVMRImageCompositor9* methods simply return *S_OK*. Here is the code for the *CompositeImage* method.

```
STDMETHODIMP CPuzzleMixer::CompositeImage(
    IUnknown *pD3DDevice, IDirect3DSurface9 *pRenderTarget,
    AM_MEDIA_TYPE *pmtRenderTarget, REFERENCE_TIME rtStart,
    REFERENCE_TIME rtEnd, D3DCOLOR dwClrBkGnd,
    VMR9VideoStreamInfo *pVideoStreamInfo, UINT cStreams)
{
    // Hold the critical section.
    CLock lock(&m_CritSec);

    CComQIPtr<IDirect3DDevice9> pDevice(pD3DDevice);
    if (!pDevice)
    {
```

(continued)

```
        return E_FAIL;
    }

    // Use the first video stream, and ignore the others.
    const VMR9VideoStreamInfo *p = pVideoStreamInfo;

    // Set the scaling sizes for the puzzle coordinates.
    RECT rcTarget;
    GetTargetRectangle(pmtRenderTarget, &rcTarget);
    m_DestRect.SetScaleSize(rcTarget.right, rcTarget.bottom);
    m_SrcRect.SetScaleSize(p->dwWidth, p->dwHeight);

    // Clear the background.
    // Note: We could just clear the empty tile space instead.
    pDevice->Clear(0, NULL, D3DCLEAR_TARGET, dwClrBkGnd, 0, 0);

    // Draw each tile.
    for (int y = 0; y < m_puzzle.Columns(); y ++)
    {
        for (int x = 0; x < m_puzzle.Rows(); x++)
        {
            CTile *pTile = m_puzzle.GetTileAt(x,y);
            if (pTile)
            {
                pTile->Update();  // Update the tile position.
                RECT rcSrc, rcDest;
                NORMALIZEDRECT rcCurrentPos, rcStartingPos;

                // Get the current and starting position of the tile.
                m_puzzle.GetStartingPosition(pTile, &rcStartingPos);
                m_puzzle.GetCurrentPosition(pTile, &rcCurrentPos);

                // Map these values to surface pixel coordinates.
                m_SrcRect.ScaleRect(rcStartingPos, &rcSrc);
                m_DestRect.ScaleRect(rcCurrentPos, &rcDest);

                // Align to even pixels.
                AlignRect(rcSrc);
                AlignRect(rcDest);

                // Stretch part of the video image to the destination surface.
                pDevice->StretchRect(p->pddsVideoSurface, &rcSrc,
                    pRenderTarget, &rcDest, D3DTEXF_NONE );
            }
        }
    }
    return S_OK;
}
```

The puzzle compositor only uses the first video stream in the *pVideoStreamInfo* array. Even if the application rendered several streams, the puzzle compositor would ignore all the rest. (In fact, you could use this feature to switch the puzzle video on the fly by rendering two streams and switching the z-order.)

For each tile in the puzzle, we map the tile's starting position to the video surface, and the current position to the render target. The *GetStartingPosition* function returns the starting position in tile coordinates [0...1], and the *dwWidth* and *dwHeight* fields of the *VMR9VideoStreamInfo* structure give the size of the video surface. The *m_SrcRect* object does the scaling. For example, if the source video is 320 × 240 pixels and the tile's starting position is (0.25, 0), the tile is drawn at pixel (80, 0). Similarly, *GetCurrentPosition* returns the tile's current position, *GetTargetRectangle* returns the region of the render target where the video should appear, and *m_DestRect* does the scaling.

The resulting rectangles, *rcSrc* and *rcDest*, are used as source and destination rectangles in the call to *StretchRect*. Note that *StretchRect* is called once for each tile, because the tiles are jumbled up after the puzzle has been shuffled.

Another approach would be to use the tile coordinates as texel coordinates and then texture the video image onto the render target. This approach is slightly more complicated than using *StretchRect*, but it opens up some interesting possibilities. For example, you could give the tiles a 3-D look with rounded corners and beveled edges. The next example uses texturing; by the time you are finished with this chapter, you'll know how to make these improvements in the FifteenPuzzle application.

As you can see, the puzzle compositor disregards all of the application's mixing preferences except for background color. However, the application still needs to set the position of the video by calling *IVMRWindowlessControl9::SetVideoPosition*. This method tells the VMR where to place the composited image in the application window. The compositor has no control over that aspect of rendering.

The FifteenPuzzle application shows that you can do some interesting things without too much code. But there's a limit to the effects that you can achieve with *StretchRect*. Textures are much more powerful, and you can use them to create almost any kind of effect that you can imagine.

Basic Video Mixing

The next sample is called BasicMixer, which shows how to mix multiple video streams according to the settings defined by the *IVMRMixerControl9* interface. You can use the BasicMixer sample as the starting point for your own compositors.

InitCompositionDevice

We use this method to cache the *IDirect3DDevice9* pointer. We also determine the best texture format that is supported by the graphics driver. This information is stored for later use.

```
STDMETHODIMP CMixer::InitCompositionDevice(IUnknown* pD3DDevice)
{
    CLock lock(&m_CritSec);
    HRESULT hr = pD3DDevice->
        QueryInterface(IID_IDirect3DDevice9, (void**)&m_pDevice);
    if (SUCCEEDED(hr))
    {
        hr = FindVideoTextureFormat();
    }
    return hr;
}
```

The *FindVideoTextureFormat* function loops through an array of texture surface formats and calls *IDirect3D9::CheckDeviceFormat*. The first texture format that is supported is stored in the *m_TexFormat* member variable.

```
HRESULT CMixer::FindVideoTextureFormat()
{
    CComPtr<IDirect3D9> pD3D;
    D3DDEVICE_CREATION_PARAMETERS params;
    D3DDISPLAYMODE mode;
    // The list of texture formats to test.
    D3DFORMAT formats[] =
    {
        D3DFMT_R8G8B8,
        D3DFMT_X8R8G8B8,
        D3DFMT_R5G6B5,
        D3DFMT_X1R5G5B5
    };

    m_pDevice->GetDirect3D(&pD3D);
    m_pDevice->GetCreationParameters(&params);
    m_pDevice->GetDisplayMode(0, &mode);
    for (int i = 0; i < ARRAY_SIZE(formats); i++)
    {
        HRESULT hr = pD3D->CheckDeviceFormat(params.AdapterOrdinal,
            D3DDEVTYPE_HAL, mode.Format, D3DUSAGE_RENDERTARGET,
            D3DRTYPE_TEXTURE, formats[i]);
        if (SUCCEEDED(hr))
        {
            // Go with this format.
            m_TexFormat = formats[i];
```

```
                return S_OK;
            }
        }
    }
    // No formats were found.
    return E_FAIL;
}
```

SetStreamMediaType

In this method, we copy the media type to an array that has one entry for each input pin, up to the maximum of 16 pins. Remember that the media type pointer (*pmt*) can be *NULL* to clear the media type. We also copy the texture flag to another array. If the texture flag is *FALSE*, we create a private texture that we'll use for our texturing operations.

```
STDMETHODIMP CMixer::SetStreamMediaType(DWORD dwStrmId,
    AM_MEDIA_TYPE *pmt, BOOL fTexture)
{
    CLock lock(&m_CritSec);
    if (pmt == NULL)
    {
        // Free the media type in the array.
        MyFreeMediaType(m_mt[dwStrmId]);
    }
    else
    {
        // Copy the media type and texture flag into the arrays.
        m_fTexture[dwStrmId] = fTexture;
        MyCopyMediaType(&m_mt[dwStrmId], *pmt);
        // If the surface is not a texture, create a private texture.
        if (!fTexture)
        {
            CreateVideoTexture(pmt);
        }
    }
    return S_OK;
}
```

The *MyCopyMediaType* and *MyFreeMediaType* functions copy and free the media type structure. These functions are necessary to avoid memory leaks, because the *AM_-MEDIA_TYPE* structure holds a pointer to a secondary structure that is allocated separately. The functions ensure that this secondary structure is allocated and released.

The *fTexture* parameter specifies whether the decoder surfaces for a given input pin are textures. If the surfaces are *not* textures, we must create a private texture for that input pin. Setting up the private texture is handled by the *CreateVideoTexture* function.

```
HRESULT CMixer::CreateVideoTexture(const AM_MEDIA_TYPE* pmt)
{
    DWORD dwWidth, dwHeight;
    GetVideoSurfaceDimensions(pmt, &dwWidth, &dwHeight);

    // Round up for POW2 textures if needed.
    AdjustTextureSize(&dwWidth, &dwHeight);

    // If we already have a texture that's as big as we need, then we're done.
    if ((dwWidth <= m_dwVideoTextureWidth) &&
        (dwHeight <= m_dwVideoTextureHeight))
    {
        return S_OK;
    }

    // Otherwise, we need to (re)allocate the texture.
    m_pVideoTexture.Release();
    HRESULT hr = m_pDevice->CreateTexture(dwWidth, dwHeight, 1,
        D3DUSAGE_RENDERTARGET, m_TexFormat, D3DPOOL_DEFAULT,
        &m_pVideoTexture, NULL);
    if (SUCCEEDED(hr))
    {
        m_dwVideoTextureWidth = dwWidth;
        m_dwVideoTextureHeight = dwHeight;
    }
    return hr;
}
```

The *GetVideoSurfaceDimensions* function returns the video size, based on the media type. If the driver requires a square or power-of-2 texture, the surface dimensions are rounded up accordingly by calling the *AdjustTextureSize* function. This function is taken directly from the TeeVee sample in Chapter 10. The compositor uses one private texture for all video streams, so after the texture has been created, we do not re-allocate it unless the next stream is larger.

CompositeImage

This is a fairly long function. It can be broken down into the following steps:

1. Clear the background, using the background color that is specified by the application. As an optimization, you can skip this step if the bottom layer has an alpha value of 1.0 and covers the entire render target.

2. For every stream, calculate the source and target rectangles. These are determined by the native video size, the video aspect ratio, the size of the render target, and the normalized position of each video stream.

3.   For each stream, get the texture from the video surface or copy the surface to the private texture. Create a set of vertices that define the four corners of the target rectangle, as shown in Figure 11.2. Using the source rectangle as the texture coordinates, place the application's alpha setting in the diffuse color component. Then draw the primitive.

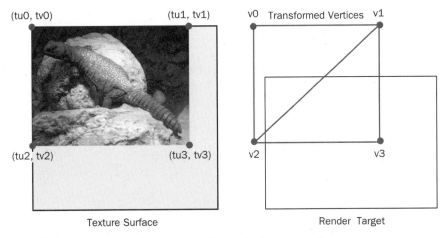

Figure 11.2   Texture and vertex coordinates in the compositor.

For each pixel, the video surface (that is, the texture) provides the diffuse color. There are two possible sources for alpha. First, there is the alpha value for the entire stream, specified by the application. This information is contained in the *VMR9VideoStreamInfo* structure. When we composite the image, we'll store this value in the diffuse color component for the vertices. Second, the video itself may contain per-pixel alpha information. If so, the diffuse alpha must be modulated with the texture alpha. This situation is not very common because most video formats do not contain an alpha channel. Here is the implementation of this method.

```
#define VERTEX_FORMAT (D3DFVF_XYZRHW | D3DFVF_DIFFUSE | D3DFVF_TEX1)

struct VERTEX
{
    float x, y, z, rhw; // Transformed vertices.
    DWORD color;        // Diffuse color (holds the alpha value).
    float tu, tv;       // Texture coordinates for the video texture.
};

HRESULT CMixer::CompositeImage(IUnknown* pD3DDevice,
    IDirect3DSurface9* pRenderTarget, AM_MEDIA_TYPE* pmtRenderTarget,
    REFERENCE_TIME rtStart, REFERENCE_TIME rtEnd, D3DCOLOR dwClrBkGnd,
    VMR9VideoStreamInfo* pVideoStreamInfo, UINT cStreams)
```

(continued)

```
    {
        CLock lock(&m_CritSec);
        // Clear the render target surface. (You may be able to skip this call.)
        m_pDevice->Clear(0, NULL, D3DCLEAR_TARGET, dwClrBkGnd, 0, 0);

        // Set the necessary render states and the flexible vertex format.
        SetRenderStates();
        m_pDevice->SetFVF(VERTEX_FORMAT);
        m_pDevice->BeginScene();

        // Loop through all of the streams.
        for (UINT iStream = 0; iStream < cStreams; iStream++)
        {
            const VMR9VideoStreamInfo *pStreamInfo = pVideoStreamInfo + iStream;

            // Place the application's alpha setting into a D3D color value.
            DWORD dwColor = D3DCOLOR_RGBA(0xFF, 0xFF, 0xFF,
                (BYTE)(0xFF * pStreamInfo->fAlpha));

            // Width and height of one texel (video pixel).
            float fTU = 1.0f, fTV = 1.0f;

            // Get the texture.
            CComPtr<IDirect3DTexture9> pTex;
            if (m_fTexture[iStream])
            {
                // This surface is a texture.
                pStreamInfo->pddsVideoSurface->GetContainer(
                    __uuidof(IDirect3DDevice9), (void**)&pTex);

                 // Calculate the texel dimensions.
                fTU = 1.0f / pStreamInfo->dwWidth;
                fTV = 1.0f / pStreamInfo->dwHeight;
            }
            else
            {
                // This surface is not a texture. Copy it to our private texture.
                RECT rc = { 0, 0, pStreamInfo->dwWidth, pStreamInfo->dwHeight };
                pTex = m_pVideoTexture;
                CComPtr<IDirect3DSurface9> pSurf;
                pTex->GetSurfaceLevel(0, &pSurf);
                m_pDevice->StretchRect(pStreamInfo->pddsVideoSurface, &rc, pSurf,
                    &rc, D3DTEXF_NONE);

                 // Calculate the texel dimensions.
                fTU = 1.0f / m_dwVideoTextureWidth;
                fTV = 1.0f / m_dwVideoTextureHeight;
            }
```

```
// Find the source rectangle from the video media type.
RECT        rcSource;
const AM_MEDIA_TYPE *pmtSource = &m_mt[pStreamInfo->dwStrmID];
GetSourceRectangle(pmtSource, &rcSource);

// Find the target rectangle from the video media type, the
// render target media type, and the application settings.
FloatRect VertexRect;
FindDestVertices(pmtSource, pmtRenderTarget, pStreamInfo->rNormal,
    &VertexRect);

// Now fill in the vertices.
VERTEX vertices[] =
{
    // Upper-left corner.
    {
        VertexRect.left, VertexRect.top, 0.5f, 1.0f,
        dwColor, fTU * rcSource.left, fTV * rcSource.top
    },
    // Upper-right corner.
    {
        VertexRect.right, VertexRect.top, 0.5f, 1.0f,
        dwColor, fTU * rcSource.right, fTV * rcSource.top
    },
    // Lower-left corner.
    {
        VertexRect.left, VertexRect.bottom, 0.5f, 1.0f,
        dwColor,fTU * rcSource.left, fTV * rcSource.bottom
    },
    // Lower-right corner.
    {
        VertexRect.right, VertexRect.bottom, 0.5f, 1.0f,
        dwColor, fTU * rcSource.right, fTV * rcSource.bottom
    }
};
WORD indices[] = { 0, 1, 3, 0, 3, 2 };

m_pDevice->SetTexture(0, pTex);
SetPerStreamRenderStates(pmtSource);
m_pDevice->DrawIndexedPrimitiveUP(D3DPT_TRIANGLELIST, 0, 4, 2,
    (void*)indices, D3DFMT_INDEX16, (void*)vertices, sizeof(VERTEX));
    }
m_pDevice->EndScene();
m_pDevice->SetTexture(0, NULL);
return S_OK;
}
```

We start by defining the flexible vertex format. We are using transformed vertex coordinates (D3DFVF_XYZRHW) because the destination rectangle is calculated in terms of screen coordinates. The diffuse color is a convenient place to store the stream alpha. (The RGB part of the diffuse color will not be used.) The texture coordinates define the source rectangle.

The *CompositeImage* function starts by clearing the render target, using the background color given in the *dwClrBkGnd* parameter. (You can optimize the function somewhat by testing whether the background color will be visible.) Next, the function loops through all of the streams in the *pVideoStreamInfo* array, and draws each frame according to the following algorithm:

1. For each frame, if the video surface is a texture, call *IDirect3DSurface9::GetContainer* to get the *IDirect3DTexture9* pointer. Otherwise, the video surface must be copied to our private texture. (Now you know why we saved the *fTexture* flag for each stream in the *SetStreamMediaType* method.)

2. Set the *fTU* and *fTV* variables to the width and height of one texel. These values are used to scale the texture coordinates. For example, suppose the video frame covers the entire destination rectangle. If the texture surface and the video image are the same size, then the texture coordinates of the lower left corner are (1.0, 1.0). But suppose the texture is 512 × 256 pixels while the video image is only 320 × 240. In that case, the coordinates must be scaled to (320/512, 240/256), or (0.625, 0.9375). Otherwise, the unused area of the texture will be visible.

3. Calculate the source and target rectangles by calling *GetSourceRectangle* and *FindDestVertices*.

4. Build the destination rectangle from two triangles with four vertices.

5. Draw the rectangle. We use the UP ("user pointer") version of *DrawIndexedPrimitive* because we're not storing the vertices in a vertex buffer. (There wouldn't be much point to doing so, because there are so few vertices and they change every frame.)

The *SetRenderStates* function sets the render states that remain constant for every video stream. We enable alpha blending but disable lighting. The diffuse color for each pixel is taken from the texture with no modulation. The texture-addressing mode in both directions is "clamp" — this lets us place the video frame inside the destination rectangle without wrapping or mirroring the texture.

```
void CMixer::SetRenderStates()
{
    // Private method, caller should hold the lock.

    // Enable alpha blending and disable lighting.
```

```cpp
    m_pDevice->SetRenderState(D3DRS_ALPHABLENDENABLE, TRUE);
    m_pDevice->SetRenderState(D3DRS_LIGHTING, FALSE);
    m_pDevice->SetRenderState(D3DRS_SRCBLEND, D3DBLEND_SRCALPHA);
    m_pDevice->SetRenderState(D3DRS_DESTBLEND, D3DBLEND_INVSRCALPHA);

    // Get the diffuse color from the texture.
    m_pDevice->SetTextureStageState(0, D3DTSS_COLOROP, D3DTOP_SELECTARG1);
    m_pDevice->SetTextureStageState(0, D3DTSS_COLORARG1, D3DTA_TEXTURE);

    // Clamp the texture addresses.
    m_pDevice->SetSamplerState(0, D3DSAMP_ADDRESSU, D3DTADDRESS_CLAMP);
    m_pDevice->SetSamplerState(0, D3DSAMP_ADDRESSV, D3DTADDRESS_CLAMP);
}
```

The *SetPerStreamRenderStates* method sets the render states that may change for each stream, depending on whether the video format contains an alpha channel. You can check this by using the *MEDIASUBTYPE_HASALPHA* macro. If the video format has an alpha channel, we enable per-pixel alpha testing and modulate the texture alpha with the diffuse alpha. Otherwise, we disable per-pixel alpha testing and just select the diffuse alpha.

```cpp
void CMixer::SetPerStreamRenderStates(const AM_MEDIA_TYPE *pmt)
{
    if (MEDIASUBTYPE_HASALPHA(*pmt))
    {
        // Modulate the diffuse alpha and the texture alpha.
        m_pDevice->SetTextureStageState(0, D3DTSS_ALPHAOP, D3DTOP_MODULATE);
        m_pDevice->SetTextureStageState(0, D3DTSS_ALPHAARG1, D3DTA_TEXTURE);
        m_pDevice->SetTextureStageState(0, D3DTSS_ALPHAARG2, D3DTA_DIFFUSE);
        // Enable per-pixel alpha testing.
        m_pDevice->SetRenderState(D3DRS_ALPHATESTENABLE, TRUE);
        // Optional: Ignore alpha below some minimum value.
        m_pDevice->SetRenderState(D3DRS_ALPHAREF, 0x10);
        m_pDevice->SetRenderState(D3DRS_ALPHAFUNC, D3DCMP_GREATER);
    }
    else
    {
        // Select the texture alpha. Disable per-pixel alpha testing.
        m_pDevice->SetTextureStageState(0, D3DTSS_ALPHAOP, D3DTOP_SELECTARG1);
        m_pDevice->SetTextureStageState(0, D3DTSS_ALPHAARG1, D3DTA_DIFFUSE);
        m_pDevice->SetRenderState(D3DRS_ALPHATESTENABLE, FALSE);
    }
}
```

TermCompositionDevice

Remember to release everything in the *TermCompositionDevice* method.

```
STDMETHODIMP CMixer::TermCompositionDevice(IUnknown* pD3DDevice)
{
    CLock lock(&m_CritSec);
    m_pDevice.Release();
    m_pVideoTexture.Release();
    for (int i = 0; i < MAX_VMR_STREAMS; i++)
    {
        MyFreeMediaType(m_mt[i]);
    }
    return S_OK;
}
```

Keep in mind that your own compositor does not have to replicate the VMR's normal behavior. You can change or omit any of the steps that you don't need. This code is simply a baseline from which to work.

Calculating Source and Target Rectangles

When the compositor mixes a video frame, it must calculate two rectangles: the *source rectangle*, which describes the portion of the video frame that should be drawn onto the render target, and the *destination rectangle*, which describes the area of the render target that should receive the video. These rectangles are derived from several pieces of information:

■ The format of the source video

■ The format of the render target

■ The stream position that was set by the application through the *IVMR-MixerControl9::SetOutputRect* method.

A video format is described with the *AM_MEDIA_TYPE* structure. This structure provides a generic way to describe any media format — whether it's audio, video, or a format that nobody has invented yet. Here is the declaration of the *AM_MEDIA_TYPE* structure.

```
typedef struct  _MediaType {
    GUID      majortype;
    GUID      subtype;
    BOOL      bFixedSizeSamples;
    BOOL      bTemporalCompression;
    ULONG     lSampleSize;
    GUID      formattype;
```

```
   IUnknown    *pUnk;
   ULONG       cbFormat;
   BYTE        *pbFormat;
} AM_MEDIA_TYPE;
```

The *majortype* and *subtype* GUIDs are used to identify formats without needing to include all of the specifics. For uncompressed video, majortype is always *MEDIA-TYPE_Video*. The subtype roughly corresponds to the *D3DFORMAT* enumeration in Direct3D. For example, 24-bit RGB is *MEDIASUBTYPE_RGB24*. You can find a list of subtype GUIDs in the DirectShow SDK documentation.

The details of the format, such as the width and height, are contained in another structure called the *format block*. This structure is allocated separately from the *AM_-MEDIA_TYPE* structure, and is stored in the *pbFormat* field as a byte array. The layout of the format block is defined by a third GUID value, the *formattype* field. For uncompressed video, the format block is one of two structures, either *VIDEOINFOHEADER* or *VIDEOINFOHEADER2*. These are identified by the GUID values *FORMAT_-VideoInfo* and *FORMAT_VideoInfo2*, respectively. The *VIDEOINFOHEADER2* structure contains all of the information in the *VIDEOINFOHEADER* structure, as well as some additional fields. However, because *VIDEOINFOHEADER2* is newer than *VIDEOINFOHEADER*, not all DirectShow filters support it.

The following list describes the structure members that are relevant for calculating the source and target rectangles:

- *bmiHeader* is a *BITMAPINFOHEADER* structure. It contains the width and height of the video surface.

- *rcTarget* is the target rectangle. In the video stream, it defines the size of the image. This may be smaller than the size defined in *bmiHeader*. For example, the surface may be wider than the image, due to stride requirements. In the render target, *rcTarget* defines the area of the surface that should receive the video. If *rcTarget* is an empty rectangle, the entire surface should be used.

- *rcSource* is the source rectangle. It defines the portion of the source video that should be placed into the render target. Decoders can set this value in order to crop a portion of the image. If this field is empty, the entire image should be used.

- *dwPictAspectRatioX* and *dwPictAspectRatioY* define the picture aspect ratio. The aspect ratio may not match the physical image size. For example, standard consumer-format DV video is 720 x 480 pixels (1.5:1) but should be displayed at a 4:3 aspect ratio (approximately 1.33:1). These fields are defined only in the *VIDEOINFOHEADER2* structure.

■   The *dwControlFlags* field may contain one of the following flags:

❏   *AMCONTROL_PAD_TO_4x3*: Pad the image to a 4 × 3 area.

❏   *AMCONTROL_PAD_TO_16x9*: Pad the image to a 16 × 9 area.

These flags are only defined in the *VIDEOINFOHEADER2* structure, and are sometimes used with DVD video content. If either of these flags is present, the target rectangle should be squeezed along one axis so that the video image retains the correct aspect ratio when the render target is displayed inside the specified area.

To summarize, here are the transformations needed to calculate the source and target rectangles:

1.   Get *rcTarget* from the video media type (T1).

2.   Get *rcTarget* from the render target media type (T2).

3.   Find the video aspect ratio from the video media type (AR).

4.   Adjust T1 for the aspect ratio by scaling horizontally (T1').

5.   Map T1 into T2 by finding the largest rectangle that fits in T2 and has the same aspect ratio as T1 (T3).

6.   If the *AMCONTROL_PAD_TO_4x3* or *AMCONTROL_PAD_TO_16x9* flag is present, the target rectangle is scaled in the opposite direction so that the image retains the correct aspect ratio (T3') when the image is stretched to the final dimensions.

7.   Map T3' into the normalized rectangle.

8.   Set the texture coordinates based on the source rectangle.

Figure 11.3 shows the intermediate results for the target rectangle calculations.

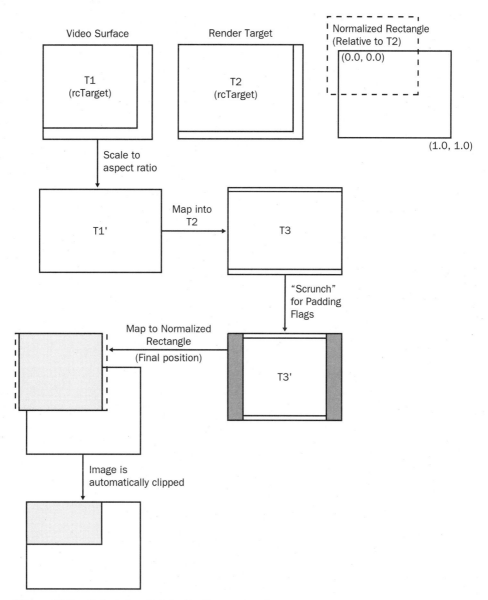

Figure 11.3   Calculating the destination rectangle.

Alpha Burst

Although the BasicMixer application provides general mixing operations, there's no point in writing a compositor just to replicate functionality already provided by the VMR. The next sample shows an interesting technique that uses an alpha map to create a circular region of video.

Run the AlphaBurst sample located in the AVBook\bin directory. When the application launches, it begins playing a video. If you click the video window, a circular transparent region appears under the mouse cursor, and a second video is visible under the first video. While the mouse button is down, the circular area follows the mouse cursor. (See Plate 9.)

The AlphaBurst compositor works by applying two texture stages to the top layer of video. The first stage contains the alpha map, and the second stage contains the video surface. The diffuse color is selected from the video surface, while the alpha value is selected from the alpha map.

The alpha map texture is stored in the AlphaMap.dds file. We created the texture by drawing a radial blend in a paint program and saving it as a bitmap. We then used the DirectX Texture tool to select the bitmap into the texture's alpha channel so that the grayscale values became alpha values. The alpha map is loaded in the *InitCompositionDevice* method.

```
STDMETHODIMP CMixer::InitCompositionDevice(IUnknown* pD3DDevice)
{
    // Load the alpha map.
    const TCHAR sz[] = TEXT("AlphaMap.dds");
    D3DXCreateTextureFromFileEx(m_pDevice, sz, D3DX_DEFAULT, D3DX_DEFAULT,
        1, 0, D3DFMT_A8R8G8B8, D3DPOOL_MANAGED, D3DX_DEFAULT,
        D3DX_DEFAULT, 0, NULL, NULL, &m_pAlphaTexture);

    // The rest of this method is the same as BasicMixer.
}
```

For the *SetStreamMediaType* method, we have arbitrarily decided that stream 0 will be the bottom layer and stream 1 will be the top layer with the alpha. The mixer ignores any other streams, and ignores the z-order settings. That means we can always use *StretchRect* for stream 0, and only worry about textures for stream 1. However, we do have to check the *fTexture* texture flag for stream 1 and create a private video texture if *fTexture* is *FALSE*.

```
STDMETHODIMP CMixer::SetStreamMediaType(DWORD dwStrmID,
    AM_MEDIA_TYPE* pmt, BOOL  fTexture
    )
{
    CLock lock(&m_CritSec);

    if (pmt == NULL)
    {
        // Clear the media type.
        MyFreeMediaType(m_mt[dwStrmID]);
    }
    else
    {
        // Save the media type.
        MyCopyMediaType(&m_mt[dwStrmID], *pmt);
    }
```

```
    // Create the video texture for stream 1 only.
    if ((dwStrmID == 1) && (pmt != NULL) && !fTexture)
    {
        CreateVideoTexture(pmt);
    }
    return S_OK;
}
```

The *CompositeImage* method for mixing the video streams is similar to the code from the BasicMixer sample. We start with a minor hack to make sure the application has rendered two video streams and did not change the z-orders. That will simplify the rest of the function because then we don't have to test for the stream IDs.

```
if (cStreams != 2)
{
    return E_FAIL;
}
if ((pVideoStreamInfo[0].dwStrmID != 0) ||
    (pVideoStreamInfo[1].dwStrmID != 1))
{
    return E_FAIL;
}
```

Now, instead of looping through the stream array in z-order, we just stretch stream 0 to fill the entire render target. Alpha blending is enabled only when the user clicks the video, so the rest of the time we can skip stream 0 entirely.

```
if (m_fShowAlpha)
{
    p = &pVideoStreamInfo[0];
    RECT rc;
    ZeroMemory(&rc, sizeof(RECT));
    rc.right = p->dwWidth;
    rc.bottom = p->dwHeight;
    pDevice->StretchRect(p->pddsVideoSurface, &rc, pddsRenderTarget,
        &rc, D3DTEXF_NONE);
    // Note: You could use a different filtering mode, such as D3DTEXF_LINEAR.
}
```

For stream 1, we use the video texture and add a second set of texture coordinates for the alpha map. The alpha map is centered around a point that is determined by the position of the mouse cursor. Here is the new definition for the vertex format and the vertices.

```
#define VERTEX_FORMAT (D3DFVF_XYZRHW | D3DFVF_TEX2)
struct VERTEX
{
    float x, y, z, rhw;
    float tu, tv;        // Alpha map.
    float tu2, tv2;      // Video texture.
};
```

(continued)

```
VERTEX vertices[] =
{
    // x        y        z      rhw    tu           tv           tu2    tv2
    { 0.0f,   0.0f,    0.5f,  1.0f,  fAlphaU_min, fAlphaV_min, 0.0f,  0.0f },
    { fWidth, 0.0f,    0.5f,  1.0f,  fAlphaU_max, fAlphaV_min,  fTU,  0.0f },
    { fWidth, fHeight, 0.5f,  1.0f,  fAlphaU_max, fAlphaV_max,  fTU,  fTV },
    { 0.0f,   0.0f,    0.5f,  1.0f,  fAlphaU_min, fAlphaV_min, 0.0f,  0.0f },
    { fWidth, fHeight, 0.5f,  1.0f,  fAlphaU_max, fAlphaV_max,  fTU,  fTV },
    { 0.0f,   fHeight, 0.5f,  1.0f,  fAlphaU_min, fAlphaV_max, 0.0f,  fTV }
};
```

The render states depend on whether alpha blending is enabled. When alpha blending is enabled, stage 0 uses the alpha map and stage 1 uses the video texture. For the alpha map, the color operation is "select current" (we overwrite it in the next texture stage in any case) and the alpha operation is "select from texture." For the video texture, the color operation is "select from texture" and the alpha operation is "select current." When alpha blending is disabled, the video texture is used in stage 0 and stage 1 is disabled. Figure 11.4 discusses texture stages.

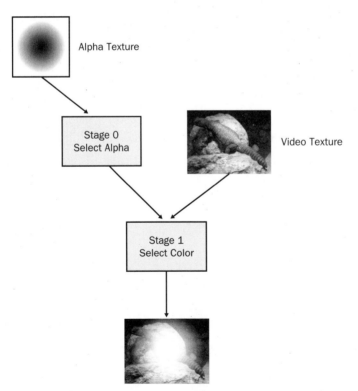

Figure 11.4   Texture stages in the AlphaBurst compositor.

Here is the code that sets the render states.

```
if (m_fShowAlpha)
{
    // Enable alpha blending.
    m_pDevice->SetRenderState(D3DRS_ALPHABLENDENABLE, TRUE);
    m_pDevice->SetRenderState(D3DRS_ALPHAREF, 0x10);
    m_pDevice->SetRenderState(D3DRS_ALPHAFUNC, D3DCMP_GREATER);

    // Texture stage 0: Select texture alpha.
    m_pDevice->SetTextureStageState(0, D3DTSS_TEXCOORDINDEX, 0);
    m_pDevice->SetTextureStageState(0, D3DTSS_COLOROP, D3DTOP_SELECTARG1);
    m_pDevice->SetTextureStageState(0, D3DTSS_COLORARG1, D3DTA_CURRENT);
    m_pDevice->SetTextureStageState(0, D3DTSS_ALPHAOP, D3DTOP_SELECTARG1);
    m_pDevice->SetTextureStageState(0, D3DTSS_ALPHAARG1, D3DTA_TEXTURE);
    m_pDevice->SetTexture(0, m_pAlphaTexture);

    // Texture stage 1: Select texture color and current alpha.
    m_pDevice->SetTextureStageState(1, D3DTSS_TEXCOORDINDEX, 1);
    m_pDevice->SetTextureStageState(1, D3DTSS_COLOROP, D3DTOP_SELECTARG1);
    m_pDevice->SetTextureStageState(1, D3DTSS_COLORARG1, D3DTA_TEXTURE);
    m_pDevice->SetTextureStageState(1, D3DTSS_ALPHAOP, D3DTOP_SELECTARG1);
    m_pDevice->SetTextureStageState(1, D3DTSS_ALPHAARG1, D3DTA_CURRENT);
    m_pDevice->SetTexture(1, pTex);
}
else
{
    // Disable alpha blending.
    m_pDevice->SetRenderState(D3DRS_ALPHABLENDENABLE, FALSE);
    m_pDevice->SetRenderState(D3DRS_ALPHATESTENABLE, FALSE);

    // Texture stage 0: Select color from the texture.
    m_pDevice->SetTextureStageState(0, D3DTSS_TEXCOORDINDEX, 1);
    m_pDevice->SetTextureStageState(0, D3DTSS_COLOROP, D3DTOP_SELECTARG1);
    m_pDevice->SetTextureStageState(0, D3DTSS_COLORARG1, D3DTA_TEXTURE);
    m_pDevice->SetTexture(0, pTex);

    // Disable texture stage 1.
    m_pDevice->SetTextureStageState(1, D3DTSS_COLOROP, D3DTOP_DISABLE);
}
```

Pixel Shaders for Video Image Manipulation

Vertex and pixel shaders are currently one of the most exciting areas in 3-D graphics. Although shaders are generally used for advanced lighting effects, pixel shaders can also be used for image processing, which opens up some interesting possibilities in the world of video. The Pixellator sample located in the AVBook\bin directory demonstrates just a few of these possibilities (see Plate 10).

Background: What's a Pixel Shader?

A *pixel shader* is a program that runs on the graphics processing unit (GPU). For every pixel that is drawn, the pixel shader receives the interpolated texture, diffuse color, and specular color values as input, and produces the final pixel color as output. The pixel shader is invoked once for every pixel that is drawn (including overdraw) on every rendering pass, so they need to be quite small — generally, anywhere from a few to a dozen lines of code, written in a strange form of assembly language. (High-level shading languages are the next logical step. They were introduced in DirectX 9, but are still something of a moving target. By the time you read this book, writing shaders in assembly language may be completely passé.)

An excellent resource for learning about vertex and pixel shaders is *Direct3D Shader X*, by Wolfgang F. Engel, ed. The chapter "Image Processing with 1.4 Pixel Shaders in Direct3D," by Jason L. Mitchell, is particularly relevant for video, although he describes processing still images. Another recent book is *Microsoft DirectX 9 Programmable Graphics Pipeline*, by Kris Gray (Microsoft Press).

Loading the Shader

Loading a pixel shader into memory is straightforward. First, check to make sure that the video adapter supports the required pixel shader version. Versions 1.1, 1.2, and 1.3 are closely related, while the instruction set in version 1.4 is much different than the other versions. (At the time that this book went to press, Nvidia drivers support 1.3 and ATI drivers support 1.4.) Here is a small helper function that checks the shader version.

```
// Queries whether the desired pixel shader version is supported.
HRESULT QueryPixelShaderVersion(
    IDirect3DDevice9 *pDevice, DWORD major, DWORD minor)
{
    if (!pDevice)
    {
        return E_POINTER;
    }
    D3DCAPS9 caps;
    pDevice->GetDeviceCaps(&caps);
    if (caps.PixelShaderVersion < D3DPS_VERSION(major, minor))
    {
        return E_FAIL;
    }
    return S_OK;
}
```

Assuming that the video adapter supports the required version, you can assemble the shader code from a text file by calling the *D3DXAssembleShaderFromFile* function, which is part of the DirectX extensions library.

```
CComPtr<ID3DXBuffer> pCode;
CComPtr<ID3DXBuffer> pErrorMessages;
hr = D3DXAssembleShaderFromFile(szFileName, 0,  NULL, 0, &pCode,
    &pErrorMessages);
if (FAILED(hr))
{
    OutputDebugString((TCHAR*)pErrorMessages->GetBufferPointer());
    return hr;
}
```

If the method succeeds, the *pCode* variable points to a buffer that contains the assembled code. If the method fails, *pErrorMessages* points to a buffer that contains an error message. (Instead of loading from a text file, you can also store the shader code in memory or in a resource file. If so, use the *D3DXAssembleShader* or *D3DXAssembleShaderFromResource* function, respectively.) Next if the assembly step was successful, create the pixel shader by calling *IDirect3DDevice9::CreatePixelShader*. Activate the pixel shader by calling *IDirect3DDevice9::SetPixelShader*.

```
// Get a pointer to the buffer that contains the assembled shader code.
DWORD *pFunction = (DWORD*)pCode->GetBufferPointer();

// Create the shader.
CComPtr<IDirect3DPixelShader9> m_pShader;
hr = m_pDevice->CreatePixelShader(pFunction, &m_pShader);
if (SUCCEEDED(hr))
{
    // Make the shader active.
    hr = m_pDevice->SetPixelShader(m_pShader);
    m_effect = iShader;
}
```

Grayscale Shader

Here is a simple shader that converts a color image to grayscale. (See Plate 11.) The idea is to multiply each RGB component by a scaling factor, sum the result to produce a luminance value, and replicate this value in all three color channels.

```
ps_1_1
def c0, 0.299, 0.587, 0.114, 1.0
tex t0
dp3 r0, t0, c0
```

The *ps* statement declares the required version number — in this case, 1.1. The *def* statement declares a set of scaling constants for the RGB components. (Each shader register contains four float values, so you can place all three scaling factors into one register.) The *tex* statement reads the color from the current texture into the t0 register. The *dp3* statement performs a dot product operation on the first three float values stored in registers t0 and c0, and places the result in r0. In other words, the *dp3* statement calculates the following sum, where .*b*, .*r*, and .*g* are the red, green, and blue values in each register:

$$(c0.r \times t0.r) + (c0.g \times t0.g) + (c0.b \times t0.b)$$

The final pixel color is always placed in the r0 register. When the pixel shader finishes executing, r0 must contain the color information for the pixel.

Sepia Tone Shader

In *Direct3D ShaderX*, Mitchell presents a technique for converting a color image to sepia tone, using a version 1.4 pixel shader. You can also achieve the same effect with a version 1.3 pixel shader. It requires a bit more work by the application, but the principle is the same. Each pixel is converted to grayscale, and the grayscale value is used to look up a color in a one-dimensional texture that holds the sepia tones. (See Figure 11.5.)

The process of looking up a texture value from a calculated result is called a *dependent read*. Version 1.4 of the pixel shader language supports dependent reads from color registers, but this capability is not available in version 1.3. Instead, we can use the *texdp3tex* instruction. This instruction calculates the dot product between a texture coordinate and a texture color value, and uses the result to perform a 1-D texture lookup. In other words, it calculates the following sum, where (x, y, z) is a texture coordinate value and (r, g, b) is a texture color value:

$$(x \times r) + (y \times g) + (z \times b)$$

The *texdp3tex* instruction uses the resulting value to look up a color in a 1-D texture. Thus, we can convert the texture color to grayscale by placing the scaling factors (0.299, 0.587, 0.114) in the texture coordinates. Here is the pixel shader.

```
ps.1.3
tex t0
texdp3tex t1, t0
mov r0, t1
```

The dot product is applied to the color value in texture stage 0 (the t0 register) and the texture coordinates in stage 1 (the t1 register). The 1-D lookup is performed on the stage 1 texture, and the result is placed in the t1 register.

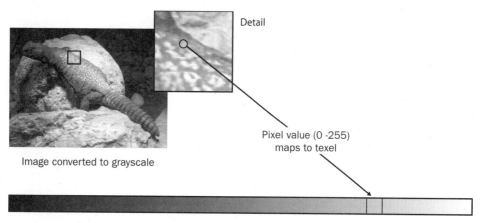

1D Texture (256 pixels x 1 pixel)

Figure 11.5   Dependent read for sepia tone shader.

In the application, we need to set up the texture stages correctly to match the shader.

```
// Define the grayscale weights.
float luma_red = 0.299f, luma_green = 0.587f, luma_blue = 0.114f;

// Define the vertex format.
const DWORD VERTEX_FORMAT =
    D3DFVF_XYZRHW | D3DFVF_TEX2 | D3DFVF_TEXCOORDSIZE3(1);
// Note: D3DFVF_TEXCOORDSIZE3(1) means texture coordinate set 1 has
// three values (u,v,w) instead of two, which is the default.

struct VERTEX
{
    float x, y, z, rhw;  // Vertex coordinates, in screen space (video).
    float tu, tv;        // Texture 0 (video).
    float tu2, tv2, tw2; // Texture 1 (grayscale conversion weights).
};

// Define the vertices.
VERTEX vertices[] =
{
  //  x        y         z     rhw   tu     tv    tu2        tv2          tv3
  { 0.0f,   0.0f,     0.5f, 1.0f, 0.0f, 0.0f, luma_red, luma_green, luma_blue},
  { fWidth, 0.0f,     0.5f, 1.0f, fTU,  0.0f, luma_red, luma_green, luma_blue},
  { fWidth, fHeight,  0.5f, 1.0f, fTU,  fTV,  luma_red, luma_green, luma_blue},
  { 0.0f,   fHeight,  0.5f, 1.0f, 0.0f, fTV,  luma_red, luma_green, luma_blue}
};
m_pDevice->SetTexture(0, pVideoTexture);
m_pDevice->SetTexture(1, m_pSepiaTexture);
m_pDevice->SetTextureStageState(1, D3DTSS_TEXCOORDINDEX, 1);
m_pDevice->SetTextureStageState(1, D3DTSS_TEXTURETRANSFORMFLAGS,
    D3DTTFF_COUNT3);
```

The tu2 texture coordinates are the same grayscale weights that we used in the previous shader. The dot product is simply an intermediate value, which is then used to look up a color value in the 1-D sepia tone texture. The stage 1 texture coordinates, therefore, are not really used as coordinates — they are just a place to store data.

You're not limited to a sepia tone with this shader. The "grue" effect in the Pixellator sample uses the same pixel shader, but maps the grayscale values to different shades of *green* and bl*ue*. (See Plate 12.)

Fuzzy Dots

Sepia tone is an interesting effect, but you can create even crazier effects with pixel shaders. We created one for the Pixellator sample that we call "fuzzy dots" (see Plate 12). Like the sepia tone shader, the fuzzy dots shader performs a dependent read to look up a texture value, but it uses a three-dimensional (volumetric) texture instead of a 1-D texture.

We used the DirectX Texture tool to create a 64 × 64 × 8 volumetric texture. Each layer of the texture consists of randomly placed red, green, and blue dots, whose density progressively decreases with each layer. The pixel shader maps the 64 × 64 bitmap to the render target, using texture coordinates that range from 0 to 8.0 horizontally and 0 to 4.0 vertically. The texture addressing mode is set to *D3DTADDRESS_WRAP*, so the bitmap is tiled 32 times. The color value for each pixel is then determined by using the grayscale value to perform a dependent read along the z-axis of the texture. Because the density of dots decreases at each layer, the dot density across the rendered image roughly corresponds to the grayscale value of the original image. (See Plate 13.)

Incidentally, we used GDI+ to generate the eight bitmaps for the texture. If your only experience till now has been with the old GDI, you should definitely check out GDI+, because it makes simple drawing applications like this one very easy.

The following shader program requires a 1.4 pixel shader.

```
ps.1.4
def c0, 0.30f, 0.59f, 0.11f, 1.0f
texld r0, t0
texcrd r1.xyz, t1
dp3 r1.z, r0, c0
phase
texld r1, r1
mov r0, r1
```

The first *texld* instruction loads the color value from video texture into register r0. The *texcrd* instruction loads the texture coordinates for the volumetric texture into register r1. The *dp3* instruction performs a dot product between the color value in t0 and the grayscale weights in register c0. The result is placed only in the z component of register r1. The r1 register contains x- and y-coordinates that were specified by the application, and a z-coordinate that equals the grayscale value of the video image. Following the *phase* instruction, the second *texld* instruction performs a dependent read from the volumetric texture, using the texture coordinates in r1. (In 1.4 pixel shaders, the *phase* instruction permits the shader program to perform texture loads after performing arithmetic operations.) The resulting RGB value is then moved into r0, where it becomes the output pixel color.

Summary

In this chapter we've shown several examples of custom mixing, ranging from the sensible (BasicMixer) to the completely gratuitous (fuzzy dots). We've only scratched the surface of what's possible, but hopefully we've inspired you to create your own mixing effects that will amaze your audience. In the next chapter, we look at some miscellaneous topics related to the VMR and video in DirectShow.

12

MultiMon, ProcAmp, Deinterlacing, and Other Odds and Ends

This chapter covers several miscellaneous topics related to the Video Mixing Renderer (VMR) and video in DirectShow:

- Video playback on multiple monitors
- Process amplification (ProcAmp)
- Advanced deinterlace controls
- Multiple VMR filters with a single allocator-presenter
- Video capture from a 3-D animation

Multimonitor Support

So far, all of the samples in this book have used the default monitor. Here are some tips on using the VMR with multiple monitors.

First, consider the case when an application runs in full-screen mode. If the monitors are on separate display adapters, each adapter requires its own Direct3D device, as well as its own resources, such as textures and vertex buffers. Therefore, if you want to switch monitors while using a custom allocator-presenter, you'll have to manage both devices yourself. Whenever you change the device, call *IVMR-SurfaceAllocatorNotify9::ChangeD3DDevice* on the VMR. Unfortunately, there is no easy way to make the video span two monitors at once; this is an inherent limitation of the Direct3D architecture.

Instead of having separate adapters, a computer might have a multihead card, which is a video card that supports two monitors. In DirectX 9.0 or later, both monitors on a multihead card can share the same device, which means you can create two swap chains for one device and share resources between them — however, not all graphics drivers support this capability. You can also treat a multihead card as if it were two display adapters, and create separate Direct3D devices. The topic "Multihead" in the DirectX SDK documentation has more information about multihead card support.

Now consider the case where the application is windowed. If you move the window to another monitor, Direct3D automatically copies the contents to the other frame buffer. However, this can severely degrade performance. The VMR's default allocator-presenter automatically handles this case by switching to another device. To maximize performance, it never renders the video on two monitors at once. If the window straddles both monitors, the VMR draws the video on whichever monitor contains a larger area of the window. (It paints the area on the other monitor with the background color.)

When the VMR connects to a decoder filter, by default it selects the primary display adapter as the device. In most cases that works fine, but you can override this behavior by calling *IVMRMonitorConfig9::SetMonitor* before the pins are connected. For example, you might want to select the best monitor based on the hardware capabilities.

If you are using a custom allocator-presenter in a windowed application, you can replicate the behavior of the VMR's default allocator-presenter by checking on each frame whether the window has moved to another monitor, or is straddling two monitors.

ProcAmp Controls

In video production, a *ProcAmp*, or processing amplifier, is a circuit that modifies a video signal to adjust qualities such as image brightness, contrast, or saturation. Some graphics cards are able to make the same types of adjustment using the graphics processing unit (GPU). If your graphics card supports this feature, you can control the image settings through the VMR's *IVMRMixerControl9* interface. This feature is demonstrated in the Amplify sample located in the AVBook\bin directory. (See Plate 15.)

Checking for ProcAmp Support

First, check for ProcAmp support on the driver. There are four ProcAmp properties — brightness, contrast, hue, and saturation — and the driver may support all, some, or none of them. The following code shows how to check for ProcAmp support.

```
// Get the ProcAmp settings from the VMR.
VMR9ProcAmpControl ProcAmp;
ZeroMemory(&ProcAmp, sizeof(VMR9ProcAmpControl));
ProcAmp.dwSize = sizeof(VMR9ProcAmpControl);
m_pMixer->GetProcAmpControl(0, &ProcAmp);

// Loop through all the properties to see which are supported.
VMR9ProcAmpControlFlags ProcAmpFlags[] =
{
    ProcAmpControl9_Brightness,
    ProcAmpControl9_Contrast,
    ProcAmpControl9_Hue,
    ProcAmpControl9_Saturation
};

for (int i = 0; i < NUM_PROCAMP_CONTROLS; i++)
{
    VMR9ProcAmpControlFlags prop = ProcAmpFlags[i];
    if ((ProcAmp.dwFlags & prop) == prop)
    {
        // This ProcAmp property is supported.
        // Get the current setting for this property.
        float val;
        switch (prop)
        {
        case ProcAmpControl9_Brightness:
            val = ProcAmp.Brightness;
            break;
        case ProcAmpControl9_Contrast:
            val = ProcAmp.Contrast;
            break;
        case ProcAmpControl9_Hue:
            val = ProcAmp.Hue;
            break;
        case ProcAmpControl9_Saturation:
            val = ProcAmp.Saturation;
            break;
        }
        // Get the allowable range of values for this property.
        VMR9ProcAmpControlRange range;
        ZeroMemory(&range, sizeof(VMR9ProcAmpControlRange));
        range.dwSize = sizeof(VMR9ProcAmpControlRange);
        range.dwProperty = prop;
        m_pMixer->GetProcAmpControlRange(0, &range);
    }
}
```

To get the current ProcAmp settings, call *IVMRMixerControl9::GetProcAmpControl* and pass in a pointer to the *VMR9ProcAmpControl* structure. You must set the structure's *dwSize* member equal to the structure size, as shown in the previous code example. Zero out the other structure members. When the method returns, the *dwFlags* field contains a bitwise OR of all the ProcAmp properties supported by the graphics card (if any). Test for each property using a bitwise AND. The *VMR9ProcAmpControl* structure also contains a separate field for each ProcAmp value. If the card supports a property, the corresponding field in the structure contains the current value. ProcAmp values are always floats.

The range of values for each property can vary depending on the driver. To get this information, call the *GetProcAmpControlRange* method. Pass in a pointer to the *VMR9ProcAmpControlRange* structure, setting the structure's *dwSize* member equal to the structure size. Specify the property that you are querying in the *dwProperty* member. When the method returns, the structure contains the minimum, maximum, and default values of the property.

The Amplify sample has a slider control for each ProcAmp property. The slider is enabled if the driver supports the property. Slider positions are expressed as *LONG* values, so the application maps the ProcAmp values (which are floats) into a range of 1 to 100, although some precision may be lost in the conversion.

Setting ProcAmp Values

To set ProcAmp properties, call the *SetProcAmpControl* method:

```
VMR9ProcAmpControl ProcAmp;
ZeroMemory(&ProcAmp, sizeof(VMR9ProcAmpControl));
ProcAmp.dwSize = sizeof(VMR9ProcAmpControl);
ProcAmp.dwFlags = prop;  // This is the property we want to set.
// Note: You can combine more than one property with a bitwise OR.

// Set the value of the property.
switch (prop)
{
    case ProcAmpControl9_Brightness:
        ProcAmp.Brightness = val;
        break;
    case ProcAmpControl9_Contrast:
        ProcAmp.Contrast = val;
        break;
    case ProcAmpControl9_Hue:
        ProcAmp.Hue = val;
        break;
    case ProcAmpControl9_Saturation:
        ProcAmp.Saturation = val;
        break;
}
hr = m_pMixer->SetProcAmpControl(0, &ProcAmp);
```

Set the *dwSize* member of the *VMR9ProcAmpControl* structure equal to the structure size before calling the method. Use the *dwFlags* member to indicate which ProcAmp properties you are changing. The example shown here sets only one property, but you can set several properties at once by combining the flags with a bitwise OR. For each property, set the new value in the corresponding structure member.

Advanced Deinterlace Settings

We have seen that the VMR supports hardware-accelerated deinterlacing, in which the GPU performs deinterlacing of interlaced content. Hardware-accelerated deinterlacing is automatically enabled whenever the graphics driver supports it. However, some cards support more than one deinterlacing technique. Therefore, you can query the VMR to get the driver's list of deinterlacing techniques and specify which technique to use. This is considered something of an advanced feature, if you want the very best rendering quality. The Amplify sample enables this feature when you play interlaced content (assuming the graphics driver also supports it).

Deinterlacing techniques include:

- Vertical stretching of the field lines, using interpolation to create missing pixel values. (This technique is a variant of bob deinterlacing.)

- Median filtering, where pixel values are recreated by taking the median value from a set of nearby pixels.

- Edge filtering, in which an edge detection filter is used to generate the missing information.

- Motion vectors, in which picture objects are tracked from one frame to the next as they move.

To get a list of the available techniques, we need to connect the decoder to the VMR, because the exact list may depend on the video format. In order to switch to a new technique, however, the decoder may need to allocate more buffers. For example, some techniques require the graphics card to examine the previous N frames. Because buffer allocation happens when the pins are connected, they must be disconnected and then reconnected before the new technique can go into effect.

Here is an outline of the process:

1. Get a list of the VMR's input pins and the corresponding output pins on the decoders. You'll need these so that you can reconnect the pins later.

2. Get the video format from the pin. The format is returned in the form of an *AM_MEDIA_TYPE* structure.

3.   Call *IVMRDeinterlaceControl9::GetNumberOfDeinterlaceModes*. This method uses a *VMR9VideoDesc* structure to describe the video format, so you need to convert the *AM_MEDIA_TYPE* structure. The *GetNumberOfDeinterlaceModes* method returns an array of GUIDs that identify the available techniques. GUIDs are used so that a driver can define its own proprietary techniques.

4.   For each deinterlacing GUID, get a description of the deinterlacing technique by calling *GetDeinterlaceModeCaps*. The method returns a *VMR9Deinterlace-Caps* structure that describes the technique.

5.   To set the deinterlacing technique, call *SetDeinterlaceMode* with the pin number and the GUID. Stop the filter graph, reconnect the pins, and start the graph again.

The next section describes each step in detail.

Get the Video Format

To get the current media type for a pin connection, call *IPin::ConnectionMediaType* on either pin. The Amplify sample only renders one video stream, so there is only a single pin. In general, you must do this for every connected input pin, because each video stream can have a different format.

```
// Find the list of input pins.
PinList pins;
GetPinList(pVMR, PINDIR_INPUT, pins);

// Look for the input pin that is connected to a decoder.
for (PinIterator iter = pins.begin(); iter != pins.end(); iter++)
{
    CComPtr<IPin> pConnected;
    hr = (*iter)->ConnectedTo(&pConnected);
    if (SUCCEEDED(hr))
    {
        m_pPinIn = *iter;
        m_pPinOut = pConnected;
        break;
    }
}

// Get the media type.
AM_MEDIA_TYPE mt;
hr = m_pPinIn->ConnectionMediaType(&mt);
```

Convert the Media Type

The VMR's deinterlace functions use a *VMR9VideoDesc* structure to describe the video format, instead of the usual DirectShow media type structure. In this section, we present some helper code to perform this conversion.

First, we need a function that checks whether a video format is interlaced. If not, there's no need to continue.

```
bool IsVideoInterlaced(const AM_MEDIA_TYPE& mt)
{
    // Is this a VideoInfo2 format?
    if ((mt.formattype == FORMAT_VideoInfo2) && (mt.pbFormat != NULL) &&
        (mt.cbFormat >= sizeof(VIDEOINFOHEADER2)))
    {
        VIDEOINFOHEADER2 *pVih = (VIDEOINFOHEADER2*)mt.pbFormat;
        if (pVih->dwInterlaceFlags & AMINTERLACE_IsInterlaced)
        {
            return true;
        }
    }
    return false;
}
```

Two format types may be used for uncompressed video, either *VIDEOINFO-HEADER* or *VIDEOINFOHEADER2*. All interlaced formats use the latter. The *AMINTERLACE_IsInterlaced* flag in the *dwInterlaceFlags* field indicates that the video is interlaced. If that flag is absent, the video is progressive.

The other flags in the *dwInterlaceFlags* field describe the type of interlacing. The *ConvertInterlaceFlags* function converts these flags into an equivalent value from the *VMR9_SampleFormat* enumeration:

```
#define IsInterlaced(x) ((x) & AMINTERLACE_IsInterlaced)
#define IsSingleField(x) ((x) & AMINTERLACE_1FieldPerSample)
#define IsField1First(x) ((x) & AMINTERLACE_Field1First)
VMR9_SampleFormat ConvertInterlaceFlags(DWORD dwInterlaceFlags)
{
    if (IsInterlaced(dwInterlaceFlags)) {
        if (IsSingleField(dwInterlaceFlags)) {
            if (IsField1First(dwInterlaceFlags)) {
                return VMR9_SampleFieldSingleEven;
            }
            else {
                return VMR9_SampleFieldSingleOdd;
            }
        }
        else {
```

(continued)

```
                    if (IsField1First(dwInterlaceFlags)) {
                        return VMR9_SampleFieldInterleavedEvenFirst;
                     }
                    else {
                        return VMR9_SampleFieldInterleavedOddFirst;
                    }
                }
            }
            else {
                return VMR9_SampleProgressiveFrame;  // Not interlaced.
            }
        }
```

The *ConvertMediaTypeToVideoDesc* function converts a media type to a *VMR9VideoDesc* structure.

```
HRESULT ConvertMediaTypeToVideoDesc(
    const AM_MEDIA_TYPE& mt, VMR9VideoDesc& desc)
{
    // Verify that the media type is VideoInfo2.
    if ((mt.formattype != FORMAT_VideoInfo2) ||
        (mt.pbFormat == NULL) ||
        (mt.cbFormat < sizeof(VIDEOINFOHEADER2)))
    {
        return E_FAIL;
    }

    VIDEOINFOHEADER2 *pVih = (VIDEOINFOHEADER2*)mt.pbFormat;
    BITMAPINFOHEADER *pBMI = &pVih->bmiHeader;

    desc.dwSize = sizeof(VMR9VideoDesc);
    desc.dwSampleWidth = abs(pBMI->biWidth);
    desc.dwSampleHeight = abs(pBMI->biHeight);
    desc.SampleFormat = ConvertInterlaceFlags(pVih->dwInterlaceFlags);
    desc.dwFourCC = pBMI->biCompression;

    // Check for well-known frame rates.
    switch (pVih->AvgTimePerFrame)
    {
        case 166833:  // NTSC, 59.94 fps.
            desc.InputSampleFreq.dwNumerator = 60000;
            desc.InputSampleFreq.dwDenominator = 1001;
            break;

        case 333667:  // NTSC, 29.97 fps.
            desc.InputSampleFreq.dwNumerator = 30000;
            desc.InputSampleFreq.dwDenominator = 1001;
            break;
```

```
    case 417188:  // NTSC, 23.97 fps.
        desc.InputSampleFreq.dwNumerator = 24000;
        desc.InputSampleFreq.dwDenominator = 1001;
        break;

    case 200000:  // PAL, 50 fps.
        desc.InputSampleFreq.dwNumerator = 50;
        desc.InputSampleFreq.dwDenominator = 1;
        break;

    case 400000:  // PAL, 25 fps.
        desc.InputSampleFreq.dwNumerator = 25;
        desc.InputSampleFreq.dwDenominator = 1;
        break;

    default:  // Unknown.
        desc.InputSampleFreq.dwNumerator = 10000000;
        desc.InputSampleFreq.dwDenominator =
            (DWORD)pVih->AvgTimePerFrame;
    }

    // Calculate the output frequency.
    if (desc.SampleFormat == VMR9_SampleFieldInterleavedEvenFirst ||
        desc.SampleFormat == VMR9_SampleFieldInterleavedOddFirst)
    {
        desc.OutputFrameFreq.dwNumerator =
            desc.InputSampleFreq.dwNumerator * 2;
    }
    else
    {
        desc.OutputFrameFreq.dwNumerator =
            desc.InputSampleFreq.dwNumerator;
    }
    return S_OK;
}
```

Note that the media type gives the *duration* of each frame, in 100-nanosecond units, while the *VMR9VideoDesc* structure gives the frame *rate*, in frames per second, expressed as a fractional value. Interlaced video generally comes in one of several standard formats, and we check for these so that we can assign a more accurate number. For example, NTSC television is 59.94 fields per second (60000/1000), which gets rounded to 166833 $\times 10^{-7}$ seconds in the media type.

With these functions defined, we can convert the video format as follows.

```
if (IsVideoInterlaced(mt))
{
    hr = ConvertMediaTypeToVideoDesc(mt, m_VideoDesc);
}
```

Query for Deinterlacing Techniques

Once you have determined whether a video is interlaced, and have filled in the *VMR9VideoDesc* structure, you can get the list of GUIDs that define the deinterlace techniques. Call *GetNumberOfDeinterlaceModes* to find out how many techniques are supported by the graphics card. If the number is more than zero, allocate an array of GUIDs and call *GetNumberOfDeinterlaceModes* again to fill in the array:

```
DWORD cModes = 0;
hr = m_pDeinterlace->GetNumberOfDeinterlaceModes(&m_VideoDesc,
    &cModes, NULL);
if (SUCCEEDED(hr) && (cModes > 0))
{
    m_pGuids = new GUID[cModes];
    m_cGuids = cModes;
    hr = m_pDeinterlace->GetNumberOfDeinterlaceModes(&m_VideoDesc,
        &cModes, m_pGuids);
}
```

The first time that we call *GetNumberOfDeinterlaceModes*, the third parameter is set to *NULL*. This call returns the number of techniques in the *cModes* parameter. If the number is more than zero, we allocate the GUID array and call *GetNumberOfDeinterlaceModes* again. This time, we pass in the address of the array as the third parameter. This second call fills in the array.

Set the Deinterlacing Technique

To change the deinterlace mode, call *SetDeinterlaceMode* with the pin number and a pointer to the GUID. Then stop the graph and reconnect the pins:

```
HRESULT CVMRGraph::SetDeinterlaceTechnique(DWORD index)
{
    if (index > m_cModes)
    {
        return E_INVALIDARG;
    }
    m_pGraph->Stop();
    m_pDeinterlace->SetDeinterlaceMode(0, m_pGuids + index);
    HRESULT hr = m_pGraph->ReconnectPins(m_pPinOut, m_pPinIn);
    if (SUCCEEDED(hr))
    {
        m_pGraph->Run();
    }
    return hr;
}
```

```
HRESULT CVMRGraph::ReconnectPins(IPin *pOut, IPin *pIn)
{
    AM_MEDIA_TYPE mt;
    HRESULT hr = pOut->ConnectionMediaType(&mt);
    if (FAILED(hr))
    {
        return hr;
    }
    m_pGraph->Disconnect(pOut);
    m_pGraph->Disconnect(pIn);
    hr = m_pGraph->ConnectDirect(pOut, pIn, &mt);
    MyFreeMediaType(mt);
    return hr;
}
```

The *IGraphBuilder::Disconnect* method disconnects a pin. You must call the method on both pins. Otherwise, one of the pins thinks it's still connected, causing unpredictable behavior in the graph. The *IGraphBuilder::ConnectDirect* method connects two pins without inserting any additional filters between them. To learn more about deinterlacing support in the VMR, refer to the topic "Setting Deinterlace Preferences" in the DirectX SDK documentation.

Multiple VMR Filters

In previous chapters, we've used the VMR filter's mixing mode to play several videos at once. An interesting alternative is to use multiple instances of the VMR, each residing in a separate filter graph (see Figure 12.1), but all connected to the same allocator-presenter. This approach gives you full control over the filter graphs, so that you can pause, start, and seek each video independently of the others.

We demonstrate this idea in the Carousel sample located in the AVBook\Video projects directory. This sample renders different videos on the sides of four objects that look vaguely like onions. (This is what happens when you let a programmer use a 3-D modeling application.) Each onion-shaped object can be brought to the foreground by pressing the 1, 2, 3, or 4 key. Pressing the 'P' key pauses or resumes the video in the foreground.

> **Note** The DirectX SDK also has a multi-VMR sample, called MultiVMR9. It is worth studying, because it provides a complete framework for creating this kind of sample application. The Carousel sample borrows a number of concepts from the MultiVMR9 sample, but has been simplified to make the code somewhat easier to follow.

In order to control the video streams independently without disrupting the frame rate of our 3-D scene, the Carousel sample does not draw any frames during the *Present-Image* method. Instead, it uses the *PresentImage* method to copy each video frame to a private texture surface. The 3-D rendering happens on the application thread, rather than the filter graph's streaming thread, and therefore the 3-D frame rate is independent of the video frame rate. The application always renders from the private textures, not from the VMR surfaces. (This can only work if all of the VMR filters are in pass-through mode. In mixing mode, the VMR makes *BeginScene* and *EndScene* calls to mix the video, and your application will end up fighting with the VMR for the device, as described in Chapter 10.)

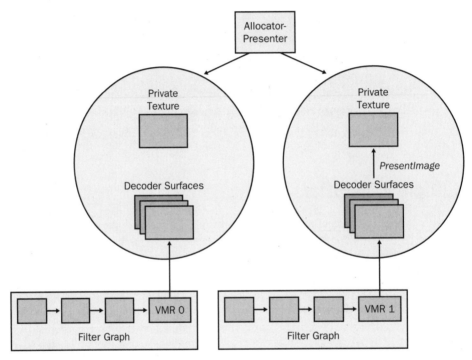

Figure 12.1   Multi-VMR application.

In a multi-VMR application, you assign a unique ID number to each VMR instance. Specify this ID when you call *IVMRSurfaceAllocatorNotify9::AdviseSurfaceAllocator*. Then, when the VMR calls methods on your allocator-presenter, it provides the ID number as the *dwUserID* parameter. (Up to now, we have ignored this parameter.) The ID gives you a way to match the method invocation with the correct VMR instance.

All of this requires some modifications to our earlier code. To begin with, the allocator-presenter must keep a separate pool of surfaces for each VMR. We therefore define a new class, named *VideoSource*, which holds an array of *IDirect3DSurface9* pointers, along with the private texture that we will use to copy the frames. Each time the application adds a new VMR instance, the allocator-presenter adds a new *VideoSource* object to an internal list:

```
HRESULT CAllocator::AttachVMR(DWORD_PTR dwUserID, IUnknown* pVMR)
{
    CLock lock(&m_CritSec);

    // First, check to see if this ID was already used.
    VideoSource *pSource = GetVideoSource(dwUserID);
    if (pSource != NULL)
    {
        return E_INVALIDARG;  // Duplicate ID.
    }

    // Add a new VideoSource object to our list.
    pSource = new VideoSource(m_pDevice, pVMR, dwUserID);
    if (!pSource)
    {
        return E_OUTOFMEMORY;
    }
    m_surfaces.push_back(pSource);
    return S_OK;
}
```

The application calls *AttachVMR* when it initializes a new VMR instance, as shown in the following code example. Note that this method replaces the *IVMRSurfaceAllocator9::AdviseNotify* method.

```
HRESULT CVmrGame::InitializeVMR()
{
    // Assign the next ID number.
    DWORD id = m_dwNextId++;

    // Create the object that manages the filter graph.
    CVMRGraph *pGraph = new CVMRGraph();
    if (!pGraph)
    {
        return E_OUTOFMEMORY;
    }

    // Create a new VMR and initialize it for renderless mode.
    CComPtr<IVMRSurfaceAllocatorNotify9> pNotify;
    HRESULT hr = pGraph->InitVMR_RenderlessMode(&pNotify);

    // Hook up the VMR and the allocator-presenter.
    HMONITOR hMonitor = g_d3d->GetAdapterMonitor(D3DADAPTER_DEFAULT);
    hr = pNotify->SetD3DDevice(m_pDevice, hMonitor);
    hr = pNotify->AdviseSurfaceAllocator(id, m_pAlloc);
    hr = m_pAlloc->AttachVMR(id, pNotify); // New method!
```

(continued)

```
    // Add the CVMRGraph object to an STL map, indexed by ID.
    m_graphs.insert(GraphMap::value_type(id, pGraph));
    return hr;
}
```

In the new version, many of the allocator-presenter methods simply call corresponding methods on the *VideoSource* object. For example, here is the new version of *InitializeDevice*.

```
STDMETHODIMP CAllocator::InitializeDevice(DWORD_PTR dwUserID,
    VMR9AllocationInfo* pAllocInfo, DWORD* pNumBuffers)
{
    CLock lock(&m_CritSec);

    // Look up the VideoSource object by the ID.
    VideoSource *pSource = GetVideoSource(dwUserID);
    if (!pSource)
    {
        return E_INVALIDARG;
    }
    // Create the surfaces.
    return pSource->CreateSurfaces(pAllocInfo, *pNumBuffers);
}
```

The *GetSurface* and *TerminateDevice* methods follow the same pattern. In each case, the corresponding method on the *VideoSource* class contains most of the code that previously was in the allocator-presenter class. For example, the *CreateBuffer* method creates the surfaces for the VMR, along with the private texture.

```
HRESULT VideoSource::CreateBuffers(VMR9AllocationInfo* pAlloc, DWORD cBuffers)
{
    // Allocate an array for the surface pointers.
    ReleaseSurfaces();
    m_pSurf = new IDirect3DSurface9* [cBuffers];
    if (m_pSurf == NULL)
    {
        return E_OUTOFMEMORY;
    }

    // Create offscreen surfaces.
    pAlloc->dwFlags = VMR9AllocFlag_OffscreenSurface;
    HRESULT hr = m_pNotify->AllocateSurfaceHelper(pAlloc, &cBuffers, m_pSurf);
    if (FAILED(hr))
    {
        return hr;
    }
    m_dwNumSurfaces = cBuffers;

    // Create the texture. It must be a render target.
    AdjustTextureSize(pAlloc);
    pAlloc->dwFlags = VMR9AllocFlag_TextureSurface |
                      VMR9AllocFlag_3DRenderTarget;
```

```
        cBuffers = 1;
        CComPtr<IDirect3DSurface9> pTexSurf;
        hr = m_pNotify->AllocateSurfaceHelper(pAlloc, &cBuffers, &pTexSurf);
        if (FAILED(hr))
        {
            return hr;
        }
        pTexSurf->GetContainer(IID_IDirect3DTexture9, (void**)&m_pTexture);
        ScaleVideoTexture();
        FixDepthBuffer(pAllocInfo);
        return hr;
    }
```

The texture is created with the *D3DUSAGE_DYNAMIC* flag, so that it can be modified. The *PresentImage* method copies the video frame to the texture.

```
STDMETHODIMP CAllocator::PresentImage(
    DWORD_PTR dwUserID,
    VMR9PresentationInfo* pPresInfo)
{
    CLock lock(&m_CritSec);
    VideoSource* pSurf = GetVideoSource(dwUserID);
    if (!pSurf)
    {
        return E_INVALIDARG;
    }
    // Copy the video surface to the texture.
    CComPtr<IDirect3DSurface9> pTexSurf;
    pSurf->GetTexture()->GetSurfaceLevel(0, &pTexSurf);
    m_pDevice->StretchRect(pPresInfo->lpSurf, NULL, pTexSurf,
        NULL, D3DTEXF_NONE);
    return S_OK;
}
```

Because the *PresentImage* method no longer draws the scene, we must provide a way for the application to get the textures from the allocator-presenter. We have added a method named *GetTexture* for this purpose. However, it's crucial that the allocator-presenter not modify any textures while the application is using them. Therefore, we also add a pair of methods named *LockTextures* and *UnlockTextures*. The first method holds the allocator-presenter's critical section, and the second releases it.

```
IDirect3DTexture9* CAllocator::GetTexture(DWORD_PTR dwUserID)
{
    VideoSource *pSource = GetVideoSource(dwUserID);
    if (!pSource)
    {
        return NULL;
    }
```

(continued)

```
        return pSource->GetTexture();
    }


void CAllocator::LockTextures() { m_CritSec.Enter(); }

void CAllocator::UnlockTextures() { m_CritSec.Leave(); }
```

Rendering the scene is now simply a matter of calling *LockTextures* to hold the critical section, calling *GetTexture* for each VMR instance, and assigning the textures to the four meshes. When we're done, we call *UnlockTextures* to release the critical section.

```
HRESULT CVmrGame::Render()
{
    m_Device.Clear(D3DCOLOR_XRGB(0x00, 0x80, 0x80));
    HRESULT hr = m_pDevice->BeginScene();
    if (FAILED(hr))
    {
        return hr;
    }
    // Lock the allocator-presenter textures.
    m_pAlloc->LockTextures();

    // Iterate through the filter graphs and get the texture for
    // each VMR. Assign the texture to a mesh.
    GraphMap::iterator iter = m_graphs.begin();
    int i = 0;
    for (; iter != m_graphs.end(); iter++, i++)
    {
        DWORD id = iter->first;
        IDirect3DTexture9 *pTex = m_pAlloc->GetTexture(iter->first);
        CMesh* pl = m_pScene->GetMesh(i);
        pl->SetTexture(1, pTex);
    }

    // Now draw the scene and unlock the textures.
    m_pScene->Render(m_pDevice);
    m_pDevice->EndScene();
    m_pAlloc->UnlockTextures();
    hr = m_pDevice->Present(NULL, NULL, NULL, NULL);
    return hr;
}
```

You can see that we've been very careful throughout about holding critical sections on any public allocator-presenter methods. This is crucial to avoid race conditions.

Creating a 3-D Animation Movie

Our final sample, ChessMen, does not use the VMR at all. DirectShow is about more than just file playback — it can also be used to create video and audio files. The ChessMen application uses this feature to create an AVI file from a Direct3D animation. All that is required is a custom DirectShow source filter to capture the frame buffer and send it down the filter graph. The rest of the process — encoding, muxing, and file writing — is done using existing DirectShow filters.

Unfortunately, it is not possible to capture the frame buffer in real time. This is a fundamental limitation of modern graphics hardware. Writing to the graphics card is fast, but reading from the graphics card is exceedingly slow. If you copy every frame into CPU memory, you cannot possibly maintain a reasonable frame rate. Our solution is to run the animation from a script, so that it can run without human intervention.

When the ChessMen application first runs, it renders normally and accepts keyboard input to control the camera movement. At every frame, it takes a snapshot of the keyboard state and writes this information to a file. If you press the F1 key, the application restarts the animation from the beginning. This time, it does not accept keyboard input. Instead, it runs the animation from the saved key strokes and captures the animation into an AVI file.

Figure 12.2 shows the DirectShow filter graph used to capture the video. The source filter is our custom capture filter, which delivers uncompressed frames to the AVI Mux filter. The AVI Mux filter outputs an AVI byte stream. The byte stream is sent to the File Writer filter, which writes the file to disk.

Figure 12.2   DirectShow filter graph for writing AVI files.

Source Filter for Capturing Animation Frames

The source filter is built with the DirectShow base class library. This library provides a set of classes for writing DirectShow filters. Although it is included in the Samples directory of the DirectShow SDK, it is meant for real-world use, and you should not hesitate to use it in your own applications.

The source filter is implemented by the *CCapSource* class, which derives from the *CSource* class. The filter has one output pin, implemented by the *CCapPin* pin, which is derived from the *CSourceStream* class. Most of the work is already done for us in the parent classes. Here are the main functions that we need to add:

- **GetMediaType.**   Proposes an output format.

- **CheckMediaType.**   Validates an output format.

■ **DecideBufferSize.** Sets the buffer size.

■ **FillBuffer.** Fills an output buffer with data.

The first three operations on this list occur when the filter connects to another filter. The last one, filling output buffers, happens on a worker thread while the filter graph runs. The parent classes implement the rest of the filter's functionality, including state transitions between running, paused, and stopped; creating the worker thread; and delivering buffers downstream to the next filter.

In the following sections, we summarize the code without getting into the internal details of the base classes. For more information, see the DirectShow SDK documentation, especially the topic "Writing DirectShow Filters". In addition, the book *Programming Microsoft DirectShow for Digital Video and Television,* by Mark Pesce (Microsoft Press), has two chapters on writing filters, including one on writing source filters.

GetMediaType

The *GetMediaType* function returns a valid output format for the pin. For this filter, the allowable format is determined by the back buffer. The filter constructs the media type when the application sets the Direct3D device on the filter.

```
HRESULT CCapPin::SetDevice(IDirect3DDevice9 *pDevice)
{
    CAutoLock cAutoLock(m_pFilter->pStateLock());
    CheckPointer(pDevice, E_POINTER);

    m_pDevice.Release();
    m_pDevice = pDevice;

    // Get the back buffer surface description.
    CComPtr<IDirect3DSurface9> pSurf;
    HRESULT hr = pDevice->GetBackBuffer(0, 0, D3DBACKBUFFER_TYPE_MONO,
        &pSurf);
    if (FAILED(hr))
    {
        return hr;
    }
    D3DSURFACE_DESC desc;
    pSurf->GetDesc(&desc);

    // Convert the surface description to a media type.
    GUID subtype;
    SubtypeFromD3DFormat(desc.Format, &subtype);
    UINT width = desc.Width;
    UINT height = desc.Height;
    CreateRGBVideoType(&m_mtFormat, subtype, width, height, m_rtFrameLength);
    return hr;
}
```

Once the media type has been defined, a copy is returned in the *GetMediaType* function.

```
HRESULT CCapPin::GetMediaType(CMediaType *pMediaType)
{
    CheckPointer(pMediaType, E_POINTER);
    CAutoLock cAutoLock(m_pFilter->pStateLock());
    *pMediaType = m_mtFormat;
    return S_OK;
}
```

The *CMediaType* class is a wrapper for the *AM_MEDIA_TYPE* structure. It overloads the assignment operator to copy the media type, including the format block.

CheckMediaType

The *CheckMediaType* function validates an output format. If the type is acceptable, the function returns S_OK. Otherwise, it returns a failure code.

```
HRESULT CCapPin::CheckMediaType(const CMediaType *pMediaType)
{
    CAutoLock lock(m_pFilter->pStateLock());
    CheckPointer(pMediaType, E_POINTER);
    if (*pMediaType == m_mtFormat)
    {
        return S_OK;
    }
    else
    {
        return VFW_E_TYPE_NOT_ACCEPTED;
    }
}
```

Because the filter accepts only one media type, the function does a straight comparison with the *m_mtFormat* variable, using the overloaded equality operator on the *CMediaType* class. The *CheckMediaType* function may seem redundant, given the *GetMediaType* function, but pin connection in DirectShow involves a certain amount of negotiation between the pins. The process is generalized enough to handle the requirements of a broad range of filters.

DecideBufferSize

The *DecideBufferSize* method sets the size of the buffers used to hold the video frames.

```
HRESULT CCapPin::DecideBufferSize(
    IMemAllocator *pAlloc, ALLOCATOR_PROPERTIES *pRequest)
{
    CAutoLock cAutoLock(m_pFilter->pStateLock());

    VIDEOINFOHEADER *pvi = (VIDEOINFOHEADER*) m_mt.Format();
```

(continued)

```
// Image size is given in the video format.
pRequest->cBuffer = pvi->bmiHeader.biSizeImage;

// We need at least one buffer.
if (pRequest->cBuffers == 0)
{
    pRequest->cBuffers = 1;
}

// Try to set the properties.
ALLOCATOR_PROPERTIES ActualProps;
HRESULT hr = pAlloc->SetProperties(pRequest, &ActualProps);
if (FAILED(hr))
{
    return hr;
}
// Check what we actually got. We accept a larger buffer than
// requested, but not a smaller buffer.
if (ActualProps.cBuffer < pRequest->cBuffer)
{
    return E_FAIL;
}
return S_OK;
}
```

Buffer allocation is performed by an object called an *allocator* that supports the *IMemAllocator* interface. The allocator is specified in the *pAlloc* parameter. The *pRequest* parameter contains the buffer properties that the downstream filter has requested.

After filling in the number of buffers (*cBuffers*) and the required buffer size (*cbBuffer*), we call the *IMemAllocator::SetProperties* method on the allocator. The results are returned in the *ActualProps* parameter, and may differ slightly from the request even if the method succeeds. For example, the buffer size may get rounded up to some even multiple, such as 512 bytes.

FillBuffer

The *FillBuffer* method is called from the source filter's worker thread in a continuous loop. In our filter, we must wait until the application has a new frame available. To synchronize these threads — the application thread and the filter's worker thread — we define a pair of event handles: *m_hEventNewFrame*, which is signaled by the application when it has a new frame, and *m_hEventStop*, which is signaled when the filter's *Stop* method is called. (The *m_hEventStop* event is needed so the worker thread doesn't block when the filter graph attempts to stop.) Here is the code for the *FillBuffer* method.

```
HRESULT CCapPin::FillBuffer(IMediaSample *pSample)
{
    HANDLE objects[] = { m_hEventStop, m_hEventNewFrame };
    DWORD result = WaitForMultipleObjects(2, objects, FALSE, INFINITE);
    if (result == WAIT_OBJECT_0)
    {
        return S_FALSE;  // End of stream.
    }
    if (result != WAIT_OBJECT_0 + 1)
    {
        return E_FAIL;
    }

    // Time stamp the sample.
    REFERENCE_TIME rtStop = m_rtStreamTime + m_rtFrameLength;
    pSample->SetTime(&m_rtStreamTime, &rtStop);
    m_rtStreamTime += m_rtFrameLength;
    pSample->SetSyncPoint(TRUE);

    return CopyFrameToSample(pSample);
}
```

If the stop event is signaled, the method returns *S_FALSE*. This informs the parent class to shut down the worker thread. Otherwise, we copy the contents of the back buffer into the sample buffer. The *CopyFrameToSample* function is straightforward, but we need to allow for the possibility that the buffer has a different pitch than the Direct3D surface, or a different image orientation.

```
HRESULT CCapPin::CopyFrameToSample(IMediaSample *pSample)
{
    HRESULT hr;

    // Get a pointer to the buffer.
    BYTE *pData;
    pSample->GetPointer(&pData);

    // Get the back buffer surface.
    CComPtr<IDirect3DSurface9> pSurf;
    hr = m_pDevice->GetBackBuffer(0, 0, D3DBACKBUFFER_TYPE_MONO, &pSurf);
    if (FAILED(hr))
    {
        return hr;
    }
    D3DLOCKED_RECT rect;
    hr = pSurf->LockRect(&rect, NULL, D3DLOCK_READONLY);
    if (SUCCEEDED(hr))
    {
```

(continued)

```
            // Copy each row of the surface into the buffer.
            // We cannot use memcpy, because the surface stride or
            // image orientation may not match.

            VIDEOINFOHEADER *pVih = (VIDEOINFOHEADER*)m_mt.pbFormat;
            DWORD dwWidth, dwHeight;
            LONG lStride;
            BYTE *pTop;
            GetVideoInfoParameters(pVih, pData, &dwWidth, &dwHeight,
                &lStride, &pTop, false);
            DWORD cbRow = (pVih->bmiHeader.biBitCount / 8) * dwWidth;

            BYTE *pSource = (BYTE*)rect.pBits;
            for (DWORD row = 0; row < dwHeight; row++)
            {
                memcpy(pTop, pSource, cbRow);
                pTop += lStride;
                pSource += rect.Pitch;
            }
            pSurf->UnlockRect();
        }
    return hr;
}
```

Building the Capture Graph

The code used to build the capture graph is quite similar to the graph-building code that we've shown in previous chapters. Some error-checking has been removed to make the code listing shorter.

```
HRESULT CGraph::BuildD3DCapGraph(IDirect3DDevice9 *pDevice)
{
    InitializeFilterGraph();

    // Add the source filter.
    m_pSource = new CCapSource(pDevice, &hr);
    m_pSource->AddRef();
    hr = m_pGraph->AddFilter(m_pSource, L"CapFilter");

    // Add the AVI Mux filter.
    CComPtr<IBaseFilter> pMux;
    hr = AddFilterByCLSID(m_pGraph, CLSID_AviDest, &pMux);

    // Add the File Writer filter and set the output file name.
    CComPtr<IBaseFilter> pWriter;
    hr = AddFilterByCLSID(m_pGraph, CLSID_FileWriter, &pWriter);
    CComQIPtr<IFileSinkFilter2> pSink(pWriter);
    pSink->SetFileName(OLESTR("d3dcap.avi"), NULL);
```

```
    // Hook up the filters.
    hr = ConnectFilters(m_pGraph, m_pSource, pMux);
    hr = ConnectFilters(m_pGraph, pMux, pWriter);
    return hr;
}
```

Because the *CCapSource* class is compiled directly into the application, we can create it with *new* instead of going through the whole COM *CoCreateInstance* process. (You can also put a filter in a DLL and register it with a CLSID, which enables the filter to be created with *CoCreateInstance*, but that's not a requirement.)

Everything else in the ChessMen application is a variation on code that you've seen before. We add the AVI Mux and File Writer filters to the graph, connect everything together, and we're ready to run the filter graph.

Note that the video files created by the ChessMen application can be quite large, because they contain uncompressed video. You could easily modify the application to insert an encoder filter before the AVI Mux filter, to reduce the file size, or else use the ASF Writer Filter to create Windows Media Video (WMV) files. Another option is to compress the file later, using a tool such as Windows Media Encoder.

Summary

This chapter concludes our discussion of video programming. In the next section, we turn to the question of how to create original audio and video content with the highest possible quality. After all, your audience doesn't see or hear any of the code that you've written. The code is only as good as the music, sound effects, and video that you provide for it.

Part III

Production Quality

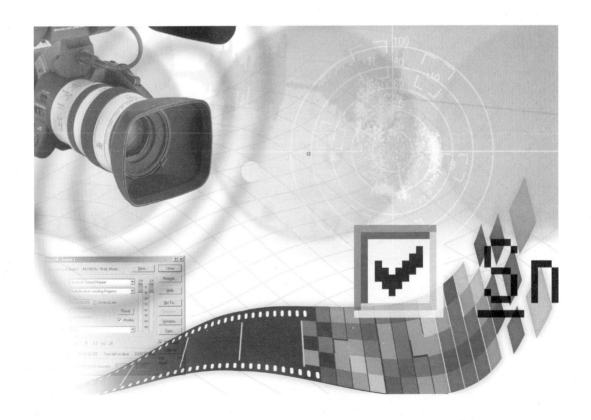

13

Producing Content with Technical Quality

In this chapter, we will explore methods and tools that you can use to optimize technical quality as you produce audio and video content. We will describe what we mean by technical quality, and then look at how to optimize it in the context of the production process. Although there are specific methods that you can use at different points in the process to improve technical quality, it's best to factor quality into every decision that you make.

The two main parts of the production process are production and postproduction. Production takes place when you record, shoot, or capture content, while postproduction occurs when you edit and distribute content. In this chapter, we will describe the production process in general. In the next chapter, we will follow the production process in detail from beginning to end, and describe how to optimize technical quality at each step.

Understanding Technical Quality

There are many different ways to measure the quality of audio and video content. For example, you can measure the artistic or creative quality of a game by how well it was designed. Technical quality, however, is concerned with the noncreative aspects of a piece of content, for example, the color quality of the video or the presence of distortion in the audio. Although these qualities describe very different aspects of a video work, they are closely related. For example, the quality of an audio recording can affect the story that you want to tell, and the artistic decision to shoot in black and white will affect technical aspects like the video format and lighting.

Technical quality is a very important aspect of an audio or video work because it carries your artistic vision. There is no rule stating that all colors must be bright and realistic, and all sounds must be clear and audible. Except for limits and standards imposed by the medium itself, such as file size, technical quality is under your control. If the technical quality of a piece is as good as it can be, it is completely transparent: only the creative qualities come through. You are the best judge of the quality of your content and are ultimately responsible for your artistic vision.

The reason for making this point is that often content creators feel bound by some arbitrary quality standard. A book about how to make movies tells them never to use this lens, or always use that kind of microphone. One of the joys of making videos and music comes with discovering that *technical quality is not dictated by a camera, or a book, or an industry professional.*

You are the one in charge of the technical quality of your production. For example, many consumer camcorders come with features that automatically control the light level entering the lens, so many consumers feel that the light levels that the camcorder sets must be right. The truth is that automatic settings are only right if they are right for *you.* You should not allow a camcorder to dictate quality just because it was expensive and has many intimidating controls. If you look through the lens and do not see what you want to see, the camcorder is wrong, regardless of how technologically advanced the automatic circuitry may be.

Optimizing is often called *cleaning.* For example, you might clean narration tracks by removing unrelated sounds like dogs barking and electronic pops, or use a clean section of video that doesn't show the camera person's thumb over the lens. The best way to determine what needs to be cleaned, and how to do it, is to put yourself in the place of the audience. You might be able to hear the narration fine over the sound of a dog barking, but what will the audience think when they listen to the narration in your game about the Civil War? They might think you are trying to make an artistic statement with the dog-barking sound, and the distraction could lead them to make a fatal mistake on the battlefield.

The term "cleaning" is not used as often when referring to video. The types of technical quality optimizations that you are most likely to do with images relate to lighting, color, and problems with equipment and physical media.

Now, let's look at what professional producers, creative people, and technicians think about when determining acceptable technical quality.

Audio

You approach the use of sound in the same way, whether you are creating a movie, video, or game, because people perceive sounds the same regardless of how the sounds come to them.

Recorded sound as used in video production falls into one of the following categories:

- Specific sound, such as the closing of a door or a passing car. Specific sounds are also called sync sounds when they are synchronized to specific events in the video.

- Background sound, such as residential neighborhood ambience (dogs barking, cars passing, birds chirping, and kids playing). The individual sounds that make up a background are not synchronized to anything in the picture, so a background can be looped or repeated.

- Music, which either originates from within a scene (source music) or from outside the scene (underscore). Examples of source music are sound from radios or marching bands, from sources that are seen in the video. Underscore can be added to enhance the emotional content of a scene.

- Dialog, which can be one or more voices synchronized to people in the picture, or a voice or voices of people who are not seen in the shot, such as narration (voice-over). A clean dialog or narration track is very important, because it is typically the most important sound and carries the meaning of a scene.

A perfectly clean audio track is one that contains only the sound(s) that you want, and the sound itself has the quality that you expect. For example, a narration track contains a good-quality recording of the narrator's voice with no distortion, no reverberation, and no barking dogs. If you want underscore music along with the voice, you can add it during the postproduction process with a multitrack editor. A multitrack editor enables you to control the placement and mix of the sounds by enabling you to work with modules or clips of sound layered on tracks. For example, you can mix sync dialog with a train station background in a multitrack editor, and it will sound like the person is in a train station.

If an audio track is not clean, you will have trouble editing and controlling the quality of the final product. For example, if you must use a narration track that includes music, you will not be able to edit the narration without also editing the music. You must be concerned with how an edit will affect the sound of both the dialog and the music. An example of this is attempting to edit video of a speech that includes a radio playing in the background. Whenever you edit the voice, the music on the radio will jump.

Unwanted, nonmusical sound in a recording is called noise. The same sound can be noise in one case and necessary in another. Audio noise can be introduced into a recording either externally or internally:

- External noise is unwanted sound that is picked up by the microphone, from sources such as air conditioners, elevator motors, refrigerators, traffic, surf, talking, wind, and music.

- Internal noise is unwanted sound that is introduced after a sound has been received by a microphone and converted to an electrical signal. This very-low-voltage audio signal is susceptible to interference from a number of sources, such as the microphone itself, cables carrying the signal, electronic components used to amplify or process the signal, the device used to convert the signal to a digital stream, or the software audio processors. Internal noise can also be generated by an external source, such as the electromagnetic radiation from power lines and transformers. Noise includes hum, hiss, pops, clicks, and distortion from electronic components and recording tape. Distortion of the audio signal is most often caused by overmodulation, when electronic components, digital processors, or recording tape receive a signal that is too high for them to effectively process.

Once noise is recorded and mixed with the desired audio, it can rarely be eliminated. It might be possible to reduce noise with software or mask it with a background sound, but the process also affects the desired sound. The best way to ensure noise-free audio is to make sure that noise is not recorded.

Video

Recorded video images are not categorized the same as audio because they are technically very different from audio, and play a different role in our perception. In audio production, you typically record elements discretely and then mix them together to create a finished piece. In video production, on the other hand, you most often do not think in terms of mixing multiple discrete elements because the process is more time-consuming and difficult. In general, photographers shoot complete images. It is typically easier to record or "shoot" an actor in a real location than it is to shoot the actor and background separately, and composite them later. Compositing is becoming more popular with inexpensive digital systems, but it will be a while before it is used as often as multitrack mixing is used with audio.

As with audio, once an image is recorded on tape or film, elements of the image are locked in place. You can use editing to cut before or after a shot that you want, but it is not easy to add to or remove parts of the actual shot. For example, if a shot of a speaker contains an unwanted airplane flying behind the person's head in the background, you cannot simply remove an airplane layer. True, there are digital video-production systems that enable you to track shapes and perform advanced compositing techniques, with which you could clean up the image. However, these systems are outside the scope of this book, and the processes are often time-consuming and expensive.

For the most part, optimizing video technical quality is limited to working with the color properties. You can do this in several ways. You can change the overall color properties of an image or create composite images using colors. If the image is digital, you can also use effects processes that change the 3-D positioning and shape of images. For example, you can enlarge and reposition an image to remove unwanted video along the edges of the frame.

The best time to optimize quality is during production when you are shooting the video. For example, it is far easier to do something to ensure that the camera does not record an airplane flying overhead than to attempt to remove it in postproduction. After the image has been recorded, you typically optimize quality during postproduction with a digital video editor, such as Avid Media Composer and Adobe Premiere. An editor enables you to apply processors to a video track and to composite images.

As with audio, problems with the technical quality of video are introduced either externally or internally. External technical problems are introduced when images are recorded, and because cameras record light, the problems are typically a result of poor lighting. Poor lighting can sometimes be corrected electronically or digitally in postproduction. There are roughly three types of poor lighting:

- Overall level of lighting is too high or too low. If it is too low, the level of lighting can be raised, however, that also increases the internal noise. If the level of lighting is too high, it can be lowered. As with audio, however, if the level is so high that it has *clipped* the video, those areas that appear washed out cannot be restored.

- *Contrast ratio* is too high. If the ratio between the dark and light areas of the image is too great, the detail in the dark areas is lost. If you increase the overall lighting level to bring out the detail, the light areas become clipped. To help correct the problem, the contrast can be reduced.

- Overall color is off. Typically, color problems are introduced by light that has a different color temperature from the type of film that is used or the white balance setting on the video camera. *Color temperature* describes the color of a light source. Incandescent light is more reddish than sunlight, so a subject that was lit with incandescent light and shot with a camera that was balanced for sunlight will appear very red. Consumer video cameras automatically compensate, but not always in the best way. For example, a camcorder might incorrectly compensate when a scene is lit by both sunlight and incandescent, or worse, adjust the color as you move the camera. In any event, overall color problems can be corrected in postproduction.

Other types of external problems, such as unwanted objects in a shot or bad camera angles, are often thought of as artistic problems. However, if the problem distracts from the central story, it can become a technical problem, and repairing the problem using electronics and software might not produce the best results.

Internal technical problems are introduced after images enter the camera lens. Unlike analog video, video that is stored digitally does not deteriorate when it is transferred or copied, so many of the internal technical problems of the old analog days are now history. For example, we no longer have to be concerned with inconsistent color caused by a consumer tape format, such as VHS. Any internal technical problems typically arise inside the camcorder before the video is converted to a digital stream. For example, problems can come from the lens, the CCD chips, the analog processors and amplifiers, and the analog to digital converter. The following list describes categories of technical problems:

- Noise. Problems appear as small flashing sparkles throughout the image. Video noise is created by electronic components that amplify or process the analog video. To minimize noise, use high-quality video hardware and minimize the number of analog components in the video-processing chain.

- Low resolution. Problems arise when detail is missing and an image appears out of focus, or *soft*. To maintain resolution, you should eliminate unnecessary video-processing steps. For example, save resolution by transferring video digitally from a tape to a computer, instead of capturing through analog composite video outputs and inputs. By transferring digitally, you bypass two converters, a number of amplifiers and processors, and a cable and connectors, all of which can lower resolution and add noise.

- Glitches and drop-outs. These are quick flashes that are usually restricted to one or two lines of a video frame. They are caused by imperfections in the videotape or some other momentary loss of signal.

- Digital artifacts. These consist of various types of aberrations caused by problems with a computer or digital device, or a codec, the most common of which include blockiness and dropped frames. Blockiness occurs when a codec is unable to reproduce the needed detail, and blocks appear in the image.

- Clipping. This problem occurs when the brightest areas of an image exceed the upper threshold of the video components, resulting in a loss of detail and a washed-out appearance. However, unlike audio, a clipped video image might not be overmodulated. Often video processors include circuitry that electronically clips or prevents the signal from going over the upper limits defined by the standard. Therefore, an image can contain clipped areas without adversely affecting the recording or transmission. In shooting high-contrast scenes, you may need to clip areas if there is no way to avoid it. For example, when shooting a shaded subject against a bright background, the best solution is to increase the light level on the subject. However, if this is not possible, you can adjust the exposure for the subject and allow the background to be slightly clipped.

Internal problems are often difficult to repair because they cannot be fixed by adjusting overall color properties. With advances in camcorder technology, tape and noise problems are becoming rarer.

The following list describes some of the basic ways to work with technical quality in postproduction:

■ Editing. The easiest way to maintain technical quality is to simply edit around the problem areas. For example, you can use a different take of a reading. If the audio portion is useable but the video is not, you can insert video of another shot.

■ Color correction. Next to editing, the easiest way to adjust technical quality is with color correction. The methods available for correcting color depend on whether the video is digital data or an analog signal and, if analog, at what point the video signal is in the processing chain. Most often, you will work with the video as digital data, which gives you a great deal of control over many details of the image. With an analog signal, you have more control early in the process when the video is in its red, green, and blue (RGB) components, but after the video has been processed into a composite signal, you have less control. Processors and filters enable you to correct the overall color of images by modifying the following video properties:

❑ Luminance or brightness. This property describes video intensity. In composite video, luminance is the black-and-white portion of the analog signal. When you adjust luminance, the image gets brighter or darker. If you turn luminance all the way off, the image is black.

❑ Chrominance or saturation. This property describes color intensity. In composite video, chrominance is the color portion of the analog signal. When you adjust chrominance, colors become more or less intense. If you turn chrominance all the way off, the image is black and white.

❑ Hue or phase. This property describes the overall hue of the colors. In composite video, the phase or timing relationship between the image portion of the chrominance signal and a reference that is called a *color burst* determines the hue. As you adjust hue, the colors change to red, green, blue, and all the shades in between.

❑ Setup. This property describes the black level. In composite video, setup is the lowest or darkest part of the black-and-white portion of the analog signal. When you increase setup, the black portions become lighter. Setup does not apply to digital video.

❑ Gamma. This property describes the mid-tone intensity. Gamma adjustments are usually made to digital and component video. Typically, gamma is used to adjust the contrast between the light and dark areas of an image. If you change gamma, the mid-tone shades become lighter or darker. You can also adjust the gamma of red, green, and blue individually.

❑ RGB. This property describes the intensity of the red, green, and blue components, which can only be adjusted if the video is analog component or digital. If you adjust the three components equally, the overall video intensity changes.

■ Compositing or layering. There are basically two ways to layer video: superimposing and keying. Superimposing is simply placing one image on top of another so they both appear together. Keying is a technique that creates transparent areas of an image based on a color or luminance level. The four frames in Figure 13.1 demonstrate a simple use of *chromakey*.

Figure 13.1   Steps for using chromakey to layer video.

The background of the first image is green. The chromakey process is applied to the image, and the keyer is carefully adjusted to create a transparent *mask,* where every instance of that shade of green is found, as in the second frame. Then the masked image is composited over the third frame, resulting in the fourth frame. Using these techniques, you could cut out a bad portion of one image by creating a mask and replacing it with something else.

■   Positioning and cropping. Positioning tools enable you to move the video frame to any location and position in three dimensions. For example, you can make a frame smaller and position it in a corner, and then add perspective so it appears that the frame is facing to the side. Cropping tools, which also only work with digital video, enable you to remove portions of the top, bottom, or sides of a frame. You can use cropping to eliminate portions or change the aspect ratio of a frame. The two images in Figure 13.2 show a frame before and after it was enlarged slightly and cropped.

Figure 13.2   Frames before and after the video was repositioned and cropped.

Judging Quality

In order to optimize the technical quality of your audio and video, you must have a clear understanding of the purpose and destination of the content. The quality decisions that you make must be driven by the creative intent of a work or a production. For example, to obtain a gritty quality, you may want a music track that contains audio distortion and unmotivated background noises. In fact, to achieve this effect, a total lack of distortion and noise may be exactly what you do *not* want. You must also be aware of the limitations imposed by your destination medium. For example, you have more flexibility with the wider dynamic range of CDs than you do with low-bit-rate streaming audio.

Optimizing is all about matching and consistency. It is more important that a clip match the quality of other clips and images within a certain work, than to have the best possible quality, because it is inconsistency that the viewer or listener will notice before a lack of quality. As stated earlier, the point of optimizing technical quality is to make it transparent, so that it does not distract the audience from the artistic aspect. For example, a high-quality, realistic, gunshot sound effect may sound bland and out of place in an action game with very stylized, animated characters. A sound that is nothing like a gunshot may actually work better, such as a distorted recording of hitting a large metal sheet with a baseball bat.

Matching means comparing the quality throughout a piece to a standard, especially your artistic standard. For example, you can ask yourself if the technical quality of a particular shot matches the quality standard that you have established for a project. The other standard is imposed by the medium, for example, a particular game platform. The limitations of a medium also impose a standard. For example, standard-definition video has a limited contrast ratio, requiring that a scene be lit more evenly in order to pick up all the detail in the dark areas.

Matching and consistency become most apparent in the editing room and in the game environment when you create transitions between video clips or attempt to mix sounds from different sources. For example, a user is likely to notice when you cut from a dark, bluish image to one that is bright and evenly colored, and that sudden shift may draw the viewer's attention away from your story or a point you want to make; in other words, that shift may take the viewer outside the experience that you are trying to create. Even though both images may be of technically good quality, it may be more important that they match and the transition appears transparent and seamless.

You should decide on your standard of technical quality, and then adhere to that standard. Maintain control, so that the technical quality of your production supports your vision throughout the creative process.

Quality in the Big Picture

In general, your original or *raw*, material should be as clean as possible. Then you can take the raw material and add effects, mix and composite it with other material, or modify properties to create a final product. For example, you should start with a clean voice recording, and then add effects in postproduction to create the sound that you want.

There are five opportunities during the life of a digital media production when you can optimize technical quality, as illustrated in Figure 13.3.

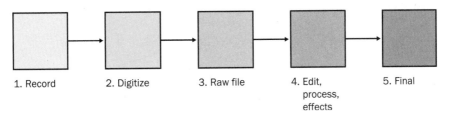

1. Record   2. Digitize   3. Raw file   4. Edit,   5. Final
                                               process,
                                               effects

Figure 13.3   Five steps of the production process.

At each point in the production process, you have different options and reasons for optimizing. For example, when shooting with a camcorder, you will optimize in different ways than when you are in the editing phase.

You can optimize quality at the following stages in the production process:

1. Production. This stage involves recording audio and video. Production is the best time to think about technical quality, because your raw material sets the standard for the entire production.

2. Acquisition. This is when you convert or copy content to a hard disk. The process is also called capturing or digitizing. At this point, there are steps that you can take to ensure that the transfer retains as much of the original quality as possible. If you are acquiring digitally, the content is not processed because the data is transferred directly. Therefore, for digital acquisition, you do not have the opportunity to either improve or degrade quality.

3. Clean-up. If your raw, digital media data contains elements that should be removed or changed, it is often easier to work with the content before post-production. If you start the editing process with clean audio and video, you can concentrate on the artistic aspects of your production rather than fight technical problems. Also, it may be easier at this point to identify content that must be rerecorded than to wait until after you start editing or mixing.

4. Postproduction. This stage involves editing, mixing, and processing the raw material into a final product. Assuming that you have done as much as possible to optimize the quality of your raw files, the technical optimization that you

perform in postproduction will most likely focus on matching and consistency: tweaking the quality of your audio and video so that the audience will not notice the transitions, and so that your audio elements work well together.

5.   Mastering. In this stage, you work with the final product before it is distributed to your audience. After your content has been edited, effects and processing applied, and the transitions smoothed out, your production should require very little additional work. Typically, any modifications that you make at this point affect the product as a whole, and are often necessitated by your destination medium. For example, you may need to raise the audio level of your entire video or decrease the dynamic range by using an audio compressor before recording the content to a CD. You may also need to make overall corrections to the color. If the content is to be used in a game, the audio quality of the many individual files must match. If files are to be played concurrently, audio levels must be adjusted so that they mix properly.

In the next section, we will look at the tools used for creating and working with audio and video.

The Tools

The tools used to create and work with content are divided between those used in the following stages:

- Production
- Postproduction

Production tools should record and store good-quality sound and images. Postproduction tools should enable you to create your final product from raw audio and video content, and to work with the technical quality to ensure that the final product is consistent with your artistic vision.

Production Tools

In the production stage, you capture images and sounds on a recording device that saves them electronically as analog signals or digital streams to a medium, such as videotape. A typical recording device for video is a camcorder, so named because it consists of a camera and videotape recorder (VTR) in one unit. Camcorders also include a microphone and playback capabilities, meaning that a camcorder is a complete video production tool in one package.

There are many types of camcorders, for many budget sizes and purposes, from manufacturers such as Sony, JVC, Panasonic, and Canon. Camcorders are the most popular video-recording device, and there is a wide range of quality among all the brands and models. Again, it is best to start production with the best technical quality because it is not possible to add quality later. For example, if you shoot low-resolution video with an inexpensive camcorder, you cannot simply add resolution later. You might be able to add sharpness with an editor plug-in, but you cannot restore detail that was not recorded.

The following describes some aspects that affect technical quality to consider when choosing a camcorder for your production:

- Number of chips. A microchip called a CCD and related electronic circuitry convert an image to an electrical signal. Consumer camcorders typically use one CCD chip. Camcorders created for professional use have three CCDs: one for each of the primary colors: red, green, and blue. With three CCDs, the camcorder produces images with truer colors and more color detail. Figure 13.4 shows examples of camcorders from Sony and Canon that lie somewhere between consumer and professional. They include three CCD chips, record in the MiniDV digital format, and provide high-quality audio and video at a price well below that of camcorders that are used in broadcast and professional video production.

Figure 13.4   Two examples of camcorders that feature three CCD chips.

- Horizontal resolution. All camcorders and televisions of a given television standard have the same vertical resolution, which is measured by the number of lines that are used to scan one frame of video. The National Television

Standards Committee (NTSC) standard consists of 525 lines. Horizontal resolution is also measured in number of lines, but it varies with the technical quality of a video source and describes the amount of sharpness and detail in an image. A professional camcorder produces images that exceed 700 lines of resolution, where a VHS videocassette recorder (VCR) has a resolution of only 240 lines.

- Tape format. The type of format and tape used to record video affect horizontal resolution, color quality, and other video properties. Format describes not only the tape, but the hardware and system used for recording and playing the video and audio. A low-quality format, such as a consumer format, is more likely to produce an inferior image because the format was designed to minimize costs, and often size. For example, video recorded on 8 mm consumer tape is more likely to contain drop-outs than professional BetaCam tape, because the format itself specifies narrower tape and smaller, lighter moving parts. In general, the quality is better with digital tape formats, such as MiniDV and DVCam, and digital video can be transferred directly to a hard disk, thereby eliminating the conversion step that lowers resolution.

- Manual control. All camcorders include a number of automatic functions, including auto-focus, auto-iris, auto white balance and others. Camcorders used by professional camera operators also include the ability to override the automatic functions, because the sensors that control the functions might not produce the desired effect. By having these manual options, you therefore have more control over technical quality.

Audio can be recorded in a number of ways. If audio is synchronized with video, it can be recorded directly on the videotape with a camcorder. If audio is to be recorded without video, it is typically recorded on an audio tape recorder, or directly to a hard disk on a computer using a digital audio workstation (DAW). One of the most popular audio recorders uses digital audio tape (DAT). One advantage of a DAT recorder is that the audio can be transferred digitally to a computer, with no loss of audio quality from the original. Not only do professional DAT machines record with very high quality, but the tape can also embed time code. Many professional video and film productions record their audio on DAT recorders, and then later synchronize the audio to film or video during postproduction. Figure 13.5 shows a portable DAT recorder from Tascam. Sony and Fostex are other companies that manufacture DAT recorders.

Figure 13.5   Example of a portable DAT recorder.

To pick up sound, you can use a high-quality *condenser* microphone. If multiple microphones are required, an audio mixer is used to blend the audio before it goes to tape. Shure, Sony and Sennheiser are several companies that manufacture good-quality microphones. Figure 13.6 shows a lavalier microphone from Tram that you can conceal underneath clothing.

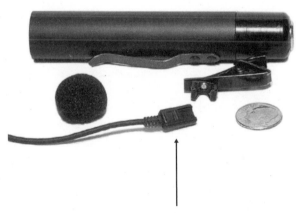

Figure 13.6   Example of a small lavalier microphone.

The following list describes the general properties of microphones and recorders that determine their technical quality:

■   Internal noise. The electronic components in microphones and recorders produce a certain amount of noise, as measured by the device's *signal-to-noise* ratio specification.

■   Dynamic range. A recorder or mixer with a high signal-to-noise ratio enables you to record with a wide dynamic range, which is the difference between the quietest sounds you can record and the loudest sounds. A wide dynamic range enables you to record with more *headroom*, which is the range between the loudest sound and digital distortion. In other words, if you use a noisy recorder, you will have to record at a higher level to avoid hearing the noise, so the recorder will have less headroom, and distortion will be more likely.

■   Analog-to-digital converter. The quality of the hardware device that converts the analog signal to a data stream and back again is measured by how accurately it makes the conversion, in other words, how close the digital sound is to the original. A converter that performs *oversampling* is capable of producing a smoother, more accurate digital waveform because it takes more samples of the analog signal during conversion.

■   Transport speed and inconsistencies. The speed of the tape in a recorder must be accurate and consistent. In an analog recorder, you can hear variations in speed. In a digital recorder, the consistency of the tape speed is not as important because the data is buffered. However, the consistency of the *clocking source* is important. A digital recorder synchronizes the delivery of its data stream to a digital clock source. If the source is unstable, the device will produce a type of distortion called *clock jitter*.

Postproduction Tools

After production, the content is acquired or digitized to a computer hard disk or a digital disk recorder (DDR). After it is has been digitized, many of the tools used to create the final product are also used to improve the technical quality or clean up the audio and video. The tools are for the most part software (programs, plug-ins, or filters) that modify the content data.

To ensure that you can effectively manage technical quality, the first set of tools you need in a postproduction workstation is a high-quality video display and audio speakers. After installing the display and speakers, make sure that they are adjusted to a known standard.

To correctly adjust audio levels, use a mixer or audio program that provides accurate VU meters. A good-quality VU meter changes rapidly enough to correctly represent how the audio level fluctuates. It also indicates at what level distortion occurs. Always use the meter when capturing analog audio content, to make sure that levels are within the desired dynamic range without distorting. Figure 13.7 shows the VU meters in a DAW.

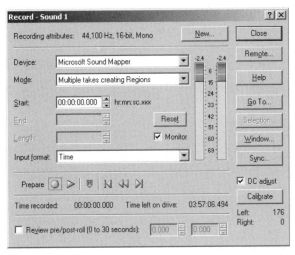

Figure 13.7   Record dialog box with VU meters that show audio levels.

To accurately adjust video properties, you can use a software waveform monitor and vectorscope. These displays work similarly to the hardware devices with the same names. The waveform monitor enables you to correctly adjust luminance and setup; the vectorscope lets you adjust chrominance and hue (phase). If this software is not available, you will have to judge video properties by viewing the content on the video display.

If you transfer digitally, for example from a camcorder or DAT recorder, the data will not change as it is being written to the hard disk. Therefore, you cannot adjust audio and video properties during acquisition.

After the content has been stored on a hard disk, you can use the following types of programs to edit, process, and convert your content:

Video

■   Video editors. The primary purpose of a video editor is to provide you with a way to edit video content into short clips, and then arrange the clips on a timeline to create a finished video. However, most high-quality video-editing programs also include many features for processing video, which enable you to add effects and different types of transitions between clips, and to composite or layer clips. The features are often included as plug-ins or filters, and a number of them enable you to work with the technical quality of your video, such as color correction. Windows-based video editors are available from such companies as Adobe and Avid. Figure 13.8 shows the Vegas video-editing program from Sonic Foundry.

Figure 13.8   Components of a video-editing program.

■ Digital effects programs. There are a number of professional-level programs that enable you to perform advanced digital compositing and apply effects, similarly to the way that you can work with still images in a graphics program. If your video requires this level of work, there are a host of third-party providers that you can contact. One such program is AfterEffects from Adobe.

Audio

■ Digital audio workstation (DAW). With these programs, you view the waveform display of an audio file and perform detailed editing and processing. The programs also include an audio-capture function and most employ good-quality VU meters. The programs typically include a number of processing features and enable you to use processing plug-ins, such as a noise reduction plug-in. You can also copy or cut and paste portions of the waveform. For fine control, many enable you to actually redraw portions of the waveform. This is often the best way to eliminate short transient clicks and pops. WaveLab from Steinberg, Sound Forge from Sonic Foundry and Cool Edit Pro from Syntrillium are examples of DAWs.

■   Multitrack programs. Use an audio workstation to make fine adjustments to a file, and a multitrack program to layer, synchronize, and mix multiple files and clips. Many multitrack programs enable you to move back and forth between it and a workstation, so that you can work with multiple tracks, and then open a piece of audio in a workstation to perform detailed work, and then move the file back to the multitrack program. Multitrack programs also include plug-ins so you can apply audio processing in real-time to one or more tracks. Steinberg and Sonic Foundry are examples of companies that offer multitrack programs for Windows-based computers.

Mastering

There are a number of tools that you can use to prepare finished content for distribution and to master content to CDs and DVDs. These tools enable you to design the layout of your media, and encode or create final distributable files. Most of these tools also include features for processing digital media for final distribution. Cleaner Pro from Discreet is an example of a tool for encoding multiple files for publishing streaming media files.

Summary

In this chapter, we explored methods and tools that you can use to optimize technical quality. The next chapter builds on the concepts and tools described in this chapter by showing you how to improve or maintain technical quality at each stage of the production process.

14

Optimizing Quality Throughout Production

In this chapter, we will follow the production process and point out what you can do to optimize quality at each step. Quality optimization begins when you first press the record button and ends when you encode or master your final product and then distribute it. Optimization should be on the mind of every creative person who produces content, especially if the content is intended for distribution to the general public. Every decision that you make is based on many factors, including technical quality. Take steps at every point in your production process to make sure that technical quality is maintained, so that technical problems do not interfere with the creative vision of your production.

Production

Production is the part of the content creation process when the technical quality bar is set. During production, technical quality may be affected by the equipment that you use to record audio and video, and by many external sources, such as unwanted sound from airplanes and bad lighting conditions.

Audio

As you prepare to shoot a scene, consider your sound source. Try to prevent sounds that are not part of the source from being picked up by the microphone, including background noise and reverberation. Also think about how you will use the sound in your final work. If a recording contains a lot of background sound, you will hear the sound change when you make a cut. Assuming your tools are adequate for the job, you can ensure a good quality recording by properly placing the microphone, eliminating background noise, and optimizing recording levels:

■ Place the microphone properly. This is the best way to optimize audio quality, since the microphone is the device that first touches the sound. By correctly placing the microphone, you get the cleanest sound pickup. A little extra work at the beginning can save you a lot of frustration later. In general, the microphone should be as close as possible with the front of the microphone facing the source. By doing this, you do not entirely eliminate the source of unwanted background sound, but you help ensure that the sound level from the desired source is sufficiently higher. Close placement also picks up a richer spectrum of sound. For example, you are more likely to pick up the high-frequency sounds that help with clarity and intelligibility. Most microphones have a cardioid pickup pattern, which means that sounds outside a heart-shaped area in front of the microphone will be reduced. Figure 14.1 shows a cardioid pickup pattern.

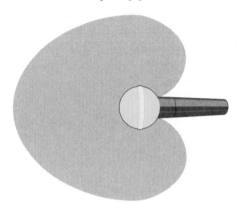

Figure 14.1   Microphone showing a cardioid pickup pattern.

■ Eliminate as many background sound distractions as possible. This includes short transient sounds like hammering, coughing, paper rustling, and footsteps, and long continuous sounds like air conditioners, traffic, and airplanes. This also includes room sounds, such as reverberation caused by the sound source reflecting off hard surfaces. You can often take direct action to eliminate a sound. For example, you can unplug a noisy refrigerator, close a door, or hang furniture blankets to cut down reverberation. If direct action is not possible, you may have to work around a distracting sound. There are some sounds, like those made by airplanes and crashing waves, that you will have no control over, regardless of the importance of your production.

■ Optimize recording levels. If you are using a good-quality recorder, typically the only way that you can optimize a recording is by making sure audio levels are set properly. Many camcorders and consumer audio recorders use circuitry that sets the audio level automatically, with an automatic gain control. If you can set levels manually with an audio meter, adjust the input control so that the audio level stays in the lower range, and uses as much of the range as possible while only rarely going over the 100% mark. If the level is too low, you will hear internal electronic noise. If the level is continually over 100%, the audio will be distorted. If you are recording on a digital device, never allow the level to hit 100%. If you do, digital clipping will occur. You may not notice a small amount of distortion with analog electronics and tape, but digital clipping is very noticeable. Clipped audio cannot be repaired or restored.

Video

Assuming that you are using a good-quality camcorder, you can either allow the camcorder to optimize quality automatically or optimize it manually. As a rule, the higher the quality of the camcorder, the more manual controls are available. The reason is that manufacturers assume consumers who purchase inexpensive camcorders will not have the expertise or desire to make manual adjustments. High-quality camcorders for professionals typically offer the choice of automatic or manual control; if a camera operator decides that an automatic adjustment is not optimal, he can override it manually. The following list describes the adjustments that must be made either automatically or manually to record video:

■ Focus. Most camcorders provide an auto-focus feature that automatically focuses the lens, so that the camera operator can be free to aim the camera and compose shots. However, the sensor that determines focus often reads only an area in the center of the image. If the part of an image that you want to be focused is not in that area, the lens will focus on the wrong thing. In those cases, you can switch to manual focus, if it is available.

■ Exposure. An optical iris mechanism opens or closes to adjust the amount of light that enters the lens and focuses on the face of the CCD chips. If the light level is too high, the bright areas of the image become clipped, and video that is clipped cannot be restored. If the light is too low, the image appears muddy or dark, and you are more likely to see video noise. As with focus, the automatic exposure system works much of the time. However, there are times when the exposure sensor adjusts for the wrong part of an image. For example, when shooting a shaded subject against a brightly lit background, many camcorders will adjust for the background and leave the subject dark. Manual override is handy in these cases.

■ White balance. An object reflects a different color depending on the color temperature of the source light. Most camcorders correct for this automatically, so that white objects always appear white. However, if a subject is lit by multiple sources with different color temperatures, the automatic white-balance circuits can correct for the wrong source, making the image appear bluish or reddish. Professional camcorders enable the camera operator to set the white balance manually.

- Shutter. The shutter adjustment controls the length of time an image is recorded in a frame of video. By default, a frame records about 1/30 of a second of an image. If objects are moving during that time, they appear blurred. However, by adjusting the shutter to 1/1000 of a second, moving objects will appear sharper. High-quality camcorders offer a number of shutter speeds.

- Gain. If the light level is insufficient even with the iris wide open, many consumer camcorders automatically add gain electronically. The main drawback of this system is that increasing gain also increases video noise. Unless you want a noisy, dark look for your video, make sure the subject is well lit. High-quality camcorders enable you to manually control gain.

Once clean audio and video have been recorded, you can further ensure that quality is optimal when you digitize your content during acquisition.

Acquisition

Acquisition is the part of the production process when the audio and video that have been recorded on tape or film are converted to digital data and saved on a computer hard disk. This task typically requires little creativity; it is often a matter of simply playing a tape and starting a capture program. However, even though it is a fairly mechanical process, the decisions made during acquisition affect the end product just as much as at any other step in the process.

The best approach for acquiring content is to decide on the parameters you want up front, and then use the same settings for everything that you digitize. With parameter standards set, the only factors that can adversely affect acquisition are mechanical or electronic problems, such as a tape creasing or a capture computer that cannot keep up with the amount of data that must be processed.

The acquisition process should be monitored and the final file spot-checked for quality. Often the only indication that you have of the quality of a capture is a display showing the number of frames dropped by the capture program. If a computer is too slow to handle the bit rate at which you are capturing, a capture program adapts by dropping frames rather than bringing the system down. There is no set rule for how many dropped frames constitute a bad capture. Often, a maximum of one or two dropped frames a minute may not be noticed. However, any number of dropped frames indicates a problem, because there should be none if your acquisition computer meets your requirements. If the number is excessive, you should use a computer with more RAM, and a faster CPU and internal bus. The write speed of the hard disk should also be adequate for the bit rate of the content. You can also monitor CPU and memory usage with Performance Monitor.

The following list describes the basic parameters you should decide before you begin acquiring analog content:

- Video frame size. Frame size is also referred to as the resolution of a video, because it determines the number of pixels that will be used in each frame. The larger the frame size, the more pixels and the higher the resolution.

- Pixel format. An analog video signal is sampled and the digital information is formatted into pixels. The pixel format defines the arrangement of the data in the pixels. Data stored in RGB formats defines pixels as values of the red, green, and blue components of the video. Data can also be arranged in a YUV format in which luminance information (Y) is separated from chrominance (UV). You can use a YUV format to save hard disk space; in most YUV formats, some chrominance detail is discarded in order to decrease the amount of data needed for each frame. If possible, use the same format that you will use in your final product to save an extra conversion step. Windows Media uses the YV12 pixel format.

- Aspect ratio. The aspect ratio is the ratio between the height and width of a frame. The standard-definition video ratio is 4:3, for example 640 pixels by 480 pixels. You might also need to consider the aspect ratio of the pixels. Square pixels are commonly used when working with digital video on a computer. However, the digital video-standard for broadcast and video production uses nonsquare pixels that are slightly narrower. Narrower pixels provide higher horizontal resolution. The resolution of 640 pixels by 480 pixels produces a frame aspect ratio of 4:3 with square pixels; a resolution of 720 pixels by 480 pixels produces the same frame aspect ratio with nonsquare pixels.

- Video frame rate. The frame rate is the number of video frames that are displayed each second. Video must be digitized at a frame rate that is no less than that of the source video in order for motion to appear as smooth as the original. The NTSC standard is roughly 30 frames per second (fps). You might also see it as 29.97 fps, which is the actual frame rate for NTSC color television. The Phase Alternating Line (PAL) standard used primarily in Europe is 25 fps.

You can improve the look and smoothness of video displayed on a computer monitor by using *deinterlacing*, a feature available on some capture cards and in Windows Media Encoder 9 Series. Analog video standards use a process called *interlacing* to create a video frame that is composed of two *fields*. One field contains odd-numbered scan lines; the other field contains even-numbered lines. The two fields displayed together produce one complete frame. Deinterlacing combines the two fields into one frame. The resulting video is then displayed using *progressive scanning*, which is the scanning method used by most computer monitors. A progressively scanned image does not contain any more image information; it just appears clearer and has less flicker. A similar method is *inverse telecine*. Film runs at 24 fps. In order to convert film to standard-definition video, redundant video fields are added so that the film appears smooth while running at 30 fps. Inverse telecine removes those fields.

■   Audio sampling rate and bit depth. The sampling rate determines the resolution of the audio. The more samples, the higher the quality. The bit depth is the number of bits used to describe one sample. Again, the more bits, the higher the quality. The Redbook standard for CDs is usually considered the benchmark for good-quality audio. It uses a sampling rate of 44.1 kHz, a bit depth of 16, and stereo. A sampling rate lower than 22 kHz or a bit depth of 8 produces noticeable audio artifacts. Professional audio sampling rates can go as high as 96 kHz.

■   Compression. If you are going to edit or process the content and then encode a final file, you will get the best quality if you work with uncompressed audio and video. After you finish editing, you can use a codec to compress the video for your destination medium, such as MPEG-2 for DVD and Windows Media Video for streaming. The disadvantage of working with uncompressed video, however, is the high bit rate and storage requirements. Therefore, a number of editing systems use proprietary software or hardware codecs with the editable digital media. Digital video formats, such as the MiniDV format, are also compressed. These compression methods are designed for editing and full-screen playback.

Digital formats make working with video and maintaining quality easy. Capturing data is less complicated than capturing and converting an analog signal, because there is no setup required. You can use an IEEE 1394 port for video formats such as MiniDV, the SDIF or AES/EBU port for digital audio, and the SDI port for the professional DV format to capture the data streams from a camcorder or recorder to a hard disk. Then you can open and work with the files in an editor or audio workstation. After you finish an edit, you can save the final product as a file or simply stream the final product back through the connector to an external recording device, such as a camcorder.

If you are working with digital content that has been recorded directly to a hard disk, such as a digital disk recorder (DDR), you can bypass the acquisition process.

The acquisition standards you set in the beginning decide the quality of the end product. After setting a standard and digitizing your content to files, you can begin the post-production phase of your production.

Clean-Up Before Postproduction

After acquiring your content, there is a point in the process when you can optimize your audio and video. While in raw digital form, there are things you can do to your content to clean it up before you start postproduction – things that would be more difficult, if not impossible to do, after you have started editing, mixing, and adding effects to create your final piece. By doing an initial clean-up, the rest of the process will often go much smoother because you can concentrate on the creative aspect. In general, if you have maintained good technical quality throughout production and acquisition, your raw files can be used directly in the editor and any quality problems can be addressed at that point. However, to help you understand methods for optimizing, we will explore what can be done prior to editing.

In each of the next three stages of the production process we will describe the types of quality problems that you should typically look for in that stage, and explore the tools and processes available.

Identifying Problems

After acquiring your content, you can check the raw files and identify problems that occurred during production that can be cleaned up before you begin the editing process. At this point, you do not necessarily know which parts of the raw material will end up in the final cut, but you may have a rough idea. Look for general problem areas that make the content difficult to work with during editing. For example, it is easier to attempt to remove a loud hum that runs through a large section of the raw content after acquisition, than to edit the content, and then attempt to edit and match each of the edited clips.

The type of video work that we will describe can be performed with fairly simple editor plug-ins that can correct the color and quality of the video frame in general. There-fore, we will wait to work with the video portion of our content until we begin editing, and then apply plug-ins at that point. However, you may choose to modify video content before you edit. The decision of whether to wait should be based on how much clean-up is required, and the complexity of your editing.

As you decide how to optimize your content, keep in mind that every time you process content, you run the risk of losing quality. If you simply copy digital media, the data is transferred bit for bit, so there is no change or loss. On the other hand, when you run content through a processor, such as a converter or color corrector, the bits are modified, so it is possible to lose quality, such as resolution or detail. Also, once applied to a file, you often cannot undo a process. Obviously, if you perform a very stylized color correction and make the image very blue with high contrast, for example, you may not be able to bring the reds and greens back in later if they have been removed. Also, the time it takes to render each process can be considerable. To help with these problems, a number of editing programs enable you to chain effects in real time, so that you can render a final file once with multiple processors and filters.

The goal of audio cleanup at this point is to remove unwanted material, reduce internal and external noise that was recorded during production, reduce the damage caused by digital distortion, and balance audio levels. You do not need to work on content that you know will not be used in the final product, but it is often easier and takes less time to simply process an entire raw file.

Exploring the Tools

Before you begin editing, you can clean up raw audio files and the audio portion of video files with an audio-editing program commonly called a digital audio workstation (DAW). This tool displays audio as a waveform. You can use the mouse to select portions, and then delete, cut, copy, or paste data. You can also mute or silence selections. The workstations also commonly include processors and plug-ins that you can apply to a selection or to the entire file.

To help you visualize working with a DAW, we will use Sound Forge from Sonic Foundry as an example. However, other audio workstations, such as Cool Edit Pro from Syntrillium software and WaveLab from Steinberg have similar functions. Figure 14.2 shows a short music segment opened in a DAW.

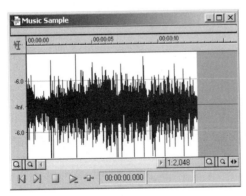

Figure 14.2 Music file opened in a digital audio workstation (DAW).

The following list describes some of the cleanup tasks that you can perform with most DAWs:

Equalization

Equalization (EQ) functions enable you to boost or lower sounds based on frequency in hertz (Hz). The most common types of equalizers are shelf, parametric, and graphic:

- Shelf equalizers are the simplest type. They raise or lower all frequencies of sound gradually above or below a certain point. The bass and treble controls in a car stereo are examples. Figure 14.3 shows an equalizer display with low-end shelf EQ applied.

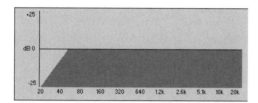

Figure 14.3   Low-end shelf EQ added with an equalizer.

The horizontal axis represents the sound spectrum from 20 Hz to 20,000 Hz; the vertical axis represents the amount of EQ that is either added to or removed from a sound, measured in decibels (dB); and sound is represented by the dark shape below the center line. If no EQ is applied, the EQ graph shows all sound at the center line. In this case, the shelf EQ begins at 55 Hz, and gradually reduces sound at frequencies below that point to a maximum of 25 dB (-25) at about 20 Hz.

- Parametric equalizers raise (boost) or lower (notch) frequencies in a selectable range, called a band. With parametric equalizers, you can work with individual tones. For example, you can lower hum from a power source by notching the sound in a narrow band at 60 Hz. Figure 14.4 shows a narrow band notched at 60 Hz and a wider band boosted at 7.5 kHz.

Figure 14.4   EQ settings in a parametric equalizer.

You can boost or notch frequencies around 7.5 kHz to bring out or lower *sibilance* in a voice recording. Sibilance is produced primarily by "s", "sh", and "t" sounds.

- Graphic equalizers boost or notch frequencies in a number of fixed bands. Typically, you use a graphic equalizer to shape the overall sound of an audio track. You could shape the equalization of a computer sound system, for example, to take into account the acoustic characteristics of the speakers and a room. Figure 14.5 shows a 20-band graphic equalizer with sound boosted in the upper and lower bands, and notched around 640 Hz.

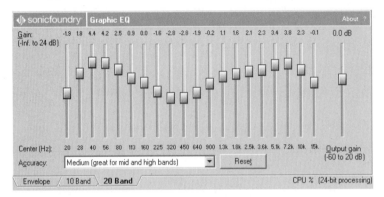

Figure 14.5 EQ settings in a graphic equalizer.

Lower Background Noise

Steady internal or external noise added during production can often be lowered to an acceptable point using equalization. However, noise-reduction programs and plug-ins target noise more precisely. These programs use a sample of the noise to create a digital sound profile. Sounds matching the profile are then removed or reduced. Figure 14.6 and 14.7 show a voice track before and after noise reduction was applied to reduce air-conditioning noise.

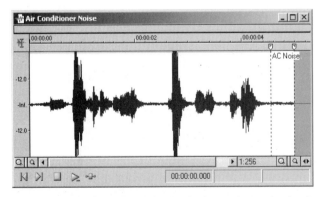

Figure 14.6 Waveform of a voice before noise reduction is applied.

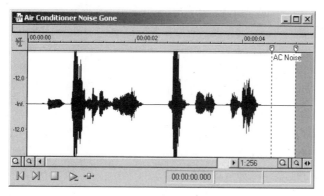

Figure 14.7 Same waveform of a voice after noise reduction is applied.

The wide variable portions of the waveform represent the parts of the sound containing the voice. Air-conditioning noise appears between vocal segments as a fairly consistent thickening of the center line. After noise reduction is applied, the portions containing air-conditioning noise can be reduced to almost nothing. Figure 14.8 shows the sound profile or noise print of the noise that was generated by the noise reduction program.

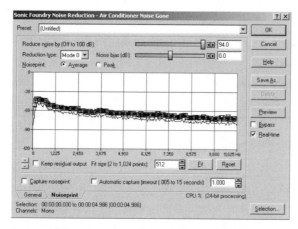

Figure 14.8 Sound profile of noise in an audio file.

A noise-reduction program does not "know" what noise is; it can only recognize sounds based on the profile. Therefore, if noise contains a wide spectrum of frequencies, such as white noise, which contains all frequencies, the program will reduce all sound, including the sound that you want to keep. Programs can solve many problems, but optimizing the use of programs is an art.

Reducing Pops and Clicks

Another type of noise-reduction function reduces pops and clicks, which are usually added to a recording internally from electronic components. They can also be added to a signal by a medium, such as static from phonograph records and broadcast reception. Figure 14.9 shows a waveform that has been zoomed-in to make a static pop easier to see. Figure 14.10 shows the same section after click-and-pop removal was applied.

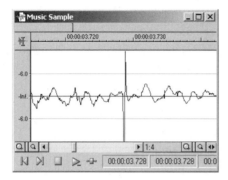

Figure 14.9 Waveform showing a static pop.

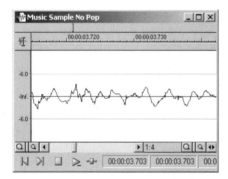

Figure 14.10 Same waveform after pop removal was applied.

This processor can be very effective at removing very short, high-frequency *transient* noises. Another way to remove noise is to manually redraw the waveform with a pencil tool. This method can be used to remove longer transient noises that are not detected by a noise-reduction program. Figures 14.11 and 14.12 show a portion of a waveform, both with a transient noise and after the transient noise has been removed with the pencil tool.

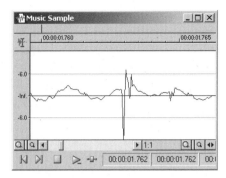

Figure 14.11 Waveform zoomed-in to show a transient noise.

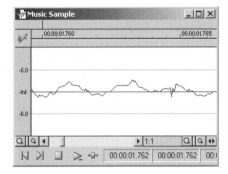

Figure 14.12 Same waveform after the pencil tool was used to remove the noise.

Help Distortion

Digital distortion, or clipping, is caused when an audio signal exceeds the upper limit of the digital range. The result is a very harsh, brittle sound. Figure 14.13 shows the waveform of some clipped audio.

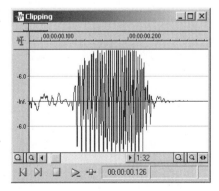

Figure 14.13 Waveform showing clipped audio.

The waveform display is adjusted so that the upper and lower edges correspond to the maximum signal that can be recorded digitally. Notice the clipped parts of the waveform that appear to be cut off evenly. The scale on the waveform is given in decibels of *attenuation*. The center line is labeled *inf* for infinite attenuation or no audio signal; the outer edges correspond to zero attenuation or the maximum signal level.

Although audio can never be restored after it is clipped, the sound can be processed so it is less distracting. You can select a clipped portion and lower the level, and then apply shelf equalization to the upper frequencies. You can also apply a clipped peak-restoration process that uses an algorithm that generates an approximation of the original sound, as in Figure 14.14.

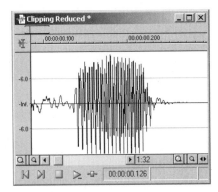

Figure 14.14   Same waveform after a restoration process is used.

If only a few peaks of the waveform are affected, you could also redraw the sections with the pencil tool.

Cut, Copy, and Paste Operations

DAWs provide the same basic tools that you will find on most computer programs. In digital form, sound can be manipulated just like any other data with cut, copy, and paste operations. For example, you can clean up a pop or remove a dog bark by simply selecting the sound and deleting it. You can also replace a sound by copying another sound over it.

After copying a sound onto the clipboard, you typically have two ways to paste it into another section of the track. You can place the cursor at a point where you want to add the sound, and click a paste operation, and the track will open up and add the clip. For example, you could paste "brown" after "quick" in "The quick fox", and get "The quick brown fox." You can also paste using overwrite or replace commands. When choosing this method, the sound replaces the sound after the cursor, but does not change the overall length of the file. For example, using replace to paste "brown" after "The," would change "The quick fox" to "The brown fox."

When working with audio in a video file, you must be careful how you use cut-and-paste operations because these functions change the length of the audio track. If you paste five seconds of audio in the middle of a video file, then all of the audio will be five seconds out of synchronization from that point to the end. Therefore, to maintain sync, you can only use *copy*-and-replace operations. To remove a section, you must replace it with something else. This is also the case when working with music in a multitrack program.

One way to remove a sound is to use a *mute* or *silence* function. Select the portion of the waveform that you want to remove, and click a mute operation. The portion isn't removed, it is silenced. The method that professional sound editors and designers use for muting sound is to replace it with *room tone*. Often when muting a track you will hear the sound go dead, which sounds unnatural. This is because every room or space, no matter how quiet it is, has a characteristic sound. You may not notice the sound because your perception tunes out continuous background noise. However, you do notice it when it disappears momentarily. To transparently mute a section, you can copy a quiet portion (the room tone) from another part of the track and paste it, using a replace operation, over the section. During production, you can also record a minute of room tone, which you can then use in postproduction. Figures 14.15, 14.16, and 14.17 show a short sound in a video track, and the waveform after the sound was replaced with room tone and by muting. Replacing the sound with room tone creates a continuous waveform that sounds less jarring.

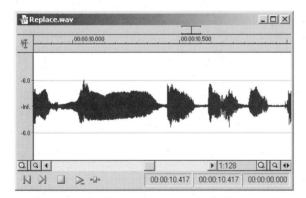

Figure 14.15   Original waveform of a voice track.

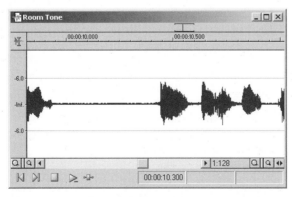

Figure 14.16   Same waveform after a portion was replaced with room tone.

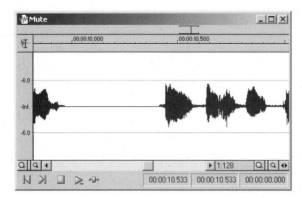

Figure 14.17   Same waveform with a portion muted or silenced.

Change Audio Volume Levels

The volume levels in a file can be changed either manually or through a process that modifies levels by using an algorithm. DAWs typically provide three functions:

- Manual volume adjustment. You simply use a slider to enter a value (number of decibels), and the program adds or subtracts that number from all samples in the waveform. Keep in mind that it is possible to subtract so much from the wave that sound data is actually deleted, or add so much that the sound becomes clipped. For this reason, percentages are often used.

- Normalizing. This is a three-step process in which the audio data is first searched for the highest value. Next, the difference between that point and the highest possible point (zero attenuation) is calculated, and then the difference is added to all the samples. Normalizing raises the audio level of a file evenly, so the highest point in the file is as high as possible before clipping. The problem with this method is that the highest point can be a very loud transient sound, such as a pop. Therefore, normalizing cannot be counted on for evening out levels.

- Dynamic level adjustment. Levels are adjusted automatically based on the settings that you enter and the actual audio level at any point in time, which makes it a dynamic process. There are many variations of dynamic processors, and as many different ways to configure them. However, they all have the following types of controls in common:

    - Input and output. Because these processors change audio levels, they typically provide controls for adjusting the amount of signal entering and leaving the device or program.

❑ Threshold. The most necessary control on a dynamic processor is the threshold setting, which determines at what volume level the processor starts working.

❑ Ratio. The amount of change the processor will perform on signals that cross the threshold.

❑ Attack time. How long it takes before the processor reacts to a signal crossing the threshold.

❑ Release. After a signal falls below the threshold, the amount of time the processor takes to return the level to the point where it was before it started changing the level.

With the common controls in mind, the following list describes the most common dynamic audio-level processors:

■ Compressor. Not to be confused with the compression applied by a codec, an audio compressor reduces the dynamics of audio content: quiet parts are less quiet, loud parts less loud. Compressors are used to even out audio content, so levels are flatter and more consistent. When the audio level rises above the threshold, the output audio is reduced based on the compression ratio. For example, if a compressor has a 3:1 ratio, a 3-dB increase in input above the threshold produces a 1-dB increase in output.

■ Expander. Increases the dynamics of audio content: quiet parts can become quieter and loud parts louder. If audio content seems too compressed, an expander can bring out more dynamics. Some noise-reduction technologies, such as Dolby, use a proprietary compressor/expander (compander) system, in which content is heavily compressed during recording and then expanded during playback, resulting in a lowering of internal noise. When the audio level crosses the threshold, the output audio is increased, based on the expansion ratio. For example, with a 1:3 ratio, a 1-dB increase in input produces a 3-dB increase in output.

■ Limiter. Restricts the audio level from going too high over the threshold point. Limiters are used to help prevent distortion. A limiter works the same as a compressor with a very high compression ratio. For example, a limiter might have an Inf:1 (infinity to 1) ratio, in which any signal over the threshold produces only a 1-dB increase in output.

■ Frequency-based dynamic processor. Confines compression or expansion to a band of frequencies. For example, if one band of frequencies has more dynamics than the rest of the sound, you can tune one of these processors to reduce the dynamics only in that band of frequencies. One example of this type of processor is a de-esser, which is tuned to reduce sibilant speech sounds, like "s" and "t" sounds. If a full-band compressor were used instead, the level of all audio would be reduced with the sibilance, so the sound would not be as natural.

- Automatic gain control. Maintains a consistent audio level. Automatic gain controls are included in consumer camcorders, for example, to keep levels consistent so that the consumer does not need to worry about audio levels. You can create your own automatic gain processor by chaining two compressors or using a compressor that enables you to enter multiple compression settings. Set one compressor with a low compression ratio and threshold. Set the second compressor to work as a limiter. Then, increase the input gain or lower the threshold so that the audio signal is always above the threshold and is therefore always compressed. You can adjust the release control to minimize the pumping effect you will hear as the level changes.

Processing the Audio

As you play back an audio file, listen for problems with the technical quality, such as transient sounds like clicks, pops, and paper rustling; long background sounds like air conditioning and traffic; and recording problems like distortion and volume levels. You should also consider the overall tone of the sound. If a person was recorded using a lavalier microphone that was buried under their clothing, the sound might be muffled. If the microphone was too far away from a source, the sound might include a lot of room sounds like reverberation, and not seem as *present*.

To describe how you might approach cleaning up a track, we will use a fictitious video recording (Speaker.avi) as an example.

1. Open Speaker.avi in the audio workstation. Except for providing a video preview window, most DAWs are designed to work with audio only. Therefore, it is often easier to work with the audio by itself, primarily because every time you save audio changes in the file, you also have to resave the video, which can take a great deal of time.

2. Save the file as Speaker.wav, to save the audio by itself in a new file.

3. Play the audio and identify quality problems. Figure 14.18 shows the entire waveform of the track.

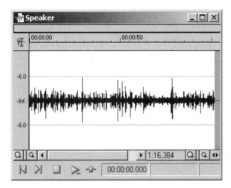

Figure 14.18   Sample waveform of a track from a video.

We decide to perform the following fixes:

■   Reduce the background noise.

■   Add clarity and presence to the voice.

■   Remove a few distracting pops.

■   Compress the sound to reduce the dynamics and bring the overall level of the file up. This is sometimes referred to as maximizing the audio. If you will be editing the file in a multitrack or editing program, you can wait until that point to add compression and maximize the audio level.

4.   Use EQ to reduce noise. Open the parametric equalizer and reduce as much noise as possible without affecting the voice. For example, remove low-frequency air-conditioning rumble, but stop before removing the rich dulcet tones of the speaker.

5.   Use EQ to add clarity. During the recording of the fictitious file, the camcorder microphone was 10 feet or more from the source, so you can boost the band of frequencies around 6 kHz a few dB to bring some sibilance back to the voice. We also tune the equalizer to prevent adding more air-conditioning noise. Process the file with the EQ settings.

6.   Noise reduction. Select a short section of room tone that contains no voice, open the noise reduction plug-in, and create a noise profile. Preview the track with the profile, and adjust parameters to balance the noise reduction effect against the artifacts that are produced. Then, process the file. It often sounds more natural to leave a little noise to mask the artifacts. By applying EQ first in Step 4, the noise reduction plug-in does not have to process as much, so the sound is often cleaner.

7.   Remove pops and transient sounds. Figures 14.19 and 14.20 show a pop that was replaced with room tone using a copy-and-replace paste operation.

Remember to not add or delete data, or the synchronization with the video will be thrown off.

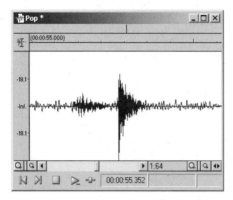

Figure 14.19 Original waveform showing a pop.

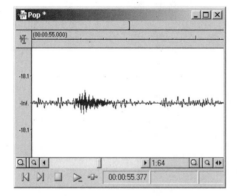

Figure 14.20 Same waveform after the pop was replaced with room tone.

8. Compress and limit the audio. Use a plug-in that provides both compressor and limiter functions. First, bypass the limiter and adjust the threshold on the compressor so that it is below the louder portions of the audio track, but higher than the noise. With this setting, the processor should compress only the speech. The best way to properly configure a compressor is by adjusting and listening. You can use the meters and preset values as a starting point, but for the best sound, you must trust your ears. If you are not sure that your ears can be trusted, get a second opinion. Figure 14.21 shows the settings on a compressor plug-in.

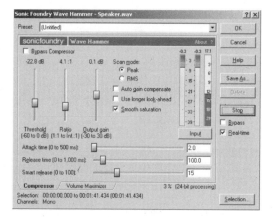

Figure 14.21   Typical audio compressor plug-in.

Notice the three, vertical audio meters on the right. The first two meters show either input or output stereo audio levels. The meter on the right appears to be upside down because it moves from the top down. This meter shows *gain reduction*: the amount of gain that is being reduced over the threshold.

After the compressor is configured, set the limiter threshold so that gain reduction occurs just before the signal reaches the point of clipping. Preview the audio to make sure that the level is as loud as possible without distorting or sounding too compressed. Adjust the input and release on the compressor so the sound is smooth.

Figure 14.22 shows Speaker.wav after it has been compressed and limited. Notice how the dynamics have been evened out and the gain has been maximized without being distorted. Compare this with the original track in Figure 14.18. You may decide that this amount of compression sounds too heavy. This is where the art of sound design comes in.

Figure 14.22   Waveform of the video track in Figure 14.18 after compression is applied.

9.   Save Speaker.wav and open an editing program, such as Vegas Video 4 or Adobe Premiere. Add Speaker.avi and Speaker.wav to tracks on the timeline, making sure that both start at the zero point, as in Figure 14.23. Then, delete the original audio track in the video file, and save a new video file, retaining the same audio and video settings. Alternatively, you can use a group function instead of saving a new video file, if such a function is available. By grouping the new audio track with the original video, you lock the two files in sync. Then you can edit and move the file and the clips made from the file without losing sync and without having to create an intermediate video file.

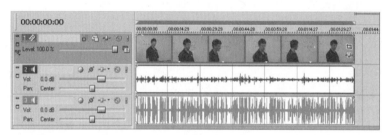

Figure 14.23   Video-editor timeline showing the original video track synchronized with the processed track.

In the next stage, you will work with Speaker.avi and other files in the editor to create a final edited and processed file.

Postproduction

After you have cleaned up the audio and re-synchronized it with the video, you can begin editing. Keep in mind that most often you will not need to clean the audio tracks prior to editing if they were recorded well. You can usually open the raw files directly in the editor.

Unlike the previous stage, the editing stage is not all about optimizing technical quality. In fact, almost all energy is spent on the creative aspect, and any further optimization is left until after the edit is finished. At that point in professional production, a sound designer or sound editor is brought in to finish the audio, and a colorist and digital effects editor are brought in to finish the video. In the process of finishing the production, they add elements and smooth out transitions to create a final product that is consistent and free of distracting problems. In audio postproduction, the audio tracks are mixed, and effects and processors are added to create a consistent experience for listeners.

Identifying the Problems

Because our focus is on technical quality, we will bypass the creative part of the postproduction process, and concentrate on optimization steps after the edit has been made. During an edit, the editor is concerned with telling a story, and selecting shots and audio elements that engage and entertain the audience. Likewise, in music production, the producer and musicians are initially concerned with performance and just getting the music on tape (or hard disk). During the creative part of the process, editors, producers, and musicians focus on the artistic aspect of their products and save the final stages of post-production for mixing and cleaning up the content so that the technical aspect is transparent.

When creating audio and video elements for a game, the process can be different. Instead of editing one final video or mixing a number of finished music files, a game may require hundreds of audio files and various unedited video files. Where a multitrack or editing program is used to create one linear experience, with a game many individual elements are integrated to create one nonlinear game experience. In a sense, the game environment can be thought of as an editing or multitrack program in which the user creates the final mix or edit. Therefore, when creating elements for a game, you often need to design the elements to be combined and layered in a number of ways.

The raw edited video and unmixed audio may contain many rough spots and distractions. As you play the content at this point, you can note the areas that will need to be cleaned to optimize technical quality. One could run into any number of potential problems at this point, many of which are related to an editor or producer who decided to wait until later to resolve a problem. During the process of editing, most creative people choose to focus on high-level decisions and not become bogged down with detailed clean-up tasks.

Most audio problems were described in the previous section. However, there are many problems that can easily be solved when working with multiple tracks and mixing. Therefore, in addition to the techniques described previously, we will explore how to work with the following problems that arise at this point:

- Uneven levels. Audio levels change from shot to shot. The mix of sounds is uneven.

- Inconsistent sound quality. The tone or texture of sound changes from shot to shot. Layered sounds do not blend.

- Audible cuts. Audio levels and quality jump on transitions, especially cuts.

By using a quality editing program, you can handle many video problems automatically during the edit process. Problems such as glitches and unwanted content can be remedied simply by using different shots or cutting around problem areas. For example, if the audio is important in a shot but you cannot use the video because it contains a distraction, you can insert different video at that point but let the audio continue.

Transitions and effects can also be used as a last resort to mask problems. For example, you could use a color or texture effect to cover a white balance problem. Also, if you need to edit out a portion of a continuous shot, but you have no other shot to which you can cut, you can use a dissolve transition to edit the two pieces together. For example, suppose the shot is a presenter giving a long speech and you edit out twenty seconds in the middle because the presenter lost his notes. When you join the two segments together, the cut, known as a *jump cut*, will appear jarring. If you have no other shot with which to cover up the cut, you can apply a dissolve transition at that point, which appears less abrupt.

There are as many creative ways to edit around problems as there are technical problems. After an edit has been finalized, you can improve the overall technical quality of a video by using effects plug-ins in editors to create a polished, final look. When using plug-ins, the focus is on consistency and matching, so that the look of the video matches from one edited clip to the next, and the overall look is consistent with the artistic vision. In a game environment, plug-ins and processors can be used to match one video element to another, and to the graphic design of the game. The objective of consistency, again, is to make the technical quality transparent, so that the audience only sees the artistic quality. For example, a shift of sharpness from cut to cut would create an inconsistency that might distract the audience from the intended focus of the piece.

Technical quality optimization at this point in postproduction focuses on the following two properties of edited video:

- Color balance. The color and luminance of images are consistent.

- Texture balance. The sharpness, detail, and resolution, grain or background noise of images are consistent.

Exploring the Audio Tools

After the initial edit, audio cleanup can be performed on the same editing program or a multitrack program that was designed for detailed audio work. There are also a number of programs that include both a video editor and a multitrack program. To help illustrate concepts, we will use Vegas Video from Sonic Foundry. However, the editing programs Adobe Premiere and Avid Xpress DV offer similar features. There are also a number of multitrack programs and systems that enable you to work with audio synchronized with video, including Syntrillium's Cool Edit Pro and Steinberg's Nuendo.

Most multitrack programs include the following methods or tools to help you work with uneven levels, inconsistent sound quality, and audible cuts:

- Audio editing and positioning

- Plug-ins

- Volume graph

Audio Editing and Positioning

As with audio workstations, you have the same level of editorial control over content in a multitrack program. The difference is in the level of detail. With a DAW, you typically work with individual files down to the detail of redrawing portions of the waveform. With a multitrack program, you work with a number of files, layering the audio vertically in tracks, and editing the files into clips and arranging them horizontally in time. You can also apply transition effects, such as dissolves.

With the flexibility provided by a multitrack, you can fix or mask the problem of audible cuts and inconsistent sound quality in a number of ways, including the following:

- Adding a background track. Often an audible bump on a cut or some other inconsistency in sound can be masked by layering background sound on another track. The background should also be consistent with the artistic vision. For example, you can add a background of a large noisy crowd and traffic over a scene that was shot on a busy street. However, the same background would not be appropriate for a speaker giving a technical seminar in a meeting room. If you need to mask inconsistent audio in this type of video, you can add a track of room tone. Figure 14.24 shows a background track containing room tone layered over an edited voice track.

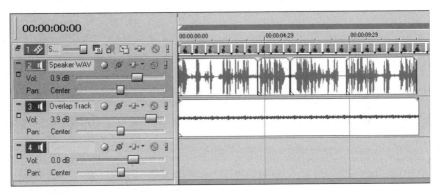

Figure 14.24   Background audio track layered with an edited voice track.

- Replacing audio. If the quality of an audio track is inadequate, a multitrack program will enable you to replace a clip or insert a completely new file. All you have to do is select the part that you want to remove and click Delete. Then, drag the new clip to the same position on a different track. You can also select the region and record directly over the clip. For example, if you need to replace a portion of a narration clip, you can bring the narrator into a studio and rerecord the section directly to the edited video. If you must replace sync sound (sound that is synchronized with the video), you can use the automatic dialog replacement (ADR) method available on a number of multitrack programs. With ADR, an actor or narrator synchronizes their reading with the person speaking in the video.

- Overlap transitions. If the sound does not match across a transition, such as a cut, and you are working with the original edit session, you can overlap the audio and create a smoother transition. To overlap the audio, move the audio on the incoming clip to another track. Then lengthen the audio on the end of the outgoing clip and the beginning of the incoming clip, as in Figure 14.25.

Figure 14.25 Using a multitrack program to overlap audio segments.

Add a fade-in to the incoming piece and a fade-out to the outgoing piece with the volume graph if necessary (see the following volume graph section). By working with the overlapping pieces and the fades, you can often smooth out a harsh transition.

Plug-Ins

Many of the same types of processor and effects plug-ins that you use in an audio workstation are available in a multitrack plug-in. The difference is that a multitrack plug-in must provide real-time processing. In an audio workstation, you preview a portion of the audio with the plug-in and then run the process, which modifies the file. In a multitrack plug-in, on the other hand, you do not modify the data in the original file, but render a final file that includes the video and audio, and all the edits, settings, and processes.

As you work with an edit session, the plug-ins must process the audio in real time, and if you have applied a number of video and audio plug-ins, as well as transitions and a large number of edits, the computer must have enough memory and CPU speed to handle a large number of calculations. For this reason, not all processors are available for multitrack editing. Also, plug-ins are often applied to an entire track. For example, if you only want to add compression to one clip, you can either process the clip in a DAW or move the clip to a new track by itself, and then apply compression to the track.

However, by working with tracks and other multitrack features, such as volume graphs, you can use plug-ins to make the sound consistent throughout. For example, you can move all clips that have the same sound problem to the same track, and apply a parametric equalizer or noise reduction. You can apply a compressor plug-in to a narration track to reduce the dynamic range, so that it mixes better with a music track. Many multitrack programs enable you to "chain" plug-ins and effects, so you can add compression, equalization, and noise reduction at once to a single track. Many multitrack programs also enable you to route the virtual audio signal in a number of ways, so you can, for example, group several tracks and then apply an effect to all of them at the same time. You can also route the entire audio signal through a plug-in, so you can, for example, apply a limiter to prevent distortion of the final mix.

Volume Graph

You can adjust the volume of a track manually with a volume slider, but this will affect the entire track. Most multitrack programs provide volume and other types of graphs with which you can modify properties of the audio over time. With a volume graph, you can draw the volume curve of the tracks. For example, you can add a volume graph to a music track, and draw a curve that gradually lowers the volume when the narration comes in and returns the music to full volume between narration clips. A volume graph can be used to even out inconsistent audio levels and match levels on transitions. You can also "duck" or reduce unwanted audio. For example, if the narrator shuffles papers between sections, you can simply fade out the track at that point.

Multitrack programs also use graphs to enable you to modify stereo positioning of a sound and to vary plug-in parameters dynamically. For example, you could automate equalizer settings or change the amount of reverberation that is applied to a track depending on how close an actor is to the camera. Graphs can also be available for video, and enable you to automate color property settings. Figure 14.26 shows a volume graph added to overlapped tracks.

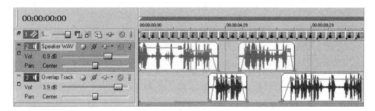

Figure 14.26   Volume graph added to overlapped audio in a multitrack program.

Exploring the Video Tools

In professional video production, a colorist is responsible for the look of an image. As data, image properties can be modified in many ways from simply tweaking the overall tint of a shot to changing properties of individual colors. Color-correction functionality is available as proprietary hardware systems and in programs that run on personal computers. Hardware systems, such as those from daVinci, are designed for use in high-end film-to-video transfer facilities called *telecines*. Much of the same functionality is available in plug-ins used in computer-based video-editing programs.

Color-correction programs and plug-ins enable you to perform the following types of processing on video:

■ Hue and saturation. Typically, a joystick style control is used to modify the overall hue or tint, and the saturation or amount of chrominance in a video image. As you move the control in a circle, the hue of the image changes gradually from red to green to blue and all the color values in between. As you move the control from the center to the edge of the circle, the saturation increases. For example, to make no change, you place the control in the center of the circle; to add a reddish tint, you would move the control toward the red part of the circle. Figure 14.27 shows a color-correction plug-in.

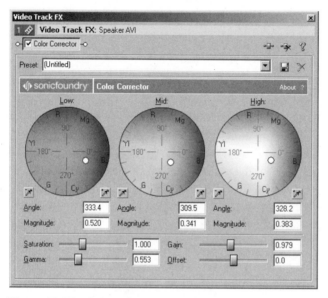

Figure 14.27 Color-correction plug-in.

■ Overall luminance. Typically, a centered slider control enables you to add or subtract luminance, which is the non-color intensity of an image, similar to a brightness control.

■ Gamma. With no gamma correction, luminance values change linearly from dark to light. By adjusting gamma, you change the linearity of luminance. If an image was very flat and washed-out, for example, you could adjust the gamma to increase the contrast. On the other hand, you could increase gamma to bring out detail in the grayscale of an image that had too much contrast.

■ Luminance ranges. An advanced color-correction control divides image luminance properties into high, middle, and low ranges, and enables you to adjust hue, saturation, and gamma in each range. For example, you could make the bright areas of an image redder, and the dark areas bluer.

■   RGB control. Typically, three slider controls are used to control red, green, and blue separately. With each slider centered, no change is made. To add a reddish tint, you move the red slider toward a positive value. An RGB control provides a less-intuitive method of color correction, but essentially does the same thing as the hue and saturation, and luminance controls.

The original intent of color correction was to provide a technical quality function. However, the controls are often used creatively to design very stylized images. Many of the other effects plug-ins are used solely for creative purposes, such as those that change the shape of an image or overlay scratches to give video the look of old film. One plug-in that can often be used to improve technical quality is a sharpness or detail enhancer plug-in, which is used to sharpen soft edges. There are also plug-ins that blur edges in an image; you could use such a plug-in to soften a very detailed, but noisy, image.

One important feature of a color-correction system is scene-by-scene correction. If the same color-correction setting was applied to every clip on a track, you would not be able to match quality from one shot to the next, so the system would be limited in its utility. By using scene-by-scene correction, you can adjust all color parameters individually for each shot. For example, if you cut from a dark, bluish shot to a bright, yellowish shot and you want them to match, you can correct each shot separately. Start by correcting one shot to your artistic standard. It could be the first shot in the timeline or another shot that is significant in some way. Then use that shot as the standard to which you match all the other shots.

You should also make sure that the artistic standard you have created will work with the limitations and standards imposed by your medium. If you are delivering your edited file on a CD-ROM with a game, for example, your primary concern may be the bit rate and size of the file. You could create a stunningly beautiful video that takes up more space on the CD than the game and requires so much CPU time and memory that the game cannot run.

To help you with video and saturation levels, you can use two types of displays: the waveform monitor and the vectorscope. These displays are available as hardware that connect directly to an analog video signal. A number of video editors provide software versions of the displays that you can use to see if your video is exceeding any limits.

Waveform Monitor

Figure 14.28 shows a software waveform monitor display.

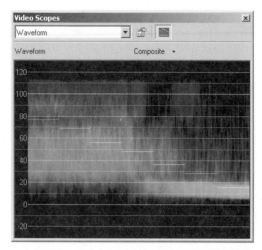

Figure 14.28   Software video waveform monitor display.

The waveform displays video frames on a graph with the vertical axis representing video gain or intensity; brighter objects appear higher on the vertical scale. A totally white frame would display as a straight horizontal line at 100%. Video that exceeds 100% will be distorted or clipped (white). If NTSC broadcast video exceeds 100%, video modulation can actually interfere with the audio signal. As you play back your video on a waveform, notice whether your video levels are too high and occasionally clipping, or too low. If they are too low, you will lose detail in the black areas of the image.

Vectorscope

Figure 14.29 shows a software vectorscope display.

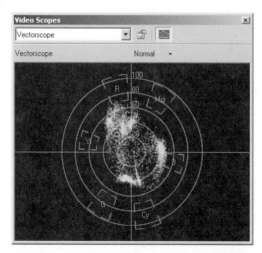

Figure 14.29   Software video vectorscope display.

Note the similarity of the video vectorscope display to the color-correction controls. A vectorscope displays the colors of a video image. The more saturated a color is, the further away it is from the center; the hue of a color is displayed on an angle of the circle. A black-and-white signal displays as a dot in the center; a true red color displays as a dot somewhere on the radius intersecting with the red point on the outer circle. As data, color saturation cannot exceed the limit of the outer circle.

After the edit is finished, and plug-ins and graphs have been applied, and after the audio is edited where necessary to create a consistent look and sound, a final audio or video file is rendered with the editor or multitrack program. In the final stage of a production, the file can go through one last quality-control stage before it is distributed.

Mastering

In general, mastering is the stage in the process of content creation when the final digital media is transferred to the medium that will be distributed to users. If it is to be streamed over a network, the file is simply copied to a media server and the URL announced to viewers. If it is part of a game, it is burned on a CD or DVD with all the other game components. If it is music destined for CD distribution, a master CD is created from the individual music tracks, and the master is used to manufacture multiple CDs, which can then enter the retail chain.

At some point then, the final edited and mixed file is converted or copied to the distribution media. This process can provide one last opportunity to optimize technical quality.

Identifying the Problems

Most often, the optimization is mandated by the limitations of the medium and the methods available to the user for playback, for example, the size of the CD and the quality of consumer sound systems. It is rare that a producer does not know early in the production process what their distribution limitations are. However, it is less rare that producers understand the limitations and take steps to optimize quality all the way through production with those limitations in mind. A good example of this problem often occurs when creating video content destined for streaming on the Internet. For video content to look its best streaming at 56 Kbps, for example, shots with fast motion that involve large portions of the frame should be minimized. Therefore, to optimize quality for low-bit-rate streaming, producers should avoid excessive and unnecessary camera movement. Streaming media codecs are improving, as well as the speed of end-user connections; nevertheless, producers can achieve the best possible quality by considering the limitations of their distribution medium throughout production.

When creating sound for games, the producer must also consider how technical quality matches from one file to the next. Often the files are recorded at different times and in different studios. Not only will the audio levels vary, but the sound quality of the files might also be different.

As you begin the process, you should plan to do test conversions or previews of the final product. For example, you should view the final, encoded streaming-media file before publishing it to the media server. If the preview does not pass your inspection, you can try different settings in the conversion tool, such as the encoder or mastering program, to improve quality. You can also process the audio or video in the file, so that the converter can do a better job.

Exploring the Tools

The conversion tools used to create distributable digital media do not inherently provide features for optimizing technical quality. Most products start with the assumption that this has already been done. Programs such as Cleaner Pro from Discreet Logic and Flip-Factory from Telestream encode content into a number of streaming media files and then publish the files to media servers. A conversion product might include an optimizing tool such as a simple compressor or normalizer to even out audio levels. However, the tools available in a conversion tool are often no better than those found in your audio workstation, multitrack program, and video editor. You may find that the best solution for preparing your digital media is to open the final audio or video file in the production tool that you have been using. To save a processing step, you can go back to your original multitrack program or editing session, make optimization changes, and then render new final files. If the files are part of a game, play the files together in the context of the game or simulate game playback by playing the files in a multitrack editor.

The following list describes the types of adjustments that you will most likely make at this stage:

- Audio volume. There are typically two reasons to adjust audio levels: to match and to maximize. The level of one file should match that of the others, especially on a CD or in a game, but also on a media server. The levels should also be maximized, so that they play back with the maximum level while maintaining an appropriate amount of dynamic range. The end user should be able to switch between files or cuts, and not have to adjust the volume control. The best way to match and maximize levels is to process files through a compressor/limiter. The WaveHammer plug-in shown in Figure 14.21 and the L2 Ultramaximizer from Waves are examples of tools designed to be all-in-one programs for reducing dynamic range, maximizing the level, and preventing distortion. If you create many streaming-media files, you can define one setting that can be used with all files.

- Audio quality. Often, overall quality mismatches can be remedied by carefully applying equalization. Assuming that the quality differences are not too extreme, you can select a standard sound, such as a particular music cut, and then use a graphic equalizer to adjust the equalization curve if necessary for the other cuts. For example, you might increase the lower frequencies and notch the file a bit at 6,000 Hz. With this type of overall equalization, you will typically apply no more than 6 dB of EQ. If a track needs more EQ help, you should consider remixing the original session.

■   Color correction. As with audio-quality modification, the amount of color correction at this point should be minimal and applied to the file overall. For example, you may find that adjusting the overall gamma slightly produces video that looks better and brings out more apparent detail after it has been encoded for streaming.

Summary

If you have optimized technical quality throughout your production process, the final product will allow the creative quality of your content to emerge, free from distractions. The technical quality should provide a transparent window through which the audience can fully experience your game, story, message, performance, or artistic statement.

Appendix A

ATL Smart Pointers

This appendix gives a quick overview of how to use the ATL smart pointer classes, *CComPtr* and *CComQIPtr*.

One of the central ideas in COM is that objects manage their own lifetimes. An object is created with a reference count of 1. Whenever a function receives an interface pointer, it must release the pointer after it's done using it. Whenever a function *gives away* an interface pointer, it must *AddRef* the pointer. Once the object's reference count goes to zero, the object deletes itself. Reference counts save you from having to figure out which code path is the last to use an object, because your code never explicitly deletes the object. As long as every function manages its own reference counts correctly, everything works.

That's the theory. In practice, getting reference counts right can be rather irritating. It's all too easy to overlook a stray *AddRef* or *Release*, and missing just one will result in memory leaks or objects that prematurely delete themselves. This is where smart pointers can make your life easier.

A smart pointer is a C++ class that manages a COM interface pointer, including the reference count. There are various smart pointer classes available. For example, Microsoft Visual C++ defines a *_com_ptr_t* class. This book uses the ATL classes, but the principles are the same.

Declare a *CComPtr* object in the following way.

```
CComPtr<ISomeInterface> pA;  // "ISomeInterface" is any COM interface.
```

The interface type is an argument to the class template, and the *CComPtr* object contains a raw interface pointer of that type. The class overloads *operator->()* and *operator&()*, so you can access the interface pointer transparently.

```
hr = GetSomeObject(&pA);  // The & operator has the expected behavior.
pA->SomeMethod();         // The '->' operator also has the expected behavior.
```

When the *CComPtr* object goes out of scope, it automatically releases the interface — but only if the interface pointer is valid. If the underlying pointer was never initialized in the first place, the *CComPtr* object safely goes out of scope without calling *Release*. That means that you can write code that looks like the following.

```
HRESULT MyFunction()
{
    CComPtr<ISomeInterface> pA;
    HRESULT hr = GetSomeObject(&pA); // Returns an interface pointer.
    if (FAILED(hr))
    {
        return hr;  // Because pA was not initialized, it is not released.
    }
    pA->SomeMethod();

    // On exit, pA is released correctly.
}
```

Without smart pointers, if you exit in the middle of a function, you have to carefully work out which pointers to release and which are still *NULL*. Or else, to avoid that problem, you end up with endlessly nested *SUCCEEDED* tests. The *CComPtr* destructor handles it all for you.

The equality and inequality operators are overloaded, and the *CComPtr* object evaluates to true only when the interface pointer is valid. With this feature, you can use an ***if*** test to check the validity of the pointer before trying to dereference it.

```
if (pControl)  // Is this a valid pointer?
{
    pControl->Run();
}
```

The *CComPtr* object also provides a helper method for calling *CoCreateInstance*. Internally, the *CComPtr::CoCreateInstance* method calls the COM function of the same name with the correct interface identifier (IID) and reasonable default values for the other parameters (*NULL* for *pUnkOuter* and CLSCTX_ALL for *dwClsContext*, although you can specify other values).

```
CComPtr<IGraphBuilder> pGraph.
pGraph.CoCreateInstance(CLSID_FilterGraph);
```

Notice that you don't have to coerce *pGraph* to a *void*** type, because the smart pointer knows what the type is. This prevents insidious errors caused by passing in the wrong pointer, which can easily happen in regular COM programming because the *void*** cast circumvents the type checking done by the compiler. The *CComPtr::QueryInterface* method works similarly.

```
CComPtr<IMediaControl> pControl.
// Query the pGraph pointer for the IMediaControl interface.
pGraph.QueryInterface(&pControl);
```

There may be times when you need to release a smart pointer explicitly, before it goes out of scope — for example, if the pointer is reinitialized inside a loop. In that case, call the *CComPtr::Release* method to release the interface. Unlike derefencing the raw pointer and calling *Release*, the smart pointer's *Release* method is always safe to call, even when the raw pointer is not valid.

```
pGraph.Release(); // Releases pGraph.
```

If you return a pointer from a function, the pointer must have an outstanding reference count according to the rules of COM. (It's the caller's responsibility to release the interface.) Use the *Detach* method to return a pointer without releasing it.

```
void GetObject(ISomeInterface **ppI)
{
    CComPtr<ISomeInterface> pI;

    // Initialize pI to a valid pointer (not shown).

    // Return the interface pointer to the caller.
    *ppI = pI.Detach();

    // When pI goes out of scope, it does not call Release.
    // The caller must release the interface.
}
```

This code is functionally equivalent to the following.

```
void GetObject(ISomeInterface **ppI)
{
    ISomeInterface *pI;

    // Initialize pI to a valid pointer (not shown).

    **ppI = pI;  // Copy the raw pointer to the [out] parameter.
}
```

Finally, if you want to be *really* terse, the *CComQIPtr* class can be used to call *QueryInterface* in zero lines of code — the class constructor automatically calls *QueryInterface*. The constructor argument is the interface pointer that you want to query.

```
// Query the pGraph pointer for the IMediaControl interface.
CComQIPtr<IMediaControl> pControl(pGraph);

if (pControl)  // Did the QueryInterface call succeed?
{
    pControl->Run();  // OK to dereference the pointer.
}
```

Smart pointers take a little while to get used to, but in the long run they can save you a lot of time debugging reference-count problems. The book *ATL Internals,* by Brent Rector and Chris Sells, has a good description of the ATL smart pointers. For a discussion of the COM reference counting rules in general, see *Inside COM,* by Dale Rogerson (Microsoft Press).

Appendix B

Multichannel Audio Tool

The MCAudio sample application is a tool for creating multichannel files in WAV and AVI format. The application is located in the AVBook/bin directory. Although MCAudio isn't particularly sophisticated — it's by no means a professional audio-editing tool — it does give you a quick way to generate 5.1 and 6.1 audio files. And best of all, we give you the source code, in case you want to modify it.

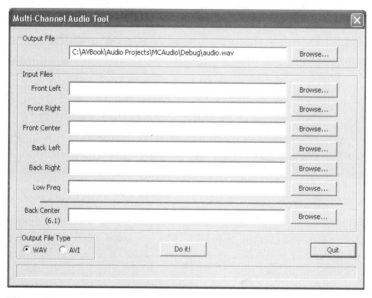

Figure B.1   **Multi-c**hannel audio tool.

Setup

The MCAudio tool requires two DLLs, MultiAudio.dll and Wavdest.ax, which are included with the executable in the binaries directory. Use the Regsvr32 utility to register these DLLs.

```
regsvr32 multiaudio.dll
regsvr32 wavdest.ax
```

(Yes, Wavdest.ax is a DLL despite the unusual file extension.)

Usage

To use the MCAudio tool, do the following:

- Choose a name for the output file in the Output File edit box. (The tool selects a default name at startup.)

- In the Input Files area, select input files for one or more audio channels. You don't have to specify a file for every channel; blank channels are simply not written into the file. For example, you can make a 5.1 file by leaving out the back center channel.

- Use the Output File Type radio buttons to switch between .wav file output and audio .avi file output.

- Click the Do It! button to write the file. A progress bar indicates the progress of the write operation.

Usage Notes

Input files must be mono or stereo. If stereo, the file is mixed down to mono before it gets written to the output file. Input files can be any format that is supported by Direct-Show, including WAV, AVI, MP3, and WMV. You can even use video files, as long as they contain an audio stream. (The video stream will be ignored.)

For the output file, the sampling rate and bits per sample are taken from the format of the first input file. If any of the other input files have a different format, they are re-sampled to match the first input file. For best results, you should use mono input files that all share the same sampling rate and bit depth.

If the input files are unequal in duration, the application writes silence into the output file to pad out the remaining time.

Programming Notes

The MultiAudio DLL is a DirectShow filter that multiplexes one or more audio streams into a single multichannel audio stream. Although the MCAudio tool uses a fixed set of channels for 5.1 and 6.1 audio, the filter supports all 18 channels that are defined for the

WAVEFORMATEXTENSIBLE structure, so you could easily convert the application to support more channels.

The Wavdest DLL is a DirectShow filter for writing .wav files. This filter is provided as an SDK sample in the DirectX SDK. The source code can be found in the Samples\C++\DirectShow\Filters\WavDest directory.

Index

Author Biographies

Illustrious authors of this book.

Dr Peter Turcan (top left) completed his BS degree in Computer Science at Edinburgh University in Scotland in 1978. He gained his PhD from Reading University in England four years later. His first venture into games immediately followed with a computer version of the Scrabble word game, which sold hundreds of thousands of copies. He then turned his attention to war games and programmed a series of seven strategy games: Borodino, Waterloo, Austerlitz, Gettysburg, Armada, Dreadnoughts, and Midway. After a run at working as a computer journalist in London, he emmigrated to the USA and joined Microsoft as a programming writer in the Digital Media Division. He has a painfully dry English sense of humor, not much of which survives the cutting board of Microsoft's ever-vigilant editors.

Mike Wasson (lower right) is a programming writer for the Microsoft DirectShow SDK. He received his BS degree in Computer Science from the University of Hawaii. Prior to joining Microsoft he worked as a copy editor. He was raised in New York and lived in Honolulu and Los Angeles before relocating to western Washington State for its bracing maritime climate. At Microsoft he has written volumes of documentation on DirectShow, and was one of the technical reviewers of *Programming Microsoft DirectShow for*

Digital Video and Television (Microsoft Press). In his spare time he listens to copious amounts of jazz and Japanese pop music.

Bill Birney (lower left) has been creating content for over 35 years. During his career, he has worked as a scriptwriter, composer, producer, director, video editor, sound designer, and creative director. As a technical writer in the Digital Media Division, Bill co-authored the books *Inside Windows Media, Windows Movie Maker Handbook* and most recently the *Windows Media Resource Kit* (all by Microsoft Press). Bill believes the goal of every writer should be to bring their readers happiness.

Jim Travis (top right) is employed by Microsoft Corporation as a lead programming writer for Windows Media technologies. Prior to working at Microsoft, Jim owned his own multimedia software company, which supplied automation software to the entertainment industry. Jim has also been a live sound engineer and video technician, and once owned and operated a multitrack recording studio.

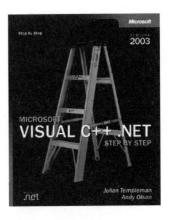

Inside information about *Microsoft .NET*

Applied Microsoft® .NET Framework Programming
ISBN 0-7356-1422-9

The expert guidance you need to succeed in .NET Framework development. The Microsoft .NET Framework allows developers to quickly build robust, secure Microsoft ASP.NET Web Forms and XML Web service applications, Windows® Forms applications, tools, and types. Find out all about its common language runtime and learn how to leverage its power to build, package, and deploy any kind of application or component. This book by renowned programming author Jeffrey Richter is ideal for anyone who understands object-oriented programming concepts such as data abstraction, inheritance, and polymorphism. The book carefully explains the extensible type system of the .NET Framework, examines how the runtime manages the behavior of types, and explores how an application manipulates types. While focusing on C#, it presents concepts applicable to all programming languages that target the .NET Framework.

Programming Microsoft .NET
ISBN 0-7356-1376-1

Learn how to develop robust, Web-enabled and Microsoft Windows–based applications by taking advantage of C# and the Microsoft .NET Framework. The Microsoft .NET initiative builds on industry standards to make interoperable software services available anywhere, on any device, over the Internet. Behind the initiative is the Microsoft .NET Framework, which combines a managed run-time environment with one of the richest class libraries ever invented to make building and deploying Web-enabled applications easier than ever. Find out how to leverage the full power of the .NET Framework with this definitive, one-stop resource, written by a leading authority in his trademark easy-to-follow, conversational style. You'll learn about the key programming models embodied in the .NET Framework, including Windows Forms, Web Forms, and XML Web services. And, you'll benefit from a wealth of how-to examples, code samples, and complete working programs in C#.

Microsoft .NET Compact Framework
ISBN 0-7356-1725-2

Build killer applications for handheld devices with the .NET Compact Framework! The Microsoft .NET Compact Framework brings the power of the .NET Framework to handheld devices such as Pocket PCs and smart phones. Learn exactly how to build killer applications—and how to solve typical problems—in developing for resource-constrained devices with this book. You'll find specifics on how to develop GUI elements with Windows Forms, access and store data with ADO.NET and integrate it across the enterprise with XML Web services, work with Microsoft SQL Server™ CE, develop applications that work across wireless networks, and more. You even get code samples plus a quick reference to differences between the .NET Compact Framework and the full .NET Framework.

To learn more about the full line of Microsoft Press® products for developers, please visit:

microsoft.com/mspress/developer

Microsoft Press

Get step-by-step instruction *plus .NET development software—all in one box!*

Microsoft® Visual C#® .NET Deluxe Learning Edition— Version 2003
ISBN: 0-7356-1910-7
U.S.A. $119.99
Canada $173.99

Microsoft® Visual Basic® .NET Deluxe Learning Edition— Version 2003
ISBN: 0-7356-1906-9
U.S.A. $119.99
Canada $173.99

Microsoft® Visual C++® .NET Deluxe Learning Edition— Version 2003
ISBN: 0-7356-1908-5
U.S.A. $119.99
Canada $173.99

Everything you need to start developing powerful applications and services for Microsoft .NET is right here in three economical training packages. DELUXE LEARNING EDITIONS give you powerful Microsoft .NET development software— Visual C# .NET 2003 Standard, Visual Basic .NET 2003 Standard, and Visual C++ .NET 2003 Standard—along with Microsoft's popular Step by Step tutorials to help you learn the languages. Work at your own pace through easy-to-follow lessons and hands-on exercises. Then apply your new expertise to full development software — not simulations or trial versions. DELUXE LEARNING EDITIONS are the ideal combination of tools and tutelage for the Microsoft .NET Framework—straight from the source!

To learn more about the full line of Microsoft Press® products for developers, please visit us at:

microsoft.com/mspress/developer

Get a **Free**

e-mail newsletter, updates,
special offers, links to related books,
and more when you

register online!

Register your Microsoft Press® title on our Web site and you'll get a FREE subscription to our e-mail newsletter, *Microsoft Press Book Connections*. You'll find out about newly released and upcoming books and learning tools, online events, software downloads, special offers and coupons for Microsoft Press customers, and information about major Microsoft® product releases. You can also read useful additional information about all the titles we publish, such as detailed book descriptions, tables of contents and indexes, sample chapters, links to related books and book series, author biographies, and reviews by other customers.

Registration is easy. Just visit this Web page and fill in your information:

http://www.microsoft.com/mspress/register

Microsoft®

- -

Proof of Purchase

Use this page as proof of purchase if participating in a promotion or rebate offer on this title. Proof of purchase must be used in conjunction with other proof(s) of payment such as your dated sales receipt—see offer details.

Fundamentals of Audio and Video Programming for Games
0-7356-1945-X

CUSTOMER NAME

Microsoft Press, PO Box 97017, Redmond, WA 98073-9830